Mad Blood Stirring

I pray thee, good Mercutio, let's retire:
The day is hot, the Capulets abroad,
And, if we meet, we shall not scape a brawl:
For now, these hot days, is the mad blood stirring.

Romeo and Juliet, 3.1.1–4

Mad Blood STIRRING

Vendetta & Factions in Friuli during the Renaissance

EDWARD MUIR

THE JOHNS HOPKINS UNIVERSITY PRESS
BALTIMORE AND LONDON

This book has been brought to publication with the generous assistance of the Gladys Krieble Delmas Foundation.

The Johns Hopkins University Press
2715 North Charles Street
Baltimore, Maryland 21218-4319
The Johns Hopkins Press Ltd., London

LIBRARY OF CONGRESS CATALOGING-IN-PUBLICATION DATA

Muir, Edward, 1946–
  Mad blood stirring : vendetta and factions in Friuli during the Renaissance / Edward Muir.
    p.   cm.
  Includes bibliographical references and index.
  ISBN 0-8018-4446-0
  1. Udine (Italy)—History.   2. Massacres—Italy—Udine.   3. Friuli (Italy)—History.   4. Vendetta—Italy—Friuli—History—16th century. 5. Savorgnan family.   6. Delle Torre family.   I. Title.
DG975.U3M85 1992   92-15211
945'.391—dc20

A catalog record for this book is available from the British Library.

To Linda

Contents

Part Three

MENTALITIES & IDEOLOGIES

Illustrations

Acknowledgments

While working on this book, I have been especially fortunate in receiving support, both financial and intellectual, from many sources. I first explored some inchoate ideas for a study of vendetta in Renaissance Italy in a seminar directed by Gene Brucker at the Southeastern Institute of Medieval and Renaissance Studies, University of North Carolina, Chapel Hill, where I was a junior fellow for the summer. During a year at the Institute for Advanced Study, Princeton, with a fellowship for independent study and research from the National Endowment for the Humanities, I was able to work on this and other projects and enjoyed the hospitality of John Elliott, Felix Gilbert, and Kenneth Setton. A grant from the Senate Research Committee of Syracuse University and a travel and research grant from the Gladys Krieble Delmas Foundation made possible two summer research trips to Italy. With the generous assistance of a fellowship from the John Simon Guggenheim Memorial Foundation and a leave from Syracuse University, I completed the necessary archival research in Italy and began to write the book. Two grants from Louisiana State University, a summer faculty research award from the Council of Research, and a sum-

mer research fellowship from the College of Arts and Sciences enabled me to complete it. I wish to thank all of these institutions for
the assistance provided for my work.

At various stages of the project I have presented the results of
research and some often less than disciplined ideas to the scrutiny
of other scholars, many of whom have added references, encouraged me to ask different questions, and forced me to rethink conclusions. A paper contributed at a very early stage of research to
the seminar of the Shelby Cullom Davis Center for Historical
Studies at Princeton University resulted in extensive criticisms that
led me to reexamine the social context of vendetta and collective
violence. The participants in seminars I directed at the Folger Institute of the Folger Shakespeare Library, Washington, D.C., and
the Newberry Library, Chicago, contributed a great deal more to
the maturing of my ideas than I probably did to theirs. To them I
owe a special debt. It would be impossible to thank individually all
the scholars from various disciplines who also responded to pre-
sentations made at several universities and conferences, especially
those who flooded me with references about pigs and dogs, species
whose role in the history of culture obviously deserves greater recognition. The discussions that followed these papers have had an
immeasurable effect on my thinking, and I wish to acknowledge
the many who have taken my efforts so seriously.

Cecil Clough sent me in advance of publication his article on the
connections between the vendetta in Friuli and the story of Romeo
and Juliet, and Thomas Scheff allowed me to look at his unpub-
lished work on the sociology of shame. Barry Barlow took out
precious time from his own research in Austria to investigate possible sources in the Kärntner Landesarchiv in Klagenfurt. Guido
Ruggiero and Charles Royster read the penultimate draft and made
many valuable suggestions. Henry Y. K. Tom of The Johns Hopkins University Press demonstrated yet again his many virtues as a
sympathetic reader and empathetic editor.

In Italy I have enjoyed associations with a remarkable group of
talented and energetic historians who, during the past generation,
have vastly expanded the horizons of historical studies in Venice
and the Veneto region. The students and faculty members at the
Universities of Venice, Padua, Trieste, and Udine must constitute

one of the most vital historical communities anywhere, and it is my hope that their work might be appreciated by a larger audience. In particular, I wish to thank Gino Benzoni, Michele Fassina, Michael Knapton, Reinhold Mueller, Giorgio Politi, Giuseppe Trebbi, and Amelio Tagliaferri. Among the treasures of Italian historical scholarship remain many *tesi di laurea*. I wish to thank Aldo Stella for allowing me to see the thesis for the University of Trieste of his student, Aurelia de Savorgnani, and Sergio Gobet for generously lending me his only copy of his own thesis for the University of Trieste. Cinzia Borghese of the University of Venice was especially open in discussing with me her thesis while it was still in progress and in presenting me with a copy when finished.

The professional expertise and cordiality of the staffs of the several archives and libraries in which I have worked have made the long hours far more productive and pleasant than they might otherwise have been. In particular, I wish to express my gratitude to Michela Dal Borgo and Sandra Sambo of the Archivio di Stato, Venice, and Marino Zorzi of the Biblioteca Nazionale Marciana. Sometime landlord and full-time friend Marino Zorzi not only helped with the collections of the Marciana but provided an introduction to dottoressa Clotilde Spanio, who gave me entrance to her private archive of family papers for the castellans of Spilimbergo. Besides the opportunity to read old parchments, dottoressa Spanio and her family offered their hospitality and assisted my researches in Spilimbergo. In that lovely town, Maria Antonietta Moro of the Biblioteca Civica Comunale volunteered to serve as my guide and supplied many kindnesses. Don Basilio Danelon gave me access to the parish archives of Santa Maria Maggiore where Arturo Bottacin patiently helped while I worked my way through that exceptional collection. Also in Spilimbergo, beside a quintessentially Friulan *fogolar*, Gianfranco Ellero enlightened me with his many insights into the dilemmas of Friulan history.

My final debt is the deepest and one impossible to repay. Were I to thank her on every point at which she deserves it, the notes to this book would be a long paean to Linda Carroll. From her expertise on dialect words to her tolerance of my moods, from her advice on prose style to her ability to make life enjoyable, and from her openness with her own researches on carnival theater to her willingness to help find some dusty field in which five hundred years ago a murder took place, she has been the best of colleagues, the most pleasant of companions. As a modest tribute this book is dedicated to her.

A Note on Names and Dates

In the documents consulted for this study, names, particularly given names, can appear in four different forms: in Friulan, Venetian, Tuscan, and Latin. For example, the name *John* might appear as Giuan, Zuan, Giovanni, or Johannes with many variant spellings of each version. There is no easy way to standardize names, especially since the nineteenth-century solution of relentless Tuscanization is offensive to history, the ear, and current Friulan sensibilities. Following fifteenth- and sixteenth-century usage, I have favored the Venetian forms but have made no attempt to impose them universally and have merely tried to be consistent in the rendering of the name of each individual. The reader will thus discover both Alvise and Luigi, Nicolò and Niccolò, and other variants.

All dates in the text have been given in the new style. In the notes, for the convenience of those who may wish to make their way through the many unpaginated volumes and boxes of documents that are cited, some dates have been left in the old style and marked with the abbreviation *m.v.* (*more veneto*). The Venetian style was to date the beginning of the year from March 1.

Abbreviations

BSU	Biblioteca del Seminario Arcivescovile, Udine
CF	*Ce fastu?*
DU	Leonardo and Gregorio Amaseo, Giovanni Antonio Azio, *Diarii udinesi dall' 1508 al 1541,* ed. Antonio Ceruti, Monumenti storici, 3d ser., vol. 2, Cronache e diarii, vol. 1 (Venice: R. Deputazione Veneta di Storia Patria, 1884).
DU, GA	Portion of diary by Gregorio Amaseo
DU, GAH	Appendix to diary by Gregorio Amaseo, *Historia della crudel zobia grassa et altri nefarii excessi et horrende calamità intervenute in la città di Udine et Patria del Friuli del 1511*
DU, LA	Portion of diary by Leonardo Amaseo
MCV	Biblioteca del Museo Civico Correr, Venice
MSF	*Memorie storico forogiuliesi*
NAV	*Nuovo archivio veneto*
ONV	Österreichische Nationalbibliothek, Vienna
QS	*Quaderni storici*
SV	*Studi veneziani*

Introduction

Men do injury through either fear or hate.

Machiavelli, *The Prince*, chap. 7

Such injury produces fear; fear seeks for defense;
for defense partisans are obtained;
from partisans rise parties in states;
from parties their ruin.

Machiavelli, *Discourses on the First Decade of
Titus Livius*, book 1, chap. 7

Late on the cold gray morning of February 27, 1511, more than a thousand militiamen, who had been searching since dawn for a raiding party of German mercenaries, stumbled back through the gates of Udine. It was the first day of carnival. The men were tired, hungry, angry. They began to drink. Through the mysterious alchemy of crowd behavior, the men ignited a conflagration, looting and burning the urban palaces of more than a score of the great lords of Friuli who were rumored to be in league with the enemy. A huge crowd of Udinesi and peasants in town for the holiday joined in, and during three days of rioting they killed between twenty-five and fifty nobles and their retainers.

As news of the wild carnival in Udine spread, peasants near and far assaulted the rural castles of the same feudal lords, all of whom were also the avowed enemies of the enormously popular militia captain, the nobleman Antonio Savorgnan, whose retainers played a suspiciously conspicuous role in the carnival violence. In a few weeks the most extensive and most damaging popular revolt in Renaissance Italy had run its course, an event that contemporaries understood both as a peasant rebellion and as the bloody backwash from a tidal wave of vendetta violence among the nobles who dominated the affairs of the region.

This book is about that event, its antecedents, and its consequences. The tale begins with the civil wars that plagued Friuli before the republic of Venice conquered the region in 1420, and it ends in 1568 when Venice finally imposed a formal peace on the vendetta clans. Although local historians have long considered the Cruel Carnival of Udine as one of the signal moments in the region's history, in the wider sphere of Italian and European concerns it has been recognized, if at all, as a minor episode in the War of the League of Cambrai, which was itself but one of several collisions at the turn of the sixteenth century among the various Italian states, France, Spain, and the Holy Roman Empire.

Nothing that happened in Friuli in the winter of 1511 altered the course of affairs in Europe or even in the republic of Venice. The significance of the Cruel Carnival lies elsewhere: in what it can reveal about the nature of vendetta conflict, the role of factions in politics, and the characteristics of a peasant revolt. The Friulan case provides a vivid look at how the hierarchic structures of noble-led factions interacted with the more egalitarian institutions of the communities and how high culture communicated with and responded to popular beliefs and practices. The Cruel Carnival provides a window on the many interconnections, the *bricolage*, among social groups in a decidedly backward society, and it also shows how fragile were the tinkering attempts at group cohesion and how social ties that reached beyond family and community could be easily broken by the miscalculations of local leaders and by intervention from outside.

Most notable is how the pressures generated by wider European events made local structures extremely vulnerable. The Italian wars of the early sixteenth century, which brought the modern European powers into their first epic clash, created a terrible and lasting fissure in the traditional patterns of living and mores in the towns and villages of Friuli. Although there has long been a tendency to minimize the violence of Renaissance warfare and to treat it as a minor sideshow to the grander achievements in the arts, humanism, and political thought, these wars hurt, and they hurt badly.

In Friuli the system of patronage embodied in two mutually antagonist factions collapsed in the years after the Cambrai wars, leaving the citizens of the region in a state of collective anomie. After the demise of the factions, through which peasant and artisan commoners had built bonds of clientage with the great feudal lords, the classes separated in various ways. Villagers achieved a modest form of representation with the institution of a peasant parliament, and nobles escaped into a fantasy world of aristocratic exclusivity, epitomized by their emulation of courtly manners. By the 1560s the traditions of vendetta, which had once bonded Friulans from all social levels in a common culture of revenge killing, dissolved as aristocrats took up dueling to settle old grievances and to counter new insults.

To make these arguments, I have organized this study according to the now-venerable principles of structuralist social history but have reached conclusions uncharacteristic of structuralism inasmuch as a single event permanently broke up traditional social forms. Change is more important here than continuity.

Chapters 1 through 3 examine the long-term structures of the geography, economy, politics, and society which underlay endemic regional feuding and show how the particular vendetta between the Savorgnan and Della Torre clans catalyzed the formation of the Zambarlano and Strumiero factions. Chapter 4 treats conjunctural changes in factional leadership, a serial crisis in agriculture, and the pressures of multiple foreign invasions which, in little more than a decade, made the Cruel Carnival probable. Chapter 5 narrates the events of the carnival. Chapters 6 through 8 explore the social changes and alteration of traditional mentalities in the half-century after 1511 when the different classes began to go their own ways.

In addition, I have benefited from poststructuralist insights. Rather than treating the historical sources as repositories of ethnographic information, I have considered them as dialogues among persons of differing cultural backgrounds who understood one another imperfectly and who sometimes had a life or death stake in what was said and written. For the rhetoric of exposition I have relied a great deal on narration, which has three distinct advantages over the analytic alternatives favored by most social historians: it makes clear how the choices of individuals, who were influenced and constrained by social conditions and cultural mores, activated the course of events even though they could never control the outcome; it emphasizes the rapidity of social change; and it lays bare the many disjunctures between events and the language available to describe them. The dizzying gap between Friulan practices and the vocabulary of official discourse is no more evident than in the poverty of humanist rhetoric for analyzing the rich culture of vendetta, a poverty that not only inhibited the rulers' understanding of the ruled but made official justice a sick joke.[1]

From the microhistorians associated with the journal *Quaderni storici* I have borrowed the investigative technique of reconstructing social groups by tracing the names of constituent individuals through all the documents the archives can supply. By analyzing the participants in the carnival massacre of 1511 (for their names see Appendix 1) and then by tracing the careers of these individuals, their ancestors, and their progeny over the course of some two hundred years, I have tried to reconstruct the history of the vendetta between the Savorgnan clansmen and their various enemies and the evolution of the factions of Zambarlani and Strumieri which formed around the two sides. Instead of beginning with a theoretical conception of agnatic kinship or a judicial definition of criminal responsibility, for example, I think one is better advised to identify participants in acts of violence and then, when possible, trace their kinsmen and women, godparents, spouses, friends, creditors, debtors, tenants, patrons, neighbors, and enemies. With these names one can reconstruct the social and political context of violent acts.

The microhistorians have intensified such a method by following the interactions of individuals in a limited geographic and temporal setting, and they have also enriched it by explicitly recognizing the criteria they employ for selecting some facts over others. Instead of relying on statistical methods that require the accumulation of quantifiable data and which minimize the importance of individual variations, microhistorians have emphasized the usefulness of the "normal exception."

In preindustrial societies in particular, exceptional events such as riots, uprisings, and crimes reveal vast areas of behavior which may usually be hidden by the social and cultural distance of the participants from the institutions of the state which produced the records. The rare and idiosyncratic record, thus, may constitute the normal exception that uncovers the lives of the vast majority of people who lived on the periphery of the society of intellectuals and officials.[2]

The persistent structures of pre-1511 Friuli subsumed an ecology of scarcity, a politics of foreign domination, and a society of intertwining patronage networks. Primarily a region defined by geographic and cultural isolation, Friuli lacked water and capitalists, which meant that it remained one of the most backwardly agrarian and feudal areas in northern Italy. The republic of Venice repeatedly fought the Holy Roman Empire for the suzerainty of the region not so much because the Venetians were lured by its potential riches as because they wanted to keep its strategic mountain passes out of the hands of the enemy.

Between the dominant city and the subordinate region, the center and periphery, lay a gap unbridged by common institutions, values, or even language. Failing in its promise to deliver equal justice and military security, Venice relied on interlocking patronage connections between members of its own patriciate and influential Friulan aristocrats, a situation that made the government hostage to private interests. When the gossamer institutions failed, patrons delivered. Given the inefficacy of both local and Venetian institutions of justice, vendetta remained the principal means for the resolution of conflicts, and factions provided the most cohesive form of collective solidarity.[3]

Because contemporaries understood these various conflicts as aspects of vendetta, they used the terminology of revenge to explain what was happening in their society. The language of vendetta employed metaphors of blood, hot blood stirred, red blood spilled, common blood of kinship shared, and blue blood exalted. Or to raise the questions encoded in these metaphors, how should a man exhibit anger, how should he react to an insult or injury to himself, how should he respond to the injury or death of a kinsman, and how should he behave toward a person of a different rank?

To respect the diversity of answers to these questions and to keep from prejudging the nature of vendetta, I have started with Renaissance rather than modern definitions of vendetta. The usual modern distinction between *vendetta*, seen as a finite conflict between individuals, and *feud*, an interminable one between groups, obscures the manifold Renaissance uses of the word *vendetta*. As the paramount means of expressing anger among males, vendetta involved individuals and groups, produced short spasms of violence and enmities lasting centuries, and created ambiguous or conflicting obligations that contemporaries struggled to resolve.[4]

Although Friulans from all social levels fought vendettas, the ones that overshadowed the affairs of the region were those among the castellans, those clans (*consorti*) that held the jurisdictional rights to castles and affiliated villages, producing a situation in which the very persons most responsible for the local administration of public justice were usually the same persons who presided over private vendettas. The Friulan castellan clan should be understood more as a dynamic process than as a fixed structure because it frequently incorporated friends and clients into what presented itself as a group of blood kin, and each clan survived through continuous negotiations with other clans, subordinates, and Venetian magistrates.

The clansmen formed alliances through marriages, but every new alliance between two clans excluded others and created the potential for new enemies. In addition, the personal retainers and familiars of the castellans often fought to preserve the honor they vicariously shared with their patrons. These élites and their men constituted the vendetta nuclei around which other social groups rotated. In conducting their affairs the castellans calculated social advantage, political connections, and economic interests but avoided the appearance of weakness even when they put off or failed to retaliate against an insult or injury. They made their own choices for their own reasons. Nevertheless, participants in vendettas followed certain patterns, especially in how they performed acts of violence. Killers murdered in public places, usually admitted the deed, normally exempted women and young boys, and maximized the amount of blood shed frequently by dismembering the victim or feeding him to animals.

The dominant way in which Friulans solidified and represented interclan alliances and enmities was through membership in a faction. Many social conflicts that had little to do on the surface with preserving aristocratic honor found an outlet in factional strife, including disputes over property, feudal dues, taxes, access to markets, appointments to public jobs, and the control of civic councils. Such conflicts resist definition in conventional terms because the vertical hierarchies supposedly embodied by the factions camouflaged many anomalies and complexities. For example, membership in the factions was so transitory that their composition can usually be discerned only at moments of confrontation when participants revealed allegiances by attacking members of the other side. One knows the factions by discovering who killed whom.

Despite the factions' amorphousness they provided shadow institutions that often substituted for the formal institutions of government at all levels, rendering necessary public services but at the same time frustrating the law and defying outside control. Within each faction protection, influence, jobs, loans, and ideas were exchanged. The factions also became the trusted executors of justice through managing vendettas. They provided more coherence and strength than any alternative form of organization or certainly any public institution above the level of the community.[5]

The communities, themselves, which took the form of rural villages (*ville*) and urban neighborhoods (*borghi*), remained vital if beleaguered sources of support, particularly for the peasants and artisans. Although most were internally divided and dominated by client brokers for the great aristocratic clans, the communities survived as the only source of cooperation besides the factions. Many communities sustained a continuous but largely futile campaign for legal redress, and after the 1470s the establishment of local militia companies enhanced the capabilities of the male citizens for collective action.

Thus, clan, faction, and community provided the three social anchors for the inhabitants of a tempestuous region. Between 1499 and 1511 a conjuncture of forces frayed these traditional safety lines. A decline in agricultural prices precipitated an economic crisis, which was aggravated by the landlords' monopolizing access to village and urban markets and increasing the fiscal demands on their tenants. Foreign invasions sharpened the sense of insecurity and forced a series of violent rural protests against the escalation of war imposts. During these critical years the paternalistic leadership of Antonio Savorgnan, head of one of the factions, offered villagers an alternative to the traditional loyalties of feudal obligation so that the accumulated grievances of the peasants found expression in 1511 in outrage against the hereditary enemies of the Savorgnan. In the collective murder and pillage the body imagery of carnival merged with the rituals of vendetta killing to create a striking vocabulary of violent protest.

In the aftermath of 1511 Friulans from various social levels struggled to find meaning in the apocalyptic violence they had inflicted on themselves, and in retracing their struggles one can uncover contemporary mentalities. Whatever the antecedent structures and precipitating causes of the 1511 carnage, events followed the inherent dialectic of violence, a pattern of stimulus and response which derived its forms of representation from the cultural precepts about how to express certain emotions.

In Friuli, as in many other places, brief moments of spontaneous violence produced awful, unanticipated consequences that haunted survivors for generations. When sufficiently endangered or provoked, a man's mad blood stirred, producing an irresistible flare of choler or anger, that emotion biologically induced by what we would call the fight response. Renaissance society greatly valued the fight over the flight response; whereas fighting always produced risks, a failure to resist perceived antagonisms guaranteed shame, a social calamity perhaps more disastrous than any other for a man's relations with his fellows, as shameful for him as impurity for a woman. Whatever the encouragements of Christian morality, a man best avoided shame and preserved honor by answering anger with anger, insult with insult, injury with injury, death with death.

Although the expression of anger was widely viewed at the time as a natural phenomenon beyond individual control, it was, in fact, permeated by cultural influences. In the course of the fifteenth and sixteenth centuries many experienced an emotional education, revealing that their blood boiled not so much for natural as for learned reasons. Anger thus had a history that altered how the emotion manifested itself, how legal authorities treated it, how thinkers understood it. In Friuli the critical changes took place after 1511, and by the middle sixteenth century one of the great transformations in the history of emotions, which had taken hold in the social hothouse of the Renaissance courts, appeared among some Friulan aristocrats, a transformation from externalizing anger and projecting it onto other persons or even animals to internalizing it by adopting the self-control of good manners.[6]

The characteristics of revenge violence in Italy have long been a subtheme in Renaissance historiography, but scholars have seldom tackled the culture of violence directly, preferring to treat it as a background problem in the battle of the city-republics and princes to gain control over their territories. An important exception was a pioneering example of the history of *mentalités* by Gabriel Maugain. His study of vengeance in Renaissance Italy, published in 1935, primarily relied on an analysis of representative literary and humanist texts, but he was also fully aware of the forms of actual practice as described in the chronicles.[7]

Despite the widespread enthusiasm in recent decades for French historiography, Maugain's study has stimulated little further work, even in the field of the *mentalités* of violence. A distinguished collection of studies by Anglo-American historians of Italy, published in 1972 and edited by Lauro Martines, focused on violence, emphasizing group violence as defined by government and the law. These scholars enveloped their examinations of violence in the institutional concerns of the state or concentrated on its social causes. More recently, Guido Ruggiero demonstrated how changing attitudes toward criminality can uncover cultural attitudes about violence and its place in human affairs. He has come closest to recapturing a history of the mentality of violence and to identifying cardinal changes, at least for Renaissance Venice.[8]

The Friulan search for the meaning of 1511 and the allure of the new aristocratic values for successive generations open windows on the shared assumptions—the *mentalités*—about violent behavior. One reaction to violence shows the processes of collective scapegoating in the search to find someone or some group to blame for the hard blows of fortune. The scapegoating process internalized within the community the causes for problems that had foreign or inexplicable origins. The opposite reaction externalized the sources of violence, projecting the anger of humans onto God or other supernatural beings by attributing deaths to the divine vendetta, to the necessary apocalyptic scourges of human sins, or to the rampages of the spectral armies of the dead.

A third common reaction was to arrange events into a story, what might be called a *revenge narrative*, which sustained vendetta obligations and provided revengers with a model for behavior. The narratives were given the form of legends continuously retold over generations on winter nights around the *fogolar*. In Friuli the *fogolar*, the large freestanding hearth surrounded by benches on three sides and located in an alcove attached to the kitchen of the great castles and even of modest rustic houses, provided the locus for social communication, much as did the piazza in the parts of Italy more urbanized and blessed with a climate hospitable to outdoor life. The intimate, private character of the *fogolar*, restricted to family, friends, servants, clients, and guests, undoubtedly contributed to the extreme cultural isolation and linguistic stratification of Friuli, the endemic distrust of strangers, the weakness of communal and public institutions, and the preservation of vendetta obligations.[9]

During the sixteenth century revenge narratives often came to be written down, usually only in private family papers, occasionally in chronicles and histories, although eventually in highly crafted polemical broadsides and pamphlets. Found in several different genres, revenge narratives commented on vendettas and often structured the accounts to evoke certain emotions in listeners and readers, much as did medieval Icelandic sagas and the tales that convicts composed in Renaissance France to obtain a royal pardon for their crimes. Closely linked to cultural fashions, the narratives often evolved to suit prevailing notions of the vendetta. Moreover, these stories encouraged mimesis in hearers and readers, providing the crucial means by which individuals, especially males, formed their identities in imitation of heroic predecessors and in opposition to hereditary enemies. The narratives also embedded individual Friulans in a story, with a defined beginning, a clear plot, identifiable characters, a consistency of setting, and an anticipated end that implied expectations about their roles in life. It is thus no accident that the most popular story about vendetta in Western literature, the tragedy of *Romeo and Juliet*, found its primary source in the writings of a participant in the vendetta in Friuli, Luigi da Porto, author of a novella about revenge and love set in Verona.[10]

The richest source for understanding the mentalities of vendetta comes not so much from what was said about the violence as from looking at the actual forms of killing. Three common and traditional practices specified how to kill humans and animals properly, thus justifying and explaining the act: vendetta established the necessary conditions for the socially acceptable murder of another human being; carnival provided a festive and ludic context for the butchery of domestic animals, especially of pigs; and hunting rituals made possible the slaughter of wild animals. These cultural seeds for the killing of humans and animals cross-fertilized one another, in particular making the butchery of animals the model for the killing of men.

Traditional Friulan vendetta practices derived their legitimacy from the accepted relationships between humans and animals, and changes in those relationships signaled changes in the legitimate forms of violence. Hunting created a hierarchic relationship between hunters and their animal prey, which was represented in the butchering of game and dividing it among the hunters. Vendetta borrowed and inverted the hierarchic practices of the hunt to transform human victims into shameful animals and to permit human killers to imitate hunting dogs, who went wild in the rabid desire for blood. Through the mimetic process of modeling vendetta killing on hunting, killers exempted themselves from the normal responsibilities of civilized mankind.

In the decades after the 1511 catastrophe, the Friulan factions began to lose their cohesion, and in turn the traditional mentality of vendetta waned, dissolving the link between the hunting band and the vendetta gang, between stalking game and ambushing men. In place of the old mentality that had been sustained by implicit rules of behavior and had been shared by all Friulans, some aristocrats adopted a new ideology that mandated highly regulated forms of behavior governed by explicit rules and which separated nobles from commoners. The new manners were disseminated by a spate of fashionable books and by Friulans exiled to the North Italian courts in which they had to conform to receive princely patronage.

Three important developments followed. First, the obsession with the collective honor of families and clans faded as concerns arose about preserving individual honor, which depended less on ancient lineage than on good manners. Second, the men who inherited family and personal obligations to avenge past injuries abandoned vendetta fighting for the duel, which regulated conflict according to precise rules and which disavowed revenge as a proper motive for a duel. Third, levels of interpersonal violence among the old vendetta clans declined precipitously in Friuli, making it possible for the Venetians to impose a permanent peace on the old combatants. The bestial cruelties of vendetta died on the domesticated fields of honor.

In writing a history of obscure events in a peripheral region of a failed state, I have tried to reexamine some of the themes of Renaissance historiography from the outside. Instead of the usual absorption with the institutions and culture of the large city-states, this book ponders the extrainstitutional, marginally literate, rural, feudal, and provincial, what might be called the other side of Renaissance Italy, the things the intellectuals and their patrons in the cities tried to forget or surmount. Whatever their rhetorical affectations, Petrarch and Machiavelli were not just conversing with dead ancients but arguing against social practices that surrounded them and which they found repulsive. Vendetta violence and factional conflict threatened the daily lives of far more people than could recite Latin orations or admire Botticelli, and the success in making safer the lives of those unnamed multitudes must be recognized. That success, however, came at the cost of the repression of individual emotions and the amassing of even more deadly powers in the hands of the state.

As is so often the case in history, apparent progress is fraught with irony, even tragedy. Here I shall attempt to cross back over a deep chasm to a lost time before good manners and the authoritarian state inhibited the expression of anger and made revenge an ugly word. Only by striving to understand the alien behavior of a remote time and place can one hope to understand whence we have come and how much of the past still lives unrecognized within us.

Mad Blood Stirring

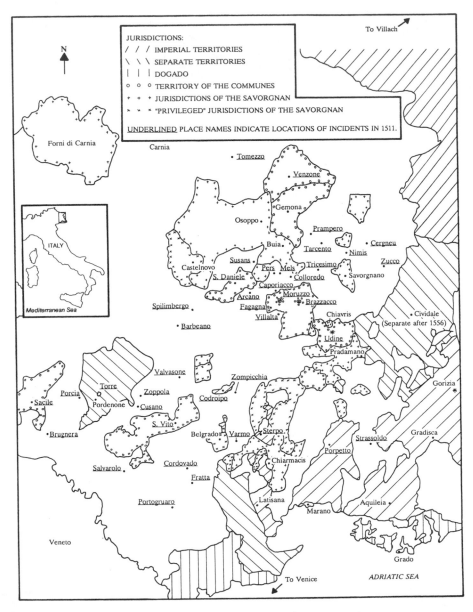

N

To Villach

Forni di Carnia

ITALY

Mediterranean Sea

Carnia

Tomezzo

Venzone

Gemona

Osoppo

Prampero

Cergneu

Buia
Tarcento
Nimis
Zucco

Susans
Pers Mels
Tricesimo
Savorgnano

Castelnovo
S. Daniele
Colloredo

Caporiacco

Arcano
Moruzzo

Spilimbergo
Fagagna
Brazzacco

Villalta
Chiavris
Cividale
(Separate after 1556)

Barbeano

Udine

Pradamano

Valvasone

Zompicchia

Gorizia

Torre
Zoppola
Codroipo

Porcia

Sacile
Pordenone
Cusano

S. Vito

Brugnera

Belgrado
Varmo
Sterpo

Gradisca

Strassoldo

Porpetto

Cordovado
Chiarmacis

Salvarolo

Fratta

Portogruaro

Latisana

Aquileia

Marano

Veneto

Grado

To Venice

ADRIATIC SEA

Map of Friuli in the sixteenth century, showing jurisdictions.

Prologue

Dead men don't fight back.
Francesco Janis di Tolmezzo[1]

Gregorio Amaseo, our principal guide to the Cruel Carnival of Udine, held an ambiguous position in his society. A notorious affair with a nun and his exceedingly modest abilities at Latin composition in the humanist mode had stymied his career as a school master, and his family's ancient patrons, the great Savorgnan clan, had abandoned him. To make matters worse, in the winter of 1511 the social fabric of his homeland began to unravel, and he held the Savorgnan responsible. Gregorio witnessed and later wrote the history of that strange unraveling, a bitter account that forms one of the most curious documents of strife and mayhem in Renaissance Italy.

Amaseo's account achieves much of its interest from the richness of its detail, its many tragic little episodes, concrete evocation of place, careful chronology, plethora of names, reports of what was said, and references to sources of information. He pushes his anti-heroic narrative through a series of edited scenes that flow from one to another with the quickening tempo of a tarantella, capturing the sickening horror of the slaughter but also constantly and tiresomely beating on the theme that that Judas, that Mohammed, that traitor, that Antonio Savorgnan, had orchestrated everything.

On the morning of Giovedì Grasso, the Thursday of carnival week, the "dogs of the house" of Savorgnan attacked young Nicolò Della Torre, son of the head of a rival clan, while he was attempting to paint the diamond blazon of his house on a well in the Savorgnan neighborhood. This little scuffle among aristocrats and their retainers (called dogs), a common enough event in Friuli, sparked something far more momentous. Nicolò quickly found himself surrounded by a crowd of artisan and peasant militiamen, many of whom had just returned from a long morning of fruitless searching for German mercenaries rumored to be in the area. The rumors also suggested that the Della Torre had rebelled against the Venetian overlords and planned to open the gates of the city to the enemy. The crowd, in Amaseo's words,

> suddenly began to yell "to arms, to arms"; at the place where the skirmish had already begun, the heads of the aforementioned peasants and plebs, who did not wait for anything else because of their desire for loot, shouted, "sack, sack, ruin the rebels"; they madly raced from everywhere and assaulted the Della Torre house with steel and fire, ringing at that point the tocsin bell in the castle to give notice to all their partisans, who rushed to the total destruction of their adversaries.[2]

The crowd rapidly grew into the thousands, surrounded the Della Torre palace, and subjected the aristocratic partisans who had found refuge there to a punishing siege:

> I, Gregorio Amaseo, a bona fide doctor, went first on that morning to the cathedral to mass with the Most Illustrious Luogotenente and then came back to the piazza with his party. Having earlier seen Savorgnan enraged . . . , I saw after dinner at the ringing of the tocsin all the armed squads march toward the houses of the Savorgnan and the Della Torre and heard from the windows of my house noises as if they were fighting. I first thought there must be a disturbance like the previous year . . . . Then seeing the flame and smoke that rose above the houses I determined to do everything possible to stop such an outrage, remembering that several times in the past the same sort of thing was remedied by my father.
> Therefore, I left the house followed by Messer Girolamo, my brother, went toward the cathedral where I saw the first

assault by the people and the firing of falconets, and it seemed
to me the people were excited with the greatest rage, and
much had already taken place. I was stirred even more by the
desire to separate them as much as was possible. So I entered
the courtyard of Savorgnan, who had just returned from the
luogotenente's castle, and seeing him so rabid, smoking with
anger, I suddenly remembered having heard from my father
that Messer Nicolò Savorgnan, father of this Antonio, said
many many times to my father because they were very close
that he was grieved by Antonio, saying that the said Antonio
had a bestial temper and was very dangerous so that Nicolò
worried there would be a day when Antonio would cause
some great trouble to the ruin of his house. Because of that
memory I did not have the boldness to confront him, as I had
first planned, especially seeing several of his close associates
who did not admonish him. From that I at once thought he
had dined with the Devil and asked two or three times several
persons especially Doctors Francesco Janis di Tolmezzo and
Girolamo Mels where the luogotenente was. Tolmezzo answered me, "What do I have to do with the luogotenente?"
and said to my brother, "Messer Gregorio would do well not
to be rash; he is looking for bad luck." Nonetheless by my
insisting to know, Tolmezzo finally indicated that the luogotenente was somewhere around the church of San Francesco.

Gregorio left, searched about, and finally found the luogotenente,
the Venetian authority in charge of maintaining order, who was
accompanied by only five or six men because he had no others to
call upon. Gregorio remembered saying to him:

What is Your Magnificence doing here? Can't you see what
ruin there will be in this place today if you don't stop them?
For the love of God don't hang around here; we'll go to Antonio Savorgnan's house, and you order them to put down the
weapons and put out this fire; let's go, let's go, don't let Your
Magnificence doubt this city, because we are all good partisans
of Saint Mark.

They went to Savorgnan's palace where they found the Venetian
treasurer, Antonio Badoer, surrounded by about fifty armed men,

who supposedly shouted a long-winded profession of loyalty, "All for one cheer, Mark, Mark; we don't want any other lords in this land than the rectors of Saint Mark." Amaseo continued a story that focused rather much on himself:

> Antonio Savorgnan ran down into the courtyard without a hat on his head as if bewitched, threatening me with words similar to these, "Messer Gregorio, Messer Gregorio, you would do well not to rush into matters that don't concern you; if you aren't smart, I'll have you killed." He shouted so that more than a hundred armed men and many others who were around there heard. Responding to that, likewise in a loud voice, I ardently said to him, "Messer Antonio, what I do, I do for your own good; you don't have any idea what the Most Illustrious Signoria intends to do; don't think that it would ever forgive you for such a thing. I am not one of your new friends; our families' friendship is an old one of more than a hundred years standing. I believe I can counsel you better about your welfare than two hundred of the best of these men who will soon go back home." Continuously imploring him to put out the above-mentioned fire, I said to them all, "You have done plenty, don't go ahead, it is enough to have shown your enemies that you could destroy them; save them now, because if you do you will regain the greatest crown of glory ever achieved by a man of your house."

Gregorio continued to plead despite Antonio's implacable anger. The luogotenente ordered Antonio in reverence of Saint Mark to cease the attack, put out the fire, lay down arms, and send away the brigades. To all this Antonio replied, "I can't do anything more, do it yourselves, do it yourselves, it's not my fault." He turned to some aides, "armored from head to foot," made certain signs, and said in a low voice that they knew their tasks: "go, go, do it, do it."

> After the first argument and seeing nothing could be worked out with him, the luogotenente returned to the street, and as I, Gregorio, remember it, he began, while grabbing hold of their shoulders, to command under penalty of the gallows and by decree of the Council of Ten that everyone put down their

arms and leave and not threaten any person because the Most Illustrious Signoria recognized them all as good and most faithful sons. He was assisted by the treasurer. Several of the heads of the mob of peasants, armed populace, and the executioners of Iscariot responded to them boastfully that the Strumieri were neither good nor faithful but all rebels and consequently the Zambarlani wanted to punish them in their own way. They called in great haste, "to the ruin, to the ruin, to the sack of the rebels." Nevertheless, many others began to withdraw in order to obey, largely because a trumpeter in Savorgnan livery played a call to retreat, an act to which he was forced by the rector, who threatened him with the gallows, although the trumpeter immediately retired to the courtyard of the Savorgnan.

However, by the instigation of many, those who had left returned to the Della Torre palace where most had remained, so that right away they stormed the doors and unloosed the falconets, at every charge shooting guns, crossbows, and bows. Seeing that, the luogotenente entered the house of Savorgnan another time, imploring him with greatest insistence that he make those companies leave and quiet the uproar, excusing him and discharging him of responsibility, as before, because the luogotenente thought Savorgnan did not want such a thing to happen; but on the contrary Savorgnan right away urged them on with glances and gestures and speaking in the ear to this person and that so they went from bad to worse. Seeing from this that he could not accomplish anything, the rector had, by my recollection, the trumpeter Ludovico come, sound the trumpet, and announce the edicts and proclamations in a loud voice. Incited by some of the leaders, among others by Giovanni Monticolo, all the rabble loudly yelled that the trumpeter could not be heard, so that despite these proclamations they did not give up their evil deeds; instead those far away interpreted the call as an order to rout out the rebels. After that incident Savorgnan went out into the street to make sure that notwithstanding the edict his men were proceeding according to the order given. The luogotenente implored him anew to stop them, and I heard Savorgnan twice say with great rage, "I am so angry that I am beside myself, and I don't know myself what I'm doing," after which it seemed of little use, so that I, Amaseo, did not remind them again of their own welfare, but because I had been threatened first by him and then by several others, especially by Vincenzo Pozzo and Ascanio Sbroiavacca, who had weapons handy to kill me, I left off saying anything else to them just as already had the treasurer, threatened with the same fate by Uccello Carneval, Pietro Justo, and Pietro Durissino, who among others burned with rabid fury. And at last the luogotenente, moreover, saw that neither edicts nor entreaties were any use; rather they provoked more evil deeds; while the traitor returned home, the luogotenente followed him and brusquely accosted him telling him in the following way, "Messer Antonio, one must have plenty of guts to take the artillery of the Council of Ten; this was an intolerable presumption. I order you under penalty of the displeasure of the Signoria and of the gallows and by decree of the Most High Council of Ten that you have all the artillery and munitions immediately returned from where you took them." He replied, "I don't know anything about it, you're mistaken."

Having already been there from [about 2:00 to 4:00 p.m.] and having continuously argued and supposing there was nothing more to do than had already been done, the luogotenente mounted his horse and rode back to the castle with his officers . . . , and Amaseo with his brother returned home by the shortest way, thinking to have done the best for the universal welfare, although nothing would be of any use to prevent Savorgnan and his accomplices from doing the worst possible, to which the awful constellation of that day largely inclined him.[3]

As artillery balls began to pound down the main door of the Della Torre palace, the company of nobles who had defended it fled through the garden or across the roofs to nearby houses. The treasures of the Della Torre were grabbed up by looters whom Amaseo described as "a number of most wicked peasants, the majority banished for thefts and assassinations, inasmuch as they have brought in the scum off the balls of the villages, castles, and towns of the Patria." The poor, however, would remember this scum

differently as heroes and patriots, as the true revengers of the
people, and more than four centuries later would still dance in their
honor every year on Giovedì Grasso.[4]

Pillage turned to slaughter. One after another, aristocratic members of the castellan clans allied to the Della Torre were dragged
from their hiding places, trampled, stoned, dismembered, and left
as food for market dogs and wild pigs. Antonio offered a few noble
refugees his protection but exacted a heavy price by shamefully
forcing them to their knees to beg for their lives.

Others died at Antonio's explicit orders. After discovering their
hiding place, Antonio promised his protection to three young nobles, Giovanni Leonardo Frattina, Teseo Colloredo, and Nicolò
Della Torre, the last having managed to escape from the scuffle that
had started the conflagration earlier in the day, but

> about two hours after sunset Savorgnan returned with a large
> number of executioners and had the three come out; seeing
> the swarm of armed men, these three were instantly fore-
> warned of their deaths, and because of this Giovanni Leonardo
> took off, was caught at the Hay Barn Square, was stopped
> by a blow from the halberd of Giovanni Pietro Fosca, and fell
> to the ground, unhappily cut to pieces by numerous blows.
> The other two, while walking down the street not far from
> Colombatto's house, were most cruelly quartered like cattle
> by . . . Vergon and others who, raising yells and screams to
> heaven, bloodied the whole street and scattered about bits of
> flesh, brains, and hair. Among these assassins was later said to
> have been one Giovanni di Leonardo Marangone di Capriglie,
> who on that night, drunk with wine and stuffed with stolen
> chickens, boasted of having hacked up Della Torre with a
> butcher's cleaver; his face covered with blood and the rings of
> the dead on his fingers, the fiend took the lighted torches from
> Giovanni Bianchino and said, "Kill! Kill those that still move!"
> At this word Vincenzo Pozzo, who had already been con-
> demned to death in Venice for rebellion, like a rabid dog tor-
> tured [the survivors] with his weapons.[5]

After two days of carnival frenzy, the allies of Antonio Savorgnan gathered to evaluate their success. One of his most ardent
partisans was Dr. Francesco Janis di Tolmezzo, a man of deep legal

learning, brother of the superintendent of the Carnia militia, re-
former of the civic statutes of Udine, and distinguished member of
the city council and the parliament of Friuli:

> With extreme elation rising up and down on his toes with his
> hands tucked in his belt and his hat pulled low over his dark
> face, averting his eyes and licking his lips, pompous and ar-
> rogant, Francesco Janis di Tolmezzo pronounced bombasti-
> cally that never had a more notable thing been achieved by a
> man of the house of Savorgnan, although they had already
> killed a patriarch [a reference to the murder of John of Moravia
> in 1394] and had removed all the bad thorns that had been such
> a nuisance over the years. By means of this action they could
> control everything without any opposition to their wishes,
> adding that he had never slept that night and blabbing on
> about every detail of what had happened.[6]

That from one of the citizens most responsible for public order.
  On Sunday the crowd celebrated the achievements of the previous days with a remarkable carnival masquerade.

> On that day, although all the rest of the city was mournful and
> sad, the sanguinary associates and followers of the most per-
> fidious assassin had a great celebration, running from one di-
> version to another, dressed in the silk clothes and livery of the
> betrayed gentlemen, calling one another by the names of those
> whose clothes they wore. The piper Sebastiano Cornetto,
> dressed in the sumptuous velvets of the Della Torre, played to
> the people who were frolicking in the square, and not a year
> passed before he suffered punishment when he was vilely
> killed near Cormons. When the rapacious clods left for their
> villages in merry gangs, mocking and jeering the miserable
> nobility, they were dressed even as doctors and their women
> as ladies so that it appeared the world was upside down.

From Udine the merry gangs of peasants brought the Cruel Carnival to the countryside, and "the peasants of all the villages as far
as Sacile took up arms against the castles to put them to sack and
burn them, and where there was no resistance they entered into the
castles to sack and burn them."[7]

As with the Udine uprising, the troubles in the countryside left a legacy of mawkish stories that the aristocratic victims told and retold to mythologize their losses. The most famous involved the escape through snow-covered fields of the children of Alvise Della Torre. Alvise and Nicolò Della Torre had left their wives, Tadea Strassoldo and Giacoma Brazzacco, at the clan's castle of Villalta where the peasants began to agitate within hours of the events in Udine. Tadea felt so threatened by the clamor that she sent her two eldest children, Raimondo and Girolamo, into the mud and snow to find refuge at Moruzzo. There they could hear the hubbub from the assault on nearby Brazzacco and went on to Colloredo di Monte Albano, where they were joined by their younger siblings, Giovanni and Ginevra, who were accompanied by two guards, a tutor, and an old family friend. From Colloredo the little band of refugees fled to Pers, then the elder two were taken to Gemona, where finally their adult cousin Giacomo Spilimbergo rescued them and with a guard of nine horsemen took them in the middle of the night to his castle. But the next morning, Spilimbergo castle also came under attack, and Giacomo had to flee with his wards and wife to Brugnera, where they arrived in time to attend a carnival ball at which many of the wives of Giovedì Grasso victims, unaware that they were newly made widows, danced away the night. The beleaguered nobles finally found safety in Pordenone, but some fled as far as Venice. In the meantime, Villalta was sacked, and the rough-handed peasants tore a fourth Della Torre infant away from his wet nurse's breast. However, they spared the child and eventually turned him over to the care of his aunt. Other castellan families produced their own stories of danger and fear.[8]

Gregorio maintained that Antonio Savorgnan coordinated even these far-flung disquiets. He supposedly sent agents out into the countryside to incite the peasants by telling them that the castellans had rebelled against Saint Mark and wanted to subject Friuli to the emperor, who would return the peasants to serfdom. Peasants had responded by attacking "like rabid dogs for they believed such things and also because of their desire for loot." On the left bank of the Tagliamento "the peasants were stirred up in a great number, armed as if for battle with artillery brought to overcome the fortresses; following them with carts came the endless numbers of their families who desired booty, and with a great outcry they thundered about the ruin of the nobles. To this end they had been inflamed by their Mohammed and his followers."[9]

These few scenes from Gregorio's angry and obviously partisan history, these few moments of confrontation in a vast wave of violence which permanently transformed Friulan society, raise numerous questions about what was going on during the Cruel Carnival. Who was rebelling against whom? Why were the Venetian authorities so inept? Why did a quarrel among a few feuding aristocrats set off such a major upheaval? How had the factions come to dominate so completely the loyalties of Friulan society? Who was in the crowd? What did they want? How much did the rioters act on their own, and how much were they merely pawns of Antonio Savorgnan as Gregorio suggests? What was the meaning of the macabre dismemberments and the feeding of corpses to animals? To answer these questions, the following chapters first take the story backward by more than a century when the Savorgnan and Della Torre vendetta began, Venice acquired Friuli, the factions formed. In searching for the answers to the little questions about this single event, a much vaster panorama unfolds, leading, I hope, to a keener sense of how vendetta operated in Renaissance Italy, how factions dominated its political life, and how contemporaries understood their own violence.

Part One

STRUCTURES
& PRACTICES

CHAPTER ONE

The Friulan Enigma

In 1420 after a long and vicious war, the republic of Venice conquered the Patria del Friuli, which had been an ecclesiastical principality ruled by the patriarch of Aquileia. The last patriarch with temporal powers, Ludwig of Teck (1412–39), went into exile in Germany, leaving his faction-ridden, mountain-ringed principality to be incorporated into the growing terraferma dominion of the maritime republic.[1]

The dramatic character of the conquest notwithstanding, the Venetian absorption of the patria did not produce a radical intensification of Venetian involvement in Friuli or an alteration in the character of Friulan society and institutions. Friuli had long been a special concern of the Venetians. Since their earliest moves out of their protective lagoon, they had struggled against the patriarchs of Aquileia and had set up a rival patriarchal seat in Grado. Venetian merchants had had extensive economic interests in Friuli since the thirteenth century, and, after the murder of Patriarch John Sobieslaw of Moravia in 1394, the republic had sought to guarantee the selection of patriarchs friendly to its interests. The conquest merely replaced the patriarch with a Venetian administrator whose powers were no greater than those of his ecclesiastical predecessor.[2]

Except for confiscating the temporal possessions of the patriarch, Venice left Friuli relatively untouched. Given the ambiguity
of its legal claims to the patriarchate, Venice did not even assert full
sovereignty over the region but merely asked the pope to accept
the reality of its occupation and gave its governor the singularly
tentative title of luogotenente (lieutenant). Friuli was just one of
several mainland territories Venice acquired during the early fifteenth century as a defensive bulwark against its many rivals, but
Venice had neither the personnel nor the bureaucracy to exploit
intensively such a vast domain.[3]

The handful of Venetian officials sent to administer Friuli after
the conquest found an impoverished, mostly arid region, inhabited
by people who spoke a strange language and practiced alien customs. Unlike the Italian-speaking, urbane citizens Venetian magistrates found in recently conquered Padua, Vicenza, and Verona,
the Friulans were inscrutable and hostile, not so much because of a
nostalgia for lost liberties, which they had never possessed, but
because their long experience with war and civil strife had left them
with a deep distrust of all strangers. Although they frequently
commented on the Friulans' peculiarities, the Venetian magistrates
and soldiers had few expectations from their subjects as long as the
region's mountain passes and fortresses provided a buffer against
potential invaders of Venice itself.

Left with their own laws largely in place, the Friulans continued
to suffer under a body of dysfunctional and conflicting feudal institutions which had made the region vulnerable to an economic
giant such as Venice in the first place. The families of the castellan
aristocracy subdivided judicial and political authority and monopolized agricultural resources, preventing the development of
effective central institutions. At the same time they used the Friulan
parliament and their local jurisdictional rights to inhibit the evolution of communal liberties and the kinds of community institutions which had given vitality to hundreds of towns elsewhere in
central and northern Italy.

THE LAND BETWEEN

"In the time of which I write," Ippolito Nievo commented concerning late eighteenth-century Friuli, "matters remained as nature
had made them and Attila had left them." Nature had fashioned

Friuli as a vast stage set for a drama of recurrent civil strife which endured almost unchanged for centuries; even the characters' given names, drawn from a small repertoire of saints and chivalric heroes attached to place-based surnames, tended to remain the same over the generations.[4]

The civil strife of fifteenth- and sixteenth-century Friuli was conditioned by geographic and ecologic circumstances that compelled a heavy concentration of settlement within a confined area; placed a premium on access to scarce water resources; demanded a careful division of the available arable land and a constant supervision of streams, ponds, bogs, pastures, and woods; and required the occupation and fortification of strategic hills for defense against neighbors and recurrent invaders. During particularly intense periods of factional strife Friuli approached the conditions of "total scarcity" Jacob Black-Michaud has posited as the necessary prerequisite for feuding, but the more common material precondition for conflict came from the habitually unequal distribution of scarce resources. The poverty of the region's subsistence economy was matched by the linguistic and cultural isolation of most of its inhabitants, who remained completely ignorant of the civic values that evolved in the cities touched by Renaissance culture.[5]

Sixteenth-century writers who described the topography of Friuli frequently relied on theatrical metaphors to convey the showy way in which the Carnic and Julian Alps created a backdrop for the events played out in the cluster of castles and towns scattered at their feet. "So this patria . . . it seems to me should be described as a theater of endless mountains," began one anonymous local in a treatise addressed to the Venetian luogotenente, the Venetian governor of the region (Figure 1). Venetians who traveled there came home praising in Petrarchan fashion the spectacular scenery but lamenting the rude, endemic poverty of Friulan villages.[6]

In 1483 Marco Sanudo and two other patricians were elected circuit judges (auditori nuovi) to tour the mainland hearing appeals to sentences delivered by local judges. When Marco left on his trip, which would last nearly six months, he brought along his seventeen-year-old nephew Marin, who kept an account of what he saw, a foretaste of his adult obsession with recording everything that passed his way in his famously verbose diaries. Notwithstanding his youthful enthusiasm for things new, he could hardly miss the

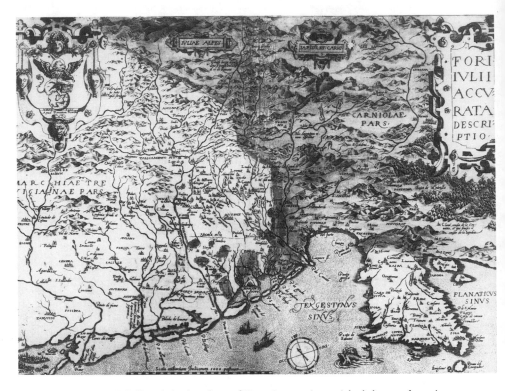

FIGURE I. Friuli and the borders of Venetian territory (*shaded areas* show imperial lands), by Donato Bertellis (sixteenth century ?).

sad ruin of many of the villages and the disease-ridden bodies of the inhabitants. Aquileia, once a "most powerful and great city," shocked him particularly. Among its ruined walls and aqueducts lived twenty-four canons, who officiated in the cathedral, preserving the liturgical functions of the much reduced and no longer princely patriarch, and a handful of fishermen and their families, most of whom suffered from the jaundice and lassitude of malaria. Later in his career, however, Marin wrote a more formal description of Friuli which revealed more about his knowledge of the ancient geographers than his ability to remember and trust in what he had actually observed:

> In Europe under the Arctic pole at the extremity and in the tenth part of beautiful Italy, irrigated by pleasant rivers, deco-

rated by opulent and rich cities, and furnished with proud castles, one sees spread out a pleasant and delightful plain . . . . It is enclosed on the northern and eastern sides by the valleys of very high mountains, on the southern by the Adriatic Sea and the western by the wide river of Livenza. The ancient cosmographers called it Carnia but now everyone knows it as the Patria del Friuli.[7]

As was the case with that of Marin Sanudo, other Renaissance descriptions of the land and its people worked at odd cross-purposes; some, especially those inspired by humanism, idealized the country that had once been a prosperous Roman province and was still so striking, whereas others, particularly those with practical problems to solve, lamented the degraded condition of the peasants and their ruthless exploitation by the castellan nobles. The idealizers remind one of those nineteenth-century Piedmontese bureaucrats who insisted that Sicily must be the breadbasket of the new Italy because that is what they had learned about the island from their classical educations.[8]

Particularly influential among Venetian and Friulan idealizers were organic descriptions, best illustrated by a remarkable topographic description called the "Anatomy of the Patria del Friuli" by an unknown Udinese of the late sixteenth century. In this description the patria takes on the "form of a human female body which has the best natural symmetry in its members and principal parts." She lay as if she were Mother Nature herself with her head toward the south wind and her feet to the north. In ancient times she married the Lombard dukes, later the emperors, the patriarchs, and most recently the doges of Venice. In her heart she held Udine, her head was old Aquileia, her right arm embraced Cividale and her left Portogruaro and ancient Concordia, and her other parts down to her toenails consisted of the many castles and villages.

The author developed his awkward and inconsistent metaphor to argue by analogy that Udine, the heart of the Friuli, should treat the other cities and the castles as its appendages and that anyone who challenged this natural arrangement was guilty of matricide. Some of her sons, he said, were too vain and thorny-tempered, and they had attacked their own mother, "cutting her with a hundred knives." Despite the author's claim that the same lifeblood pumped by the capital-city heart flowed through all Friuli, he nearly dismembered his own image under the pressure of incompatible reality, and his goal in describing his land as one body was itself polemical and divisive inasmuch as it supported the claims of Udine against its rival cities (particularly its bitter enemy Cividale) and against the castellans who controlled the parliament and who saw themselves at the heart of things. In fact, this description reinterpreted the official emblem of Friuli, which consisted of a female figure whose many-colored dress denoted the qualities of the noble lords who lived there, whose crown of towers represented the nobles' castles, and whose lance stood for the obligations and privileges of the castellans.[9]

In contrast, Luigi da Porto, the author of *Giulietta e Romeo*, wrote more directly and with less fancy. The castles and many of the towns spread over the plain are pleasant, he said, but the "villages are more for utility than for beauty," and he missed the palaces and gardens of his native Vicentino. With equal frankness the Venetian luogotenenti presented to the Senate at the end of their terms of office summary reports (*relazioni*) about conditions in Friuli, and these became a genre of lamentations.[10]

Girolamo Mocenigo wrote in 1574, "the peasants are all poor, and a few of them hang around the taverns and often make the women and children work the fields." The demands of Venetian wartime taxation, he added, were so onerous that they made life impossible for the peasants, many of whom abandoned their houses and emigrated. "The peasantry, principal nerve of public service in that patria," Tommaso Morosini continued in 1601, "finds itself because of a thousand adverse conditions in manifest ruin with little hope of improvement." Because of scarcities of virtually all goods as well as exactions from Venice, emigration had risen to such a point that the inhabitants had abandoned entire villages, weeds choked the fields, and aristocrats deserted their castles, leaving the few remaining peasants "in a thousand ways oppressed."

Just four years before the fall of the republic in 1797, Paolo Erizzo recapitulated the observation made by his predecessors over the previous four centuries, saying "the peasant lives vegetating like his sterile field, brutalized by ignorance and misery." These luogotenenti reported on a forsaken wasteland that contrasted with the euphoric floridity of the humanist descriptions. However, the

sparsely inhabited, economically depressed region continued to attract the attention of Venice on the one hand and of the archdukes
of Austria and the emperors on the other through its important
commercial roads and its strategic position as the "great open
door" to Italy.[11]

The door to Italy opens onto the three morphologic zones of
Friuli. In the south of the region lies a broad flat land, the eastern
extreme of the great Po Valley–Veneto Plain that stretches more
than three hundred miles from just west of Turin. The plain, which
constitutes more than a third of Friuli's area, rises from the lagoons
of Caorle, Marano, and Grado in places merging with swamps,
flood-plagued lowlands, and sand dunes. This region, known as
lower Friuli, where in Roman times settlements had concentrated,
suffered beginning in the early Middle Ages from continuous shifting in the courses of the Livenza, Tagliamento, and Isonzo Rivers,
whose sedimentary deposits and swamp-creating overflows made
permanent habitation tenuous. Malarial ponds and difficulties in
transportation limited exploitation of the lower plain's resources—
wild game, fish, woods, canes, and arable land—so that most of the
area remained sparsely inhabited until the great land-reclamation
projects of the nineteenth and twentieth centuries.[12]

In the Renaissance the principal city of the lower plain was Portogruaro, a trading emporium and stopover near the old Concordia
road. The vital ports were Caorle; Monfalcone, which was isolated
from the rest of the patria by the imperial county of Gorizia which
surrounded it; and Marano, a lagoon-edge fortress that during the
sixteenth century was traded back and forth between the Venetians
and Austrians because of sieges and betrayals.

The second and central morphologic zone consists of three concentric arcs, called the morainic amphitheater of the Tagliamento,
located to the north of Udine. The highest hills found in the outer
arc rise, sometimes precipitously, three hundred feet above the
plain's surface whereas those of the two inner bands are more lobe-
like, some mere ripples, and among the three cordons of hills were
once dispersed several lakes that have gradually become bogs. The
soils of these hills are poor and dry, producing only a natural covering of thin grass and requiring wells and irrigation for settlement
and agriculture. The area on the left bank of the Tagliamento,
blessed with a greater variety of minerals for the soil, offers the

best prospects for crops, and here most of the 835 villages of sixteenth-century Friuli clustered.[13]

Conflicts of interest, particularly between the requirements of lumber transport and those of agriculture, prevented the improvements proposed by generation after generation of reformers who envisioned the potential benefits of irrigation and land reclamation in the hill region. Such conflicts are emblematic of a social and political system that had difficulty resolving the internal discord which, more than anything else, bears the burden of blame for the continued agrarian poverty. Altering a water course in the slightest way could set in motion bloody confrontations and a deluge of protest. In 1482 when one of the nobles of Spilimbergo had some ditches dug without the consent of his neighbors, the citizens rose up in open rebellion, claiming he had abused his right of access to the commons.[14]

As a result of such defensive habits, agricultural productivity in central Friuli before the introduction of maize and rice remained at the subsistence level. Locally grown grains, vegetables, and fodder could sustain the population and their domestic animals except when the harvests failed, as they often did during the early sixteenth century, or when grain dealers sold or were forced by the Venetians to sell their reserves to Venice or occasionally to Belluno. In Udine the bread supply was notoriously uncertain, falling short with any major economic downturn, "a thing too miserable and dangerous" admitted the city council, and when bread was available "one could not find a blacker or nastier" loaf than that made and sold in Udine. The Friulan wines, however, were famous if not overly plentiful. The young Marin Sanudo found the whites of Cividale "most perfect" and heard it claimed that they were the best in Italy.[15]

Plenty of wood for lumber and fuel was available although the demands of Venetian shipbuilding began to use up the better timber during the sixteenth century, and arsenal officials had to return again and again to find new sources. The land produced fruit, olives, flax, hay, and straw and provided pasture for mules, donkeys, horses, and draft oxen. Cattle were rarely grazed for slaughter, the available beef coming from animals driven over the passes from Austrian mountain pastures. Sheep could be found, but their wool was coarse and woven only for peasant clothing. Pork, kid, veal, fish, chicken, and other poultry supplemented the diets of the rich and occasionally the poor. Hunters caught partridges, pheasants, wild cocks, deer, fallow deer, wild goats, hares, boars, foxes, wolves, and bears, producing grand sport and a modest variety for the table. Twelve annual fairs held in Aquileia, Cividale, Udine, Codroipo, Portogruaro, Sacile, Roveri, and Villafredda traded available products, especially livestock, but few luxury goods or imported items could be found.[16]

Friulan craftsmen produced little for export except scythes, which they traded throughout Italy; there were no organized industries save for a few isolated mines and small workshops in metals; and commercial crops did not exist. Initially dominated by Florentines, the woolen cloth industry never developed an export market, and the silk industry, introduced in 1515, took nearly a century to become viable. The rigidity of the regional economy, committed chiefly to direct subsistence agriculture, provided few cushions to absorb the shocks of weather, war, and exploitation. As long as social organization remained static, the potential riches of these modest hills remained buried.[17]

Numerous fortifications still appear on the tops of the thinly green hills and in a few locations across the lower soggy plain. Some of these are mere earthworks barely traceable among the brush; others are no more than a single ruined tower that seems to grow from the rock; some are pleasant country villas protected by entrenchments and a strong door; and still others are massive gray piles, proper castles complete with moat and drawbridges, battlements and ramparts, towers and keep. The governing rules of location for all of the fortifications were strategic value, proximity to habitation, and access to water to make a moat. The better sites had been occupied at least since the terrifying Hungarian invasions that came with the fall of the Ottonian Empire. Girolamo Porcìa (1531–1601) distinguished forty-four modest castles, used primarily as noble residences; eleven large ones, some of which served as garrisons; and thirteen walled towns, which also had castles within them. In his time many scores more of old fortifications were abandoned or in ruins. Palmanova, the showpiece of Renaissance military architecture, was the only completely new location in the sixteenth century.[18]

The fortifications testify to the insecurity of Friulan life, but the threat as often as not came from within, from the castles' inhabitants, whose violent passions sometimes flamed forth. These lumps of stone served the decaying power of the nobles who prized them as signs of honor and who seldom risked closing their gates and manning their towers against attackers more dangerous than their own peasant tenants or their castellan neighbors. By the sixteenth century only a handful of the castles retained any authentic military value, and most castellans quickly capitulated before they would face a siege from a real army. The castellans formed a privileged military class that had lost its military functions and ability but that still dominated the hill country around Udine. Members of this class kept the vendettas alive, and their battles made the hill region the locus of most violent conflicts. Thus, the geographic concentration of feuding in the Friulan hills contrasts with the typical Mediterranean pattern of mountain feuds.[19]

To the north and east of the plain and hill regions appears the third morphologic zone of the Carnic and Julian Alps, which covers more than two fifths of the land surface of the region. The mountains provided the Venetians with meager riches beyond timber and iron, but the real allure came from the prospect of controlling the passes into Carinthia, Styria, and upper Austria and of assuring transit for Venetian commerce.[20]

Despite the forbidding obstacles—the arduous climbs, rutted roads, disgusting inns, snow, rock slides, and sudden storms—the rewards for merchants who reached the other side of the mountains had long been great. Even in Roman times seventeen out of the twenty-three major passes through the Alps proper were in regular use, and the Romans built two roads through the passes of Carnia. The Imperial or Iron Road outstripped all others in commercial significance. Several feeder routes crossed the Friulan plain from south to north to join the Imperial Road near Gemona. This well-situated, properly walled town had a warehouse for merchants traveling to and from German lands and a jurisdictional privilege that required all commercial travelers to lodge overnight there. Sanudo reported in 1503 that the privilege, for which the town paid sixty ducats annually to the fiscal chamber of Udine, brought between five hundred and six hundred ducats extra income per year. Venzone, a few miles further north up the road, had a similar privilege to frustrate trade.[21]

Just beyond Venzone the road divided. The Imperial Road on the right fork followed the course of the Fella up the Canale di Ferro along a narrow cliff-hugging track, through the guard fortress at Chiusaforte, and after Pontebba on toward Villach, Klagenfurt, Graz, and Vienna. The left fork meandered beside the Tagliamento to Tolmezzo where most travelers turned north along the But, passed the ancient Roman settlement at Zuglio, crossed the pass at Monte Croce (Plöckenpass), and continued toward Lienz, Salzburg, and Munich. The Monte Croce pass could only be crossed on horseback, a disadvantage that also limited the usefulness of the routes to the west of Tolmezzo, one following the Degan toward a cluster of passes into Austria and the other tracing the Tagliamento to its source then crossing the Mauria pass into Cadore.[22]

The Venetians sought control of mountain passes for both commercial advantages and military defense. Almost every description of Friuli dwells at length on the opportunities the passes provided for the enemy—Turks, Hungarians, or Austrians—to bring troops, provisions, and artillery into Italy. Because geographic studies were the stepchild of military science, one expects such a preoccupation, but the recurrent invasions and threats of invasion, particularly in the late fifteenth and early sixteenth centuries, created a monomaniacal concern with the condition of mountain roads and with provisions for fortifications guarding access to Italy.

The excessive focus on passes led to some disastrous follies. Seldom were the Venetians able to ward off with mountain defenses a well-organized invasion—the famous victory of Cadore in 1508 was the exception—but they continued to delude themselves that mountain defenses could provide security on the cheap. Partly as a result of his observations of the manifold failures of Venetian policy during the War of the League of Cambrai, Machiavelli disparaged guarding passes, pointing out that the most one could accomplish was to prevent the enemy from crossing one pass rather than another. "If, then, you lose a pass which you have set out to hold and which your people and your army trust, almost every time such great terror seizes your people and the remainder of your soldiers that, without a chance to test their valor, you become a loser. Thus you lose all of your fortune with part of your forces."[23]

The Venetians tried to guard the Carnic mountain passes in two ways. One was to garrison the fortress at Chiusaforte, built at a point at which the canyon walls close in around the river, to control completely all traffic on the Imperial Road. The road itself, which was the only way down the canyon, passed directly through the strongly built fortress protected by drawbridges. No fortification, however, guards better than the men who defend it, and on several critical occasions during the War of the League of Cambrai the garrison fled in the face of superior numbers. The second strategy relied on local mountain militias. The 180 villages of Carnia were grouped into four valleys (*canali*), each of which contributed men to a militia company. In theory a force of three thousand should have been available, but such a level of strength was seldom achieved, and the men who did appear were only able to drill in the late summer when they returned from work in Germany. One luogotenente described them to the doge of Venice:

> This nation consists of robust people, and many of them are as clever as university graduates without having ever opened a book. From among these Carnians, who travel all over the place and then come home during the months of July and August, Your Serenity can glean five hundred soldiers, all harquebusmen, for your militia company, but given the short time available to train them and even though the men are imposing and very strong, they handle the harquebuses very badly, and I judge that training them would serve for little. At present the said company is led by Captain Ottavio da Macerata, who does what he can.

Whatever the merits of the militiamen of Carnia, amply proved at the battle of Rio Secco during the 1508 campaign in Cadore, their lack of numbers, discipline, and availability made them an unreliable defense force, and the failure of the strategy of defending mountain passes made the plain of Friuli particularly vulnerable to invasion. After 1485 Venice fought a long series of bloody wars on Friulan soil against the emperor, his allies, and surrogates, all of whom sent troops and supplies through the mountains.[24]

Once their mountain defenses had been breached, the Venetians had to rely on a cordon of fortified positions on the Friulan plain. Because the eastern edge of the plain was occupied by the county of Gorizia, allied to the empire and after the extinction of the counts directly ruled by Emperor Maximilian, the mountains provided no protection on that side except for the fact that the routes from Austria and Hungary to Gorizia were so rocky and difficult that artillery could not be transported along them.[25]

As early as 1474 Venice began a defensive line of trenches and earthworks on the right bank of the Isonzo from just below Gorizia to Aquileia, but the Turks easily breached these in 1477. As an alternative, Venice built up the fortresses at Foglianica and especially Gradisca, but these again proved to be inadequate when the Turks returned in 1499. The next year the Senate hired Leonardo da Vinci to make recommendations about the Isonzo defenses, but even his advice produced no effective improvements. After Maximilian's captains seized Gradisca in 1509, the Venetians were never again able to recover it permanently.

The sea access found protection at Marano and the western plain in the fortified city of Sacile and the line of stockades along the Livenza River although strategists intended these to protect the approaches to Venice after the enemy had already overrun Friuli. Any significant army invading from Austria, however, would have to use the Imperial Road to bring in artillery; and when the strategy of guarding mountain passes failed, the defenders of Friuli fell back upon Osoppo.[26]

The rock of Osoppo is a place of many fables. Occupied before the Romans came, used by the Lombards to defend themselves against the Avars and by 364 revolutionaries against a long Austrian siege in 1848, garrisoned in the First World War and bombed in the Second, Osoppo has long been the keystone of Friulan and northeastern Italian defenses. In 1513 and 1514 after Marano and Gradisca had fallen to the Austrians, Venetian forces had abandoned Udine, and nearly all the castellans had gone over to the enemy, Girolamo Savorgnan and a few hundred men held out at Osoppo against the siege of the combined imperial armies and forced the enemy to abandon Friuli and return most of it to Venetian rule. Situated between the Imperial Road and the Tagliamento River a few miles below where the river breaks onto the plain, the moraine rises precipitously some 350 feet above the fields, providing a strategic position from which all movement to and from the mountains could be observed (Figure 2). Girolamo Savorgnan described it as he found it:

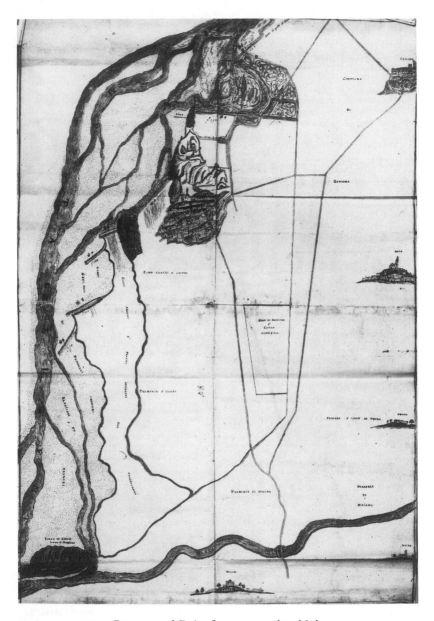

FIGURE 2. Osoppo and Buia, from a map dated July 30, 1714.

This mountain, located in such a convenient and opportune place, so strongly protected, and one can truly say built by Nature in the model of a marvelous fortress, has three faces: that which looks toward the East is 450 *passa* [765 meters] long, the other toward the North is 200 [340 meters], and on these two faces the living rock has been so cut and broken up that it is impossible to imagine it, let alone climb up it; the third face toward the West, on which Nature left for the convenience of the inhabitants a ridge for a cart road, is so well defended by various sentry posts and many towers of living rock that no architect could possibly want them in more opportune locations, and this third face covers 405 *passa* [688.5 meters]. This place from all that I have been able to find was held in great esteem by the ancients, a fact which is demonstrated to me by certain stones found with some most beautiful Roman epitaphs, some mosaic pavements, and two very large cisterns cut into the rock, made in the Roman fashion with an artificial wall and at great expense. There is still a most lovely pond, completely round, that is seventy *passa* [119 meters] across, for use of the animals, and there is still a large stand of trees so that we shall have plenty of water and fuel.

With its extraordinary strategic value Osoppo gave its possessor military primacy in Friuli, a primacy as useful in times of peace as in war.[27]

Osoppo was, significantly, a fief of the Savorgnan family. Accumulators of vast possessions, honorary members of the Venetian patriciate, veritable lords of Friuli, the Savorgnan held fast to Osoppo like hounds to prey. The family used this precious prize in their collection of fiefs to play for concessions from the Venetians. The Venetians, in turn, recognized that their continued dominion over Friuli was hostage to the lords of Osoppo and always had to tailor their rule to satisfy whichever member of the Savorgnan clan held the fortress.

Friulan topography, in sum, created a peculiar environment that, by cutting the landscape into radically distinct zones, forced most of the populace to inhabit a scattering of hills around Udine. From these ramparted mounds the castellans looked with vigilance toward their noble neighbors on the nearby rises, with severity down on the peasants living in squalid wooden huts below them, and with jealousy at privileged Udine and the ambitious Savorgnan. From the luogotenente's hilltop palace in Udine many of these castles could be watched and the immense alpine peaks observed and feared. This little land, dwarfed by mountains and gigantic enemies, the home of scrubby poverty and deceptive greenery, of ignorant arrogance and tattered chivalry, constituted a house divided against itself, ever at war within, and from without vulnerable to the ruses and assaults of greedy foreigners.

"The people are handsome," wrote Count Girolamo of Porcìa of his fellow Friulans, "especially the nobility, the women as much as the men. They possess good blood, are vigorous, but the people have an obstinate pride and are given to the vendetta; they are a coarse people and have quasi-barbarian customs, particularly those that a few let slip out. They have a difficult language, and to be understood they speak Italian." In the sixteenth century the population of the patria varied in cycles between 140,000 and 194,000 people, rising gradually and falling precipitously as in 1570 when more than 25,000 people died from famine. The whole region put together had about as many persons as lived in the city of Venice itself, which in 1553 hosted 153,397 inhabitants, a figure that placed it among the ten most populous cities in Europe. Among the terraferma subjects of La Serenissima, the number of residents in the patria was second only to the Bresciano, but the population was overwhelmingly rural, and urban structures were less well developed than in any other area in the Veneto. In 1548 Udine had a population of 14,597, making it the sixth largest terraferma city after Verona (52,109), Brescia (42,660), Padua (34,075), Vicenza (21,268), and Bergamo (17,707). Udine, however, was far larger than any other town in Friuli: Portogruaro had only 3,500 souls; Cividale, 2,903; Pordenone, 2,710; Gemona, 2,070; and Spilimbergo, 1,285. The distribution of the population mirrored the geographic characteristics that made the hilly area around Udine most suitable for settlement.[28]

Although they were said to have German customs and dress and had strong Lombard vestiges in their common law, the region's inhabitants identified themselves at least by the sixteenth century as "faithful and good Friulans" and somewhat defensively as "legitimate Italians." The success of Italian culture in the region had been a gradual and furtive process that only slightly quickened after the Venetian conquest. Educated Friulans went to Padua to study, and political interests, fashion, and economic opportunity drew some to Venice, but the absence of a large middle class that could mediate between the peasants and artisans on the one hand and Latin humanism on the other prevented the evolution of the civic culture which appeared elsewhere in central and northern Italy.[29]

In the sixteenth century four linguistic strata can be identified among the general population. At the base were speakers of Friulan or Furlan, the language of the mass of uneducated peasants and artisans. Friulan survived as a language in opposition to those employed by the authorities, and nearly all examples of written Friulan from this period were by persons of limited literacy who used writing for practical and personal reasons. The monolingualism of most of the Friulans segregated them from outside influences. A peasant defendant before the tribunal of the Holy Office in 1649, for example, asked the court to provide an interpreter because he could not understand the questions put to him by the inquisitor from Orvieto. At the more elevated social levels of the peasant-artisan group, some, who needed to work in a wider ambit and were at least marginally literate such as the heretic Menocchio studied by Carlo Ginzburg, also spoke Veneto when necessary. A third linguistic level consisted of those who habitually spoke Veneto. A tiny fourth group knew Tuscan and maybe Latin. In his 1484 rendering into the vernacular tongue of the *Constitutions of the Patria del Friuli*, humanist Pietro Capretto discussed the problems he faced in deciding which vernacular to choose. Tuscan, he wrote, was too obscure for the Friulan people, but Friulan itself presented problems: "Furlana is not universally spoken in all Friuli, and one can write it poorly and even worse pronounce it by reading." He finally chose the Trevisan form of Veneto, the *lingua franca* of the Venetian mainland.[30]

There were also two other distinct language groups isolated among the Friulan-speaking masses. One of the four quarters of Cividale consisted largely of Slovenes, and outside the city walls on the far side of a small stream called the Rossimigliano, were seventy-three Slovenian-speaking villages that in 1588 had a total population of 3,904. The much smaller islands of German speakers, which still survive today, comprised three extremely remote villages in the mountains of Carnia and Cadore, each probably founded between 1100 and 1300 by the counts of Gorizia to secure communications among their separate domains and fiefs. Many of the castellans of Friuli, however, claimed German ancestors and continued to maintain strong ties through friendship, marriage, and even vassalage to the German aristocracy of the empire; as a result some of them were as much drawn to German as to Italian.[31]

Friuli constituted a land between, both in the literal sense that it was a border region in which the Venetian republic and Holy Roman Empire met, and in a metaphoric one that its leaders were suspended between, on the one hand, a population whose rural poverty and linguistic isolation underlay a feudal and archaic culture and, on the other, a sophisticated, capitalist, imperialist city-republic that had become the paragon of Renaissance civic culture. Topography and culture also conspired to keep Friuli divided within itself. Residential location and class had dramatic correlates in speech, dividing some groups from one another so completely that there was little common ground for communication or mutual understanding. Despite centuries of independence under the patriarchs of Aquileia, Friuli was bound together by phantom institutional threads that were easily broken and, more substantially, by the webs of factional clientage.

INSTITUTIONAL LABYRINTH

Among all of the territories in the Venetian terraferma dominion, Friuli alone had been a feudal principality rather than a city-state prior to conquest. Elsewhere during the twelfth- and thirteenth-century heyday of the communes, cities such as Verona, Vicenza, and Padua had politically absorbed the surrounding rural *contado* and smaller towns in the vicinity. In Friuli towns were communal islands in a still feudal countryside, which had long been formally unified around its ecclesiastical prince, a titular unity recognized after the conquest by the official designation of the region as a patria. However, when the Venetians conquered Friuli, its unity, undermined by decades of civil war, had become a legal fiction, and government at all levels failed to function effectively as

subjects and officials alike wandered through a labyrinth of discor-
dant institutions and procedures.[32]

To Venetian officials, Friuli was a special enigma, in part because
of their own ignorance. Despite an order of 1460 to all rectors on
the mainland to map their jurisdictions for the information of senators and members of councils, Venetian patricians understood
little about Friulan geography. Many Venetian families had villas
in the lush lands between the Piave and the Adige, but few owned
land, had business dealings, or even made visits along the Tagliamento or Isonzo, a fact that led Giulio Savorgnan in 1566 to have
maps made up again for his Venetian masters.[33]

Venetians were also bigoted about the Friulans. One magistrate
summarized the report of his service there by saying that the Friulans were dirty by nature.[34]

But most of all, Venetians were indifferent. Few of the rectors
sent to Friuli displayed great merits, most were lazy, many stuffed
with pretensions, and a very few well enough disposed to the na-
tives to act as their representative to Venice rather than Venice's
local strongman.[35]

The absence of a clear hierarchy of authority weakened Venetian
rule. Although the Venetian luogotenente in Udine had general
responsibility for all Friuli, he could not supervise other Venetian
rectors in the region effectively because they too were patricians
elected to their post. Because they reported directly to the college
of the Senate and Council of Ten, they could easily outmaneuver
or ignore the luogotenente's orders. Venice subdivided its administration among the provveditore of Marano, the podestà of Ca-
neva, the podestà of Monfalcone, the podestà of Portogruaro, the
podestà and captain of Sacile, the castellan of Chiusa di Venzone,
the captain of Cadore, the provveditore and captain of Pordenone
(after 1508), the provveditore of Cividale del Friuli (after 1553),
and the provveditore generale of Palmanova (after 1593). The luogotenente's authority in Udine and its immediate environs was
clearer: he could hear criminal appeals and major civil cases; and he
supervised the treasury, the public pawn shop (Monte di Pietà,
founded in 1496), grain supply, Lazarus house during plagues, and
all military matters including border patrols, local militias, and
fortresses.[36]

However, procedural red tape often tied his hands because, as one luogotenente observed, when Venice conquered Friuli it only added new institutions without eliminating the old, making the new system even less effective than the patriarch's. The layering of institutions created a Byzantine obscurity about most issues.

In the sixteenth century jurisdictional lines divided Friuli into 816 communities (*ville*): Venice governed 49 of these directly, the empire controlled 29, the patriarch of Aquileia retained 10, and the luogotenente had appellant jurisdiction over the remaining 728. Subinfeudations parceled out the luogotenente's territory into 60 or more subjurisdictions, each with its own privileges and powers. Feudal lords or their deputies held most of these subjurisdictions, prelates had some, and independent towns controlled quite a few. Some judged cases only in the first instance, some also heard the first appeal, some acted only in civil cases, most had jurisdiction in both civil and criminal, many could exact the death penalty, and most retained the right to torture. The local jurisdictions were not even obliged to inform the luogotenente of their decisions, and if on appeal he disagreed with a decision, he usually just returned the case to the court of first instance.

The size of these many subjurisdictions also complicated the situation because there were extensive districts, such as that of the counts of Prata, which dominated more than thirty-two villages whereas others, such as the lords of Toppo, judged only a few of the inhabitants of a single village. The complications seemed endless to outside observers. In Soffumbergo a gastaldo appointed by the luogotenente sat on the bench with the counts of Strassoldo but could not vote. For their part, the counts appointed a member of their own clan to the captaincy of the jurisdiction, but he could not execute any orders without the agreement of the village mayors (*decani*) and judges (*giurati*). The town of La Motta had thirty-one villages under its jurisdiction, but fifteen of these were in Friuli and sixteen in the Trevigiana, which had a very different legal system. The many jurisdictions made justice a particularly rare commodity for peasants because when they appealed their cases, they usually came before their own lord, and they could seldom afford to go to Udine to plead before the luogotenente. In 1553 a former luogotenente, Francesco Sanudo, identified the many jurisdictions as the principal cause of strife: "with the many doctors of law and advocates clear matters are made obscure, and all esteem their own privileges too highly so that for every minor cause conflicts arise among them for which they then kill one another."[37]

Particularly troublesome were the contrasts between the feudal jurisdictions and the independent communities (*ville comuni*). Venice usually sold feudal jurisdictions to the highest bidder, which meant, of course, that the new lords had to recover their expenses through the corruption of justice. In these jurisdictions official justice became merely a form of extortion. Although in some feudal jurisdictions such as Valvasone lord and populace stood on equal footing before the law, in most the lords claimed to be exempt from arrest and could hardly be sued by their subjects inasmuch as they were the judges. Latisana, on the other hand, governed itself in complete independence of any lord and did not even have a resident Venetian rector. Although a fief of the Savorgnan, Buia had exemplary communal statutes that permitted a considerable amount of autonomy when the local notables were strong enough to stand up to their lord. And there were freakish anomalies such as Aviano. The community lacked jurisdictional rights which the Venetians granted to the count of San Polo, but the community retained a vote in the Friulan parliament, a privilege the counts lacked.[38]

Among all the various institutions, both Friulan and Venetian, only the parliament encompassed all of Friuli. Officially founded by the patriarch in 1269, the parliament assumed great prestige and authority, especially over financial affairs, and, until the arrival of the Venetians, constituted the most successful feudal assembly in Italy. Under the Venetians, however, the parliament became primarily a forum for the castellan nobles whose worst excesses could be checked by Venice through the luogotenente's presence in parliamentary sessions, a development that made its activities mere routine and its prestige hollow.

Consisting of the traditional three estates, the parliament included twelve prelates, forty-five castellan lords, and thirteen representatives of towns. After 1446 the membership divided into two parties on most issues: one made up of the luogotenente, the Savorgnan family, and the representatives of Udine; and the other of most of the castellan lords and the delegates of a few communities, especially Cividale. During the fifteenth and sixteenth centuries, the parliament's only significant achievement was a reform of the constitution of the patria, accomplished by a series of parliamentary commissions manned by castellans with law degrees. These various commissions took more than a century to complete their work, an odd hybrid of common law principles. In marriage law, for example, part of the population retained the Lombard practice of the *morgengabe*, part employed the Roman system of dowries, and part mixed the two practices.[39]

Even after the defeat of the patriarch of Aquileia, he continued to be the head of the first estate. Until his death in exile in 1439, Ludwig of Teck persisted in trying to recapture his secular powers, keeping the Friulan church in a continuous uproar. Venice pared down the jurisdictions of his successors, themselves cooperative Venetian patricians, until the surviving jurisdictions consisted of only the two towns of San Vito and San Daniele and a handful of villages in which the patriarchs remained autonomous, if exceedingly modest, ecclesiastical lords. The citizens of San Daniele, in particular, used the political emasculation of the patriarchs to their own advantage: when appeals to the patriarch did not satisfy them, they went behind his back to the Venetians and even beyond them both to the Holy See. The Sandanielesi pushed Venice to dismantle more of the patriarch's temporal authority than perhaps the dominant city itself had wanted.[40]

The Friulan church failed especially to fulfill its spiritual responsibilities. At the end of the fifteenth century the patriarch's vicar reported that churches were used as barns or had been completely abandoned and that priests survived by running hostels or providing refuge for bandits. Deprived of liturgical services, peasants substituted magical incantations and a rich folklore.[41]

In Udine secular clerics became extremely scarce, and those few survived by selling the sacraments. Only the mendicant orders consistently and freely provided spiritual services to the laity, but the secular priests retained enough influence to lobby the city council to prohibit such pious competition. After a visit Cardinal Alessandrino observed that the patriarch paid little attention to his spiritual duties whereas his canons scandalized the people with their insolence. Examples abounded. In 1500 a cathedral deacon played the part of a prostitute in a presentation of Terence's *The Eunuch*; in 1531 a priest died from wounds received in a street fight; and in 1565, while leaving a ball, a canon assaulted and wounded a man in a dispute over who should go through a door first. In the same year the luogotenente and his soldiers had to force their way into the monastery of Saint Peter Martyr to put down an armed rebellion by the monks against the prior and his partisans. Liturgical processions and the masses of major feast days were notorious for occasioning shoving matches between civic deputies and cathedral canons over precedence. A 1567 description summarizes well the degraded condition of the church in Udine: the cathedral "is in such a state that not only does it lack many things necessary for the divine cult, the roof also leaks and threatens to collapse so that one can not stay under it without manifest danger to life and without such a soaking when it rains as one might get in the middle of the street."[42]

A stunning indifference to ecclesiastical affairs, let alone to the spiritual welfare of the laity, meant that the Friulan church abdicated its leadership role in the community, eliminating the possibility of the kind of popular protests led by priests and friars in the principalities of Germany or the peacemaking role the church sometimes played in Tuscany.[43]

To ensure their loyalty after the conquest, Venice promised the members of the second estate that their "libertates, iura et consuetudines" would be respected. Although Venice honored these liberties, rights, and customs with legalistic formality and never challenged the castellans outright, the dominant city encouraged as much as possible Udine's claims against the castellans, a situation that left them prickly about the slightest infringement of their position. Udine threatened their privileges because it wanted to break the castellans' economic stranglehold on the city. The castellans regulated the flow of products from the country to the city through protectionist laws, tolls, judicial regulations, and the confiscation of goods. Conflict between the city and the lords intensified during the sixteenth century, particularly when inflation diluted the castellans' fixed incomes, forcing them to alienate some of their lands and to send younger sons away to seek their own fortunes in foreign courts.[44]

During the Renaissance the great castles, such as those at Villalta, Colloredo, Spilimbergo, Valvasone, and Zoppola, flew red flags as signs of the personal inviolability of the inhabitants and housed the nobles, their retainers, and servants. The various nuclear families of the noble clans usually lived in a common residence on the premises. The clansmen were bound together by blood ties that could extend as far as first- and second-degree cousins. Occasionally affines or even unrelated persons who had bought their way in or taken possession upon the default of a loan subdivided the castle with proper members of the clan. The nobles who lived together in the same castle and exercised its jurisdictional rights called themselves castellans (*castellani*) or consorts (*consorti*). The consorts often established different apartments or even different houses within a castle complex for each nuclear family, and these separate units could be alienated, sold, and willed away. The social ideal was one of patrilocality and of solidarity among consorts, but social ideals, especially in Friuli, often had little relationship to reality.[45]

The castellans derived their status from the possession of fiefs, which were confirmed or granted by the luogotenente, or in the case of strategic border areas, by the Council of Ten itself. In some cases more than one group of consorts shared the jurisdictional rights within a fief, as was the case in several villages near Villalta in which the consorts of the Della Torre and those of the Villalta practiced a yearly exchange of the villages in which they exercised jurisdiction.[46]

The consorts in possession of a fief looked to a senior male as the *maior domus* who had legal authority over his brothers, sons, and nephews. Reforms of the fifteenth century made it easier to break the control of property by an incompetent or corrupt *maior*, but rebellion against him was difficult because he could enact severe sanctions against disobedient minors and could hunt down family rebels. At the death of a *maior*, surviving males formed a *tacita societas*, but the very tacitness of this fraternal community of property caused such endless problems that a reform law required brothers to cohabit if the *societas* were to have contractual value. A principle of *dismontadure* prohibited female succession to the property of a *societas*.[47]

The property the males inherited, however, was in no sense unconditionally theirs to do with as they pleased. Contemporary property laws recognized two basic kinds of rights to most property: the lord's *dominium directum*, or the right to collect some form of rent from a property; and the peasant's *dominium utile*, or the right to harvest and live off of the land. Whoever had the right of usage could sublease, divide, or sell that right, subject only to a promise to improve the land and to recognize the lordship of whomever had the *dominium directum*. Rarely were these two rights in the hands of the same person, and neither party could obtain the rights of the other without compensation. Other claims to property included the right to collect a *decima* or an excise tax on certain products, a right possessed by ecclesiastics, towns, and Venice itself in some cases. Collective rights to pasture encumbered other lands, and the commons belonged to all the citizens of a community, lord and commoner alike.[48]

The various consorts displayed very different styles of lordship in managing their properties. Those with princely ambitions, such as the Savorgnan, used their holdings as a source of clients and retainers who could be tied to them through indebtedness and other forms of assistance such as advances of grain just before harvest and loans of tools and plow animals. The more typical and less ambitious castellans looked to their land almost exclusively as a source of income. Virtually none of these Friulan lords, however, sought to build uniform estates but held lands widely dispersed about the countryside. Although some properties were concentrated near the castle, most lords possessed scattered holdings in many different villages in which there may have been only two or three manses that owed rents to the same lord.

Quite unlike latifundia, Friulan patrimonies maximized diversity at the expense of uniformity. The Strassoldo estates, for example, were concentrated on the lower plain south of Udine between the Torre and Tagliamento, but within this area the patrimony was highly diversified. There were two large complexes of substantial holdings, but the consorts also had tenants in six wine-producing villages, fourteen villages devoted to heavy irrigation, and eight dry farming settlements. Other castellans, including the numerous Savorgnan and Colloredo consorts, also collected rents from many of these same villages.[49]

Whereas jurisdictional rights came with a particular fief, lords independently acquired actual property rights of *dominium directum* through inheritance or purchase. The jurisdictional territory of a lord and many of the farms from which he derived his income might be in different places, a situation typical of feudal landhold-

ing patterns but atypical of the tendency in much of the rest of the
Veneto to build coherent estates. Friulan lords suffered from extreme disjunctures among their own institutions of social and economic control, disjunctures that made a mockery of their pleni-
potentiary pufferies and contributed to their habitual feelings of
insecurity.

A lord's control of his own lands depended heavily on the men
who actually handled the day-to-day management of his affairs.
One of the lord's familiars served as steward (*caniparius, canipario,
canevar*) who collected and registered rents (*censi*) from the peasants
on the appointed day of payment. In most cases, however, the
steward relied on a local peasant deputized to collect the rents and
to transport them to the lord's castle. Usually the village head (*decano, jurato, brico, meriga,* or *massaro*), the local collector served as
the linchpin in the whole manorial system. Lords and stewards
might cultivate personal ties with him especially in the villages in
which the consorts had jurisdictional rights, but the *decano* labored
in an ambiguous position inasmuch as he represented both the lord
to the village and the village to the lord. The Savorgnan carefully
nurtured their relationship with such men, who could then be relied upon to bring out the villagers in support of the lord in his
fights with his castellan enemies. Less effective proprietors than the
Savorgnan, however, might find the *decani* leading the peasants
against them during one of the rural rebellions. Usually elected for
one- or two-year terms by the village assembly (*vicinia*), the *decano*
handled civil and criminal matters at the most basic level, organized public works, and collected the *estimo*. In a few places the
lords had the right to appoint a *gastaldo* to exercise authority more
directly than was possible when the villagers chose their own
leader.[50]

The villages led by these *decani* and *gastaldi* were in most
cases physically dispersed, and their administration was subdivided
among several competing institutions. Friulan place names differ
from those found elsewhere in Italy by referring not just to a single
concentration of buildings but to a concentration and the nearby
zone of lands or even to several separately located groupings of
houses. Fields included individual plots of unfenced arable land
(*masi*) cultivated according to a system of triennial rotation by each
peasant family (*massaro*) and communally owned *taviela* land di-

vided up each year at a village assembly among those with full rights of residence. Each manse had its own modest piece of garden or orchard land (*bearz*) contiguous with the house and possibly some enclosed land at the edges of the village used for orchards (*braida*). Most *massari* also enjoyed membership in a pasture association (*compascuo*) which gave them access to the common pastures for their animals, a resource of particular importance in the poor lands of Friuli in which husbandry was vital. Border disputes often embroiled an association with other competing associations, but the husbandmen usually lacked support from their village neighbors in these disputes because the confines of the *compascuo* did not always correspond to and often subdivided those of the village.[51]

In other words, the peasant family found itself enmeshed in several distinct and sometimes quite incompatible institutional structures: the feudal jurisdiction, a contractual obligation to pay rents to a lord who may or may not have been the judge of his jurisdiction, the *vicinia* headed by a neighbor who was *decano*, a pasture association, a fiscal unit for taxation, and a *pieve* of the church. Until the organization of the peasant militias at the end of the fifteenth century and the creation of the peasants' parliament, the *contadinanza*, in the middle of the sixteenth, villages offered few consistent sources of solidarity beyond kin groups.

Given the varieties of settlements, there may not have been a typical Friulan village except in those traits created by the miseries of poverty. Orzano, between Udine and Cividale at the meeting point of several roads, boasted a piazza and church, cemetery, and well. Buildings clustered wall to wall so that those around the piazza could form a defensive barrier behind which inhabitants and animals might find refuge from bandits and marauding soldiers. Built of wood with roofs of thatch, the peasants' houses sheltered animals in the same rooms as humans. Ignoring the more heavily trafficked east–west road, the inhabitants had aligned their houses on a north–south axis so that the morning and afternoon sun fell on one of the two principal facades, testimony to the premium placed on heat and light in this subalpine land.[52]

In contrast to Orzano's clustered pattern, Buia, in the hills to the northwest of Udine, spread out among several modest concentrations of houses scattered miles apart. A substantial church, a dark tavern, and even a simple town hall created a center at Santo Stefano, but by the fifteenth century the only defensive works consisted of some long-abandoned ruins on one of the nearby hills. Buia's pattern may have evolved in service of the stock-raising economy memorialized in its name, but other communities with similar economic interests developed other patterns of settlement.[53]

Although Friuli had been one of the last regions in Italy to abandon serfdom, most peasants were free by the fifteenth century. During the last decades of the patriarchate, Friulan serfdom (*servitù di masnada*) had begun to disappear because of collective manumissions, and after a rebellion of serfs in 1424, lords no longer fought to preserve the institution. The last serfs disappeared around 1460.[54]

Most of the free peasants worked land as tenants under one- to twenty-nine-year contracts in which they were obligated to pay rent in fixed quantities of cereals, principally wheat, and frequently some poultry and wine. Chronic indebtedness among the tenants, who often had to be carried over from one harvest to the next with loans of grain from their lord, produced endemic instability among the agrarian population. The image of a poor but geographically immobile peasantry, tied generation after generation to the same plot of land, finds little confirmation in fifteenth- and sixteenth-century Friuli in which flight from the village and fields often provided the only means of escaping ruinous levels of insolvency. Short-term crises could mean that nearly the entire population of a village disappeared as a result of starvation and migration. If, however, a peasant family managed to survive a generation on its plot, the heirs of the tenant usually continued to occupy the manse, even though the law did not guarantee it. Given the shortage of rural labor, lords could not afford to drive away too many able-bodied tenants. In the normal course of things, when a father died his sons would collectively carry on the obligations of the manse until one of them became the legal tenant after which the others would either work with him or divide up the mobile property according to local unwritten customs.[55]

Besides the contractual obligations to pay rent, peasants had to perform a long list of corvées and other duties including the *albergaria* or provision of housing and abundant food and wine to judges and tax collectors, free transportation of lumber and ship's stores for the Venetian arsenal, service as galley oarsmen, ditch digging for Venetian hydrology projects and fortresses, free transit for nuns, and carting of salt. The Venetian Senate occasionally passed laws protecting peasants from the worst abuses of their creditors, such as the demanding of work animals, tools, hay, or straw as collateral for loans, but by the late sixteenth century the requirements of Venice itself became one of the worst causes of rural impoverishment.[56]

More than the first and second estates, which had the most to lose to Venetian domination, or the impoverished peasants who bore the burden of Venetian taxation, the natural ally of Venice in Friuli was Udine, the city that could best profit from the eclipse of the castellans and from commercial ties to the great entrepôt. When the patriarch of Aquileia transferred his seat there in 1238 he granted commercial privileges and guaranteed a protected market that helped Udine surpass Cividale, Venzone, and San Daniele and become the primary commercial intermediary between the northern Adriatic and Germany, attracting Lombard, Florentine, and Jewish merchants. But, unlike many other cities in central and northern Italy, Udine failed to establish itself as a free commune, become an independent city-state, control much of its own contado, conquer other cities, or defeat the regional landed aristocracy.[57]

Although it was the only town in Friuli large enough to be called a city, modest Udine retained a strongly rural orientation, enclosing large tracts of farm land within the outer circuit of its walls. Based on the observations from his visit in 1483, Marin Sanudo described the city as composed of three concentric circles defined by walls. Within the inner circle around a hill were the luogotenente's castle and two churches. The second circuit of walls enclosed the *citadella* of noble palaces, and the third protected the *borghi* inhabited by artisans and peasants.[58]

Although some of the stone palaces impressed visitors, most of the housing resembled farm dwellings and consisted of wood and thatch, creating a terrible fire hazard realized in 1419 when a conflagration destroyed the *borghi* of Gemona, Villalta, and San Lazzaro. A communal decree of 1502 prohibited new straw roofs or the repairing of old ones, but thatched houses still existed at the end of the century. Most were roughcast affairs of one story without such amenities as windows. They lined dusty or muddy streets and fetid little alleys so clogged with refuse that passage was sometimes impossible. City workers drained the open latrines irregularly, and the small streams that passed through the city came to smell like sewers as they filled with garbage and dead animals. Even by the standards of the fifteenth century Udine was a squalid place.[59]

Udine had its own jealously guarded definitions of class. The civic nobility consisted of descendants of the vassals of the patriarchs, members of the liberal professions, communal office holders, and some castellan aristocrats who had obtained citizenship in the city, usually before 1392. A 1518 list included 111 families with 275 members able to sit in the communal council. Most of these families reportedly lived within the *citadella*, separated from the popular *borghi* by the second circuit of walls. The *popolari* included artisans, workers, and peasants who lived in the *borghi*, each of which was organized like a rural *vicinia* headed by a *decano*. In contrast to the great Renaissance cities such as Florence and Venice, Udine had marked residential segregation along class lines and lacked the industrial and commercial middle classes who had been the dynamic force in the city-republics. The few Udinesi in trade devoted themselves to the local market and never rose above the level of shopkeepers whereas banking and international commerce rested after the midthirteenth century in the hands of Tuscan immigrants who for generations maintained their connections with Florence, Lucca, and Siena.

During the Florentine-Venetian War of 1450 the Florentines were banished from Udine, which resulted in a financial disaster for all Friuli but especially for the city, which lost its most productive sector. Venetians failed to step into the place vacated by the Florentines, whose businesses were only partially taken over by an enlarged community of Jews. Contributing to the highly segmented nature of Friulan society, the absence of a native entrepreneurial class meant that there were very few possibilities for social mobility. No one moved from the artisan or peasant classes to bourgeois comfort, and the few middle-class individuals who could bought land and imitated nobles by withdrawing from trade.

Udine also lacked regularly available credit services, a lacuna that placed a heavy burden on the peasants, who had to depend either on their own lord or the limited resources of the Jewish lenders who in hard times also had to support the aristocracy. Besides land acquisition, the preferred forms of investment were in monopolies, fiscal exemptions, hoarding of foodstuffs, the importation of German cloth, and horse breeding.[60]

Udine financed its public treasury through direct imposts (*gravezze*), indirect levies on consumer goods (*dazi*), and income from communal properties (*livelli*) in the city and seventy-nine other hamlets and towns in central Friuli. Neither Udine nor Venice was willing to concede to the other any of its own taxation rights, and Venice failed to coordinate the tax policies of the two cities so that *gravezze* and *dazi* were collected twice. Until the 1570s the levels of taxation did not seriously exceed the ability of the population to pay, but when the population of Udine began to decline, tax levels remained the same, making the burden more onerous. Before the late sixteenth century, confiscatory taxation was perhaps less of a problem for Udine than inadequate investment and productivity.[61]

Although the Venetians sponsored a reform of the statutes of Udine in 1425, the principal institutions of civic government remained unchanged between 1356 and 1513. In effect, there were two tiers: at the top the Venetian luogotenente inherited the position of the patriarch's *gastaldo* as a judicial and military officer; and on a second level the city government consisted of two bodies, an assembly (*arengo*) and a minor council. The assembly met each year on Michaelmas and on rare special occasions during a plague or war to legislate and to elect members of the minor council and other administrative officers. The minor council consisted of one *popolano* and six noble deputies and occasional ad hoc commissions of jurists and notaries who drafted legislation. Although the deputies had to be available every day, the minor council normally met once a week and handled most of the routine business of government. They could meet without the presence or permission of the luogotenente.[62]

Udine's civic honor heavily depended on the autonomy theoretically guaranteed by these communal institutions. In a revealing apology for Udine, Romanello Manin employed the form of a dialogue between a citizen and a castellan to explore the implications of Udine's claims for primacy in Friuli. Relying on a historical argument about early privileges granted the city by the patriarchs, a description of the greater size of the city in comparison with any single castle, and an analysis of the noble origins of its citizens,

Manin produced a diatribe against castellan arrogance and a pane-gyric to the city's moderation, especially in reducing the factional violence of the castellans. In fact Manin's argument could bear little weight inasmuch as it tried to place Udine in the company of the great Italian communes, where it hardly belonged. His dialogue, however, sums up the simple truth that Udine provided the only indigenous counterweight to the castellans.[63]

Friulan and Udinese institutions failed to function very effi-ciently. They created an oppressive burden of vested interests in which every obscure office and every procedure were the privi-leged rights of someone; moreover, institutions worked against one another, furthering rather than resolving conflicts. As a result, noninstitutional relationships comprised the real life of the society.

The creation of influential relationships came partly from family background, wealth, status, and official position but also from more fleeting characteristics such as the strength of personality and talent, the ability to recognize and grasp opportunity, the judicious building of friendships and alliances, and the willingness to use force appropriately. Every Friulan lived within multiple, overlap-ping, sometimes competing networks, some cohesive enough to constitute groups, others loose connections among individuals. Vertical bonds between patrons and clients or fathers and sons co-existed with horizontal ones among friends, siblings, and neigh-bors. The small communities of Friuli defined themselves through these ties as much as through legal definitions of citizenship, but individuals within each community were also linked outside it to trading partners, debtors and creditors, clients and patrons, fellow militiamen, and factional comrades. In the villages each individual lived within several shifting, noncorporate associations, in what Giovanni Levi has called a system of continuous tensions. In mo-ments of crisis, groups might temporarily form along class lines, but these could easily decompose and recompose into clientage groups or factions.[64]

The family had a central position in the social webs entangling each individual. In Friuli the family cannot be reduced simply to the household, a fiscal unit useful for taxation and agricultural management, or consanguinity, so valued in the rhetoric of patri-archy. The family was both of these and a range of alliances created through intermarriage, patronage, and friendship as well. Individuals did not act within their social world in isolation but in continuous reference to the interests of the family knot. Even economic choices depended less on the legal or market forces that determined price than on the social implications of any given decision for relatives, allies, and clients. However, on many occasions in Friuli the family knot unraveled, forcing individuals to seek solidarity elsewhere. Such a system of tensions placed heavy burdens on the intermediaries among the networks, especially on those who mediated between artisan-peasant clients and aristocratic patrons—the local notables, those men of relatively substantial property, the *decani*, militia captains, and notaries.

Faced with extraordinary opportunities resulting from their brokerage of resources and protection of local rights and privileges, these men also subjected themselves to great dangers inasmuch as the disgrace or treason of a protector might be as disastrous for them as for him. Trapped into serving multiple masters, including their own townsmen, feudal lords, factional chiefs, and Venetian officials, the intermediaries sometimes acted as enforcers but more often as patrons with a constituency and interests of their own. For the clever ones, the disruptions of vendetta violence and of war created special opportunities by occupying the powerful figures from outside the villages in other matters.[65]

The language available for describing social relations, however, paid little attention to these ambiguities. Social rhetoric dramatized opposites to explain behavior: loyalty and disloyalty, honor and shame, justice and injustice, revenge and weakness. But a language of stark alternatives failed to explain a situation plagued with contradictions. It schematized the indeterminate. Rather than adhering to absolute loyalties, one pursued a strategy. The simplest attitude, found among the weak, was hardly a strategy at all but a series of tactical maneuvers devoted to following the path of least resistance and giving in to whomever pushed the hardest. A more common attitude might be to avoid committing oneself irrevocably to any one group in a conflict, simply keeping options open until it was clear who was most likely to win. Those who aspired to any level of leadership, however, had to follow a more complex and difficult strategy of simultaneously maintaining conflicting loyalties, of playing a double or triple game of intrigue and deception. These strategies constituted different social styles of behavior which were far more important in accounting for Friulan factional violence than any particular set of institutional arrangements.

CHAPTER TWO

Regulating Conflicts

In recent years historians have devoted a great deal of attention to the relationships between the dominant cities and their subject territories in the states of central and northern Italy during the late medieval and early modern periods. Jacob Burckhardt's model for the Renaissance state, encapsulated in the famous phrase, "the state as a work of art," suggested that rational, calculating princes and oligarchs consciously crafted new political institutions much like the architects who worked for them turned rough stone into geometrically precise, classically inspired palaces and churches. Many historians have become dissatisfied with this model that made a radical chronological break between the city-republics of the twelfth and thirteenth centuries and the city-states of the late fourteenth and fifteenth, which for the most part continued to rely on antecedent institutions and practices. Historians have also found that humanism had far less to do with actual political practice than once assumed.[1]

In the labor of wearing away the Burckhardtian scheme, most historians have followed the lead of Federico Chabod and adopted an evolutionary view of political development, which they have examined through detailed institutional studies that attempt to

measure the modernity of the various states by examining practices
that enhanced centralization and bureaucratic growth. The result
has been various alternative models, perhaps the most influential
the concept of the regional state, formulated by Giorgio Chittolini
for Lombardy. By concentrating on judicial and administrative
connections between the center and the periphery, Chittolini and
others have argued that the regional state can be characterized by
its heterogeneity, informality, and limited centralization, a state
neither medieval in its extreme subdivision of authority nor modern in its tendency toward absolutism. Students of the Venetian
state have emphasized how its hodgepodge of institutions, the
prevalence of aristocratic privilege, and widespread cultural differences created a "diarchy" in which local oligarchs shared authority
with Venetian officials. Most recently, Osvaldo Raggio, in his
study of the daily and local exercise of power in a provincial area
of the Genoese state, has employed the term *indirect government*.[2]

Venice's rule of Friuli is an extreme example of diarchy or indirect government, an example that illustrates the relationship between two very different societies. Except for military matters,
these two came into contact primarily through Venice's attempts
to enforce criminal penalties for vendetta violence. The objective
of Venetian government in Friuli was almost exclusively to control
and even to obliterate the inconvenient aspects of another culture,
which emphasized male aggressiveness and obligations of honorable revenge.[3]

VENICE AND THE TERRAFERMA

The contrast between Venetian and Friulan political culture and
institutions presented both rulers and ruled with vexing problems
for centuries after the 1420 conquest. Although the distinctiveness
of Venice's civic culture has often been exaggerated to the level of
myth, there can be no doubt that its institutions were remarkably
successful in reducing the level of political violence within the city
itself and in mediating disputes especially when compared with
those of other contemporary regimes. The institutions of Friuli, in
contrast, were notoriously feeble, weakened by generations of civil
war and largely incapable of regulating conflicts, which were governed by the implicit rules of vendetta. The pursuit and preserva-

tion of power in Friuli depended on one's influence over friends and clients whose armed assistance was frequently necessary. Venetians treated Friuli, as they did all their terraferma lands, as a source of revenue and a military buffer zone, an approach that failed to unify the dominion in a way that would either bring a true *pax Veneta* to the countryside or permit Friuli to evolve autonomously under Venetian patronage. Thus, Venice's habits of provincial rule became part of Friuli's problem.[4]

The Venetian republic's most worthy claim to political success in the capital city itself came from replacing the feuds of its own magnate clans with a system of elections and the distribution of preferments (*grazie*). Certainly the early political history of Venice was violent enough. If the chronicles can be trusted, between 697 and 1172 five doges were forced to abdicate, nine exiled or deposed, five blinded, and five murdered. The early doges and their families were famous for their involvement in conspiracies and vendettas. In the late twelfth and thirteenth centuries, however, new families who had made fortunes in trade with the levant seized the dogeship and transformed the institutions of Venice to serve their interests. They found that domestic political violence hurt business. Moreover, generations of experience at sea, where the captain of a ship had nearly absolute power over and responsibility for the entire crew and where the fastest ship in a convoy had to accommodate itself to the slowest, had created psychological unity and habits of collective obedience which were transferred to political behavior. The hegemonic families accepted the rule of law over most aspects of life, building a political consensus that supplanted the feuding of the past. There were still significant internal enmities, especially between the factions headed by the Tiepolo and Dandolo families, factions whose composition showed signs of masking class antagonisms, but quarrels neither threatened the electoral system nor produced a tyrant as happened in so many mainland cities.[5]

The decisive confrontation came at the ducal election in 1229. The nominating committee deadlocked at a twenty to twenty tie between Jacopo Tiepolo, the hero of the conquest of Crete, and Marino Dandolo, the nephew of old, blind Doge Enrico who had led the Venetians over the walls of Constantinople in 1204. After a casting of lots made Tiepolo the winner, Dandolo peacefully accepted the result. Personal restraint on both sides prevented fighting and perhaps even a civil war. Tiepolo went on to encourage political equilibrium in Venice through the implementation of new statutes. When Venetian law was codified in 1242 new social groups were allowed to rise to political influence, but at the same time all those living outside of the Rialto city, even the inhabitants of the lagoon settlements of Chioggia, Murano, Torcello, and Grado, lost their right to be consulted about their own affairs and had to accept the rule of a podestà sent out from the capital city. Peaceful behavior came from the policing of the *signori di notte* and a social ethic of tranquility inculcated by images of the Virgin and saints (*capitelli*) placed in the streets of the city and lit at night to deter fighting. The new state of affairs in Venice is best represented by Doge Lorenzo Tiepolo's actions in 1268. Open fighting between his supporters and enemies had preceded the election, but after the announcement of his accession he had all his enemies brought to the palace, embraced them, made peace, and assured them of his good will and friendship.[6]

Venetian oligarchs became so concerned about the danger of vendetta in their city that they systematically attacked the social customs associated with factional identity. A law in 1266 banned all displays of the armorial insignia of the magnate families. After the defeat in 1310 of the conspiracy of Marco Querini and Baiamonte Tiepolo, the city prohibited the bearing of the blazons of either family for more than a century. Because large banquets, ideal for the building of factional alliances, were deemed especially dangerous the law limited guest lists to immediate kinsmen, even for weddings. Godparentage solidified bonds between an infant's parents and others. Some children had as many as 150 godparents until a 1505 law prohibited nobles from serving as the godparents of the children of other nobles.

Verbal, gestural, pictorial, and written insults came to be seen as even more subversive than street violence. Once the open factional clashes disappeared, Venetian magistrates were relatively tolerant of assaults by nobles, which were considered normal if regrettable behavior, especially among youths; but officials were very hard on public insults that could lead to vendetta. Laws protecting the

doge, his counselors, and the signoria from insults, which threatened the honor of the government as a whole, were more readily
enforced than laws against crimes of violence such as rape, which
merely hurt the personal honor of the victim and by extension her
male relatives who should have protected her from harm. For example, a man who drew insulting caricatures of the doge and other
officials in 1464 had his right hand cut off.

As the work of Guido Ruggiero has shown, Venice remained
a crime-ridden city, but Venetian nobles found it more useful to
exact vengeance through the courts or the political process than
to assault enemies or hire assassins. Gangs of young nobles still
roamed the streets, especially at night, getting themselves into
brawls with members of other gangs and attacking defenseless by-
standers, but these activities were treated as crimes rather than as
political threats. In 1494 a fight between some young Venetian
nobles backed up by their artisan friends on one side and the retainers of the ambassador of the Duke of Milan on the other, which
left one man dead, was quite exceptional in its political overtones
but did not involve discord among domestic factions.[7]

The values of Venetian nobles came to have a particularly civic
cast which prized their collective honor as civilized men over the
visceral protection of personal honor and which found the chivalrous fantasies of the rural nobility increasingly alien. Even as early
as the thirteenth century Venetians were defensive about their inability to compete in tournaments—that is, to act like true nobles—
as ably as neighboring Trevisans or Friulans. For the carnival festivities in 1272, Venetians had to rely for entertainment on six
young Friulan nobles who came to the city to joust.[8]

The cultural gap between provincial and Venetian nobles only
widened. By the fifteenth century the most characteristic feature
of the Venetian civic ideal became *unanimitas*, "the convergence of
a multitude of wants and aspirations into a single will," as Margaret King has defined it. The ideal of *unanimitas* permeated the
writings of Venetian humanists, influencing how they understood
their own politics and depriving all dissenters of legitimacy. The
principle inspired the most important Venetian treatise on the subject of factions. Bishop Pietro Barozzi wrote *On the Extirpation of
Factions and Recalling and Compelling the Citizens to Obedience* in 1489

as advice to his friend Bernardo Bembo who had been elected podestà of strife-torn Bergamo. As Bishop of Padua, Barozzi had
demonstrated his ability as an effective administrator, gaining such
a reputation that he became the model for the ideal bishop in Gasparo Contarini's *The Office of the Bishop*. Although he had had
ample practical experience and understood the historical causes,
Barozzi chose to diagnose the disease of factionalism in moral and
spiritual terms: "certainly there has been in Italy, as long as men
can remember, no plague more pernicious," a plague caused by the
greed of the poor, the pride of the rich, and the envy of the middle
classes. From these deadly vices derived nine ordinary and eleven
extraordinary causes of factionalism, which could be checked by
the secular and ecclesiastical authorities' effective employment of
the virtues of liberality, humility, and charity. Underlying these
spiritual concerns, however, was the single principle of the consensus of all parties (*consensus partium*), the ideal of the city as a balanced organism found in Aristotle's *Politics*.[9]

The Aristotelian principle of unity continued to dominate Venetian political thought in the following century, most notably in
Gasparo Contarini's influential *The Commonwealth and Government
of Venice*. Book Five treats the government of subject cities which,
he argues, Venice acquired reluctantly, "yielding to the instant petition of the oppressed bordering people, who could not endure
the rapines and cruelties of severall tyrants, that had brought them
into subiection. . . . With an infinite applause and willingnes of the
people," Venice brought the mainland cities under its protection,
"as though they had never beene disunited thereby setting them
free from out the servitude of insolent strangers, which being the
remainder & offspring of those Barbarians, that had wrought that
general devastation in *Italy*, had then nestled themselves and helde
the people in a most cruell and miserable bondage." Venice sought
to "comfort and cherish" its terraferma subjects by maintaining
"wholesome and profitable lawes" that respected municipal privileges and traditional institutions. According to Contarini, the towns
of the dominion were self-governed but guided by doctors of law
and natural principles of moderation.[10]

The humanist ideals of Barozzi and Contarini, however, had
very little to do with the realities of terraferma life or the character
of the Venetian dominion. Although they provided ethical guide-

lines that the occasional Venetian governor may have actually tried to follow, the humanist ideals of civic unity led, most often, to a dangerous cleavage between the operations of Venetian government and the rhetoric used to talk about it. Despite the promptings of the Aristotelian tradition to analyze government as a united body politic, the Venetian dominion never became very unified. The fashionable and flattering eloquence of the humanists obscured the real world in which Venetian aristocrats acted, and Venice never produced its own Machiavelli whose practical experience wedded with an exceptional intelligence enabled him to see through political discourse to the necessities demanded by his times. So apparently successful at home, Venetian rule in the terraferma dominion had an odd splintered quality, marked by a disconnection between language and action, a political malady that often had tragic results. Perhaps the greatest of these tragedies was that despite its promises of justice and peace, Venice consistently achieved neither and often failed to perform the most elementary functions of government. Fear festered in defenselessness. And from fear came vendettas.[11]

As Machiavelli argued, the foundations of a successful state are good laws and good arms. The myth of Venice, which has for so long been employed to explain the republic's successes, emphasized the quality of its laws and ignored the failures of its arms. Recent scholarship, however, has turned the myth on its head. On the mainland, Venetian legal institutions largely failed whereas the city's army, so often maligned in those centuries of jokes about a Venetian on horseback, has come to be understood as the best organized force in Italy.

Among the many problems the republic faced during the early fifteenth century when it conquered the terraferma was the diversity of laws and institutions in cities from Cividale to Bergamo, institutions which in most cases Venice left in place, merely substituting itself for the previous lord. In attempting to objectify and depersonalize its regime, Venice argued that its "most sacred laws" embodied the common interests of all these cities. But this was never the case in practice. A variety of laws and innumerable special privileges characterized the patchwork dominion. Even the political and fiscal advantages that came with citizenship in the various towns were controlled locally, and unlike in Tuscany where

Siena and Florence permitted citizenship in the capital city to notables from the subject towns, Venice rarely made a similar concession. Instead the Venetian patriciate established contractual relationships with local self-defining oligarchies composed of a few noble and citizen families who had controlled the administration and economy under the previous lords. The Venetian diarchy, in effect, linked two systems of families, one composed of Venetian patricians and the other of local notables who allied themselves with the Venetian families to continue their supervision of local affairs. The situation in the Veneto did not have the legal formality of Liguria where the Genoese *alberghi* governed through their connections to the provincial clans (*parentele*), but the creation of networks of families was similar.[12]

In some times and places the rapport between these two groupings was mostly harmonious; in others it was forced, masking severe conflicts. Venetian propaganda, however, promised a rather different regime in which *popolani* and peasants could expect impartial justice through the right to appeal cases to Venetian tribunals, a right that has led some to assume that the basis of Venetian hegemony on the mainland was an alliance between the republic and the lower classes of the countryside. Venetian justice may have offered provincials certain tactical opportunities for furthering their own interests, but Venetian promises were at best erratically kept. As J. R. Hale has recently characterized it, "the Venetian patriciate's instinct was to survive and prosper on the cheap." Even more than Venetian justice, Venetian failures to protect the rural population and terraferma towns during times of war prove the truth of this proposition. The terraferma was not so much to be defended as to provide a line of defense for Venice itself. However good were Venetian laws and arms in protecting the lagoon, they were all too often meager bulwarks for the terraferma populations.[13]

Venetians governed the mainland more through administrative habits forced on them by long-standing local practice than through a coherent policy and system. Each subject town had its own past glories, intense pride, corporate rights, and privileges. Each honored its own statutes, distinctively blended from Roman, common, canon, and Lombard law. To defend its local interests, each hired its own professional experts, usually trained in law at Padua. Vene-

tian laws were dramatically different from those found in the terraferma cities because Venice incorporated few Lombard and Frankish
principles in its statutes, Venetian jurists had ignored the reintroduction of Roman law during the twelfth and thirteenth centuries
when it was associated with the extension of imperial rights, and
Venetian merchants abhorred the influence of lawyers in their affairs. To dilute opposition to its initial conquest, Venice asked the
subject towns to sign a formal pact in which they agreed to accept
Venetian sovereignty in return for a guarantee that the Venetian
signoria would respect local statutes. Where local laws interfered
too gravely with Venetian prerogatives, as in Verona, Padua, Vicenza, Brescia, Bergamo, Udine, and the Patria del Friuli, the signoria formed an ad hoc board of local jurists who rendered local
government more accessible to Venetian influence, but there was
no wholesale reconciliation of differences in legal systems.[14]

In Friuli the reformed statutes were translated and published in
the Veneto vernacular as the *Constitutioni de la Patria de Friuli*
(Udine, 1484), but they still embodied numerous contradictions
which Venice failed to eliminate despite repeated Friulan complaints. The signoria gave the luogotenente of Friuli the self-
contradictory charge to rule according to "their and our statutes,
ordinances, and customs."[15]

The result of Venice's failure to create its own coherent system
of rule was that its officials were hostage to the advice of local
lawyers who mediated between Venice and the provincial oligarchs, a situation that had both technical and political consequences. Venetian jurists and appellate judges had little contact
with their colleagues on the terraferma, reinforcing the dishar-
mony between these two judicial worlds. The business of government became so inefficient that Venetian rulership appeared at best
arbitrary and at worst grossly exploitative.[16]

No one but the members of the highest councils of the Venetian
regime could have created governmental efficiency. Although a
body of *savii* in the administrative college of the Venetian Senate
had the responsibility to oversee affairs in the terraferma dominion, the authority of the *savii* began to be usurped during the late
fifteenth century by the Council of Ten, which had a general interest in strategic and defense matters. The council interpreted its

charge broadly to include the distribution of fiefs, creation of maps, conservation of woodlands, supervision of the hydrology of the lagoon, surveillance of fortifications and the arsenal, acquisition and storing of munitions, drilling of provincial militias, and custody of political prisoners. All of these functions involved the ten in terraferma affairs. The regulations of the council, however, were inconsistent and arbitrary, and the habit of members of the council to seek clients among the provincial élites meant that they frequently defended local privileges against encroachments by other Venetian officials. Despite a dramatic expansion in the number and function of regulatory offices during the sixteenth century, the closed nature of the Venetian patriciate so severely restricted the size of the bureaucracy that the government had to rely heavily on local officials.[17]

Nevertheless, Venetian rectors were found in all of the principal terraferma cities. The biggest cities had two: one a podestà in charge of civil and juridical matters, and the other a captain responsible for military and financial affairs. In the smaller cities one man combined both jobs, as was the case in Udine, where the luogotenente served as rector. Terms of office were for sixteen months but often lasted longer when replacements refused to accept the office or failed to take up duties that could be a financial and personal burden.

Three or four assessors (Udine had two), perhaps two chamberlains, and a chancellor assisted the rectors. The assessors were often the most influential of these assistants inasmuch as they were recruited locally and had to possess a law degree and political experience. These men mediated on a day-to-day basis between the statutes and customs of the subject city and those of Venice, a particularly vital function because in most places the rectors could only act as judges and could not legislate. In Friuli, where local jurisdictional privileges survived more fully intact than elsewhere, the assessors were particularly important because the luogotenente's powers were so severely restricted.

Venetian rule also gave privileged place to the local colleges of notaries, especially the notaries *ad acta* who had the exclusive right to positions in the administrative bureaucracy. More prestigious than remunerative, these notarial offices were considered personal and hereditary sinecures that betokened notability and were often occupied, therefore, by ignorant and irresponsible men whose excruciatingly slow pace of work constituted a kind of mental torture for any citizen with a problem to solve.[18]

The absence of sufficient and competent police forces also hindered Venetian justice. The rectors relied on *sbirri* or *zaffi* in the towns and on *campagnoli* who patrolled, if one can so dignify the wanderings of licensed thugs, the rural districts. Usually recruited from among the ranks of criminals who were offered the jobs as alternatives to punishment, their proverbial brutishness and lack of discipline were hardly discouraged by a level of pay so low that robbery or extortion was necessary for survival. The people thoroughly feared and hated them. It was not unusual for a company of *sbirri* sent by the rector on a legitimate mission to be met by the sounding of the tocsin and armed opposition of hostile townsmen. Tommaso Garzoni described a *sbirro* as

> truly malicious in every action, no matter what one is talking about, because to steal he becomes the friend of thieves, carries the torch to light the way for all their plunderings, keeps company with them, serves them as a spy. . . . Everyone is ashamed to deal with the cops, so marked are they by such an ugly and shameful character.

The rectors, moreover, suffered from a chronic shortage of men willing to accept the dubious attractions of the profession and often had to rely on unemployed soldiers of fortune or, worst of all, on Croatian and Albanian shepherds recruited, often at the point of a sword, for the task. If these substitutes failed, as they often did, rectors accepted the voluntary collaboration of private persons who agreed to help, usually for pay but also for the cover such assignments provided for private vendettas. No matter how responsible a podestà, captain, or luogotenente was, no matter how benevolent his intentions or great his wisdom, he simply lacked the forces necessary to police his territory; and in the more feudal areas such as Friuli he could not compete with, let alone confront, local lords capable of assembling scores of mounted retainers.[19]

The available methods for investigating crimes were equally inadequate. Three types of penal procedures could initiate a trial: a secret denunciation, an inquisition in which a judge proceeded *ex officio*, or a mixture of the two in which the judge relied for information on local functionaries such as village mayors, neighborhood chiefs in the cities, or surgeons who treated the wounded. The system thrived on rumor, innuendo, personal animosities, and public reputations with little sifting of evidence until the trial stage, if then. Even after a trial and sentencing Venetian procedures permitted if not encouraged violence and endemic criminality through the absence of enough prisons; a typical sentence for a crime of violence involved a fine and exile. Exiles became bandits who by the late sixteenth century were so numerous they formed private armies that turned Venetian law and order into a dead letter outside of the walled cities. As Gaetano Cozzi and his students characterize it, the Venetian judiciary was one of the most peculiar in Europe, providing a quick and severe punishment for any crime that threatened Venice's hegemony, but in most other cases the weakness or laziness of officials and a heavy reliance on provincial functionaries made it one of the most permissive systems anywhere. In addition, Venetian nobles who served as judges brought to their task a fathomless ignorance of the law and a defensive cunning that led them to subordinate legal principles to political expediency.[20]

The only means the republic devised to achieve some measure of legal uniformity in its terraferma dominion was through judicial appeals. The advocates of the commune (*avvogadori di comun*) in theory defended proper procedures by intervening in cases appealed to the provincial rectors. However, the advocates frequently found themselves in conflict with the auditors (*auditori nuovi*), patrician circuit judges who were supposed to respond to the grievances of the terraferma population by hearing appeals from any court including those of the rectors. Their annual circuits gave provincials access to the highest levels of Venetian judicial authority because the auditors acted as agents of the *quarantia*, the major Venetian court of appeals. Although they had the potential to become quite powerful on the terraferma by reducing the competence of both the local courts and the Venetian rectors, the auditors were hampered by the superior efficiency of the local courts and by the contradictions of their mission. On the one hand, they were supposed to ensure that uniform principles applied through the entire appeals process, but on the other, the initial agreements be-

tween Venice and the conquered territories obliged them to adhere
to the customs and statutes of the subject cities. However, because
the auditors were never in one town for more than a few days, they
could hardly master the local statutes in such a short time and were
at the mercy of local attorneys and notaries for advice. Locals,
moreover, could exploit the right of appeal as a means of evading
the law and delaying judgments.[21]

Good laws and good arms cost a great deal. From a financial
point of view, the Venetian republic can best be understood as a
large corporation devoted to the economic well-being of its patrician shareholders who sought on the mainland access to markets,
landed estates, salaried jobs, and graft. If they profited individually, they may not have been too concerned about the financial
health of the republic itself. In addition, many sources of income
from Venice and the terraferma were designated to cover specific
expenses such as salaries and do not appear on the balance sheet of
the state. It is impossible, therefore, to determine if the revenues
from the terraferma ever actually compensated Venice for the administrative burdens and military costs of acquiring the lands. Before the seventeenth century general budgets are extant for only a
few scattered years (1469, 1500, 1559, and 1582–83; see Tables 1,
2, 3, and 4, respectively), and they show net revenues varying
greatly from year to year. In 1469 the total general revenues of the
republic were 1,033,211 ducats, of which 59.6 percent came from
the capital city, 17.4 percent from the maritime colonies, and 23.0
percent from the terraferma. In 1500 the terraferma share of general revenues grew to 38.4 percent.

From the provincials' perspective the flow of ducats to Venice
could represent an enormous drain. It has been estimated that
Udine, for example, retained for local needs only about ten to fifteen percent of its own revenues from *dazi* and other exactions
placed on more than one hundred products including such necessities as bread, salt, and wine. Most of the extant general budgets
of Venice (Tables 1 through 4), on the other hand, show substantial
expenditures deducted from the gross revenue of each mainland
city, leaving Venice a significantly reduced net income and in 1559
a net loss from Padua and Udine. In addition, direct taxes and
forced loans collected on the mainland seldom met the established
quotas.[22]

TABLE I. Income from the Terraferma in Venetian Budgets, 1469[1]

City or Territory	Gross in Ducats	(%)	Net in Ducats	(%)
Bassano				
Belluno				
Bergamo				
Brescia	75,000	(24.9)	58,991	(24.8)
Cologna				
Crema	7,400	(2.5)	3,500	(1.5)
Feltre				
Padovano				
Padua	65,500	(21.7)	50,900	(21.4)
Patria del Friuli	**7,500**	**(2.5)**	**1,100**	**(0.5)**
Polesine and Rovigo				
Ravenna	9,140	(3.0)	6,290	(2.6)
Rovigo				
Trevigiano				
Treviso	49,850	(16.5)	38,530	(16.2)
Udine				
Verona	52,800	(17.5)	51,000	(21.5)
Vicentino				
Vicenza	34,600	(11.5)	27,150	(11.4)
Totals	301,790		237,461	

Source: *Bilanci generali della Repubblica di Venezia*, Regia commissione per la pubblicazione dei documenti finanziari della Repubblica Veneta, 2d ser., vol. 1, tomo 1 (Venice: Stabl. Visentina, 1912), doc. 123, pp. 148–50.

[1] In only four cases do the figures given in the document for net return correspond exactly to the figures derived from subtracting the listed expenses from the listed gross income. I have ignored the column of net figures and created a new one based on subtracting expenses from income. The sum of these new net figures is 237,461 ducats, much closer to the net sum of 236,220 ducats listed in the document than the actual sum of the listed figures, which is only 177,220 ducats.

Even though the figures do not permit us to estimate accurately the overall value to Venice of the terraferma dominion, they do show the comparative value of each city or region. Throughout the period Brescia remained the most lucrative of the Venetian possessions, usually supplying nearly one quarter of all the terraferma revenues. During the fifteenth century Padua produced

TABLE 2. Income from the Terraferma in Venetian Budgets, 1500[1]

City or Territory	Gross in Ducats	(%)	Net in Ducats	(%)
Bassano				
Belluno				
Bergamo	25,500	(7.7)	16,000	(6.7)
Brescia	75,000	(22.7)	59,000	(24.8)
Cologna				
Crema	7,400	(2.2)	3,500	(1.5)
Feltre				
Padovano				
Padua	65,600	(19.9)	51,000	(21.4)
Patria del Friuli	**7,550**	**(2.3)**	**1,150**	**(0.5)**
Polesine and Rovigo				
Ravenna	11,830	(3.6)	6,990	(2.9)
Rovigo				
Trevigiano				
Treviso	49,850	(15.1)	38,530	(16.2)
Udine				
Verona	52,500	(15.9)	34,500	(14.5)
Vicentino				
Vicenza	34,600	(10.5)	27,150	(11.4)
Totals	329,830		237,820	

Source: *Bilanci generali*, vol. 1, tomo 1, doc. 134, pp. 172–73.
[1] Includes the contado of all towns.

about one fifth of the return, but in the sixteenth it lost position to Verona, which underwent a remarkable population increase. Treviso and Vicenza were always important. Udine and the patria, on the other hand, were consistently among the least remunerative, despite the vast amount of territory they comprised. (To this day, Udine is the largest commune in the size of its territory in Italy.) In 1469 and 1500 Friuli provided only 0.5 percent of net terraferma revenues. In 1559 Venetian expenses in Friuli exceeded income from it by 1,943 ducats.[23]

The low level of income from Friuli becomes especially revealing when the military expenditures in this frontier region are taken into account. In 1582–83 to drill the necessary troops the patria

TABLE 3. Income from the Terraferma in Venetian Budgets, 1559

City or Territory	Gross in Ducats	(%)	Net in Ducats	(%)
Bassano	5,038	(1.1)	1,547	(11.0)
Belluno				
Bergamo	39,680	(8.3)	0	(0.0)
Brescia	104,497	(22.0)	47	(0.3)
Cologna	2,818	(0.6)	169	(1.2)
Crema	16,377	(3.4)	1,445	(10.3)
Feltre				
Padovano				
Padua	68,846	(14.5)	−3,813	(−27.2)
Patria del Friuli				
Polesine and Rovigo				
Ravenna				
Rovigo	8,172	(1.7)	352	(2.5)
Trevigiano				
Treviso	56,522	(11.9)	12,443	(88.7)
Udine	**13,074**	**(2.7)**	**−1,943**	**(−13.9)**
Verona	101,771	(21.4)	42	(0.3)
Vicentino				
Vicenza	59,017	(12.4)	3,733	(26.6)
Totals	475,812		14,022	

Source: *Bilanci generali*, vol. 1, tomo 1, doc. 166, pp. 222–31.

required twenty captains who accounted for nearly one fifth of all monies spent on captains (Table 5). Likewise, 18.5 percent of the budget for fortress garrisons went to Friuli (Table 6). Given the region's position as a buffer for Venice against the Turks, Austrians, and Hungarians, the high ratio of military costs to revenues may not be remarkable, but the patria was still fiscally unhealthy. In 1606 a Venetian auditor of terraferma finances (*Provveditore sopra le camere in Terraferma*), Carlo Ruzzini, pointed out that whereas the expenses of government were not much less in Udine than in the more populous terraferma cities, its maximum revenues were greatly less, about one fifth of what could be expected from Brescia or Verona. Treviso, which had the same level of annual expenditures as Udine, could anticipate more than double the income.[24]

TABLE 4. Income from the Terraferma in Venetian Budgets, 1582–83[1]

City or Territory	Gross in Ducats	(%)
Bassano		
Belluno	5,842	(1.0)
Bergamo	33,114	(5.8)
Brescia	145,591	(25.4)
Cologna		
Crema	74,662	(13.0)
Feltre	4,620	(0.8)
Padovano	12,803	(2.2)
Padua	44,836	(7.8)
Patria del Friuli[2]	**10,225**	**(1.8)**
Polesine and Rovigo	3,251	(0.6)
Ravenna		
Rovigo	9,206	(1.6)
Trevigiano	23,618	(4.1)
Treviso	25,876	(4.5)
Udine	**12,290**	**(2.1)**
Verona	122,861	(21.4)
Vicentino	1,992	(0.3)
Vicenza	42,697	(7.4)
Totals	573,484	

Source: *Bilanci generali*, vol. 1, tomo 1, doc. 189, pp. 283–323.

[1] Figures listed only include gross income. Some entries give only one year, which cannot be distinguished between 1582 and 1583, and others give both years. In the latter cases, figures for 1583 have been used.

[2] The entry "Castelle della Patria" lists Cividale (2,808), Portogruaro (1,406), Monfalcone (1,124), Chiusa (710), Pordenone (4,117).

For provincial subjects the Venetian dominion was probably at best a mixed blessing, at worst a terrible financial drain, which gave little in return for taxes except for the dubious protection of the Venetian military. Although it is obviously true that the Venetians ruled the terraferma according to their own perception of their own interests, self-interest hardly accounts for the obscurity, inefficiency, and contradictory nature of Venetian practice. One need not apply some anachronistic modern standard to Renaissance Venice but only listen to the voices of the Venetian rectors them-

TABLE 5. Costs of Maintaining Captains on the Terraferma, 1582–83

Location and Number of Captains	Ducats per Year	(%)
Bresciano (20)	4,000	(18.9)
Cividal di Belluno (2)	560	(2.7)
Cremasco (6)	1,960	(9.3)
Feltre (2)	560	(2.7)
Istria (4)	960	(4.5)
Padua (7)	1,640	(7.8)
Patria del Friuli (20)	**4,160**	**(19.7)**
Polesine di Rovigo (8)	2,000	(9.5)
Trevigiano (8)	1,920	(9.1)
Veronese (8)	1,920	(9.1)
Vicentino (6)	1,440	(6.8)
Total	21,120	

Source: *Bilanci generali*, vol. 1, tomo 1, doc. 190, pp. 323–39.

TABLE 6. Colonels, Governors, Captains, and Other Officials Paid to Garrison Fortresses and Cities on the Terraferma, 1582–83

Fortress or Fortified City	Ducats per Year	(%)
Asola di Bresciana	2,318	(2.9)
Bergamo	11,329	(14.1)
Brescia	10,989	(13.7)
Cadore	942	(1.2)
Chiusa	**864**	**(1.1)**
Crema	8,319	(10.3)
Este	2,318	(2.9)
Marano	4,216	(5.2)
Padua	6,437	(8.0)
Pontevico	1,611	(2.0)
Rovigo	2,919	(3.6)
Salo	1,884	(2.3)
Treviso	2,318	(2.9)
Udine	**10,700**	**(13.3)**
Verona	10,941	(13.6)
Vicenza	2,318	(2.9)
Total	80,483	

Source: *Bilanci generali*, vol. 1, tomo 1, doc. 190, pp. 329–30.

selves, who mastered a kind of doublespeak in which they parroted verses in praise of their singular city while they discussed the sad consequences of its rule of the mainland. Although Venetian justice promised more than could be delivered, it did provide mainland subjects with additional room to maneuver in seeking a resolution of disputes. Some appealed to Venetian magistrates as a means of resisting local oligarchs, but others surely exploited the courts to evade local laws. There was no redress for any of them when Venetians thought their own security was at stake, and little hope in reducing fiscal burdens.

In many ways Friuli was the oddest piece in Venice's heterogeneous collection of territories, the vital piece to be deployed against the ever-menacing German and Ottoman Empires, but nevertheless a distinctly difficult land.

VENDETTA

One of the most common kinds of conflict and certainly the most troublesome one Venetian magistrates faced in Friuli was vendetta. In the attempts to control vendetta through administrative decrees and criminal prosecutions, Venetians encountered a system of primitive law and a form of social organization governed by implicit rules that provided models for individual behavior, defined the membership in social groups, and, most importantly, regulated conflicts by promising retaliatory punishment for insults and aggression. Theoretically, official justice and vendetta justice were incompatible because, on the one hand, private vendettas impinged upon the most basic prerogatives of the state and, on the other, avengers who relied on the courts rather than their own valor could be seen as shameful cowards. However, in the real world of fifteenth- and early sixteenth-century Friuli the two forms of justice often worked hand in hand, the Venetians going easy on friendly families and relying on modest judicial punishments of exile, which permitted many vendettas to continue, and the Friulans manipulating and corrupting the courts when it was to their advantage to do so. For more than a century after the Venetian conquest, the two systems of law cohabited in an inconsistent yet symbiotic relationship.[25]

Friuli shared in the Mediterranean-wide culture of feuding which has been studied by legions of anthropologists and historians. In such cultures persons assume that disputes of any sort will inevitably take the form of a feud or vendetta and that all calculations about power and honor are based on the status of ongoing vendettas. The pursuit of vendettas was inextricably linked to the Mediterranean ideal of masculinity, which David Gilmore has characterized as striving for "performative excellence." A man who is "good at being a man" follows a script that involves him in public displays of physical risk, which he meets with decision and useful action—that is, behavior directed toward a specific purpose, such as protecting vulnerable family members. The "good" man is neither a saint nor a bully but someone who employs aggressiveness to deter challenges and is above all loyal to his own. When he or someone close to him is hurt by another, either in word or deed, the good man seeks revenge by which he retaliates in an appropriate way, ideally matching the injury with an equal or slightly greater injury. By pulling off such performances well he acquires honor, that most precious and perishable of social attributes, and the reputation for being an honorable man helps him avoid further challenges. The performative aspect of masculine honor is embodied in the very word, *vendetta*, which implied a forceful demonstration of potency, and its Friulan variant, *svindic*, conveyed an especially strong message of anger.[26]

Found in Mosaic, Roman, and particularly Lombard law, vendetta embodied a principle of compensation, "eye for eye, tooth for tooth," for a debt created by an insult or injury. Throughout the Mediterranean and the Middle East, people have long conceived of revenge as an exchange that followed the general economic rule that the transfer of any value should be returned in kind and with an increment if possible; the escalation of retaliatory killings was, therefore, a kind of interest payment, and the commodity exchanged was blood. Just as in the marketplace where every transaction implies the possibility of future transactions—indeed, makes them more likely—each assault or killing in a vendetta makes future acts of violence more likely. The principle of compensation, generally called the *contrappasso*, found its way into the customs and sometimes common law of many medieval and Renaissance Italian towns.[27]

The common law of Friuli retained many vestiges of Lombard principles, which recognized the Old German concept of *faida*, the requirement of revenge that fell on the closest blood relative of a victim, who in effect replaced the dead man in the household. Early Lombard edicts attempted to limit the effects of *faida* by confining it to a very narrow range of participants but recognized it as a popular custom. Although no longer a necessity as it had been among the ancient Germans, *faida* remained an important means of personal defense parallel to judicial combat and private pledges. Friulan law went far in prohibiting the behavioral legacy of *faida* but implicitly recognized that vendettas still served as a system of private justice, a legal situation that reflected a deep ambivalence about vendetta in Friulan society.[28]

Ambivalence about the role of vengeance also persisted in other areas of Italy, especially among the educated elite most influenced by Christian and humanist culture. A double-tongued attitude can be found in the combined heritage, on the one hand, of the early Christian moralists and Stoics, who treated all anger as a passion unworthy of humanity and, on the other, of Aristotle, who distinguished a form of righteous anger from the extremes of spiritless passivity and unreasonable anger. Aquinas probably went farther than any other Christian thinker in justifying lawful vengeance, which he called a special virtue and a form of charity, but he stipulated various conditions that would guarantee the avenger's pious intentions: the avenger must act only in keeping with his rank and position, should bear with wrongs committed against his person, and should retaliate only against those who had wronged God, the church, or a neighbor. Excessive punishment such as cruelty and deficient punishment such as improper leniency both violated true vengeance. The Thomist criterion for virtuous vengeance consisted "in observing the due measure of vengeance with regard to all the circumstances." Saint Thomas defended the principle of exact parity between the assault and the retaliation, a principle that quixotically struggled against the exchange character of vendetta, which assumed a continuous escalation of insults and assaults. Although he sanctioned righteous anger, Aquinas's distinctions had so little to do with actual practice that they merely contributed to the ambivalence of the educated, especially the clergy, toward vendetta.[29]

For the less philosophically minded, however, divine precepts mirrored human practices. Florentines of the fourteenth century, for example, equated divine justice with the phrase "vendetta di

Dio," a justice that the agents of God pursued with a righteous ferocity. One Luca di Totto da Panzano, a distinguished Florentine citizen who between 1355 and 1371 enjoyed four terms as prior and one as a standard-bearer of justice, described in his matter-of-fact diary how he and his relatives murdered numerous enemies. Luca never bothered to justify his blood lust save to point out that one of his relatives had been murdered first. He needed no further explanation. In contrast to Aquinas's, his might represent the untutored attitude, an unambiguous acceptance of the personal obligation to avenge a wrong: "I retaliate, therefore I am."[30]

A greater ambivalence can be found in *The Divine Comedy*. Beatrice assured Dante that those responsible for the Babylonian captivity of the papacy would not escape God's vengeance (*Purgatorio*, canto 33, lines 35–36), but Dante himself was less certain about his own personal obligation to pursue vengeance. In the *Inferno* (canto 29, lines 31–36) a cousin of Dante's father, Geri del Bello, who had been murdered by a member of the Sachetti family, reminds the poet that his violent end had not been avenged. The meaning of this episode is unusually obscure. Did Dante intend to demonstrate his piety for the memory of his ancestor, to condemn those who pursued the vendetta, or to express the struggle in his own mind between the religious command to forgive wrongs and his personal shame for failing to satisfy an obligation that common opinion condoned?[31]

Whereas fourteenth-century humanists, as opposed to Thomist scholastics, accepted the Stoic rejection of all anger as contrary to the dictates of reason, in the fifteenth century some humanists came to defend anger openly, creating a form of revenge humanism. Leonardo Bruni, unable to separate justifiable wrath from the emotions of devotion and bravery so necessary for the ideal civic life, argued that moral strength had to be nourished by the passions, which gave commitment to the course set out by reason.[32]

In addition, the examples of antiquity justified the actions of some Renaissance conspirators, who were undoubtedly also motivated by personal desires for revenge. Pomponius Laetus and other humanists cited the ancients in defending their plan to assassinate Pope Paul II, as did both Girolamo Olgiati in his assault on Galeazzo Maria Visconti and Jacopo da Diaceto in attacking Cardinal Giulio de' Medici. Plutarch, Livy, and Tacitus supplied the favored texts, some of which Francesco Burlamacchi cited in giving grounds for his conspiracy against the Grand Duke of Tuscany. Contemporary humanist philology also helped. Stefano Porcari took Lorenzo Valla's demolition of the Donation of Constantine so seriously that he saw himself as another Cato in his plot against Pope Nicholas V.[33]

Although one should be cautious in taking the humanists at face value by believing the justifications put out under the guise of antique culture by these professional propagandists, there is no doubt that many Italian aristocrats found in pagan antiquity a society the values of which paralleled their own. From the ancients they acquired a language that articulated what they already knew: the desire for revenge was a passion, the stirring of mad blood. But humanist notions of honorable revenge became at best a thin patina covering deep and rough angers. Even those who had never heard of Plutarch understood that vendetta had an emotional basis. Some might use such emotional knowledge as an excuse—"I was almost beside myself, and I wanted to go out and cause some harm. . . . I wanted to kill priests and set fire to churches and do something crazy: but because of my two little children, I restrained myself"—and others as a lament—"I want you to feel how the crude and vain passions of the parties and factions, which in miserable Italy rule, can possess human minds." The widespread contemporary understanding of the emotional components of vendetta may help explain further the plasticity of the term, applied to so many different situations, and any explanation of vendetta must rely on an appreciation for these feelings as well. The very wildness of revenge ought to caution us to avoid defining it so precisely that we fail to appreciate its passionate madness as well as its sociological reasonableness.[34]

A vendetta need not have begun with assault or murder but only required a perceived insult. An affronted man becomes very dangerous, especially if his honor has been questioned by calumnies against his female relatives or his own lack of courage. Insults could be symbolic, physical, or verbal, and the laws promised heavy penalties for those who affronted another. In areas most influenced by Roman legal learning, the statutory rubrics distinguished between simple derision, which attributed to the offended person physical or moral defects or compared him with an animal, and more threatening imputations against his honor. The law demanded in the latter case that proof of the charge be forthcoming and provided heavy sentences for false accusations. Friulan codes were especially rich in statutory provisions against various kinds of ridicule. In Udine the scale of penalties enacted higher fines for taunts heard in the public streets, and threats spoken in the city square, communal council, or the courts received the heaviest punishments. Fines for verbal abuse (*rusticitates iniuriosae*) applied only to the aggressor and not to the person provoked even if he replied in kind. In cases in which it was unclear who started the confrontation the court divided the fine between the two. The statute listed the scornful words that should not be spoken and provided penalties for knocking off someone's hat or jerking down his hood. It exacted special punishments for abuse committed by women and treated with unusual severity Tuscans domiciled in Udine who threatened their countrymen.[35]

The authorities remained vigilant for verbal affronts and symbolic acts of calumny which publicly unbalanced the delicate relationships of the community. As a result, people had to be cautious about what was said to whom, and aggressive joking, in particular, required a sensitivity to the style of native discourse, to what Basil Bernstein calls "restricted codes," which are peculiar to all local and class relationships and which employ condensed symbols and metaphors that contrast with the elaborate linguistic codes of the learned. The more restricted the verbal codes of the community, the more likely creative forms of abuse and plays upon everyday imagery might be both valued and dangerous if taken too far. At the most extreme, insults could be understood as similar to curses, words spoken in such a way that they conveyed a malevolent power through their very utterance. Illiteracy and cultural isolation, thus, contributed to the hothouse atmosphere of Friuli, leaving the Friulans with a body of concrete images, usually about animals, which, when spoken in derision, left little room for the ambiguous interpretations that contemporary diplomats, for example, found so useful for avoiding confrontations.[36]

The principal means available to Venetian magistrates and local Friulan judges for controlling vendetta was to sentence culprits to exile, an act that put them outside of the protection of the law and made them, as far as the law was concerned, members of "the living dead." In outlawing men for crimes of violence the government sought not only to rid itself of public nuisances but also to focus the wrath of the community on guilty scapegoats whose legal death would have a healing effect for the community as a whole.[37]

Exile may be the oldest legal method for dealing with disturbances of the peace and for preserving the borders of society. Ancient Roman law distinguished between simple exile, the expulsion from the place where one normally lived; relegation, the obligation to remain in a defined place; and deportation, the forced removal across the sea. The outlaw might suffer the loss of his property, and others were prohibited from giving him water or fire, depriving him in effect of the benefits of membership in the human community. He would be denied access to all sacred sites and ceremonies because he was a source of pollution. If anything, Germanic custom was even more thorough in denying the humanity of a person banished for crime. His chief considered him dead, his wife became a widow, his children orphans, and his property was either destroyed or returned to the tribe. If he were caught and killed, his captors left the corpse in the wilds to be ravaged by animals. If he escaped, he became a *wargus* or werewolf who must be attacked and killed by anyone who found him; in fact in many medieval statutes the head of an outlaw brought the same reward as the head of a wolf. Banishment, thus, constituted legal, social, and very often literal death. The Edict of Theodoric of 507 combined Roman imperial and German tribal principles, creating the concept of banishment passed on by the Carolingian codes. In following these traditions, Friuli and Venice employed relegation, deportation, and (because most offenders were contumacious) simple exile as the normal penalties for almost all crimes of violence.[38]

The connotations of the word *bandit* reveal the kind of life that awaited most banished persons. Up until about the middle of the fifteenth century, bandits in northern Italy often joined others who had suffered the same fate and formed armed companies to plot their return or to raid their enemies, robbing to survive. Bandits had traditionally been able to rely on the aid and comfort of foreign princes who used them to stir up trouble in the territory of their neighbors; but after the Peace of Lodi in 1454 resident ambassadors helped guarantee the prohibitions of the Italic League against supporting the exiles of a neighboring prince.[39]

This salutary general development only marginally touched Friuli, in which imperial enclaves and the difficult terrain continued to provide a ready refuge. At no time during the fifteenth and sixteenth centuries, moreover, did Venice have the police forces necessary to catch culprits. By making proclamations and offering bounties Venice had to rely on subjects rather than officials to apprehend or kill delinquents, and the city seldom employed the army, even when it was at full strength and in the field, to capture fleeing criminals or to combat brigands. The authorities had little choice but to rely on the time-honored expedient of banishment as a means of controlling and punishing crimes, but the system created a vicious circle in which an exile had few incentives to keep from continuing his violence because he could do so without hindrance unless some private citizen determined to stop him.[40]

The statutes of Venice and Udine devote a great deal of space to regulating banishment and to the treatment of bandits. Before the Venetian conquest, Friuli had a draconian version of the *interdictio aquae et ignis* according to which judges had a ditch dug around a culprit's house and private citizens could neither give him water and fire nor speak with him. After the conquest, Udine's revised statutes eliminated the *interdictio* and provided for two kinds of exile: ordinary banishment for life, in which the condemned suffered the effects of a civil death, and capital banishment, in which anyone could kill the exile without criminal penalty. But in one of the typical contradictions of Venetian rule, Venetian law failed to make the same distinctions as Udinese law, meaning that anyone banished from Venetian territories could, in many cases, be legally assassinated. The question thus became which laws should apply to Friulan cases; there was never a consistent answer. Moreover, Venetian authorities had the flexibility to apply the law as they wished, offering bounties on the heads of exiles according to political considerations.

The Venetian provisions that allowed the killing of declared bandits and those who helped them caused enormous problems that reveal the dilemmas produced by the system. For a few years Venice experimented with a rule that allowed an exiled person to escape his ban by bringing in the head of another exile, but this law provoked so much crime it had to be revoked. The Council of Ten found itself repeating a cycle of expanding the right to assassinate exiles and then revoking it a few years later as the number of assaults and murders increased. The privilege of some Friulan castellans, such as the lords of Spilimbergo, to offer refuge to outlaws especially troubled the Venetian rectors who recurrently tried to circumscribe the practice, but the council did not definitively abrogate the entitlement until 1581. In the most atrocious cases a banned person lost his property; but in Friuli, where brothers jointly held most private property, carrying out this provision against one member of a fraternal consortium might prove difficult and encourage relatives to assist the exile.[41]

An exiled person was banished beyond a fifteen-mile perimeter around the territory; but unless specifically stated otherwise, the ban only applied to the territory of the jurisdiction in which the crime had been committed. The multiple jurisdictions in Friuli produced a nightmare, especially because many jurisdictions were not even fifteen miles across. Moreover, a loophole in the law which was not corrected until 1541 permitted persons banished from a terraferma jurisdiction to find refuge in Venice itself, a rather pleasant prospect for many rural ruffians. As if these complications did not inhibit enforcement enough, rectors issued many safe conducts to those banished from other jurisdictions, a practice that may have been lucrative enough for the rectors but made a mockery of justice.

The numerous anomalies in the Venetian provisions against vendetta permitted even a modestly clever outlaw considerable freedom of movement and action. A law of 1504, for example, stipulated that persons banished *ad inquirendum* (awaiting judgment), presumably because they were contumacious, had up to sixteen months after the term of office of the rector who banished them ended to present themselves to the court or face banishment for life. By 1524, however, numerous criminals had complained that because they had been away when banished, they had not known about their own exile and had not returned in time to defend themselves against false accusations. The Senate, therefore, revoked the 1504 law. It soon became evident, however, that the very persons whose complaints had led to the revocation had in fact conspired with other exiles to take advantage of the opportunity to return to commit crimes in Venetian territories. The 1504 statute had to be reinstituted.

Another trick was to apply to several different Venetian councils for a pardon, to appeal rejections of pardons several times, and to use a pardon, once granted, to exact revenge on old enemies. Only in 1565 did the Council of Ten reserve for itself the right to issue pardons from sentences of exile.[42]

Despite the ancient traditions behind the scapegoating of outlaws, the process largely failed in Friuli. Exiled persons very often remained members of society, even when absent, and sentences of exile seldom turned communities against culprits. Exiling failed for several reasons. First, although exiles might be legal nonpersons, their sentences merely put them in trouble with the distant and vague Venetians; and if outlaws had strong local support, they were relatively safe. Second, many of the castellans who administered the lower levels of justice were themselves participants in feuds. As a result outlaw proclamations often lacked legitimacy and were unenforceable in the villages and castles in which more informal social pressures governed behavior. Third, Venetian law was not very intimidating, especially compared with the dangers that came from ignoring a personal affront. Notwithstanding the many disjunctures in Friulan kinship patterns, the internal clan ruptures among brothers and cousins, and the dereliction of allied families in defending their friends, vendetta constituted the real law and often the only justice. Through vendetta the fictive dead men of exile and literal dead men of combat could fight back.

CHAPTER THREE

Factions in the Fifteenth Century

In Friuli many forms of conflict found meaning in the ethos of vendetta, including not only disputes between families and clans but conflicts within clans, among communities, and especially among the classes. Most of these struggles originated in competition for material resources under conditions of scarcity—competition over water supplies, collective rights to pastures, or the distribution of patronage jobs. Vendetta contained and regulated these clashes, but it also aggravated them because the language of honorable retaliation which helped persons conceptualize quarrels and the stories of valor that nourished the factions masked the material and social sources of discord.

Several castellan lineages, which were akin to clans in the Scottish fashion, dominated the vendettas and formed the core group of the factions. However, members of the castellan clans also had a tendency to fight among themselves, undermining the strength of lineages as a pervasive source of stability, a tendency that makes them less cohesive, for example, than the *parentele* of Liguria, which provided a language and structure for all political and economic relationships.[1]

The castellan clans of Friuli might best be understood as the manifestations of a dynamic process that can be traced through marriage choices, which reveal the changing identities of the clans. Given the apparent fragility of clan solidarity, the factions became the most potent organizations for regulating local conflicts, protecting the vulnerable and weak, and providing a source of collective identity. These factions consisted of a variety of persons allied to but not usually related by blood or marriage to a dominant family, and in Friuli the membership of the two dominant factions coalesced primarily along class lines, divisions that also expressed community tensions. Although Friulans habitually described their struggles as vendettas, these vendettas cast a wide net that gathered in most of the tensions of the society, many of which had little to do with the technical obligations of personal revenge.

SAVORGNAN AND DELLA TORRE

For more than two centuries the Savorgnan and Della Torre clans fought an on-again, off-again vendetta that recurrently expanded into factional warfare. The followers of the Savorgnan called themselves the Zambarlani, those of the Della Torre the Strumieri. The pervasive, dominating extralegal influence of the Savorgnan and challenges to that influence stimulated the formation of the factions and created the central political fact of Friulan internal history, both before and after the Venetian conquest. Beginning in the thirteenth century, the Savorgnan fortified their position through the acquisition of lands, control of lucrative investments, accumulation of jurisdictions, and cultivation of useful friendships, especially in Venice. Although others feared they would transform themselves into princes, they never acquired a lordship as did the Carrara in Padua, Della Scala in Verona, Este in Ferrara, or Visconti in Milan, but they came close to the kind of covert hegemony the Medici achieved in fifteenth-century Florence.

Considering the aridity of the Friulan plain, it is perhaps not surprising that the Savorgnan based their power in the control of water supplies. In the thirteenth century Udine had only five wells, then considered very old and inadequate because only one was reliable. Besides these, the most important source of water was an aqueduct from the Torre River, a modest but vital stream that begins on the slopes of Mount Musi in the Julian Alps. As the Torre passes out of the foothills, its channel narrows; dropping below the level of the plain, the river becomes too low for gravity-flow aqueducts and irrigation ditches, a situation that made control of its upper reaches particularly valuable.

In 921 the Emperor Berengarius granted to a canon of the church of Aquileia the right to fortify a small castle at a narrow place just above where the Torre drops below the plain, a spot called Savorgnan del Torre. Thereafter, whoever possessed this insignificant-looking location would be the master of the water supply for much of the high plain and especially for Udine. In the thirteenth century an already prominent Udinese family acquired the fief of Savorgnan del Torre, which supplied them with a surname and castellan status. Finally, they saw in the battles against Patriarch Philippe d'Alençon in 1383 the opportunity to designate themselves absolute lords over the waters of the Torre, making *de jure* what had already existed *de facto*. From this position of ecologic arbiter, the clan built an impressive domain.[2]

Between 1315 and 1344, with profits acquired in Udine (especially through associations with Tuscans in the woolen-cloth trade), the Savorgnan bought up enormous amounts of land, at first along the Torre downstream from their castle and then in Udine itself. A 1396 record of their holdings in Udine lists houses, a monopoly of lucrative water-driven mills, warehouses of grain reserves, farms directly cultivated for them in the semirural *borghi*, and *livello* rents from other farms. They owned lands acquired from the counts of Gorizia in Pradamano, Cussignacco, and Terenzano. From the castle at Savorgnan their estate fanned out into the nearby towns of Nimis and Tarcento and into the villages of the foothills and mountains where they owned farms, pastures, stands of timber, and peat bogs. A second concentration in the valleys of the Alps made them predominant in Carnia, where they controlled vast herds of sheep and goats and cut forest timber essential for Venice's shipping. But they also had extensive properties dispersed throughout Friuli in dozens of little villages. After 1428, in fulfillment of a long penance imposed by Pope Martin V on Tristano Savorgnan for having murdered Patriarch John Sobieslaw of Moravia, the Savorgnan became the major patrons of churches in Udine. Their gifts gave them rights to name priests to parishes, canons to the cathedral, and abbots to monasteries.[3]

One of the common characteristics of factions in Mediterranean societies was the convergence of friendship and patronage ties with economic transactions. Leaders traded with and lent money and goods to their colleagues and clients. Essential to Savorgnan success in building a vast clientele were their ties to the bankers of Friuli. Although far too little is known about this aspect of their activities, it appears that the family managed the distribution of credit in Udine and environs. They did not act as bankers themselves but protected first Tuscan and, after 1450, Jewish bankers who provided short-term loans to the poor.

The largest community of Jews was in San Daniele, but in the late fifteenth and early sixteenth centuries Cividale, Venzone, Gemona, and Udine all had contracts with Ashkenazim to operate pawn shops for small loans. As was the case elsewhere in northern Italy, hostility toward the Jews and their purportedly usurious hold on the poor led to the establishment of a Christian charitable lending agency, a Monte di Pietà, first set up in Udine in 1496. However, until the 1540s, partly as a result of Savorgnan resistance, the Monte di Pietà failed to generate enough capital to play a very significant role in the economy, and the Jewish bankers continued to function without molestation.

The Savorgnan profited from the Jews' business activities by granting for a fee the contract that permitted them to live in Udine and by acting as their protectors, both directly as in 1511 when Antonio Savorgnan prevented the looting of Jewish property during the Cruel Carnival and indirectly through Udine's minor council which, despite promptings from Venice, failed to curtail Jewish activities in the city. The Jews served the useful double function of supplying much-needed liquid capital and of serving as scapegoats during periods of discontent.

By the midsixteenth century, however, the perceived need to scapegoat Jews outstripped the need for Jewish capital, and in 1556, after a severe epidemic, Udine expelled the Jews. Cividale drove them out by 1571, and thereafter they confined their banking activities to the smaller towns and the countryside, the larger towns relying on the Monti di Pietà.[4]

From their unmatched financial base the Savorgnan wove together a network of political and jurisdictional privileges. In Udine the family considered the right to appoint the city's chancellor "an ancient inherited practice," nearly always had a family member among the deputies, and even had the city adopt the Savorgnan blazon as its own. In the fifteenth and sixteenth centuries the Savorgnan were one of the few Friulan clans to enjoy more than one feudal jurisdiction. They had twelve. Osoppo was the most important strategically, but within the fiefs of Belgrado and Castelnovo with some twenty-two subject villages, the Savorgnan were autonomous princes, legally separate from the patria and the supervision of the luogotenente and subject only to the ultimate authority of the Savorgnans' feudal lord, the doge of Venice (see map "Friuli in the Sixteenth Century"). Their privileges in their fiefs included the monopoly of salt supplies; the collecting of tolls at the crossing points of the Tagliamento, Isonzo, Cosa, Arzino Rivers and several smaller streams; the issuing of licenses for keeping sheep, harvesting grapes, hunting and fishing, and operating a bakery or tavern; and the appointment of podestà, *decani*, judges, and priests in more than fifty localities. A 1470 census listed 5,328 people under the direct jurisdiction of the Savorgnan.[5]

Even before the conquest, Venice had solidified its position in Friuli by granting them membership in the Venetian patriciate, a status that made them, as Mallett and Hale put it, the "most prominent and the most controversial" of all the terraferma families allied to Venice. Their exceptional autonomy and near-princely powers in Friuli made their loyalty essential to Venetian interests, which was precisely why the Venetians tolerated and humored them for so long; but to many other Friulan castellans, their usurpations and petty tyrannies made them insufferable.[6]

The Savorgnan, however, recurrently divided into mutually antagonistic branches. The repeated schisms of the Savorgnan and many other Friulan clans illustrate a pattern commonly found in societies with partible inheritance customs. Where the entire patrimony including castles, lands, livestock, liquid capital, water and pasturage rights, rents, and levies belongs to the family as a whole, conflict within the family, even violent conflict, is part of an inevitable and even necessary process that balances resources with the optimal number of family members. The successful resolution of tensions might become a source of future clan and family cohesion, but at the point of fission family conflicts disrupted other social ties of patronage and clientage which normally brought stability to the society as a whole.[7]

As early as the thirteenth century, members of the separate Savorgnan branches resident in Udine and Savorgnan del Torre were murdering one another. After 1260 the Della Bandiera branch located themselves in Savorgnan del Torre, Artegna, and Cividale whereas the Dello Scaglione, which produced most of the family members discussed in this book, resided in Udine. In the fifteenth century the Savorgnan Dello Scaglione themselves split after Tristano, who had assassinated a patriarch and helped Venice in its conquest, divided his properties between two principal heirs (Table 7). The descendants of his son Urbano (died 1464) formed the Torre di Zuino subbranch and possessed the fiefs of Bibano, Buia, Pinzano, Pradamano, and Zuino. The progeny of Pagano (died 1470) became the Monte d'Osoppo subbranch and held the fiefs of Ariis, Forni, Osoppo, and after 1515 Belgrado, Castelnovo, and Palazzolo. During the early sixteenth century, when the factional conflicts of Friuli reached such a violent peak, the rivalry between the head of the Savorgnan del Torre di Zuino, Antonio (1458–1512), and the Savorgnan di Monte d'Osoppo, Girolamo (1466–1529), dramatically complicated the position of the clan, confusing the loyalties of the antagonistic factions and threatening the very survival of Venetian dominion. One of the ironies of Friulan vendettas was that while revenge assaults and killings were carried on in the name of clan solidarity, many clans suffered deep internal antagonisms and recurrent schisms that make a static portrait of the social structure deceptive.[8]

Whereas the Savorgnan enhanced their influence after the Venetian conquest, the Della Torre were among the principal losers. Originally coming from Milan where several Della Torre had served as the captain of the people, the clan rose to prominence in Friuli with the tenure of Patriarch Raimondo Della Torre (1273–99). The Della Torre produced three more patriarchs: Castone (1317), Pagano (1320–31), and Lodovico (1359–63). They accumulated extensive properties in Friuli and Gorizia and, with the acquisition through marriage of the castle of Duino, found themselves frequently in conflict with the Venetians, especially over the possession of nearby Monfalcone. Their hostility toward the Vene-

TABLE 7. Family Tree of the Savorgnan Dello Scaglione[1]

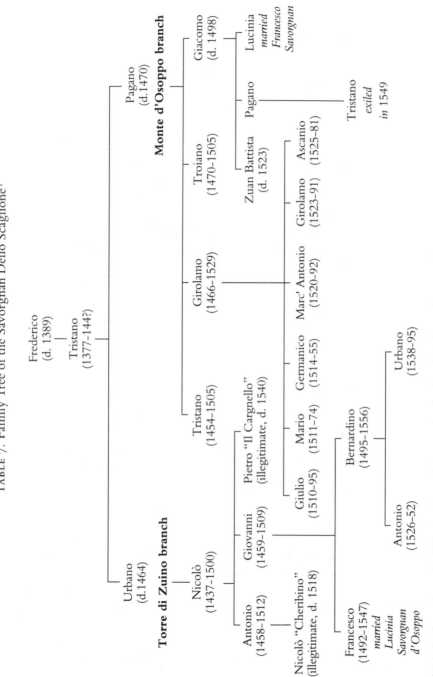

[1]Only family members who fell in the direct male line or who played a role in the vendetta are included.

FIGURE 3. Della Torre coat of arms in relief over the main
portal of the castle at Villalta.

tians was not consistent, however, and for a brief time after 1340
one branch of the Della Torre received honorary membership in
the Venetian Great Council, a right that disappeared by the early
fifteenth century when the Savorgnan became Venice's favored
Friulan clan.[9]

The centerpiece of Della Torre clan identity became the magnifi-
cent castle of Villalta obtained as part of the dowry of Giovannina
q. Andreuzio di Villalta who married Ottolino q. Nicolino Della
Torre in 1398 (Figure 3). With the castle came jurisdictional rights
in several villages in the environs and *livello* rents from properties
in twenty-two villages scattered among the surrounding hills. The
patrimony also included rents from properties in Udine and substantial holdings in Muggia. Just as the Savorgnan had relied on
connections with Venice to further themselves in Friuli, the Della
Torre, especially after the Venetian conquest, maintained ties with
the imperial household in Austria.[10]

Although both the Savorgnan and the Della Torre were lineages
whose members recognized a common ancestor, their collective

identities as clans were not foreordained. Aristocratic men and women found themselves tossed about by competing vortices of the clan, branch, sibling group, and nuclear family, any one of which could dominate under certain circumstances. The centripetal force of clan or branch cohesion strengthened under outside pressures such as vendetta or peasant rebellion, weakened when the death of the senior male brought the division of a patrimony, expanded its range with a marriage, and lost its power when a superabundance of sons or daughters placed strains on patrimonial resources. The clan and the family were dynamic processes rather than fixed structures and can only be understood in the historical context that forced members to make recurrent, often uncomfortable, choices.

The most important of these choices involved the selection of marriage partners. Knowledge of who married whom helps to fix the position of a family vis-à-vis its friends and enemies and to determine the composition of factions. According to traditional feuding theory, failed or ambiguous marriage alliances could cause animosities that resulted in vendetta violence, just as the end of a vendetta was often signaled by a marriage arranged between former enemies. The theoretical position might be summed up by the admonition to marry one's enemies. But this theoretical supposition about the relationship between feuding and marriage is not borne out by the patterns found in Friuli, in which major families practiced divergent marriage strategies that had important implications for the family's political position but did not characteristically bind together former enemies.[11]

Factional endogamies can be reconstructed from the alignment of Friulan families in 1511 when one can determine who was on which side by establishing who killed whom in the Cruel Carnival (see Appendix 1). Those affiliated in 1511 with the Zambarlani of the Savorgnan family included some forty-six men with thirty-seven different surnames (some surnames are not known). Only five of these surnames were those of Friulan castellans, the rest were of either Udinese noble citizens (seventeen surnames) or commoners from various backgrounds. Three of the five castellan surnames also appear on that occasion on the list of enemy Strumieri, revealing the internal divisions within these clans. The 113 Strumiero supporters of the Della Torre in 1511 had forty-three different surnames (almost all of castellan origin), which provide the basis for defining the composition of the faction.

The two factions that evolved out of the rivalry between the Della Torre and the Savorgnan differed primarily in their social composition, especially with respect to class. The chroniclers identify the Zambarlani as "all the citizens, all the plebs, and all the city [of Udine] with some castellans." The Strumieri, on the other hand, included "nearly all the castellans, a few citizens [of Udine], and some plebs." Thus, the Zambarlani followed a vertically arranged clientage system with the Savorgnan indisputably at the head whereas the Strumieri largely consisted of an association of aristocrats who were at least formal equals. Because of the social differences between the factions the Savorgnan and Della Torre followed distinct marriage strategies with regard to their followers.[12]

Of thirty-five Savorgnan marriages known for the period from 1420 to 1595, none was with families identified as Zambarlani in 1511. Such a finding supports the contemporary impression that the Savorgnan led a faction composed of subordinates from families unsuitable for intermarriage. The strongest form of endogamy in Savorgnan marriage patterns was within their own class of Friulan castellans, a group that produced twelve (34 percent) spouses. These endogamous marriages, however, created a feeble solidarity because most of the families thus allied to the Savorgnan joined the enemy Strumieri in 1511. Even more prominent were exogamous marriages, eight (23 percent) with Venetian patrician families and another twelve (34 percent) with neither Venetian nor Friulan families. Thus, more than half of the known Savorgnan marriages formed connections with families outside of the region, usually from the nobility of northern Italy. None was with Austrians.[13]

Whereas the Savorgnan pattern of exogamies was an adaptation to the Venetian conquest, the more endogamous Della Torre failed to take account of the growing power of the Venetians, as the records of fifty Della Torre marriages between 1147 and 1420 show. In the late thirteenth and early fourteenth centuries, they habitually married among the seigneurial families of northern Italy—the counts of Gorizia and Ceneda, the Carrara of Padua, Soresina of Cortellana, Montefeltro of Urbino, and Della Scala of Verona. In the 1330s, after the tenure of Patriarch Pagano Della Torre, the strategy shifted to one of building connections within Friuli through marriages with other castellan families. Between 1333 and 1420 seventy-five percent of Della Torre marriages followed that endogamous pattern. Of the twenty-five known marriages in the post-conquest period between 1420 and 1511, seventy-two percent were with other Friulan castellan families and sixty-four percent of the total with castellans who were also members of the Strumiero faction. All of the remaining marriages were exogamous, mostly with high-ranking foreign noble families including the Este of Ferrara, Piatti of Milan, Sanguin and Fontellis of Paris, and the Thiene of Vicenza. The only Della Torre marriage into a Venetian family took place after 1511 when one of the sons of the murdered Alvise Della Torre married a Bembo.[14]

The marriage practices of the Della Torre and Savorgnan evolved in opposite directions. From the 1330s through the fifteenth and early sixteenth centuries the Della Torre progressively contracted the geographic range of their marriage connections, becoming more endogamous and declining from a princely family that built alliances of equality among the lordly despots of Romagna, Lombardy, and the Veneto to an aristocratic family of merely local significance with no effective primacy in the region. The Della Torre confined their choices to a very restricted marriage market. In contrast, the Savorgnan progressively expanded their alliances to families in the dominant city of Venice and other towns in the Venetian terraferma while they still retained a strong commitment to other castellans within Friuli. The Della Torre acted defensively, the Savorgnan expansively and opportunistically. The Della Torre, moreover, employed marriage connections to create cohesion among their Strumiero colleagues whereas the Savorgnan avoided marriage to other Zambarlani.

The Friulan patterns parallel those Stanley Chojnacki found among the patrician families in early fifteenth-century Venice. The old families with the most prestigious lineages, the *case vecchie*, formed endogamous marriage alliances much more frequently than the *case nuove*, which were economically ascendant, or the sub-group of the *nuovi*, the *case ducali*, which dominated the highest public offices. Endogamies among old families enhanced the value of social prestige by making it more difficult to marry into them, but at the same time the more exogamous families had a broader

range of commercial and political ties which expanded their influence and power.[15]

On a few occasions the Della Torre and Savorgnan did marry
their enemies. In the fifteenth century, over the course of three
generations, there were three weddings between the two rival clans.
A brother of Tristano Savorgnan married a Della Torre, as did one
of Tristano's sons, and a grandson. This last marriage, between
Girolamo q. Pagano Savorgnan (who would eventually head the
Monte d'Osoppo branch) and Maddalena Della Torre, the cousin
of Alvise (who served as head of his clan) is perhaps the most significant. One cannot judge the original intention of the alliance,
but it signaled the growing split between the Monte d'Osoppo and
Torre di Zuino branches of the Savorgnan.[16]

After Maddalena's premature death Girolamo continued to be
friendly with his former in-laws and was alienated from his powerful cousin Antonio who headed the Zambarlani. During the
great assault on the Strumieri led by Antonio in 1511 Girolamo
stayed aloof from the slaughter. In Girolamo's case, ties with affines, even those from a previous marriage, counterbalanced the
claims of blood enough to allow him to remain neutral in a fight
between his family's traditional enemies and his own cousin.

The gathering of relatives, friends, clients, and allies at the signing of a nuptial contract and at wedding festivities generally served,
of course, to solidify their relationships. However, the strength-
ening of such ties also provoked other clans because the very act
of demonstrating collective vigor threatened not only traditional
enemies but also anyone not included in the alliance. The mentality
of social relations involved a kind of zero sum game in which a
gain for one group must inevitably be seen as a loss for another,
especially given the castellans' habits of class endogamy, which
severely restricted the number of potential marriage partners.[17]

Although marriages have traditionally been seen as a means of
building group cohesion and especially as the way to finalize a
peace among feuding families, such gatherings also brought out
the potential for the feud to reemerge from the peace. Thus, both
the Savorgnan and the Della Torre marriage strategies, but particularly the endogamous one of the Della Torre, created enemies as
well as friends. The mixed lineage of the inhabitants of many
castles and the castellans' characteristic endogamy also worked

against a strictly bilateral kinship system that would have sustained distinct lineages and small, cohesive vengeance groups.[18]

Even though the rhetoric of kinship obligations pervaded Friulan society, the fragility of clan structures necessitated the extension of revenge obligations to others who were not strictly agnatic kin. Ad hoc vengeance groups consisted of "friends," a broad category that might include affines and distant cousins as well as persons dependent in some way on the principals in the vendetta. Thus, vengeance groups and the larger factions built around them converged more along lines of dependence than of blood. Whether composed of equals allied through marriage or clients devoted to a powerful patron, both factions relied heavily on the familiars and servants (*famegli, buli, cani della casa*) of the noble lords, subordinates known elsewhere as *bravi* who played a significant role in the vendetta violence of both sides. Originally denoting the squires of knights in battle, the term *familiar* came to be applied to any armed follower of the great lords, and although most of these remain anonymous, those who can be identified primarily seem to have been foreign adventurers hired to serve the grand families. The familiars, often in conjunction with the young men of the aristocratic houses, perpetrated many of the most notorious acts of violence.[19]

Each faction developed a public identity that could not entirely be separated from personal loyalties to Savorgnan or Della Torre but had its own form of representation. The origins of the terms *Zambarlano* and *Strumiero* are obscure, but the best informed contemporary diarist, Gregorio Amaseo, used them as local equivalents of *Guelf* (meaning in this case philo-Venetian) and *Ghibelline* (meaning proimperial). The partisans of the two factions identified themselves with cheers, "Savorgnan, Savorgnan" countered by "Struma, Struma" or "Torre, Torre," and a variety of fanciful insignia. Herbs, flowers, or ribbons worn over the appropriate ear, on a hat, in the hair, on a shoe, or elsewhere served as declarations of allegiance.[20]

Beginning at least as early as 1468, the Venetian authorities recurrently tried to prohibit all signs of factional affiliation, but partisans invented new ones as soon as the old ones could be identified and made illegal. In May 1480 the provveditore in Cividale decreed that no one could carry flowers or fern fronds of any sort, wear blazons, or chant, "Strumer," "Zambarlan," or anything else. The prohibition applied to all men, women, and children and threatened a fine of 100 lire and four lashes for violators. The same month an inhabitant of San Daniele was condemned for dressing a child in a pair of shoes that had the signs of a faction on them. By 1482 the fine had doubled, and banishment for a year had been added. Records for 1486 alone show that kerchiefs displayed in a certain fashion had become a declaration of affiliation, the traditional arbor bows displayed at weddings were employed as insignia, a servant of Ippolito di Valvasone went to prison for wearing a carnation on the left side of his cap, and a hunchback was banished for three years for carrying a vase of flowers on his hump. As futile as their prohibitions may seem, the Venetians recognized that factions throve on a kind of street theater, where the display of large followings could intimidate rivals and demarcate turf. Solidarity had to be shown, publicly and provocatively, in part because without such demonstrations cohesion rapidly disintegrated, and followers reverted to the safety of ambiguous loyalties.[21]

Although the Savorgnan and Della Torre vendetta evolved from the feudal wars of the late patriarchate and revealed deep structural contradictions in Friulan society, contemporaries saw the struggle as an intensely personal affair among people with identifiable names and faces, with known histories, and with acknowledged friends. Vendetta was not just a social phenomenon for resolving group conflict or a form of primitive justice but a medium of collective memory, a way of structuring clan history around deeds of infamy and of valor. Vendettas were stories.

The story of the Savorgnan and Della Torre vendetta began in 1339 when Ettore Savorgnan bought from a rich Udinese the castle of Ariis in lower Friuli. Because the Della Torre claimed to possess rights to the castle, they disputed the purchase, and Ermacore Della Torre defended his family's interests by attacking Ettore Savorgnan. By 1346 there had been several brawls between the two clans during one of which Ettore's nephew Pietro lost an eye. Ettore and Ermacore established the pattern that would be repeated again and again in the confrontations between their descendants when each accused the other of planning his assassination and of inciting the peasants.

Other individuals, groups, and even cities fueled the struggle around which the factions evolved, especially Udine by defending the Savorgnan and Cividale the Della Torre. The excommunication of Cividale in the autumn of 1346 by Patriarch Bertrand, allied to the Savorgnan, probably occurred because Cividale had provided a refuge for Ermacore Della Torre. On October 9 Cividale declared war on Udine.

The form of the declaration brings to light how participants understood the fight; rather than the legalistic document that one commune was expected to send to another, Cividale dispatched two knights to challenge Ettore and Federico Savorgnan, Ermanno di Carnia, and the commune of Udine to personal combat. Rules of chivalry structured the declaration of war, which was hardly very chivalrous in execution. Sackings, arson, and atrocities by both sides lasted until March 10, 1347, when Ermacore Della Torre and Ettore Savorgnan concluded a truce. According to the mythology of the two sides, the factions originated in this little war— one faction centered on the Savorgnan and the citizens of Udine, the other on the Della Torre and their allies in Cividale.[22]

During the endemic civil wars of the last half of the fourteenth century and the first two decades of the fifteenth, the Savorgnan and Della Torre pursued their vendetta by expanding their range of allies in Friuli and by finding foreign patrons who wanted to influence events in the strategic region. Although the Savorgnan had once been the chamberlains and principal defenders of the patriarchs, during the patriarchate of Ludovico Della Torre (1359–65) they switched to an alliance with the republic of Venice, a move that forced the Della Torre to find benefactors among Venice's enemies, the Genoese, the counts of Gorizia, the Carrara of Padua, the Della Scala of Verona, and the kings of Hungary. With the Venetian victory in 1420, the Savorgnan achieved a dominant, if not commanding, position of privilege.[23]

In the period immediately after the Venetian conquest the Savorgnan and Della Torre lived in relative peace with one another. The quiescence after many years of endemic violence came as a byproduct of a peace imposed by Venice, but it is also typical of long feuds for there to be cycles of violence, one phase of which can comprise many years of apparent reconciliation.[24]

During the 1470s and 1480s, a phase of renewed violence started when disputes between the two factions arose which involved an expanded range of clients and friends including even the Venetian luogotenente. During these years the powerful and numerous Colloredo clan matched the Della Torre in animosity toward the Savorgnan. Despite the many ties forged by intermarriage between the Colloredo and Savorgnan, the clans split apart in 1470 when Ghibellino Savorgnan tore down the gallows that the lords of Colloredo and Mels had erected in various parts of their jurisdiction to intimidate the population. The bad blood between the two clans intensified after the Colloredo moved to Savorgnan-dominated Udine where, at about the same time, Tristano Savorgnan, accompanied by his familiars and some of his peasant subjects, attacked the Della Torre brothers during a carnival ball held under the loggia of the city council. By the time young Marin Sanudo visited Udine in 1483 the Strumieri and Zambarlani conflict had reached such a pitch that sections of the city were chained off to members of the opposing faction.[25]

This series of assaults, accusations, and countercharges between the factions was probably precipitated by the destructive Turkish raids into Friuli between 1470 and 1478, which intensified the perpetual Friulan struggle over scarce material resources made scarcer by the raids. The incursions left the indelible impression of unbelievable horror brought on by Venice's long war with the Turks and the dominant city's unwillingness or inability to protect its provincial subjects.

After the Turkish army broke into Carniola and Istria in 1470, irregular bands began to make repeated raids from the Slovenian valleys, pillaging the land and enslaving the rural Friulan population. In 1472 the Turks crossed the Isonzo and blocked up the undermanned and unpaid Venetian army in a stronghold at Cervignano while they plundered right to the gates of Cividale and Udine where women and children mobbed the churches in search of refuge. The approach of the local militia of peasants, more valiant in taking to the field than the Venetian army, drove the raiders off.

In October 1477 a much larger force of Turkish foot soldiers crossed the Isonzo, defeated the Venetian mercenaries, killed or captured several of their captains, and, bypassing Cividale and Udine, marched as far as Pordenone, burning as it went an estimated one hundred villages. The eminent Friulan humanist, Marc Antonio Sabellico, witnessed the carnage from the safety of the castle at Tarcento and described how at night he could see a continuous line of flames across all of lower Friuli.

To divert the Venetians from their siege of Scutari the Turks sent an even larger force into Friuli the next summer, but the Venetian army and Friulan militias deflected the enemy into a circuitous and ineffective expedition into the mountains. In February 1479 Venice and the Ottomans made a truce that ended the immediate threat to Friuli.[26]

Besides disrupting the local economy, causing widespread suffering, demonstrating the incapacity of the Venetian defensive system, and illuminating the irresponsibility of most of the castellans who only looked after themselves, the first Turkish invasion helped stimulate the development of an important new institution, the local militias or *cernide*. During the 1470s, under Venetian encouragement, the villages formed militias, elected captains, and began to drill. Even though these impoverished units often had little more than farm tools to use as weapons and were of limited military value, they built village cohesion by giving the young men some training in handling weapons and in drilling, and expanded the villagers' experience in autonomous decision making.

When the Venetians named a Savorgnan the head of the collective militias, the other castellans felt particularly threatened because they lost direct control of their peasant subjects, who were armed and drawn into the Zambarlano orbit. After the Turkish invasions, the Della Torre became increasingly strident in attempting to counter the perceived threat of Savorgnan-dominated militias.[27]

The Della Torre and their friends responded to this threat with an intensification of what contemporaries described as vendetta violence. Particularly revealing of the ways in which the mentality of vendetta shapes all kinds of conflict are the allegations two Della Torre brothers, Francesco and Isidoro, made about Luogotenente Giovanni Emo's favoritism toward the Savorgnan. Emo went to Udine in 1478 and soon found himself embroiled in a personal dispute with the Della Torre over his policies. According to depositions the Della Torre submitted to the Avogaria di Comun, Emo showed a "capital hatred" toward them from the very beginning and acted against them "without any justice."

At a meeting of the minor council of Udine one Piero del Ongaro publicly impugned the brothers' loyalty, asserting that "because in the time of the patriarchs these Della Torre were in the habit of getting their own way in the city and the patria, they regret the passing of that time and this is the cause of their fury." He went on to express his wish to cut off their heads. Emo apparently accepted this simple and logical explanation for the continuous hostility of the Della Torre and, again in the words of the Della Torre deposition, sought to "shame us publicly" by making an announcement, "accusing us of being heads of the Strumieri and of having organized a sect and mob of people to assault the Zambarlani, but we have never thought of such a thing much less done it." Whatever the truth of Emo's allegations, Francesco and Isidoro took them as a personal insult. After Francesco went to Venice to complain about the luogotenente's attitude, it was said that Emo "had decided to avenge himself in every possible way," and he was quoted as having declared, "I know very well what I think, and for a vendetta to last five, indeed, ten years is not too long." Although all we have is the Della Torre version of the conflict, it appears that they, at least, could only conceive of Venetian policies they did not like in personal terms as a manifestation of vendetta.

To document their case against the luogotenente, the Della Torre brothers presented depositions recounting how he had purportedly used torture and undue influence to turn one of their own partisans against them. (The irony that this charge assumes in light of their assertion that they did not head any faction at all was apparently lost on the pair.) One Leonardo di Cichiare, resident of Colloredo, was arrested in the jurisdiction of Cividale and personally interrogated by Emo. He admitted to involvement in a series of brawls at various country fairs in Nimis, Fagagna, and Attimis but insisted that he always acted in self-defense, once against some twenty Zambarlano peasants from Pradamano. Liberally applying the lash to gain a confession, Emo tried to get Leonardo to admit that Francesco Della Torre and Giacomo Giusto had ordered him to assassinate Nicolò Savorgnan and his consorts. Leonardo held out for two days but seems to have finally given in and changed his testimony under the influence of some friends to whom the luogotenente released him. Leonardo went on to declare that the Della Torre did indeed captain a faction and asked the councilors of Cividale and some peasants from Momiacco to provide corroboration. The Della Torre later insisted that only Emo's tortures forced Leo-

nardo to change his story and that the record of the interrogation
had been falsified to cover up the excessive lashings and water torture personally applied by the luogotenente.

In contrast to Emo's hostility toward them, the Della Torre repeated, he had never proceeded on any of the allegations against
the Savorgnan. In fact, he "wants to make the said Savorgnan another Lorenzo di Cosimo [de' Medici]," and they quoted a report
in which Emo had asserted that every city needs a leading citizen
like those in Florence and Bologna. But in their eyes Nicolò Savorgnan was far from worthy of such an honor. The Della Torre
deposition complained that whereas Francesco Della Torre had always valiantly served Venice against its enemies, Nicolò Savorgnan
during the Turkish invasion promised to supply three hundred
men but showed up with thirteen and fled when nine Turks approached. The deposition went on to charge that Nicolò and his
cousin Tristano had broken the law by manipulating the elections
of Udinese officials, monopolizing the hay market, evading communal taxes, stealing two hundred ducats worth of arms from
Udine, hiring banished persons to serve them, and abetting the
Jews "with extraordinary extortions of money and in drinking the
blood of poor Christians." The valiant Della Torre lords summarized their charges thus:

> It is good that the Magnificent Luogotenente has shown the
> desire to eradicate the factions and troublesome companies.
> However, he has not wanted to anticipate where the need
> would be and still is, something he can very well see, because
> he would have to investigate and denounce some seditious,
> homicidal peasants of evil reputation who form factions and
> companies from which come many murders and disturbances
> across the whole land. Since His Magnificence understands
> that these are the tenants and subjects of the Savorgnan, he
> has never wanted to proceed against or affront them. And yet
> against us from whom there has never been any trouble or fail-
> ing, he has intensified his own fury and anger. Whereas we are
> innocent and averse to any discord, he has sought to treat us as
> guilty and troublemakers. Thus, we pray Your Magnificences
> will deign to honor the justice and esteem of Our Most Illus-
> trious Lordship by wanting to look into such things and by

preventing the worst wishes of the traitors who try to suppress those who seek to live in peace as is our hope and desire.[28]

After the departure of Emo, however, the issue between the Della Torre and the Savorgnan only grew more violent. According to the Della Torre account, upon returning to Udine from Venice on November 6, 1480, Isidoro Della Torre went to the castle to pay his respects to the luogotenente. About an hour after sunset he left the castle to walk home unarmed because he had no reason to suspect an attack. As he passed the house of a Jew, assassins sprung on him from its shadows, wounded him, and left him for dead while they escaped to the house of Ghibellino Savorgnan. A few days before, so claimed the wounded man's brother Francesco, Tristano Savorgnan had also come from Venice but in disguise and without showing himself in public so he could plot the assassination with others in his family. The suspected swordsman was Nicolò Savorgnan's son, Antonio, who, twenty years later, would achieve the greatest influence ever of any Savorgnan and who would preside over the virtual annihilation of the Della Torre.

The evidence against him, however, was decidedly thin. The assault had taken place near the house of a Jew, and the Savorgnan were known protectors of the Jews; therefore, the Savorgnan must have done it, or so ran the logic of the account. The attempt at murder also had public and factional dimensions because while Francesco Della Torre and Giacomo Giusto were giving evidence about the attack in the luogotenente's chambers, a large crowd formed outside the castle chanting against the Strumieri. The Council of Ten authorized the banishment of the unidentified assailants of Isidoro but never gathered enough evidence against anyone to charge with the crime. For their part, the Della Torre had to go back to writing letters to each new luogotenente warning him not to believe anything the Savorgnan said about them.[29]

Dating back to at least the 1330s the Savorgnan and Della Torre vendetta became during the civil wars of the late patriarchate the central dispute around which all other conflicts in Friuli found expression. When the Turkish raids of the 1470s disrupted the fragile equilibrium imposed by the Venetian conquest, the vendetta revived, and the factions attached to the two great families became the dominant forces in regional and local politics.

As the focus of individual loyalties, the factions necessarily supplemented the lineages, especially given the diversity of Friulan settlement patterns, the weakness of clan cohesion, and the endogamy of most castellan families, all of which worked against a strongly bilateral kinship system. In many places the factions came to have a life of their own because individuals allied with one or the other faction to defend themselves against rivals in their own community, expressing animosities that had nothing directly to do with the Savorgnan–Della Torre vendetta. Joining a faction became a means for finding assistance from outside the community, and thus many persons involved themselves for their own reasons in the affairs of the great castellan clans.

COMMUNITIES: THE CASE OF SPILIMBERGO

The classic social anthropology theory of feuding, inspired by Evans-Pritchard, assumed that an organized community could not sustain feuds because the daily need to cooperate, to move freely about the village or town, and to have access to the fields and pastures precluded such sustained conflicts. More recent work, especially Wilson's study of Corsica, shows that communities do not necessarily disintegrate even when subjected to recurrent retaliatory killings over many generations. The history of the Italian communes of the twelfth through fourteenth centuries reveals that such conflicts may disrupt the economy, corrupt justice, and turn the streets into dangerous places, but they do not destroy community life altogether.[30]

In Friuli violent factional strife became an extension of normal community processes for the resolution of disputes, in some cases ameliorating castellan abuses of power, in others acting as a kind of safety valve for a social system that provided limited means of judicial redress, and in exceptional cases forcing the redistribution of communal jobs and resources. Factions embraced tenants protesting against their lord, rural subjects rebelling against an oppressive town, neighborhoods competing with other neighborhoods, whole communities struggling against corrupt feudal judges or the tax assessors of Venice. Examples of vendetta and factional strife in communities could be multiplied a hundredfold, but it may be more instructive to examine one particularly troubled town in some detail.[31]

The town of Spilimbergo lay on a rise overlooking a ford across the Tagliamento. Although the fief of Spilimbergo was one of the largest in area in all Friuli, it was sparsely populated, incorporating only twenty small villages besides the town of some 1,200 souls. Outside Carnia the environs of Spilimbergo comprised the poorest area of the patria, largely because of the absence of a dependable water supply. The bluffs on the right bank of the Tagliamento blocked diversions of water from the great river to the dry soils around Spilimbergo, and although the land to the west of town was relatively flat and gradually merged into the sandy bed of the Meduna, the waters of that river usually sank underground before they got near arable land. (The area has supplied modern Italian with the word *magredo*, meaning alluvial lands that are highly permeable and deprived of vegetation.) Nevertheless, peasants grew the usual variety of grains and produce—wheat, oats, rye, barley, millet, vetch, buckwheat, beans, sorghum, flax, wine grapes, lentils, kale, legumes, and panic grass—but the demands of the lords usually outstripped the ability of the peasants to provide. The large size of the castellan clan and the poverty of the land combined to put a premium on the exploitation of common pasture lands, which were divided up according to an elaborate system of usage rights. Uncertain rainfall and the meanderings of the Meduna meant that the greenness of the various pastures shifted unpredictably from season to season and year to year, which wrought havoc with usage rights. In addition, the only way to expand arable land and personal income was to encroach on the pastures, which the consorts of the castle persistently attempted to do.[32]

At the highest point in the town, on a stony knoll made precipitous by a deep, man-made ditch, sat the castle of Spilimbergo. Access was possible only across a narrow drawbridge, which was guarded by a towered gatehouse that opened into a large courtyard enclosed on three sides by the separate multistoried houses of the castellan consorts. The separateness of these houses exemplified the very divisions among the consorts. Bound together on the castle hill by blood and their shared rights to the jurisdiction of the fief, the consorts of Spilimbergo underwent numerous schisms that subdivided their properties and condemned them to perpetual conflicts among themselves.[33]

The exceptional jurisdictional privileges of the lords gave them, besides the usual rights to *mero e misto imperio* (civil and criminal jurisdiction), the ability to enact the death penalty. The common-law statutes of Spilimbergo listed four types of crimes which fell under the jurisdiction of the consorts: crimes against God, including blasphemy, witchcraft, and perjury; crimes against the public interest, such as tax fraud, use of false measures, breaches of official duty, and threats to the public health; crimes against private persons ranging from false accusation and theft to homicide; and a special class of crimes against the lords of the castle, loosely defined acts left to the lord-judges themselves to clarify. In addition to these statutes, which allowed considerable room for abuse, the consorts retained a special right of asylum whereby a person exiled from Friuli for a homicide that had not been premeditated but resulted from a fair fight could pledge all his property as a surety and ask the lords for refuge. As a result of this special right, Spilimbergo became a quasi-legal haven for bandits, and the granting of asylum to those involved in vendetta violence became a lucrative source of income for the lords.[34]

The lords' exercise of their rights to prosecute and judge criminal offenses often precipitated violent conflicts with the citizens and peasants of the jurisdiction. The spare language of the judicial records usually leaves unclear exactly what issues stimulated the outbursts of violence, but more often than not criminal charges mask deeper social discontents with the lords.

On June 3, 1443, the consorts tried to arrest on the charge of theft Leonardo Molinari of Rivis, but a crowd prevented the lords' men from making the arrest and sounded the tocsin of revolt. When the crowd ignored the lords' orders to disperse, both sides quickly accepted a peace pact to prevent an escalation of violence on the spot. During the night, however, citizens from Spilimbergo fanned out into the countryside, inviting the peasants to help expel the consorts from the castle. The men of Vivaro (an arid outpost between the sinks of the Meduna and Cellina Rivers), Barbeano, and Maniago agreed to come, and the next day some five hundred men armed with bows, swords, and guns drove the lords from the town square to refuge behind the drawbridge of their castle. The rioters lifted their two-day siege only when the luogotenente's marshal arrived with a squad of soldiers. The subsequent investigation revealed that the consorts had been ignoring the judicial decisions of their own podestà and judges and making arrests contrary to the statutes. The Venetian doge ordered them to follow the law. This would not be the last time, however, that Leonardo Molinari would lead the citizens against the consorts; in fact, he and his son would be the principal figures in popular agitation for the next forty years.[35]

The lords built a small bureaucracy to keep surveillance over their possessions, but the statutes of the town obliged the lords to consult with the civic council in making appointments of the podestà and judges, notaries, and other public officials. This theoretical obligation was frequently ignored. Between 1423 and 1440 the consorts refused to receive the recommendations of the council until an appeal to the doge of Venice resulted in a decree ordering the consorts to adhere to their own statutes. A concord between the council and the lords in 1445 established the principle that the council would nominate candidates to the lords, but by 1450 the lords had reverted to their old habits, which led to another futile agreement in 1456. At issue were not only the rights of patronage for the few meagerly paid public jobs but control of the collection of duties, taxes, and fees. Extraordinary expenses such as those necessary to pay mercenaries and repair fortifications during the Turkish invasions almost inevitably set off a confrontation between the citizens and lords, who pleaded their own poverty and accused the "rich and opulent citizens" of avoiding the obligation to pay.[36]

The 1445 agreement gives further insight into the nature of the contentions between the citizens and lords of Spilimbergo. Foremost among the complaints were financial issues: the consorts had been making extraordinary demands for the maintenance of the town's defenses, abrogating peasants' rights for pasture, collecting unusual penalties from market sellers, raising *livello* and *affittanza* rates for peasants, and charging fees for the use of the Tagliamento ferry, which had forced the poor to try to ford the river despite the peril of drowning. In addition the citizens demanded that the lords close their open latrines, allow the people to keep orchards illegally planted in the castle moat, restore the right of judicial appeal, employ a regular teacher for the church school, and follow the statutes in every detail, repaying any penalties that had been exacted without legal justification. For their part the consorts provided documents justifying their right to charge fees for the river ferry. The

luogotenente arbitrated the dispute and imposed nine conditions
on citizens and lords: he guaranteed the citizens a limited right to
assemble and to ring the tocsin but prohibited them from ringing
the church, clock, or castle bell; subject to his review, he gave the
council the right to legislate new laws that did not accord with the
statutes; he limited the consorts to choosing officials from among
twenty nominated by the council and allowed the chamberlain of
the church to serve for only a one-year term; he permitted *livelli*
rents for houses or farms to be paid in money rather than in kind
and exempted tenants from the obligation to repair houses; he restricted levies for the maintenance of fortifications to times of necessity; he ordered the consorts to let citizens and peasants graze
their animals within defined pastures and to negotiate with their
tenants before imposing extra rent charges; and finally he agreed
to permit orchards as long as they did not block the moats.[37]

Some of these issues involved the usual complaints of any rural
community, especially those over use of the land. The right to use
pastures and plant orchards and to keep rent payments predictable
were issues of survival for most of the inhabitants. The consorts'
violations of electoral procedures and local laws probably concerned a much smaller group, those better-off commoners who
naturally led the citizens against the nobles and who found it in
their own interest to defend the privileges of the community,
people like Leonardo Molinari. These men whose knowledge of
letters placed them above their neighbors recognized the potential
value of calling on the Venetian luogotenente to adhere to the
promises of his regime to uphold customary and statutory laws. In
other towns in Friuli these men had some success; in Spilimbergo
where the lords were seldom reluctant to employ the force available to them, the citizen élite nearly always failed.

The request to pay *livello* rents in coin rather than in kind raised
an entirely different set of issues. It implied a desire to sell grains
and foodstuffs for money and to speculate on grain prices as the
lords were able to do with the rents they received in kind. From
other examples we know that Friulan lords withheld their grain
reserves from the market to induce shortages and drive up prices.
If tenants could do the same, they would have the financial benefits
of speculation previously limited to the lords. Because the demand
to pay in specie may be considered a measure of the penetration of

a market economy into the countryside, it would be useful to know exactly who pushed for this provision, the average tenants or merely the relatively affluent townsmen who employed day laborers to work farms they held in fee from the lords. Whoever was behind the demand, it is clear that despite its poverty and backwardness even Spilimbergo had become enmeshed in the thriving commercialism of the late fifteenth century.

An unusually detailed account of unrest in 1482 further illustrates the gravity of disputes over the use of land and reveals the inner workings of the community. The central figure was one Giovanni Molinari, son of the earlier rebel leader, Leonardo. After spending several years studying philosophy and medicine in Padua, where he developed a reputation for violence and had reportedly killed a soldier, Giovanni returned to Spilimbergo and began to have trouble with the consort lords of the castle. He found himself in several scrapes with them, including an open assault on Francesco Picinino, captain of the local militias. On another occasion he argued with Francesco q. Antonio of the consorts about abuses of their jurisdictional rights and ended by calling Francesco a "rebellious traitor." Although the consorts tried to buy him off with a stipend as the town physician, he did not stop his opposition to them.

The conflict escalated after the arrest of Filippo Droghiere and Bartolo q. Bertoli del Cos for abducting a young girl with a false promise of marriage. Molinari demanded that Francesco Picinino, who was serving as the rector for that year, and his fellow consorts, Giovanni, Francesco, and Orlando, be removed from judging the case because of bias, but Picinino remained firm despite popular demonstrations on behalf of the two defendants who, in fact, managed to escape with the help of their neighbors. This seemingly minor episode finally brought out the true issues.[38]

Giovanni Molinari and a priest, Father Dionisio, jointly called for a town assembly to be held in the presence of the consorts. Their complaint was straightforward enough. Ser Concordio of the consorts had started to plow parts of the common pasture for his own use, had dug ditches and built dikes around the appropriated land, and was now attempting to lay claim to the land he had usurped. The consorts put off the assembly by promising to examine the case and noted that inasmuch as others were said to have expropriated common pasture lands, they would submit all charges of a usurpation that had lasted more than a year to a committee of lords and commoners for adjudication. Apparently, Concordio had only plowed the pastures for the previous year, but other consorts, including Francesco Picinino, had been doing so for some time, and they wanted to postpone a reckoning. The next day, however, under the leadership of the unstoppable Giovanni, a band of armed men, forty from Spilimbergo and seven from Baseglia, went out to the disputed pastures and filled in the ditches Francesco Picinino had used to irrigate fields he had been plowing for four years. After Picinino presented his claim to the land to the luogotenente, the real fighting began, which at first consisted only of a small skirmish in the castle courtyard.

Several days after this fight Messer Jacopo Pituzzo of Padua, the vicar of Luogotenente Benedetto Trevisan, arrived to inventory the property of Albertino di Spilimbergo who was under arrest in the castle. Albertino played a mysterious role in the conflict. He was apparently one of the consorts, locked up by his fellows because they said he had wandered naked through the woods and mountains like a madman. It seems more likely that he had in some way befriended the popular cause against his fellow consorts and was therefore locked up as if he were crazy. On several occasions the popular conspirators tried either to throw letters through his window or to talk to him despite a specific order from the vicar not to do so. During a dinner for the vicar, Francesco Picinino caught Father Dionisio and Giovanni Molinari talking to Albertino through the window of the room in which he was imprisoned. Picinino attacked Giovanni, who retreated to a heap of stones in the courtyard of the castle and began hurling them at the well-armed lords. He was badly outnumbered, and his followers ignored his calls for help. One of the consorts, Eduardo, finally wounded Giovanni with a halberd, and while he writhed in agony on the ground, another lord, Agostino, finished him off with a stab to the heart.

Although none had come to his aid when he needed it, Giovanni Molinari's death spurred the people of Spilimbergo into a violent retaliation. They surrounded the castle all that night, but the two murderers, Francesco Picinino, and several other consorts managed to effect their escape, and the next night several of the remaining lords stole away. When the luogotenente's vicemarshal arrived with two hundred infantrymen, the crowds withdrew although some minor looting and vandalism continued. After stopping the siege, the vicemarshal's first task was to find the murderers of Giovanni Molinari, but inasmuch as these had already escaped and he needed to placate the crowd, he locked up all the remaining consorts in the castle prison, even those he knew to be innocent. With the apparent support of the Venetians, Father Dionisio was emboldened to call for the institution of a Venetian podestà to replace the lords of Spilimbergo, probably the most revolutionary demand anyone could have made in Spilimbergo in 1482.

Two days after the arrival of the vicemarshal, the luogotenente himself rode in as did many of the castellans of the patria responding to the news that the consorts of Spilimbergo had been imprisoned. It is difficult to imagine a more difficult position for the luogotenente, a situation that would have tested the mettle of the most able of men. Benedetto Trevisan stayed for three days while he held a trial for homicide which resulted in the release of all of the consorts except for two taken to prison in Udine. Both sides sent delegations first to Udine and then to Venice arguing their respective cases, but the popular side soon transformed their plea for a just punishment of the murderers of Giovanni Molinari into a political cause in which they asked to abrogate the community's agreement with the lords and to be ruled by their own council.

Meanwhile, the criminal case dragged on. When the luogotenente appeared to be about to free the two imprisoned consorts, the relatives of the deceased came up with new charges that there were more wounds on the body than accounted for in the proceedings. When the luogotenente demanded proof, the dead man's father admitted in a macabre twist that another son and some others had opened Giovanni's tomb and stabbed him nine more times to make it look as if others besides Eduardo and Agostino had been involved in the murder. Finally on August 3, 1482, the luogotenente pronounced sentence. Declaring it a premeditated homicide, he banished for life six of the consorts but freed the two in prison, who had probably been held only as hostages in place of the guilty, and required two of the remaining lords to feed and clothe the wife and family of the dead man and to provide his daughter with a dowry. Giovanni's father appealed the case on the grounds that the sentence was too light while the consorts appealed to relieve themselves of the obligation to provide for Giovanni's survivors. But the case against Giovanni's murderers was only one phase of a much larger struggle.

By the end of the summer the Spilimberghesi seem to have divided again, this time into three groups. Led by Father Dionisio, the previously imprisoned alleged madman Albertino, and two other renegade consorts, one faction demanded that the lords consult the citizens on all decisions in the future, hold no trials without the inclusion of judges from the citizenry, permit no torture without consultation with the citizens, and levy no new imposts without public approval. A second group headed by one Urbano q. Domenico del Cos stated that the people had no desire to interfere with the privileges of the consorts, but they did want a council as in previous years. The last party consisted of the remaining consorts who intransigently opposed all of the demands of Father Dionisio's group and put off Urbano del Cos's request as a matter of grave importance that needed to be studied. The situation remained confused. After several minor incidents the luogotenente sent yet another vicar to conduct an investigation, and castellans from other places came to help the consorts defend themselves; but nearly all the Spilimbergo lords' subjects, with the sole exception of the peasants of Sequals and a few favored artisans in Spilimbergo itself, remained hostile to them.

The rebels then turned to find professional help. They established a hideout in a remote house in which they gathered at night and from which they launched an occasional raid. Their plans became excessively grand. They wanted to kill all of the consorts and demolish the castle completely, but they needed the advice of an expert in military affairs to bring it off. They chose Liberale Trevisini, a soldier in the service of Count Antonio di Maniago and husband of the widow of a Spilimbergo man. Although Liberale tried to talk them out of their plan, he gave them very precise advice. They needed to wait for a feast day and time when most of the consorts would be in church. Two men should watch the lords in church while a contingent of the strongest and bravest secretly entered the castle and seized the gate. At a predetermined signal the others must storm the church and kill every noble there. Then the entire populace should be aroused to arms by ringing the tocsin.

With the whole city behind them and the gate securely in the hands of their confederates, the castle was to be stormed and every male child put to death. The older men and women were to be spared so that they could suffer from the shock of witnessing the destruction of their clan. The population must be allowed time to loot the palace completely, and then it should be burned and the remaining stones torn down to the foundations so that no one would ever think of living there again. Finally Liberale warned the conspirators not to leave town or celebrate for three days. The rebels accepted the plan and fixed the date for the fair of Saint Michael when probably all of the consorts would be in Spilimbergo.

An examination of the identities of the rebels reveals the composition of the rebel faction, which represented the interests of low-level artisans. The occupations of twenty-one of the conspirators are known. The largest single professional group consisted of five shoemakers, but there were also a blacksmith, miller, clerk, tanner, tailor, son of an official of Portogruaro, son of a locksmith, a purported counterfeiter, and several persons with criminal records. Conspicuously missing from the list were merchants, shopkeepers, and professionals, the citizen élite who may have wished to avoid putting their property in jeopardy. When the appointed day arrived, however, even the conspirators' resolve weakened when it appeared that their own business might suffer from a precipitous act. One Giovanni Toniutti argued that on the festival day there would be many visitors to Spilimbergo and business would be good, a plea that apparently convinced the others to put off the attack. A rumor that the vicar knew what was afoot forced them to postpone a second time; but between then and the third appointed date the vicar began to collect testimony about the disturbances in the town. Fearing that someone had revealed the plans while testifying, one of the conspirators panicked and told the consorts everything. To prevent the riot that would have taken place had he arrested them all in Spilimbergo, the luogotenente summoned each of the conspirators, one by one, to Udine to depose on another matter, and after they had all arrived arrested them *en masse.* Just as after the death of Giovanni Molinari, each side sent delegations to Udine and Venice, extending and complicating the case. Luogotenente Trevisan eventually banished twenty-two men.

The story has a coda. On the night of December 30, 1485, the banished twenty-two returned and found refuge in the inn run by Giovanni Molinari's father, Leonardo. The next morning they gathered in the church of San Pantaleone but soon found themselves surrounded by the consorts' mercenaries. By ringing the church bell they brought to their aid friends who were able to force the consorts' men to flee to the castle. But the exiles' raid counted for nothing. This time they did not even try to seize the castle but took flight and headed for refuge in the lands of the count of Gorizia.[39]

The strife of Spilimbergo was complex and multifaceted and only loosely connected at this time to the wider factional battles of Friuli; but by the turn of the century, "all of the plebs of Spilimbergo and their followers," had become Zambarlani. In the course of the fifteenth century the Zambarlano and Strumiero factions annexed to themselves the disparate elements of many little local struggles, each of which had its own issues and social complexities, as in Spilimbergo.[40]

The horizontal loyalties of neighbors and co-workers, limited though they were in geographic scope and in the consciousness of the common interests of a class, found a home within the vertical hierarchy of aristocratically dominated factions. The factions thrived from their ability to represent a diversity of interests and to give leadership to the expression of collective grievances. The elaboration of the factions had been activated by outside events, especially the Turkish raids. Even more powerful pressures from outside the region and the appearance of an extraordinary charismatic leader of the Zambarlano faction during the first decade of the new century created an explosive situation.

Part Two

CONJUNCTURES
& EVENTS

CHAPTER FOUR

Approaching Thunder

The deep structures that had channeled most Friulan social and political disputes into the cultural ambit of vendetta kept the castellan clans in an uneasy balance for some eighty years after the Venetian conquest. However, during the first decade of the sixteenth century external pressures on the region conjoined with a serial crisis in agriculture to bring the factions to the verge of civil war. A youthful, charismatic head of the Zambarlani, Antonio Savorgnan, offered the artisans of Udine and Spilimbergo and the peasants from all over Friuli a leader who seemed to speak for them and who defied the other lords in a succession of public quarrels. His leadership created a vastly expanded network of Savorgnan clients among the peasants, who supported the Zambarlano faction as a means of resisting the escalating demands of Strumiero landlords. A renewed series of invasions by Turkish and then imperialist forces not only devastated crops and increased taxation to pay for the defense against the invaders but stimulated the growth and expanded the fighting experience of the militias, making them a potential armed threat to the knights of the Strumieri. Finally, grain prices fell precipitously over the decade, forcing landlords to attempt to wring more income out of their tenants and to solidify their control of markets. The peasants responded first with legal petitions to the parliament and Venice and then with a violent confrontation that resulted in the sacking of the castle of Sterpo in 1509, actions that reveal the desire among the well-off peasants to gain unrestricted access to the market economy of Udine. During this decade the Friulan factions became more militarized than before, in large part because of invasion and war, a development that intensified the potential for disruptive violence over local political and economic issues.

THE RISE OF ANTONIO SAVORGNAN

The most enigmatic of the enigmas of Friuli, Antonio Savorgnan became the greatest master of the agon of vendetta and its most celebrated victim. Beginning with the death of his father in 1500, his brief tenure as head of his branch of the Savorgnan and of the Zambarlano faction saw Antonio come closer than anyone else since the end of the patriarchate to establishing himself as the prince of Friuli, and yet his behavior could be quite erratic, his loyalties equivocal.

He had the singular advantage of looking like a prince (Figure 4). Although strong and robust, he had a head that seemed too large for his body, even when armored in breastplate. He wore his hair in the close-cropped fashion of the ancient Romans, a style he probably adopted during his student days in Padua, and his broad forehead appeared only more prominent as his hairline receded with age. His huge, aquiline nose and strong chin gave his face a certain angularity made severe by recessed, dark eyes surmounted by bushy eyebrows. He kept his beard short and always looked like a soldier, even though he was educated as a lawyer. The extant copy of his portrait depicts him standing dressed in full armor and pointing with lordly hauteur down at his subject city of Udine, shown in the diminished scale of distant perspective.

Contemporaries had strong opinions about him, and even in tempestuous Friuli his character was especially divisive, his reputation particularly threatening to his enemies. However, he was the only person, aristocrat or commoner, cleric or layman, ever to create a mass following among the peasants and artisans. His admiring nephew, Luigi da Porto, who would become one of the

FIGURE 4. Drawing of Antonio Savorgnan.

eminent literary men of his day, grew up in the Vicentino and as a youth went to Udine to serve his uncle. Luigi described Antonio thus:

> There was in Friuli a very great man of the house of Savorgnan whose authority in that region is still greater than any other, as is his name, called . . . Messer Antonio. Sustaining the Guelf cause, he is of such power in those parts that none of the other lords in Italy are greater in their own states than he nor do they have subjects who are so obedient as the Friulan people and peasants have been, and perhaps still are, to the aforementioned whom they hold in such veneration.

Although widespread, veneration of Antonio was never universal even among those who had their own grievances against other castellan lords. Cividale, ever the archrival of Udine, felt especially threatened by Savorgnan's presumptions. The syndics and deputies of the city wrote to the doge of Venice complaining that "in all his duties he always conducts himself with little honor and intolerable damage to us and our subjects." They went on to ask the doge "to silence the said Messer Antonio so that he can no longer call assemblies of the people of this land or have the opportunity to agitate them as the head of anything, since in all the important enterprises he has always conducted himself poorly and shamefully and to our damage." The animosity of the city fathers of Cividale, however, might best be read as a measure of Antonio's power, inasmuch as they obviously felt threatened by his popularity among and leadership of the poor.[1]

Such was Antonio's influence that even his enemies attributed to him far more power than any man could muster. In their eyes he fostered all the evils of the age. Perhaps the most revealing example of their attitude is found in the magnificently malevolent opening sentence of Gregorio Amaseo's *History of the Cruel Fat Thursday and Other Nefarious Excesses and Horrendous Calamities That Occurred in the City of Udine and Patria del Friuli in 1511*:

> In the time of the famous war made by the great league of the Supreme Pontiff Julius II, Maximilian the emperor-elect, Louis XII the king of France, and Ferdinand the king of Spain, Sicily, and Naples with all their allies against only the Illustrious Venetian Republic, the parties and factions of Guelfs and Ghibellines in the Patria del Friuli were inflamed and enraged, much more than they had ever been before, by the forceful instigation of Antonio Savorgnan, Doctor of Laws and son of Messer Nicolò the knight, who through his following of plebeian Guelfs of Udine and peasants of the patria and with all ingenuity and cunning promoted discord and hatred between them and the nobility of citizens and castellans so as then to be able to overwhelm his rivals and enemies and in that fashion to bring down the nobility so that there was no longer anyone who dared raise his eyebrows or open his mouth against even Antonio's slightest gesture, thus assuming for himself much greater impudence than authority, which had been conceded and permitted him on the occasion of that war by the Most Illustrious Signoria of Venice for a good end and with hope of improved results, especially to muster and su-

pervise the militias of the patria, commanding and governing them according to his will, although then he followed completely the opposite end, that is doing no good and a great deal of evil especially against his own compatriots, searching to suppress all the rest and to exalt only himself, which was the most powerful way to alienate the minds of the most faithful, seeing themselves to be more oppressed by the insolent tyranny of him alone than by all the hostile army.

Amaseo made his assessment of Antonio's character, however, after the lord's death when hindsight offered a certain clarity. At one time even the vitriolic Gregorio had been a fawning follower of Antonio Savorgnan.[2]

Born in 1457, Antonio went to study at the University of Padua at which he earned his doctor of laws degree in about 1485. Hardly an intellectual, he seems to have been utterly indifferent to the fine points of the law and to the new humanist learning, which captivated some of his closest associates and his cousin, Girolamo. During his student days his mistress, a certain Paduan woman called Chiribina, said to have been a nun, bore him a child named in memory of the boy's grandfather Nicolò. Antonio never married, and he recognized no other children.

Soon after his return to Friuli he began to represent Pinzano, Ariis, and Osoppo in the parliament. In 1489 he served as a special envoy to Venice, where he obtained the approval of new laws requested by the artisans of Udine and with the success of this trip began to cultivate his reputation as the protector of the common people. After his father died in 1500, Antonio inherited the leadership of the faction and the family's influence in Udine, where nothing passed through the councils of the city without his consent and where he found ample opportunity to exercise his fabled persuasive prowess: "He knew well how to change black into white," as Gregorio Amaseo described his rhetorical gifts.[3]

The Savorgnan legacy, however, was a mixed one because poor management of the family's estates had heavily indebted heirs to Venetian bankers. Revealing an estrangement from his cousins of the Monte d'Osoppo branch, Antonio refused to accept full responsibility for these debts, arguing that his father had managed affairs well and that uncles and cousins had contracted the obligations. But he also blamed the usury of the Venetians for his family's plight:

> And I, Antonio Savorgnan, doctor, with true testimony can tell it straight and have brought up the painful issues. I exhort and pray anyone who will ever read this memorial that if ever for any reason whatsoever he wants to buy anything whatsoever on credit in Venice or to stand surety for a living person in Venice, make any other bad deal and sell one's goods and portions of land rather than begin to take a loan in Venice, because I affirm that from 1475 up until today [July 12, 1500] Messer Tristano and brothers of the Savorgnan and my father have paid in Venice for various loans more than fourteen thousand ducats. And, moreover, in effect no more than eight thousand of these ducats counted toward the principal and the rest went to sterile cows.

Despite their fabled riches in Friuli, the Savorgnan thus had a heavy burden of debt in Venice. Antonio's indebtedness bound him to Venetian policies just as so many peasants bound themselves to the Savorgnan through debt peonage. Probably more important than the formal jurisdictional lines between Venice and the Friuli were these informal and yet quite binding economic moorings that gave Venetian bankers a subtle means of influencing events on the mainland.[4]

Thus, Antonio lived at the center of a vast web of financial, political, and personal ties which stretched from the highest councils of Venice to the peasant villages of Friuli. By 1501 he obtained from the luogotenente a blanket investiture of the fiefs he jointly possessed with his brother. He developed notably cordial relations with Pietro Capello, who held office as luogotenente in 1506 and 1507, but his most influential Venetian friend was Andrea Loredan, who served in the same capacity in Friuli from 1507 to 1509. The careers of the three men intertwined through the difficult war years that followed. The two Venetians encouraged Antonio Savorgnan's ambitions and became something like Friuli specialists in the Venetian councils, furthering their own political careers through their standing in the troublesome but strategic region.

Capello and Loredan seem to have been allies in their own right, and their careers moved notably in tandem. After Capello's term as podestà in Brescia between 1501 and 1503, Loredan replaced him. In a similar way Loredan followed Capello into the office of luogotenente of Friuli. Both enjoyed a nearly uninterrupted string of prestigious offices.

Capello served on the Council of Ten or in the college of the Senate almost continuously between his service in Brescia and Friuli. After his return from Udine he held such offices as ducal counselor and *savio* of the college for four years without break, gaining a reputation as a pragmatist in planning Venetian war policy, especially for Friuli and Istria.[5]

Loredan served as a *savio* of the college in 1505 and as a head of the Council of Ten in 1506 and again after his return from Friuli in 1509. Because he was only a very distant kinsman of Doge Leonardo Loredan, Andrea's career prospered not so much from his family connections as from his own abilities and fabulous wealth. During his term of office in Friuli, he earned a reputation as a "most active man" in both his capacity as a judge and as captain of the war effort. The members of the Savorgnan clan even chose him to arbitrate their family quarrels. He and Antonio Savorgnan personally lent money to the city of Udine to pay for soldiers during the campaigns of 1508. Loredan left Friuli with the best reputation of any luogotenente in memory; and in 1511, at the darkest moment as imperial troops closed in, Udine, Cividale, Portogruaro, and Marano sent delegations to Venice to request that Loredan be sent back to organize the defense. This request may have been the only time in centuries that Udine and Cividale agreed on anything.[6]

After his return from Friuli, however, a nasty episode temporarily interrupted Andrea's career. On August 1, 1509, he became one of the three heads of the Council of Ten, the most powerful office in Venice, especially during the war crisis of that summer. Ten days later he was elected provveditor general for the Venetian military in Friuli, but he refused the new office "saying he was in the Council of Ten and a provveditor of the Arsenal" and would have to pay a penalty if he gave up the latter responsibility. In a second vote Francesco Capello was elected. Nevertheless, four days later one of the state attorneys entered the council to remove Loredan from the ten because he had refused the election as provveditor to Friuli. Failure to accept such an position was against the law, and serving on the Council of Ten no excuse. The statutory penalty included a fine and deportation for six months.

In a personal appeal to the Senate Andrea insisted that he was ignorant of the law, but he was deported anyway—not abroad as the statute required but to the little island of Mazzorbo in the Venetian lagoon where he could stay in contact with political events and entertain friends in his accustomed lavish style. Twice during the deportation allies tried to arrange deals for his freedom, but threats to penalize them as well ended such proposals. Shortly after Andrea's return to Venice, the Great Council elected him to a new office, and by October 1510 he was back on the Council of Ten with his old colleague Pietro Capello.[7]

Loredan had apparently become used to getting his own way in elections and had made powerful enemies who knew how to use the law against him. Moreover, he was not as enthusiastic about returning to Friuli as the Friulans were about having him there.

Andrea Loredan was certainly not afraid to employ his wealth to promote his own political career. In the election of the podestà of Padua held by the Great Council during November 1510, Andrea came in second in the balloting. Sanudo reported, however, that as the nobles filed into the council hall before the election many stood on the stairs offering bribes in return for votes, and supporters of Loredan were among the most actively involved. The diarist commented that it was "with the greatest shame to the city that in these times when the state has been lost, they made such offers. First of all, in this solicitation for the Padua job one clearly sees that corruption is at a peak and the old families are ambitious. God help this republic; it really needs it!"[8]

More impressive were Loredan's activities as a patron. As one of those most responsible for the introduction of Renaissance artistic styles in Venice, he earned a certain fame as a sponsor of architects, in particular. Through connections made by his marriage to Maria Badoer, he became involved in her family's patronage of the Scuola Grande di San Giovanni Evangelista, but most intriguingly he associated with the group of intellectuals who frequented San Michele, the island monastery where Fra Mauro had made his famous map of the world. A small group of laymen and monks interested in the recent revivals of the antique and in Florentine humanism gathered at San Michele for discussions, and there Loredan probably met Mauro Codussi, who was transforming San Michele into Venice's first humanistically inspired building. Loredan became one of the most generous benefactors of San Michele and chose to be buried there; but in going far beyond what had been accomplished there, he hired Codussi to build a grand palace at San Marcuola on the Grand Canal.

Now known as the Palazzo Vendramin-Calergi, which houses Venice's winter casino, the spectacular palace broke with the usual Venetian traditions of restraint in private residences and evoked the antique style more completely than any contemporary palace except possibly the more modest Palazzo Zorzi at San Severo, also by Codussi. Loredan's palace was a much more dramatic statement of the new values than were those of the well-known patrician humanists of his day, such as Bernardo Bembo and Ermolao Barbaro, which followed the self-effacing pattern of Venetian tradition. The splendor of Loredan's palace conveyed an unseemly pride, perhaps the sinful pride of *superbia*, which seems to have been his dominant character trait. Even Loredan showed discomfort with his own violation of the patriciate's egalitarian standards that discouraged excessive displays of personal wealth; inscribed in large letters on the facade is the disclaimer, "Non nobis Domine sed nomini tuo da gloriam" ("It is not our name, Oh Lord, but yours glorified here"). But Andrea's compulsive briberies, his piling of office upon office, and his cultivation of powerful men on the mainland, such as Antonio Savorgnan, leave his protestations of modesty empty.[9]

Andrea Loredan's interest in the new culture of humanism failed to rub off on Antonio Savorgnan, who remained oblivious, despite his Caesarean haircut, to the many ways in which the imitation of ancient Romans could legitimate a usurper such as he. In this he was quite unlike many other petty pseudoprinces of Italy or even his cousin, Girolamo, who knew just how to embellish his letters with the appropriate learned allusions as he threatened treason or worse if he did not get his way. A blunter, rougher man than his refined friends from Venice, Antonio found in Andrea Loredan if not a kindred spirit, at least a powerful acquaintance who acted almost as imperiously in Venice's highest councils as did Antonio in Udine's. Antonio would find Loredan's friendship very helpful when the Friulan attempted his *coup de main* against the Strumieri. For his part Andrea stuck by Savorgnan, barely avoiding the destruction of career that befell other Venetian patricians under Antonio Savorgnan's spell.

Antonio's power in Friuli can be measured in many ways: through his domination of the most important deliberative institutions, his range of friends and clients, his reputation as the protector of the poor, and his ability to call upon thousands of armed citizens and peasants. In the 1503 meeting of the Friulan parliament he had four and one-half votes (for Carnia, Pinzano, Osoppo, Ariis, and he shared the vote of Udine with Rizzardo Fontanabuona, one of his partisans). His close associate, Francesco Janis di Tolmezzo, who had been a law student at Padua with Antonio, also controlled three votes. Almost continuously on the Council of Udine, he ranked first on the list of deputies and between 1505 and 1511 proposed legislation more often than any other person.[10]

In most matters, Antonio usually got his way. He pushed through the election of Giovanni Monticolo as chancellor of the commune over the objections of the notaries who quite properly pointed out that Monticolo had not been admitted into their guild. But since Monticolo was Savorgnan's man, he got the job. In 1507 Antonio advocated the reform of the statutes of Udine according to the principles followed in Padua, Verona, Brescia, and Bergamo, and the council accepted his proposal without dissent but never put the reform into effect because of opposition from Venice.[11]

During the first decade of the century, Antonio created a close-knit cadre of factional associates. The inner circle comprised Francesco Janis di Tolmezzo, Giovanni Monticolo, Nicolò Zanni da Cortona, Ippolito Valvasone, and Antonio's bastard son, Nicolò Chiribin, who entered the priesthood and for whom Antonio obtained the benefice of Buia, a deaconate at the cathedral in Udine, and a canonate of Aquileia. Other allies in Udine included Rizzardo Fontanabuona, Girolamo Mels (not among the consorts of Colloredo and Mels), and Bartolomeo Brugno da Gemona, all of whom held university degrees; and Odorico Susanna, Giovanni Francesco Torso, Ascanio Sbroiavacca, Odorico Scraiber, Alessandro Filitino, and Giovanni Monticolo's brother, Nicolò, all of whom were citizens of Udine. The heads of the suburban *borghi* of Udine also declared themselves supporters of Antonio. Outside the city he favored two castellans who captained rural militias, Asquinio and Federico Varmo; an ardent group of plebeians from Spilimbergo; and artisans, notaries, and peasants from all over the patria.[12]

Antonio carefully nourished the loyalty of the artisans and plebeians of Udine through his advocacy of legislation and reforms that served their interests. As early as 1490 he intervened to support the free market sale of wine, thus breaking the aristocratic monopoly on profits made in its trade. Many of his proposals attempted to alleviate famine and to improve the quality of available food. He proposed that the city buy fodder during a shortage in July 1494 and advocated prohibiting the sale of wheat, millet, and rye to foreigners or to Venice during a later famine. During a meat shortage in 1504 and 1505, Savorgnan accused the butchers of selling at elevated prices meat fit only for dogs and banned the marketing of meat from sick cattle. The next year he accused the guild bakers of selling poorly cooked, nearly rotten bread made from black flour which had damaged the health of the poor; to improve the bread supply he proposed that the city set up a communal bakery in addition to granting free licenses to private bakers who wanted to compete with the established guild bakeries. Finally, it was Antonio who paid the communal physician to inspect medicines sold by pharmacists to guarantee their quality and Antonio who insisted that the school master accept as students "sons of the artisans and common people just like those of the citizens and the little people like the big shots without any particular payment."[13]

Savorgnan's advocacy for the poor of Udine built a vast following without costing him much personally because in most cases the financial burden of his reforms fell on the commune. Maintaining the loyalty of peasants, on the other hand, was an entirely different matter inasmuch as his own economic interests and theirs were inevitably opposed, especially in light of the debts Antonio had inherited. Nevertheless, on general policy matters regarding agriculture, even where his own finances could suffer, he backed the peasants over his fellow lords. In 1501 and 1502 he spoke up in defense of the peasants against new taxes and obligatory public work obligations for military purposes imposed by the Venetians, and in 1503 he involved himself in a vicious struggle with the other castellans in the Friulan parliament over their attempts to require tenants to make improvements to their leaseholds without compensation.[14]

In advocating reforms Antonio introduced a new strategy of cultivating clients among the peasantry which contrasted with Savorgnan family traditions of lordship which were far from magnanimous. In 1488 Antonio's cousin Tristano di Pagano had demanded a larger than usual *decima* on wine from the peasants in Vito d'Asio near Osoppo, a demand that precipitated a minor rebellion after which several tenants were beaten and imprisoned. On his own estates, in contrast, Antonio seems to have been a relatively gentle landlord, a fact that enhanced his reputation among the peasants. His motives were not so much benevolent as calculated to acquire clients. Given the absence of any institutional alternative to the system in place, Antonio's personal reputation helped considerably in establishing him as the leader of the peasant movement.[15]

Antonio's policies toward his tenants emphasized the bonds of clientage over economic advantage. During the agrarian crisis of the early sixteenth century he loaned money with great liberality and no rigid expectations of repayment, a policy that allowed peasants to survive during a period of depressed agricultural prices and to counter the effects of a rural rent structure that overvalued the productive capacity of the land. Although Antonio's profits suffered, the loyalty of his followers intensified. In examining the rent-rolls for Antonio's landholdings in Buia, for example, one finds a very high level of personal indebtedness to him. Between 1500, when Antonio became the lord of Buia at his father's death, and 1508 the levels of tenant indebtedness increased steadily, in part because of the poor harvests and disruptions of war but also because Antonio tolerated unpaid debts. In 1508 one peasant had ten outstanding loans. Most of these were advances of wheat, rye, oats, and millet made in June just before the harvest, but there were also loans of wine, straw, tools, shoes, and pieces of cloth. Of the 145 Savorgnan tenants in 1508, 53 obtained loans from the landlord that year. Many of these were never repaid in full, and the rent-roll shows a net loss of 35.8 percent on loans made to tenants that year. In addition, only 68 (46.9 percent) of the 145 were able to pay their land rents in full in 1508, and some 10 (6.9 percent) paid nothing at all. Antonio also made approximately ninety-one loans in Buia to nontenants, and a sample of these reveals a net loss of about 12.4 percent on the principal alone. Antonio permitted repayment in extra labor at harvest time or in cheap oats rather than the expensive wheat originally advanced. The economic loss entailed by these lending practices was even greater than appears in the figures of amounts lent and repaid because the loans were originally made in kind just before harvest when commodities were dear, but repayment was accepted after harvest when market prices were low.[16]

Antonio's paternalism, in effect, subsidized his tenants during the most difficult parts of the year and maintained a policy of repayment which contrasted sharply with that of other castellans, such as the neighboring Colloredo, whose rent-rolls have been studied. Savorgnan certainly knew what he was doing because the rent-rolls list a monetary value for all commodities and quote current market values of both loans and repayments in kind. His estate managers, therefore, had a keen sensitivity to the market economy and to values as determined by price, but they did not exploit these loans to make a profit. By lending to tenants and others on such a vast scale, Antonio acquired dependents rather than profits. Despite the systematic record keeping and other modern techniques, his practice was closer to a potlatch than a business enterprise. Antonio's loan practices redistributed wealth, revealing an objective more social than economic, the accumulation of what might be called social capital, which would have been squandered by precipitously demanding timely repayments.[17]

Besides his advocacy of popular issues in the councils of Udine and the parliament of Friuli and the easy credit he made available to his tenants and followers, Antonio cultivated the rural militias more systematically than any of his predecessors. Venice's 1487 decree naming Antonio's father, Nicolò, the permanent captain of the Friulan militias provoked a riot when it was read in the parliament because the other castellans could easily envision the extraordinary power the Savorgnan would acquire from such a position. But Nicolò had never made his captaincy a reality, and the militias existed largely on paper until the wars of the first decade of the new century, when Antonio transformed them into a private army.[18]

Antonio's opportunities came from changes in military practice stimulated by the Swiss victories of the late fifteenth century and the invasion of King Charles VIII in 1494. The Swiss example encouraged the integration of mercenary troops among soldiers recruited from the local population with an eye to providing professional officers for the militiamen. Venice called these units *ordinanze* and commissioned an officer, the *contestabile*, for every one hundred men and a corporal for every twenty-five. Because recruits were not paid in peacetime, the only incentives to join came from the exemption from labor services such as carting and work on fortifications, the opportunity to obtain weapons, and whatever rewards or punishments local recruiters or a lord such as Antonio Savorgnan could offer.[19]

Antonio and his cousin Girolamo came to monopolize the recruitment of militiamen so that in 1510 when Venice tried to create its own *ordinanza marchesca* in Friuli quotas fell short because the available men had already enrolled under the Savorgnan. Militiamen performed admirably on occasion but were prone to desert at harvest time or when their home villages were threatened. Later in the century a Venetian rector observed that not even "another Mars" could discipline these ragged bands, and although Antonio Savorgnan succeeded in bringing together hundreds of men from many villages, he was no Mars himself.[20]

Estimates of the number of men Antonio could muster varied greatly from five hundred to six thousand, but a reasonable guess might put the maximum ever in the field at about fifteen hundred. Supplies for the peasant militia often came from the larders of Antonio Savorgnan himself, as can be seen in 1508 when he lent flour and wine to the communes of Buia and Maiano to provide for their men leaving for Gorizia on the campaign. In July 1509, when foreign armies controlled much of the terraferma dominion, Venice could spare only two hundred extra mercenaries to defend Udine. In addition to these professionals, fifty artisan militiamen were available to guard the castle of the luogotenente, leaving the manning of the town walls to the peasant militias. Savorgnan mustered the peasants at two locations in the environs of Udine, but during a heavy rain many of them wandered away. Evil rumors spread panic among those who remained. One peasant who was on the run told Leonardo Amaseo that he was fleeing not because anyone was actually chasing him but out of fear that someone would. Amaseo commented, "it is a bad business to defend the patria with peasants, and this comes from bad government." The next spring

Antonio called up a huge but undisciplined horde to expel the enemy from the castle at Cormons, but they performed with little honor and fled in the face of any opposition.[21]

However unsuccessful their efforts against foreign enemies, the militias under Antonio Savorgnan altered the balance of factional forces in Friuli. In building up the militias he not only relied on his own peasants but made clients out of the feudal subjects of his traditional Strumiero enemies. Although recruits from the tenants of the Strumiero lords may have considered their adventures away from their home villages dreary, they learned how to follow a leader other than their landlord, one who did not demand forced labor or extra rents and who might even provide a weapon, food, and wine. In causing the peasants to step outside of their normal social roles for a brief period and experience a certain autonomy, a certain breath of freedom, the wartime musters created a liminal state, which contributed to the vast uprising of 1511. Although we have no direct information about Friuli, in other regions of Europe militia companies usually also acted as festive companies, organizing carnival revelries and often initiating riots, as the Friulan militias would do in 1511.

Liminal states and liminal groups—those periods such as festivals and those persons such as young soldiers who had not yet acquired the responsibilities of adult life—often stimulated reform in premodern Europe. By participating in liminal experiences promoted by Antonio Savorgnan, the peasants of Friuli began to build bonds outside of their own villages. They became a rebellious political force, the Zambarlani.[22]

Antonio Savorgnan's expansive incorporation of artisans and peasants into the Zambarlani disturbed not only the Strumieri but also his equally ambitious cousin Girolamo. Hindsight has produced stark contrasts between these two men: Antonio the cruel, wicked, and audacious tyrant whose character opposed Girolamo's, the pious, heroic, and faithful "paragon of true soldierly temperament." But matters were hardly that simple. The tensions between them were, in many ways, the inevitable result of the clan's inheritance patterns, which forced them to share large parts of the Savorgnan patrimony. Each struggled to carve out of this collectivity his own portion, creating a rivalry that intensified during the wars with the empire. Both instinctively served Venice, but neither was above making overtures to the emperor when it seemed useful. Both relied on the same circle of men for their principal servants and allies. Whereas Antonio's chief aid was Francesco Janis di Tolmezzo, Girolamo's was Francesco's brother, Giacomo, who even suffered imprisonment in Girolamo's service. Both Savorgnan captained their own companies in the militia. In 1509, as a reward for their service to Venice, they jointly received the fief of Castelnovo, a possession that soon drove them apart because Girolamo felt slighted by Antonio's quick grabbing of booty and ransoming of prisoners who surrendered with the castle's conquest.[23]

Until his death, Antonio remained the dominant figure of the two. His personality, which was sometimes courageously magnanimous, especially toward his clients, and sometimes treacherously mean-spirited, his constant calculations of advantage and disadvantage, and his arrogant ambition help explain the intensity of the factional struggle during his lifetime. A clash between the Zambarlani and Strumieri may have become highly likely because of the conjuncture of war and an agrarian crisis, but the timing of their battles, not to say the intensity and form of their violence toward one another, had a great deal to do with the elusive character traits that made Antonio Savorgnan a brilliant and yet deeply flawed leader, the only Italian nobleman of his age to guide a mass movement of peasants, a movement that would produce the greatest conflagration in Friulan history.

INVASIONS, 1499–1509

While Antonio Savorgnan was making himself a prince without title, a storm was gathering over Friuli. Unresolved and opposing legal claims to the patriarchate and the disputed division of the region into territories occupied by Venice, the empire, and the counts of Gorizia, who remained closely tied to the Hapsburgs, had been building pressure since 1420.

Two new developments released the pressure. Maximilian Hapsburg's grandiose ambitions lured him to reassert imperial rights in the regions of northern Italy conquered by Venice. At the same time the Turks attacked Venetian possessions on several fronts. Friuli was the only place among Venice's far-flung lands which suffered assaults by both of the republic's enemies. The Turks laid waste to the countryside in 1499, and before recovery could take hold, Emperor-Elect Maximilian and Venice escalated their conflict by moving from clandestine interference in the affairs of each others' dominions and border skirmishes to open warfare.

Until these wars, the most important of the empire's enclaves in Friuli were Pordenone in western Friuli, Latisana and Belgrado on the lower Tagliamento, Castelnovo in the mountains north of Spilimbergo, and Codroipo southwest of Udine on the road to Venice (see map, "Friuli in the Sixteenth Century"). Also outside of Venetian control was the county of Gorizia, which dominated the Isonzo River valley and extended westward to include Cormons and southwestward to Aquileia itself.[24]

The counts of Gorizia and many of the Strumiero castellans had feudal or marriage ties that enmeshed them in a web of anti-Venetian loyalties. As early as 1438, the luogotenente prohibited Venetian subjects from accepting titles, offices, or positions from the counts, and in 1467 the Senate forbade feudal investitures from them; but the lure of Gorizian and imperial fiefs continued to nourish Strumiero hopes for the removal of the Venetians.[25]

The proximity of the enclaves facilitated employing them as refuges for those banished from the Venetian dominions, making it profitable for the Austrian *gastaldi* who administered them to welcome exiles in return for a fee. Assassins found these enclaves particularly convenient because if they could manage to ambush an enemy close to a border, a secure haven might be only a few steps away. Pordenone, situated in the midst of the western plain without any natural borders, was particularly notorious as a roost for bandits, with those exiled from Venetian Friuli living in the town and others exiled from imperial territories congregating on the Venetian side of the border in the castles at Porcìa, Torre, Cusano, and Zoppola.[26]

When Count Johann of Gorizia died in 1468 the county passed to his son Ludwig, who lived in Lienz because he feared the Turkish threat to Gorizia. Insecure and unlikely to leave an heir, Ludwig agreed to cede Gorizia to Maximilian Hapsburg in exchange for safer lands across the Alps, a transfer that intensified the legal and military confrontation in Friuli between Venice and the Hapsburgs.

The Venetians argued that the county had been a fief of the patriarch of Aquileia, and therefore should pass to them when Count Ludwig died no matter what he himself desired. Venice's case was

based on the fact that after the conquest of the patriarchate the doge
had invested Ludwig's ancestor with the county in a grand public
ceremony in San Marco. By participating in the investiture ceremony the count had recognized the republic as his feudal lord.
Pope Alexander VI supported Venice's claim, pointing out that
fiefs can not be reassigned by vassals. Maximilian, on the other
hand, argued that the German emperors had originally invested the
patriarchs with their territories, which the Venetians had illegally
usurped. By insisting on irreconcilable positions, the two sides
committed themselves to a fight.

Tension stayed at a high level throughout 1497 and 1498 by a
series of provocations and raids from both sides. At one point,
when false news arrived that the count was dying, Venice commissioned Nicolò Savorgnan to muster his militiamen to take the
county, but renewed Turkish threats forced them to withdraw.[27]

In the summer of 1499 Venice focused its attention on an invasion of Milan planned with its new ally, France. The enterprise
enfeebled the eastern frontier defenses despite recurring reports in
August of numerous imperial detachments in the vicinity and rumors from Bosnia that a large Turkish force anticipated invading
Friuli as soon as the weather cooled off. On August 26 a delegation
of Friulans spoke to the Venetian college of the Senate about the
very poor condition of Udine's fortifications and the lack of sufficient troops to defend against the expected Turkish assault. But
with offensive ambitions elsewhere, Venice was in no position to
offer any assistance. On September 28 a force of more than ten
thousand Turks camped outside of Gorizia. Sanudo recorded a rumor that they had with them thousands of huge attack dogs, two
or three for every man, a story that spread panic. Crying for help,
peasants from the surrounding countryside flocked to the Venetian
fortress at Gradisca, but the provveditor, Andrea Zoncani, refused
to help, saying reportedly, "I don't want to get myself killed." Except for a few stradiots who disobeyed orders (probably because
their own families were threatened) none of the Venetian forces put
up the slightest resistance when Skander, the Turkish general, and
his troops entered Venetian Friuli.

The invaders formed a fifteen-mile-wide front of infantrymen
who advanced to the Livenza River, destroying or looting everything in their path and spreading panic as far as the Marghera ferry

stations to Venice. Reports of the numbers of their victims are un-
trustworthy, but the figures certainly imply massive devastation:
twelve hundred slaughtered at Cordenons, one thousand killed in
a field outside of Roveredo, two thousand massacred or taken prisoner from the Aviano district. The village of San Martino outside
of Aviano lost 420 of its 500 inhabitants. Near Valvasone the Turks
put to flight a poorly armed and even more poorly led company of
peasant militiamen and brought back some 260 heads on their
lances. Detachments of Turks lingered around Valvasone for four
days, and while the nobles locked themselves up in their castle,
approximately five hundred of their subjects hid in woods and
ditches. During the night two bands of Turks rode up to the castle
gate and plumbed the depths of the moat but found it too deep to
ford; lacking the necessary artillery for a siege, they were forced to
retire. Before recrossing the Tagliamento, Skander divided his cap-
tives into two groups in anticipation of a final sickening spectacle:
the young men and women who could be sold into slavery were
taken away, and the remaining old people, estimated at between
fifteen hundred and two thousand, were beheaded on the banks of
the river. After an investigation, Venetian officials estimated that
during the eight-day rampage the Turks killed or captured more
than ten thousand people and burned 132 villages. This singularly
horrible invasion etched itself in the collective memory of the
Friulans. The village of Vigonovo, for example, continued to
mourn its dead every year on September 30 until late in the nineteenth century.[28]

The results of these terrible eight days can hardly be overesti-
mated. Some of the peasant villages in the Turks' path never recov-
ered. As the ensuing decade brought increasing fiscal demands
both from the landlords and the Venetians, many villagers found
themselves faced with starvation, others were forced to give up
their leaseholds, and many gravitated for protection to the Zambarlani of Antonio Savorgnan. The Venetians' failure to provide
efficient frontier defenses undermined confidence in their leadership, particularly because they seemed to be locked in a permanent
struggle with the Turks, who could again assault Venice by invading Friuli. The empire was at peace with the sultan, a fact that
made Maximilian's claims to Friuli ever more alluring to his local
supporters.

Even before the Turkish invasion, a Friulan castellan with a humanist education, Jacopo di Porcìa, composed a learned critique of Venetian rule in Friuli, *De reipublicae Venetae administratione*. Porcìa advocated the complete reorganization of the Venetian military in particular by rejecting the reliance on mercenaries along lines Machiavelli would later recommend for all Italy. Porcìa followed the feudal traditions of his family and class by arguing that experienced Friulan knights be systematically integrated into the forces and preferred over young, inexperienced Venetians. However, despite the merits of Porcìa's views, Venetian politicians completely ignored his advice and relied even more on mercenaries and the Savorgnan militias.[29]

In addition, until the Turks came to terms in 1503, their continued threat prevented Venice from countering Maximilian's intrigues in Friuli. When Count Ludwig finally died on April 12, 1500, Maximilian sent representatives to Friuli to seize his inheritance, and the Venetians, still faced with rumors of another Turkish invasion, did nothing to stop them. The initiative and the lands of Gorizia thus slipped out of Venice's grasp. The way was now open for Maximilian to act out his fantasy of reviving the German empire of Otto the Great by using Friuli as his base for the reconquest of imperial Italy, lost so many centuries before to the Lombard League. In both Venetian and Austrian Friuli factions were encouraged by the trouble brewing between La Serenissima and Maximilian. Even the castle at Gorizia was divided into two parties when the imperial counts arrived to take possession after the death of Ludwig.

Antonio Savorgnan, dismayed by the arrival of the Hapsburgs on his doorstep, pointed out that the prospect of Austrian domination frightened the peasants in particular because they assumed that an imperial victory would lead to a reintroduction of serfdom. The same prospect encouraged the Strumiero lords. At the Treaty of Blois in 1504 Maximilian and King Louis XII of France secretly agreed to conquer and divide up the mainland territories of Venice, and concentrations of imperial forces in Villach alerted Venice to an impending invasion throughout 1506 and 1507. Maximilian requested permission to make an armed march through Venetian territory on his way to Rome for his coronation. Venice refused and amassed its forces in the Veronese, anticipating an invasion through the Brenner Pass.[30]

War came in early 1508 resulting in a quick Venetian victory in the Cadore and, after a brief siege, the capture of Gorizia itself. The imperial enclaves of Pordenone, Castelnovo, Codroipo, and Belgrado fell as prizes to the victorious captains, including the Savorgnan cousins.

Although Venice celebrated a stunning victory, several signs already foretold future troubles. Despite new revenues from the conquered towns, the cost of the campaign and the expenditures necessary to defend the new territories put Venetian finances under a tremendous strain. Supporting the army in 1508 consumed one fifth of the entire Venetian state budget even though the campaign had been relatively brief. As early as May, Antonio Savorgnan and Andrea Loredan had to pay out of their own pockets the troops of Francesco Sbroiavacca to keep the men fighting for another month.[31]

Maximilian, the one truly humiliated, began to plot his revenge. On December 10, 1508, he and King Louis of France signed a treaty in Cambrai which broke the truce with Venice of the previous June. Soon after, the marquis of Mantua, the duke of Ferrara, Pope Julius II, and Ferdinand of Aragon joined the new league, officially formed against the Turks but secretly designed to divide up the dominion Venice had conquered during the previous century. The treaty assigned spoils in advance to each signatory. Among other spoils Maximilian would get Friuli.[32]

When news of the League of Cambrai arrived in Venice, the government undertook hurried preparations in an attempt to stave off the inevitable, but on May 14 disaster struck. The French crushed Venetian forces at Agnadello. Bartolomeo d'Alviano, one of the victors for Venice the previous year, was taken prisoner. As fast as the news could spread, town after town capitulated to the enemy, and in a few days Venice lost almost all its mainland empire. Excited by the news, Maximilian proposed to go beyond the treaty by taking the city of Venice itself and dividing it into four quarters to be administered by the four principal allies in the league.[33]

Venetian forces regrouped for a strategic withdrawal to the edge of the lagoon, and a nervous Senate voted to abandon without further fighting more than thirty-six subject towns. Such defeatist behavior did not encourage Venice's supporters on the mainland, and until the Council of Ten seized the initiative and began to dictate a new policy, towns such as Verona, Vicenza, and Padua stayed in the enemy fold.[34]

In Friuli imperial troops recaptured the towns lost the year before and ranged throughout the countryside without opposition, threatening to besiege at any moment the cities remaining in the Venetian camp. Imperial heralds approached the walls of the fortified cities and demanded that they send representatives to Padua to make a formal submission or face sacking and burning. Udine remained loyal despite the abject fear felt throughout June and July. The Savorgnan, Della Torre, and many others sent their wives and movable property to the safety of Venice. On June 14 rumors of a pending attack spread waves of panic through the city. We are told that the populace began to run hither and yon through the streets, fighting among themselves with sticks and clubs. As soon as calm prevailed in one area another tumult broke out elsewhere. Five or six times during the night a suburban village's tocsin rung in response to approaching phantoms, echoed in Udine by a call to arms. Fits of fear became so common that Luogotenente Giovanni Paolo Gradenigo was forced to decree on the twenty-eighth that "the first person who speaks about surrendering to the king of the Romans, no matter what social position he has, will be hung, and whoever accuses him will have a one-hundred ducat reward from the public treasury." The general nervousness seriously undermined the discipline necessary to defend the city when the enemy finally did arrive. A false alarm or even a drunken brawl would draw militiamen in the direction of the noise, abandoning the gate they were assigned to guard. To protect their palaces, the great families brought in heavily armed *bravi* who aroused the suspicions of the citizens worried that their city might be betrayed from within.

The situation was just as bad if not worse in Spilimbergo, where the deep distrust between the consorts and the citizens led each to suspect the other of betrayal. Leonardo Amaseo recounted in his diary "that all Spilimbergo turned upside down. There are evil people everywhere."[35]

The uncertainties of the spring and summer of 1509 opened

an extraordinary period of internal disintegration in Friuli which lasted for more than two years. All the social tensions between peasants and castellans, between Zambarlani and Strumieri, between Antonio Savorgnan and his many enemies, and between Venice and its Friulan subjects came into the open. The war introduced the possibility that the whole system of patronage and allegiances would be changed by an imperial victory, which would certainly have meant the destruction of Antonio Savorgnan and his friends, unless, of course, they switched to the imperial side first.

As the external controls by the Venetians loosened from the spring of 1509 to the winter of 1511–12, Friuli became a society governed almost entirely by its factions and serves, therefore, as a revealing historical laboratory for the scrutiny of vendetta and factional relationships. During this period, Friuli suffered from cycles of violence, generated by the internal logic of vendetta, which alternated periods of fearful social tension with demonstrations of pacification and unity. The war often quickened the periods of tension, and the Venetians tried to draw out those of domestic peace. But the cycles had a life of their own, often operating quite independently of the pressures of war and the policies of Venice.

The first signs of renewed factional conflict appeared in June, when many castellans, despite their assurances of loyalty to Venice, conspired with the imperialists, inhibited the Venetian defense, or abstained from fighting. Most, in fact, never took up arms until it appeared as though the Austrians might be defeated. Soon after the fall of Padua in June, Antonio Savorgnan presented the luogotenente with a list of castellans whom he said had been dealing with the enemy and should be sent to Venice for the security of the patria. The list included the houses of Colloredo (except for Camillo), Mels, Strassoldo (except for Giovanni), Candido, Gorghi, Arcoloniano, Brazzacco, Cergneu, Frattina, Zucco, Cucagna, Partistagno, Bertolino, Castello, Soldonieri, Sbrugli, and Guarienti and the individuals Martino Valentinis and Francesco Pavona. Among the great families of the Strumieri the only names missing were the Della Torre, who were left off, according to Gregorio Amaseo, because Savorgnan knew the list was a fraud and he did not want "to put too much wood on the fire the first time around." Later in the summer, however, his cousin Girolamo, who had no reason to make Antonio look good, implicated Alvise Della Torre

in treasonous activities. Despite Amaseo's opinion, the list has a
certain credibility, especially given the decidedly tardy appearance
of these castellans on the field of battle. Nevertheless, the traitors
named were all Antonio's personal Strumiero enemies, and one
cannot blame the luogotenente for having some doubts about
Savorgnan's motives.[36]

Quite unlike his predecessor Andrea Loredan, who had befriended and defended Antonio, Giovanni Paolo Gradenigo suspected the Strumieri less than the Zambarlano leader himself. Late
in June a rumor spread that Antonio's brother, Giovanni, had gone
to negotiate with the imperialists. In response some nobles attempted to elect a citizen to govern Udine over Antonio's head,
but a member of Antonio's inner circle, Giovanni Monticolo, sabo-
taged the election. Even the Austrians' failure to attack Udine for
so long was attributed to Antonio Savorgnan's supposed dealings
with them. Instead of forwarding Savorgnan's list of purported
traitors, Gradenigo wrote to the Council of Ten about his own
suspicions of Antonio. The council replied that although it appreciated the luogotenente's vigilance,

> every day we see and understand the actions of the above men-
> tioned Lord Antonio we neither are persuaded to believe these
> charges nor do we expect from him anything that is not faith-
> ful and that does not conform to that which he and all his
> house have always shown and done for our state. And this
> single doubt should not permit you to show any ambiguities
> and suspicions about his faithfulness to this patria because it
> could well push him to some thoughts alien to his nature and
> disposition, which would be dangerous for the following he
> has in the whole patria.

The council thought the rumors about Antonio originated with his
enemies and ordered, "you must use every sweet and kindly office
with the said Lord Antonio in such a way that he knows that we
and you love and admire him." Although Gradenigo repeated his
suspicions, the council again warned him against alienating the
head of the Savorgnan clan in any way. Given the ambiguity of the
situation in Friuli, the confidence of the council in the loyalty of
Antonio Savorgnan seems remarkable, even foolhardy, but it rec-

ognized better than Gradenigo that Venice had few alternatives to trusting Antonio given the strain on its military resources. Moreover, Antonio's friend and patron, Andrea Loredan, was on the council that summer, and his influence in defending Antonio was undoubtedly strong.[37]

While imperial and French armies roamed almost at will across Venice's mainland territories and Friuli disintegrated into its component parts, the Venetians worried about what had gone wrong. There were many diagnoses, some of which were not far off the mark. Girolamo Priuli confided to his diary that the attack and failure to defend the mainland dominion were the fault of his fellow patricians. They had been victims of their own arrogance, which had led them to neglect justice, live in a splendor fed by bribes, avoid civic duties, rely on mercenaries rather than fatigue themselves in mastering the arts of war, indulge in sexual exploits with nuns and young boys, and search for the easy life in country villas rather than bear the hardships of maritime trade. Although some mainlanders, such as Luigi da Porto, were fatalistic, blaming the stars and indecipherable fortune, most critics from the terraferma were inclined, at least in their first reactions, to blame the Venetians themselves, echoing Priuli's themes of haughtiness, pride, and obliviousness to the truth. Despite the fact that some saw precisely what had gone wrong, reforms faltered, and Venice stumbled through the next eight years of war, separating its enemies from one another by either bribing them or playing upon their mutual suspicions.[38]

AGRARIAN CRISIS: THE PILLAGE OF STERPO

While the Venetians agonized over their own failings in provincial administration and international diplomacy which had brought on the disaster of 1509, a peasant uprising took place in Friuli in July of the same year. The uprising, which culminated in the burning of Sterpo castle, was fueled by an agrarian crisis that began with the Turkish invasion of 1499 and was sparked by the War of the League of Cambrai. The disruptions of the war finally permitted the peasants from this tiny village and its environs to confront their lord in a way that anticipated the more general agrarian revolt that was to occur in 1511. Because the Colloredo fief of Sterpo can be reconstructed in some detail, the situation there helps explain the more widespread peasant discontent that characterized the agrarian crisis.

One needs to distinguish between the agrarian structures that had impoverished rural Friuli for centuries and the more immediate precipitants of the violent attacks on castellan property and privilege. The ubiquity of malaria, absence of irrigation projects, frequent flooding, lack of roads and bridges, indebtedness, and manifold financial exactions from foreign overlords had plagued the region for centuries. During the fifteenth and sixteenth centuries high taxes on milling forced many peasants to haul their grain long distances to one of the exempt mills in the imperial enclaves, the patriarchal towns of San Vito or San Daniele, or the Savorgnan fief at Belgrado. Although these long-term conditions produced a rural economy with little ability to cushion crises, they did not alone stimulate rebellion. However, during the first decade of the sixteenth century, several other kinds of developments made some kind of rural disturbance likely. First, a dramatic drop in agricultural prices prompted landlords to increase income from agrarian holdings by monopolizing access to markets and guaranteeing control over the labor force, actions that led to a growing insecurity of tenure for leaseholders. In addition, war pressures forced the Venetians to increase fiscal and work obligations and rural billets for mercenaries. And finally the Zambarlano faction under the leadership of Antonio Savorgnan offered some kind of redress of grievances.

As early as 1501 the Friulan parliament heard a proposal to send a delegation to the new doge, Leonardo Loredan, to complain about the progressive impoverishment of the peasants caused by the heavy demands of military projects such as requirements to cut wood for the arsenal and to billet stradiots in the villages. Complaints to Venice, however, masked the conflict between the castellan landlords and the peasant tenants which came out in the open during the parliamentary sessions in 1502 and 1503.

The central issue involved the improvements that peasants made to the leasehold. Traditional *livello* contracts had an *ad meliorandum* clause that obligated the tenant to improve the land with capital and material provided by the landlord. The peasants came to see the reciprocity guaranteed in the clause as a right that meant they could clear new land if it were available and use the resources of the lord to build new houses for their children. By the early sixteenth century, most leaseholds had been converted from *livello* to *affittanza* contracts, which were for a shorter term and which offered tenants compensation for any improvements they made inasmuch as there was no guarantee that children could inherit the same leasehold. Compensation for improvements was a price landlords had to pay for the greater flexibility *affittanza* contracts provided them, but, also, the contracts implied that they alone could decide what improvements were to be made and eliminated peasant rights to use the land's building resources, particularly lumber and thatch. In a series of proposals to the parliament, the lords sought to deny tenants reimbursement for improvements or to lower the value of the repayments. Ascanio Sbroiavacca argued that because stradiots had begun to be billeted in the villages, some peasants had used the stipend Venice provided to build new houses and had then gone to the landlord and asked for compensation for improving the leasehold. His assertion that the peasants had received double payment for their improvements could have applied to only a very few, but his proposal would have eliminated the lords' payments for all improvements by all peasant tenants. After much discussion and study a bill was drawn up for the session held in March 1503. The new law prohibited tenants from making any improvements, especially constructing rental buildings without the permission of their landlord; provided for an evaluation of work already done by a committee of men from the village; and established standards for future improvements such as the quality of the thatch for roofing.[39]

By November the castellans complained in parliament that the peasants had formed various subversive "conventicles," some with as many as two thousand members, and had "used some nefarious and diabolical words, especially about cutting to pieces priests, gentlemen, castellans, and citizens and even about launching a Sicilian Vespers." A member of parliament proposed a bill to send a delegation to Venice to notify the signoria of the threats, but Antonio Savorgnan arose to support the peasants, saying they needed to be helped rather than driven to destitution. Antonio lost. Parliament instructed the castellan delegation to request that peasants who billeted Venice's soldiers be required to pay a rent to their

landlords; in other words rather than address the peasants' grievances the lords sought to exploit their tenants even further.[40]

Rebuffed by the parliament, the peasants turned, probably under
the guidance of Antonio Savorgnan, to the deputies of Udine for
help in sending to Venice a delegation representing the peasants'
views. In the list of requests drawn up for the delegation, the peasants placed on paper for the first time a plan that went beyond
immediate grievances to propose institutional changes. Their first
recommendation was for the formation of a peasant assembly composed of village syndics who would meet annually in Udine in the
presence of the luogotenente to deliberate on issues vital to the
peasants, especially on the distribution of the fees and work demanded of them. The countrymen also wanted the delegates from
Udine to defend them in Venice against the false accusations made
by the castellans of the parliament, to ask for relief from their obligations of lumber cutting for the arsenal and levee building on the
banks of the distant Brenta River, and to request the right to cut
oak trees to build mills, bridges, and carts for their own use. In a
deferential spirit, the peasant syndics returned to the parliament to
repudiate their more rebellious fellows who had threatened violence against the landlords and to ask the castellans "to embrace us
as a father does his family." In response to this plea for a return to
paternalism, Alvise Della Torre spoke against all the peasants and
demanded that for the dignity of the parliament immediate action
be taken against them. Just as Antonio Savorgnan had already become the defender of the peasants, after this incident Alvise Della
Torre became their *bête noire*.[41]

In Venice Doge Loredan suffered through long harangues from
both castellan and Udinese delegations, then dismissed them all
cryptically saying that although the leaders of the protests would
be punished "peasants must be peasants." The doge's attitude
merely postponed the problems to a time when Venice would be
far less able to deal with them.[42]

Once the wars began, the general collapse of order permitted
numerous atrocities that, if nothing else, contributed to a widespread sense of insecurity in the undefended villages. The soldiers
from both sides made a bad situation worse. Armies tried to live
off the land in the enemy's territory, and much of what passed for
warfare consisted of raids to plunder villagers. In March 1508 Aus-

trians from the castle at Gorizia destroyed three villages near Monfalcone, "taking a great booty of goods and animals, burning
houses, and killing two men and one woman." Three weeks later
Venetian soldiers pillaged three towns and nearby villages in Gorizian territory. The most infamous incident was the sacking of
Cormons after d'Alviano's men took the town in April 1508. Because the Cormonesi had been looting villages in Venetian Friuli
for some weeks, their former victims wanted to retaliate, and because many peasants from the surrounding *contado* had brought
their goods to Cormons for safekeeping, there were prospects for
rich booty. The citizens of Cormons suffered horribly. While the
soldiers concentrated on the town of Cormons, peasants from all
over Venetian Friuli sacked the villages in imperial territory, "and
it is said that the peasants are a thousand times worse than the
soldiers."

The same area of borderlands near the Isonzo was pillaged again
the next year when imperial forces recaptured Gorizia and Cormons. Saddened by the loss of so many of his men during the
imperial reconquest, the Venetian commander at Gradisca "thought
that this rout justified a vendetta." He sent out his cavalry not
against his military foes but against the villagers under the jurisdiction of Gorizia and Cormons and ordered his men to take as many
prisoners as possible and to burn everything. The imperialists
again retaliated by following the same scorched-earth policy in
Venetian territories:

> The Friulan region was afflicted by the most terrible calami-
> ties: thefts, pillages, burnings, murders, assassinations, and
> sacrileges were everyday things; there was nothing inviolable
> any more or any restraint to crimes. With the offenses and
> reprisals not a day passed without horrors. The most beautiful
> countryside came no less under that accumulation of scourges,
> and he who from the tops of the highest hills looked down
> upon the plains below was not able to hold back tears pro-
> duced by the view in every direction of towns, villages, and
> farm-houses that burned and smoked. These were, thus, the
> first examples of the furious war, since on both sides spirits
> were agitated by the vendetta which began after the Venetians
> had restored to the emperor his cities.

Contemporaries thus saw an intimate relationship between the scourges of war and the pursuit of vendetta, which influenced soldiers and peasants alike.[43]

A climate of vendetta, of mutual reprisals, and of extensive suffering at the hands of soldiers and enemy peasants probably contributed more than anything else to the Friulan peasants' famous loyalty to Venice, a dedication that contrasted with the fickle commitment of nobles and townsmen throughout the terraferma dominion. Unlike the powerful who defended themselves in castles and behind town walls and who could always bargain with the enemy if necessary, the peasants had nothing to gain and much to lose from foreign armies. When Venice lost, they lost; very often they lost everything because of the ravages of the invading armies. When Venice won, they could join the soldiers in plundering the villages of the enemy, recover from their own privations, and pay back those who had pillaged them.

The stalwart farmers of the Veneto and Friuli, who amazed Machiavelli and who have puzzled modern scholars unable to see what they got out of the arrangement, stood by Venice during the War of the League of Cambrai not because of some mysterious ideological bond but because it was simply in their interest to do so. Although Venice seldom protected the country people effectively, the townsmen and castellans never offered any help and often actively assisted the enemy. Despite all the pompous cant about aristocratic honor and the true word of a knight, in Friuli loyalty was almost exclusively a trait of the men and women of the little farm communities. They seldom rebelled against Venice because they knew who had left them vulnerable to an enemy who only promised a return to serfdom, and when they plundered property or besieged a castle because, they said, the aristocrats had betrayed Saint Mark, one should take their words seriously. Despite the many inadequacies of the Venetian regime, the peasants understood quite well how incorporation into the empire would have strengthened the hands of their own castellan lords.[44]

Although peasants had been threatening violence against the castellans since at least 1503, no actual attacks took place until 1509 when peasant militiamen destroyed the little castle at Sterpo, an imperial fief granted to the Colloredo lords and surrounded by Venetian territory. Perhaps second only to the Savorgnan in the extensiveness of their holdings and closely allied to the Della Torre through several marriages, the Colloredo clan took its name and collective identity from the vast fortified complex at Colloredo di Monte Albano in the morainic hills. Like the Savorgnan, they held properties both in the Carnic alpine valleys from which they collected mutton and cheeses and in various places on the Friulan plain which provided them with grains, poultry, and wine. Unlike the Savorgnan, however, they owned little in Udine besides their palace.

The lands of Albertino Colloredo's branch were concentrated among the marshes on the left bank of the lower Tagliamento. The Colloredo also held six jurisdictions including Sterpo, all located on the lower plain. In 1502 Albertino obtained from his grandfather Febo Della Torre additional lands, the fortified house, and landworks in Sterpo; in 1508 he conceded them to his own son, Teseo. They remained in Colloredo hands until 1959. Because Sterpo was a fief of the count of Gorizia, Albertino carefully arranged to have Emperor-Elect Maximilian ratify Teseo's succession. During the campaign of 1509, moreover, Albertino and his son Odorico both served with the imperial forces, more openly declaring their allegiance than did most of their fellow castellans; Odorico died in 1510 fighting at Cormons on the imperialist side. The open affiliation of Albertino and his sons with the emperor became one of the principal motives in the 1509 assault, which combined an act of war with a rebellion over economic grievances.[45]

A document drawn up in 1502 for the imperial court describes Sterpo (Figure 5). Situated on wooded land between the Bua and Roia, streams which converged just below it, the castle had a circle of walls, themselves encircled by a moat fed by a ditch from the Bua. The only entrance was through a tower that guarded a bridge over the moat and the Roia. The modest castle buildings consisted of a cooking shed with attached pigeon roost, a three-room house with two roof terraces, a barn, and a minuscule chapel. The haphazardly built defensive works were uneven in height and strength. On the chapel side of the entrance tower the walls consisted of an earth embankment that merged into a more substantial wall of stone and rubble. Between the barn and the house there were no barriers at all, but in the final section between the house and the entrance tower stretched a foot-wide wall about five or six feet

FIGURE 5. Sterpo; moat and castle rebuilt after 1509.

high. Outside the walls on one side a natural swamp had been ex-
cavated to make a deep pond, and on the other the moat was deep
enough to prevent both men and horses from wading across. The
water barriers formed the real protection from intruders, and the
uneven walls seem to have been intended to provide cover from
shot and bombardment. Outside the moat a second, higher circuit
of walls offered some safety for the people of the village and their
animals, and if the additional, partially finished towers, walls, and
ditches had been completed there would have been better security
and more room for livestock. Near these walls clustered a handful
of rough-hewn, thatched hovels for the tenants. As insubstantial as
these fortifications may seem, during the Turkish invasion of 1499

they succeeded in providing a refuge for the peasants and livestock from many nearby villages.[46]

Compared with the grander castles of the hill country around Udine, humble Sterpo must have appeared almost ignoble. The swampy, mosquito-infested terrain and the climate, miasmal in summer and murky cold in winter, offered few allurements for pleasant living. Sterpo's principal attraction came from a location that made it a convenient place for gentlemen to stop over on the route between Udine and Venice.

Nevertheless, in the seven years before the peasant rebellion Albertino Colloredo and his sons attempted to transform Sterpo into the centerpiece of a more unified estate, even into a local market town. They required peasants from their widely separated properties to cart their rent payments to Sterpo, to mill their grain there (in an open challenge to the nearby Savorgnan mills at Belgrado, which charged cheaper rates), and to fulfill most of their *corvée* obligations in improving the fortifications and ditches around the castle.

Unfortunately, the Colloredos' attempts to commercialize their agricultural income, if indeed they had such coherent plans, took place during a period of depressed farm prices. The average price of wheat on the Udine market in the five-year period of 1501–5 compared with the 1506–10 period dropped by 18 percent (from 106 *soldi*, 2 *denari* to 84 *soldi* per *staro udinese*). During the same period rye fell nearly 15 percent (from 77s, 10d to 65s, 7d) and millet by 9 percent (from 50s, 10d to 45s, 5d). Only wine prices remained stable (falling only from 59s, 10d to 59s, 2d per *conzo udinese*). Although we cannot know how much Colloredo stewards sold on the Udine market, any attempt to raise capital through the rationalization of agricultural income would have involved carting commodities to sell in Udine, the only substantial market in the region. In addition, because Friulans preferred the white wines from the hill regions, lowland Sterpo was perforce grain country and thus was especially hurt by weak grain prices.[47]

In 1502 Albertino Colloredo's tenants consisted of 26 families in Sterpo proper and 143 others scattered among about forty villages throughout the lower plain. By 1509 the number of tenants increased in Sterpo to 29 but dropped to 129 in the other villages.

There were two types of proprietor-tenant contracts in force on the Colloredo estates, *affittanza* and *livello*, the simple *affittanza* far more numerous than *livello* contracts. The *affittanza* or *fitto* contracts were of variable duration, most commonly of nine years, and required the tenant to pay a fixed rent in kind at a defined place on a certain date. A *livello* contract lasted for twenty-nine years, which was approximately the working life of each generation, and would usually be considered by both proprietor and tenant to be perpetual and inheritable. *Livello* tenants paid a rent in kind similar to those under *affittanza*. Peasants who worked the land under the more common *affittanza* contracts suffered from greater insecurity of tenure than did those who enjoyed the longer terms of the *livello*, but these distinctions were often legal fictions because most peasants, no matter what their contractual status, were permanently subject to eviction because of their chronic inability to keep up with rent payments. The usual rent, in fact, significantly overvalued the productive capacity of the land. Although a few cultivators on the Colloredo rolls were able to pay their rents at the required level, many others never could, and nearly all might fall behind in a crisis year.[48]

In a study of other Friulan estates made from the extant rent-rolls dating between 1371 and 1453, yields in the three principal categories of grains—wheat, oats, and millet—exceeded the mandated level only in wheat on one estate in one year, the Strassoldo properties in 1435. The partial payments made in other years varied from only 9 percent of the millet due to the De Portis in 1447 to 97 percent of the wheat due to the Strassoldo in 1433 and 1434. On average only 67 percent of the wheat, 66 percent of the oats, and 59 percent of the millet due were ever paid. Permanent indebtedness was thus built into the agrarian rent structure. Proprietors did not just tolerate indebtedness, they required it, probably for social rather than economic reasons. Once a tenant family fell behind on their rent payments, they survived at the sufferance of the lord, who could legally evict them at any time. He could demand other kinds of services in lieu of rents and rid himself of troublesome, sick, or aging tenants. The system maximized the options open to the lord and eliminated almost all security of tenure for the peasants.[49]

Farmers in the lower Friulan plain rotated their crops in a three-field system, sowing wheat in one field in November and harvesting it in late July, oats in another field in November and reaping in May or June, and planting minor grains, such as millet, sorghum, rye, spelt, barley, or panic grass, in a third field later in the winter or even early spring. In Sterpo a typical tenant paid a rent composed of cereals and possibly some beans, wine, poultry, money, and labor services. For example, his contract obliged one Jacomo da Talmasons, nicknamed "the bishop" (Vescul), to two *stazi* of wheat, two of oats, one of beans, one of millet, three *conzi* of wine, two chickens, one ham, three guinea hens, thirty eggs, two cartloads of firewood, and two days work mowing hay.[50]

But neither Jacomo nor most of his neighbors were able to keep up. In 1497 in Sterpo proper six of the nine Colloredo tenants paid nothing at all whereas outside Sterpo about 36 percent failed to pay, and 28 managed only a partial payment. 1502 was one of the better years, but still only about half of the tenants brought full payments.

When rents came due in 1509, the Colloredo tenants faced a disaster. Barely more than one in ten had harvested enough to pay a full rent, and about two thirds would pay nothing at all that year. The precise motives for failure to pay in 1509 are hidden behind laconic notes in the rent-roll: "agreed that he need not pay," and the more common phrases, "he owes past rents," "he owes for last year," "he owes all the past rents," "she owes," "he owes," "they owe." The tenants from larger leaseholds were more likely to pay in full than the smaller, more marginal cultivators, who probably leased less productive land. The harvest of 1509 may have been particularly poor, but the major problem does not seem to have been just the bad harvest or a debt crunch, but Albertino and Teseo Colloredo's attitude toward their debtors.[51]

As we have seen, Antonio Savorgnan carried the debts of a large number of his own tenants and lent to many persons who were not tenants because such debtors became client followers. The Colloredo had no such interests. Whereas in 1508 Antonio Savorgnan made ninety-one loans to persons who were not his tenants in the jurisdiction of Buia alone, the Colloredo lords did not make a single loan to a nontenant in any of the years for which rent-rolls survive. Savorgnan's policy had been to provide relief in the form of loans for the overvaluation of the productive capacity of the land, thereby guaranteeing a large following of peasant-clients, whereas the Colloredo sought to maximize their profits and their ability to pick and choose tenants from among the pool of impoverished, landless peasants.[52]

The more traditional, aristocratic Colloredo were ironically making a more rational adjustment to the market than Antonio Savorgnan, himself a client of capitalist Venice. By the war years the Colloredo and perhaps many of their castellan colleagues, as well, had come to treat their estates as economic resources rather than as repositories for loyal clients and followers. It may not be an accident that all the Sterpo rent-rolls between 1503 and 1508 are missing. Obliterating records of debts was probably one of the motives for the 1509 assault on Sterpo castle.

The attack had both economic and military precipitants. Rents came due in July. Payments had been trickling in right up to the day of the assault, but many tenants were obviously not going to be able to pay. The military situation, however, provided both an excuse and the necessary organizational structure and leadership for measures against the landlords. The rural militias under the general captaincy of Antonio Savorgnan had been called up during the month in anticipation of the imperial army's siege of Udine.[53]

On July 14 under the pretext of needing to drill, a company of militiamen attempted to gain access to the castle at Valvasone, but a wary lord raised the drawbridge against them and ordered them to drill outside in the village streets. On July 30 Asquinio and Federico Varmo brought several hundred militiamen from Belgrado and Ariis to imperial Sterpo on the pretext that they needed to search the castle for munitions reportedly stored there to aid the enemy. Asquinio and Federico were influential leaders of the militias of the lower plain and well-known as clients of Antonio Savorgnan. Three of Antonio's closest associates, Ippolito Valvasone, Francesco Cortona, and Vicenzo Pozzo, joined the local forces. Although Belgrado and Ariis were Savorgnan jurisdictions, Albertino Colloredo had at least eighteen tenants in Belgrado and environs, but of course there is no way of knowing if any of them joined the militiamen at Sterpo. In any event, the leaders told the militiamen that Albertino Colloredo was a "rebel and had assembled a great deal of munitions to requisition to the enemy for use against Saint Mark." At the time only Albertino's son, Nicolò, and four retainers manned the castle. When they saw the peasants approaching, they raised the drawbridge quickly enough to block entry. Negotiating across the moat, the Varmo captains apparently convinced Nicolò that they merely wanted to search for weapons and would not harm him or the castle, but when he lowered the bridge, the peasant militiamen swarmed across. They seized the tower, sacked the castle, and set it afire. During the following days they and other local peasants tore the remains down to the foundations. Nicolò was captured and taken as a prisoner to Udine.[54]

The destruction of Sterpo castle permanently ruined the Colloredos' plans for the village. The rent-roll of 1513 notes "that the castle, mills, and houses that were in that place were ruined at the time that the nobles were persecuted by the peasants." Soon after the event Gregorio Amaseo estimated the damage at ten thousand ducats, but in 1530 when the heirs were finally able to submit claims for restitution, the estimate increased to fifteen thousand. The 1530 document lists as destroyed the castle "ruined down to its foundations," two towers, one mill, a house for the overseer, and other houses. Taken as plunder were 400 *stazi* of wheat, 100 of rye, 160 of spelt, 111 of millet, 13 beds, and blankets, sheets, table linens, wine, carts, cattle, horses, pigs, geese, and a deep-red cloak lined with the fur of a marten.[55]

Just as dramatic was the decline in the number of Colloredo tenants after 1509, a decline revealed by tracing the names of tenants from one rent-roll to the next. In Sterpo proper the number dropped from 29 in 1509 to 13 in 1510 and 1512 and only 6 by 1513. In the surrounding villages the number also lowered precipitously from 129 in 1509 to around 80 in the following years. But most of the tenants who disappeared from the Colloredo rolls were the least successful farmers, many of whom had obtained leases on marginal, perhaps newly cleared land. In fact the expansion of the number of leaseholds in Sterpo between 1502 and 1509 may indicate that the Colloredo were usurping parts of the common land for arable, which is precisely what the peasant syndics had been charging for years. The marginality of the new tenants put to farm the reclaimed commons can be shown by looking at the rent-rolls for the years after 1509. Although the total number of tenants declined, the percentage of those who could pay full rents increased markedly. In Sterpo in 1509 only 10 percent had been able to pay all the rent due, but by 1510 and 1512 about one third managed to pay a full rent, and by 1513 only one of the few remaining tenants could not manage to pay in full. In the other villages the percentage of surviving tenants who could pay in full increased from only 13 percent in 1509 to nearly 70 percent by 1512. In other words, those who survived were those who were most likely to be able to pay all their rents, and they could probably do so because they had the best land and labor resources.

If one looks only at those tenant families that remained on the same leasehold from one year to the next, the stable long-term tenants, the pattern becomes clearer. Although the ability of the tenants to pay a full rent increased after 1509, the lives of the tenants in Sterpo were seriously disrupted because more than three quarters of the long-term tenants disappeared after the destruction of the castle, and many more who survived 1509 left or died between 1510 and 1512. The good land was left, but the old families were gone.

In the other villages there was far greater stability, shown by the fact that about 90 percent of the tenants retained their leaseholds between 1509 and 1510 and a similar percentage between 1510 and 1512. Among these long-term tenants, in fact, the ability to pay off debts and to make up for rents missed in the past rose significantly after the destruction of Sterpo and again after the 1511 conflagration. Whereas between 1502 and 1509 only 13 percent of the surviving tenants outside Sterpo paid full rents in both years or increased their payments from one year to the next, between 1509 and 1510 and again between 1510 and 1512 more than 78 percent were able to do so. Finally, the loss of Sterpo as a center for Colloredo agricultural activities after 1509 can be confirmed by looking at the places to which tenants carted their produce to pay annual rents. In 1502 only four of all the tenants of Albertino Colloredo paid their rents in a place other than Sterpo. In 1509 there were only five. But by 1510 the number jumped to fifty-seven and by 1512 to seventy-eight, most of them hauling their rents to Udine, Colloredo di Monte Albano, or Zopolla.

The Colloredo lost nearly all that they had acquired at Sterpo, not only the castle fortifications and their own houses, but much of the income from their tenants, this at a time when their military obligations to the empire left them hard-pressed for cash. In the other villages, as in Sterpo, many of those who had owed back rents and who were burdened with debts disappeared from the rolls, and it seems likely that these indebted peasants, relegated to the inferior or smaller leaseholds, were the ones who looted and destroyed Sterpo castle and the rent-rolls listing their debts. Nevertheless, someone, perhaps Nicolò Colloredo himself, escaped with the 1509 roll, from which the situation can be reconstructed.

Although Luogotenente Gradenigo condemned the attack and conducted an investigation, the Venetian signoria tacitly excused it, probably because Albertino Colloredo was a public rebel and the leaders of the assault had Antonio Savorgnan's protection. No one ever suffered punishment. The Strumieri vainly demanded justice, and the Colloredo pursued legal channels to have their jurisdictional rights reestablished. About a year later, Pope Julius II excommunicated those who had pillaged Sterpo, but inasmuch as Sterpo lacked a priest no one suffered much from the distant indignation of His Holiness.

The attack on Sterpo castle, however, had wide-ranging effects in Friuli. Their success in challenging the Colloredo helped the peasants better articulate their needs and emboldened them to put together a list of demands, presented to the luogotenente in November. Sterpo also represented a crossing of the Rubicon for the Friulan factions. Both sides later looked to this event as the beginning of an almost inevitable slide into factional civil war.[56]

The peasants' November demands, the Eleven Articles or "supplication from every village in the patria," broaden the picture of general rural discontent of which the attack on Sterpo was only the most violent example. First, the most pressing demands of the twenty representatives who spoke before the luogotenente concerned the distribution of the Venetian *gravezze* and other taxes, which they argued were corruptly collected by deputies who made the peasants bear an unfair portion of the burden. Pointing out how loyal they had been in opposing the enemy during the past year, how they had shed blood and lost their property, they requested that a chancellor be appointed at their own expense to audit the accounts. Second, they complained that frequently the luogotenente had required them to sell their grain to him at a fixed price but later he would resell it at a higher price, defrauding them of any chance to make a profit. Third, they requested that there be a limit to the amount that itinerant judges (*gastaldi*) could charge communities when they came to represent the luogotenente in court cases. Fourth, notwithstanding the many prohibitions to the contrary, they wanted the right to sell bread, wine, and other necessities at market prices in their own villages. Fifth, noting that many lords had usurped the commons for their own use, thus making it impossible for the peasants to graze their animals, they asked that these communal lands be returned to their original state. Sixth, many villages had suffered considerable expenses when soldiers had passed through in transit, and these villagers wanted some consideration in the distribution of future taxes. Seventh, other villages had been pillaged by the stradiots serving Venice, and these victims deserved compensation. Eighth, some villages on the east side of the Tagliamento had already been given exemptions from some taxes because of storm damage to their crops, but the luogotenente had ignored these exemptions, which they wished to have restored. Ninth, inasmuch as many persons in the countryside were indebted to Jews from Udine who had sent out agents to confiscate collateral at a time when repayment was impossible because of the war, the peasants wanted one or two accountants paid by the debtors to examine the books and calculate the debts. Tenth, because many poor peasants had been paying extraordinary taxes, had borne the expenses of the war, and more often than not had lost their crops to the enemy, they wanted a moratorium on paying debts, "except for payments they wanted to make." And last, because some creditors had even sequestered crops in the fields of debtors, the peasants wanted all creditors to be required to go to court before they could confiscate unharvested crops.[57]

The Eleven Articles of the Friulan peasants are almost exclusively concerned with short-term economic problems engendered by the war and attempts to gain fuller access to the markets. In every case, they demand justice and fairness, envisioning practical reforms of society rather than a turning of the world upside-down. Theirs is a conflict within the social system, an attempt to make it work for themselves. Moreover, the complaints in the Eleven Articles are mostly about abuses by Venice and its agents—the luogotenente, his *gastaldi*, and soldiers fighting Venice's wars—or by the merchants of Udine, especially the Jewish bankers. The only antifeudal provision is the perennial complaint about the alienation of commons for private use. Thus, in many ways these articles represent a set of problems which did not entirely correspond to the situation in Sterpo. The burdens of indebtedness and the ravages of war were the same, but the articles address issues that would have been most important to the substantial farmers and independent peasants who sold produce on the Udine market and who dominated the village assemblies that wrote up the list of demands. The small cottagers of Sterpo who risked slipping into the fetid pool of day laborers suffered more from the exploitation of the Colloredo lords than from the bureaucrats of Venice and bankers of Udine and had to rely on their own collective force rather than legalistic petitions.

The articulate authors of the Eleven Articles, however, anticipated the peasants and townsmen who launched the great rebellions in the south Tyrol and upper Swabia during the 1520s and who went beyond their Friulan fellows by employing religious language to envision a different, more godly society. Protestantism provided a new law by which to measure the world. In contrast to the famous rebels inspired by Luther, neither the rebels of Sterpo nor the supplicants to the luogotenente made even the most conventional references to God, the Virgin, the saints, or the Bible. Their mental horizons limited what they thought could be done because no common religious or ideological aspirations bound together these various peasant groups, each with divergent economic grievances. But Antonio Savorgnan did. Speaking of all the castellans of Friuli in the aftermath of Sterpo, a contemporary commented, "the men of their jurisdictions do not want to obey their lords any more, and they recognize no other lord than Messer Antonio Savorgnan." The idea of a loyalty based on personal choice rather than tenant obligation was a revolutionary new concept, akin to the doctrine of election in its effect on the peasants. The peasants and their leader freely entered into a reciprocal relationship of mutual help which undermined the traditional hierarchy of feudal society. By giving shape to the peasants' desires, Antonio Savorgnan promised the only kind of salvation imaginable in Friuli, the salvation of revenge.[58]

CHAPTER FIVE

The Tempest of 1511

The gradually intensifying pressures of the Savorgnan-Della Torre vendetta, the polarization of the Zambarlano and Strumiero factions, the turbulence of war between Venice and the League of Cambrai, and the accumulated economic grievances of the Friulan peasants merged to create a terrible tempest during the carnival of 1511. What began as a clash in the streets of Udine between the followers of Antonio Savorgnan and the youthful enthusiasts of the Strumieri rapidly spread beyond the city and became the largest and most destructive peasant uprising in Renaissance Italy. The composite sources of the violence, finally let loose by the gathering for a festival of thousands of armed men, produced oddly hybrid forms of violence, in which participants improvised murder and mayhem, pillage and arson according to the ritual structures of vendetta practices and carnival.

Under the factional leadership of the Zambarlani, crowds in the city collectively murdered the Strumiero leaders whereas in the rural areas the faction soon dissolved into its component communities. There rioters pursued their own specific grievances against individual Strumiero landlords and limited themselves to pillage, arson, and a few rapes. The complexity of the forms of violence and the specificity of the objects of attack reveal how opportunity had created a strange coalition of Friulans who acted in concert not so much because they shared common objectives as because they shared a common culture of violence and found their mutual enemies suddenly vulnerable. After the Cruel Carnival the fragile Zambarlano hierarchy quickly disintegrated from the centrifugal forces of its own violence. The vendetta-revolt of 1511 followed more the logic of violence than the leadership of men or the dictates of a political agenda.

Armed Tension

Since the Sterpo assault, "all the poor castellans have stayed in their castles in great fear," as a contingent of Strumieri put it, "anxious not to be cut to pieces by the peasants and burned out as happened at Sterpo." The threat was not an idle one. In March 1510, peasants from Zompicchia, led by the militia captains who had been at Sterpo, attacked Alvise Della Torre, the Strumiero leader, and other castellans on the road from Venice where they had gone to complain about Antonio Savorgnan. Although the Strumieri escaped, the incident provoked several days of street fighting in Udine. Commenting about Venice's inability to pacify the factions after the Zompicchia confrontation, Gregorio Amaseo wrote that "one could accurately say that the lovely state of Venice lost her virginity on this one."[1]

With the Strumieri and Zambarlani testing and accusing one another, Antonio Savorgnan threatening a coup, and the enemy pillaging the countryside, ravished Venice allowed great pressures to build up in Friuli. An inept shuffle of provincial administrators did not help matters much. In October 1510 the latest vice luogotenente, Antonio Giustiniani, who had "in the turbulent past and dangerous times" earned a high reputation for himself back home, asked to return to Venice to take up a new position on the Council of Ten. Granting his request became problematic when the luogotenente himself, Alvise Gradenigo, who had been recovering from wounds received at the siege of Cividale in 1509, announced he could not yet assume his office. Despite the misgivings of a few, the Senate agreed to make some temporary arrangement. It sent Giustiniani's brother Orsato, without salary, expense account, or title, to govern Friuli until Alvise Gradenigo could resume his duties. During his brief stay Orsato failed to keep the disputants under surveillance.[2]

When Alvise finally arrived in Udine during the first week of the new year, one of the saluting cannons misfired, injuring five men, an accident "reputed by all to be the worst portent, as subsequent events would show." That very day, partisans of one faction killed a miller from the other. Gradenigo issued the usual New Year's decree against petty crimes such as blasphemy and impersonating priests and friars, to which he added provisions designed to prevent factional violence, such as orders against assembling without permission, assisting exiles, carrying weapons at night, and fighting. Public officials, surgeons, and grave diggers all had to report any injury or death that came to their notice. The government made its intentions clear, but that was about as far as it could go. In fact, the luogotenente faced the rapid deterioration of public order and lacked sufficient time to reestablish the delicate personal ties necessary to hold together the capricious collectivity and to keep the factions from one another's throats.[3]

In January when Venice finally lured Pope Julius II into a separate peace with a rich bribe of salt from the Comacchio beds, Venetian politicians relaxed with a false sense of security. Although the new peace brought some quiet to the southern front, Maximilian's mercenaries raided eastern Friuli with impunity from their winter quarters in Cormons and Gorizia. They specialized in nighttime sorties that terrorized helpless civilians, plundering, murdering, and burning whole villages while the Venetian army slept safely in garrisons and refused to go out on night patrols because of the difficulty of tracking the enemy in the dark. Even though the damage was limited to a small area, the surprise appearance of probable death and certain ruin, one night here the next there, thoroughly panicked the peasants and demoralized even those protected by city walls. Officials sent numerous letters and a delegation to Venice to plead for assistance, and finally on February 3 Giovanni Vitturi was promoted to provveditor general. On February 11 the Udine city council voted to send him on retaliatory strikes against the Cormons raiders.[4]

During the months of Venice's weakness and inaction each faction built up its forces. "Occasioned by that war, during which the authority of the glorious state of the Most Illustrious Venetian signoria ceased because it was overwhelmed," commented the diarist Gregorio Amaseo, "everyone took license and were prompted to push the government around and to abuse their adversaries." Antonio Savorgnan, or so his enemies asserted, provoked matters during the *interregnum* between luogotenenti by hiring fifty *bravi* in Venice and elsewhere and sending them to Spilimbergo to assist his followers there against exiles who were returning with forged safe conducts. The prickly castellans of Spilimbergo reacted quickly, secreting into their towers during the night two hundred peasant retainers from Zoppola and Fanna and securing the city gates. The *bravi* managed to talk their way out of town and retired to Udine where they spent their time swaggering about and daily provoking Savorgnan's enemies.

Toward the end of December, the *bravi* killed a Strumiero retainer, and on New Year's Eve Nicolò Maria Caporiacco, a member of Nicolò Colloredo's company, was assaulted and murdered in his own house. On Epiphany the Savorgnan thugs happened upon the unarmed, sixteen-year-old Francesco Candido, attacked him, and chased him into the courtyard of his father's palace. The Epiphany outrage prompted Teseo Colloredo and Sebastiano Monfalcone, perennial mainstays among the Strumieri, to hire their own squad of fifty foot soldiers.[5]

On January 25 Antonio Savorgnan, feeling secure and knowing that the Venetians needed him more than he needed them, tried a daring bluff. Claiming that the four leading Strumieri—Giacomo Castello, Alvise Della Torre, Teseo Colloredo, and Francesco Cergneu—"undoubtedly await Mysia and the coming of the Germans and are the worst enemies" of Venice, Savorgnan asked the signoria either to remove them or him from Friuli. Otherwise, he warned, the peace could not be maintained. Ignoring his advice, Venice exiled no one, encouraged all of the principals to reconcile themselves, and implored them to unite against the common enemy. His bluff having failed, Antonio and his retainers left Udine on February 15 to avoid a confrontation during the dangerous carnival holidays and went to Marano where, following a request from the Council of Ten, he was to supervise work on the fortifications.[6]

While he was gone, both sides continued to build up their forces, each claiming that whatever they did was merely for its own defense. Strumiero brigades formed under the leadership of the Candido, the Brazzacco, the Sandanieli, the Frattina, Sebastiano Monfalcone, and Francesco Pavona. The most noteworthy, however, were Teseo Colloredo and Nicolò Della Torre, who strutted about Udine with a band of forty men brandishing weapons, "bragging, and threatening." Giacomo Spilimbergo put together a force of five hundred infantrymen and fifty cavalry to defend his relatives and friends, and throughout the land people commented on the fact that in time of open war the castellans had failed to provide any contributions of soldiers but now found it so easy to put armed companies together.[7]

For his part, Antonio Savorgnan sent his favorite, Dr. Francesco Janis di Tolmezzo, back to Udine to organize the Zambarlano artisans and to gather a large company of peasant militiamen and followers to be billeted in Chiavris, a village on the outskirts of Udine in which the Savorgnan operated one of their mills. The ostensible reason for the mobilization was to guard the city against Austrian raiders. Other groups of Savorgnan supporters gathered in San Daniele, Venzone, Spilimbergo, Cividale, and elsewhere. On Sunday the twenty-third the luogotenente in Udine desperately tried to prohibit anyone of any rank from carrying arms day or night, but despite the assertion that the edict would be enforced "without respect of any person," no one was arrested.[8]

It is difficult to tell just what the factional leaders, let alone their many followers and friends, had in mind in these days before Giovedì Grasso. Later, with benefit of hindsight and under the necessity of justifying themselves, each side would accuse the other of following out a prearranged nefarious plan. Apologists for each charged the other with elaborate conspiracies devoted to taking advantage of Venetian irresolution and to fulfilling ancient dreams of total revenge.

The situation was, in fact, far less starkly clear. Charges of conspiracy were in part outright fabrications and in part self-delusions, guesses filtered through prejudice about what the others must have been up to. At the beginning of the week each faction looked toward Giovedì Grasso, the principal carnival day of revelry, as the time when the throngs of outsiders gathered to feast and play in Udine would give the other side special opportunities. Everyone wanted to be prepared for the worst. Although the events that followed could hardly have been fully planned by anyone, they could not have been entirely accidental either. Two pieces of evidence, a letter supposedly written by Alvise Della Torre and the surprising success of the Zambarlani, point to foreknowledge that there would be some sort of showdown on carnival Thursday.[9]

On Tuesday the twenty-fifth there was no overt violence, but brigade after brigade of armed peasant militiamen marched through town chanting "Savorgnan, Savorgnan" in open violation of Gradenigo's decree and in obvious provocation of the Strumieri. Many citizens hastened up the hill to the luogotenente's palace and urged him to do something. In the meantime, Antonio Savorgnan, forced, he said, by pleas from his friends that as long as he stayed away the entire populace of Udine was unprotected, returned from Marano accompanied by only five retainers. He knew "for certain" that the Strumieri conspired to kill him, but "wanting to come back to town in order not to lose reputation during the present war," he alerted some of his subjects along the way, and when he arrived in Udine a great gathering of followers protected him. He immediately conferred with Gradenigo to explain his reappearance, and although Antonio wanted first to consult with the signoria in Venice, the luogotenente insisted that he disband his followers immediately and accept a peace with the Strumieri. Antonio finally agreed, asking only to defer the peace pact until the next day. The luogotenente also convinced the Strumiero leaders to dismiss their men and join in a pact.[10]

By Wednesday a large crowd of outsiders, mostly Antonio's peasant clients and militiamen armed and ready for combat with someone, had arrived in town. Mingling with local artisans, they were unlikely to disband quietly and leave the city the day before the most Dionysian festival of the year. Antonio knew this. In an attempt to make the peace pact work, or so he later swore, Antonio invited about one hundred citizen and artisan leaders to his palace to persuade them to join him in an honest peace with the Strumieri. At sunset the luogotenente gathered the deputies and elders of Udine in one room, Antonio Savorgnan and his friends in another, and in a third the Strumiero leaders, Alvise and Nicolò Della Torre, Giovanni and Giovanni Battista Candido, Teseo Colloredo, Francesco Cergneu, Giovanni Leonardo Frattina, and Sebastiano Monfalcone. After separately haranguing each group, Gradenigo brought the principals together to solemnize the peace. They embraced and kissed one another on the mouth in front of a group of distinguished witnesses. It is not certain that the host was broken and shared at this peace ceremony, creating the "terrible obligation" of Florentine peace pacts, but the pledge was a serious matter, and those who blamed Savorgnan for breaking it thereafter called him Antonio Iscariot.[11]

The pact may not have been, as partisans of both sides later claimed, an empty ritual that masked the devious intentions of some of the participants, as much as an utterly inadequate resolution of a perilous situation. Alvise Gradenigo had neither guaranteed the safety of anyone nor had he the manpower to divide up the many dangerous groups and force them out of the city. And that very night the Austrians mounted another raid.

During the evening the leaders of each faction gathered separately to assess the prospects for a lasting peace and found themselves pessimistic about the chances that the other side would keep the pact it had sworn to preserve. To some, the peace may have just bought time, but none could have avoided the appearance of keeping the peace. Antonio Savorgnan, at least formally, dismissed his followers. One of these, Sebastiano Vicentino from Paperiano near Fiumicello where Antonio had some properties, later testified that he arrived that day with twenty armed men and went to the Savorgnan palace. He recalled that after the peace Antonio's son Nicolò thanked them for their support and announced that in the morning they were to go home. They were then billeted out for the night. Antonio seemed sincere about the peace, but he sent a message to the luogotenente asking him to advise Alvise and Nicolò Della Torre and Teseo Colloredo to leave town the next morning and to spend carnival on their estates to prevent any "outrage," indicating that he must have known that even if he had wanted to, he could not control his followers. Unfortunately none of the three lived to confirm whether or not he received any warning from the luogotenente.[12]

That evening, however, witnessed a sweet interlude. The Savorgnan clan, their friends, and guests gathered for a ball that lasted late into the night at the house of Maria Savorgnan, widow of Girolamo's brother Giacomo and sometime mistress of the famous humanist, Pietro Bembo, who was also a mentor to Luigi da

Porto, the nephew of Antonio Savorgnan. Singing to the accompaniment of a clavichord, a rare sixteen-year-old beauty cast a delicious spell over the evening. Even sour Gregorio Amaseo interrupted his long invective against the Judas Antonio to recall her enchantments, and at least one young soldier fell in love with her, probably on that evening. She was Maria and Giacomo's daughter Lucina, the second cousin of Antonio. The love-smitten soldier was da Porto, who had already earned local acclaim for his courage in the guerrilla skirmishes against the imperial mercenaries on the eastern frontier and would later achieve lasting fame for his literary and historical writings. Luigi was close to Antonio, who had entrusted the youth with delicate and difficult missions.

As Cecil Clough has cleverly argued, the memory of this magical evening, framed as it was by anxiety and blood, became the seed for a great story. Years later, half-paralyzed by a battle wound from which no one thought he could recover, Luigi sat in his villa in the Vicentino and wrote a *novella* about love and hate set among the towers of Verona, which he could see from his convalescent's window. He titled it *Giulietta e Romeo*. Shakespeare, of course, would later transform Luigi's story into a far greater play. He dedicated the *novella* to none other than Lucina Savorgnan, by then married off to another of Antonio's nephews, Francesco, and the dedication barely disguises in Petrarchan dress Luigi's lost love for her. Perhaps in memory of his mentor's past love affair with Lucina's mother, he sent one of the first copies to Pietro Bembo for comment.[13]

Although da Porto's *Giulietta e Romeo* was a literary creation rather than disguised history, and fortunately neither Lucina nor Luigi met Juliet's or Romeo's fates, their separation was a sad and probably inevitable one. Although they were not members of opposing factions as were the star-crossed lovers, they belonged to a badly divided clan; Girolamo Savorgnan was Lucina's guardian, and Luigi had the misfortune to meet her when his uncle and patron Antonio's relations with Girolamo were at their nadir.

During the evening the Strumieri celebrated carnival with a banquet hosted by Alvise Della Torre. In an after-dinner palaver Francesco Cergneu recommended that each lord remove himself to his country castle as the best way of guaranteeing safety and as the only way of making the peace work. Francesco was an unlikely

pacifist; unlettered and quarrelsome, he was known for his soldierly abilities, having commanded the reluctant feudal cavalry at
the defense of Udine in 1509, and for his animosity toward Antonio Savorgnan, who in turn described Francesco as "seditious,
wretched, and beggarly."[14]

The voice of reason which he uncharacteristically offered was
quickly hushed. Opposed to Francesco's counsel was Teseo Colloredo, who had first hired foreign *bravi* back in January and who
arrived that evening with a large company of armed retainers.
Both Francesco Cergneu and Teseo Colloredo included themselves
in the inner circle of leaders around Alvise Della Torre, and each
had his own constituency. Teseo argued that he would not allow
himself to be dishonored by fleeing, and he soon convinced the
others, isolating Francesco, who reluctantly agreed to stay.

That night Alvise Della Torre wrote a letter to report the news
of peace to the lords of Spilimbergo, who still waited at their castle
with a large following of *bravi*. Later the letter became the critical
piece of evidence used to document Strumiero bad faith. Everyone,
even partisans of the Della Torre, accepted its authenticity. In it
Alvise abused the Zambarlani and minimized their threat: "this
beast of Antonio Savorgnan . . . has been put to such flight that he
does not dare show his face." According to the letter, although
Savorgnan brought eight hundred peasants in by various roads,
when he saw how well prepared the Strumieri were he ran to the
luogotenente to beg for a peace. Alvise, averring that he himself
had accepted the peace only for convenience's sake because he did
not believe it would last long, asserted that the other side wanted
it not only as a deception but to gain reputation. Finally, warning
the Spilimbergo lords to keep their eyes open and to stand united
with him because their mutual enemies wished to rob them of all
power and honor, Alvise offered the military services of his own
friends and servants. Alvise entrusted the letter to a servant of
the Spilimbergo lords, who was to slip out of Udine when the
city gates opened at dawn. Neither messenger nor message ever
arrived.[15]

THE CRUEL CARNIVAL OF UDINE

The next day was Giovedì Grasso. In normal times gluttonous,
drunken Fat Thursday was the favorite festival in Udine, but in-

stead of playing light music, as Giovanni Battista Cergneu would later put it, the Udinesi gathered for war. Antonio Savorgnan would also later recall several Strumiero predictions of a slaughter for that day, declarations of intent which shifted blame from himself to the victims of the massacre. It was reported that public physician Leonardo Guberto, a passionate devotee of the Strumieri, had said a few days before, "I have studied this matter and I find that on Giovedì Grasso there will be revenge by massacre which in Udine will be extensive, and many people will be killed." The recollections of others suffered from the excessive appositeness of hindsight. Former grand captain of Udine and future prisoner for treason Giovanni Candido declared on Thursday morning that his enemies "long to have a delightful Giovedì Grasso, but they are going to eat the bitterest fritters they have ever eaten in their lives." And finally but least probably the *enfant terrible* of the Della Torre clan, Nicolò, declaimed as he slipped on his woolen gloves to go outside on the last day of his life, "today we are going to have a Sicilian Vespers."[16]

The Strumiero prognostications alluded to the faction's own alleged plan to help imperial troops capture the city while the Zambarlano militiamen debauched themselves in festive revelry. There is some evidence to support the idea of a Strumiero conspiracy with the imperialist captains. Antonio Savorgnan cited several witnesses who reported that one hour after sunrise fifteen hundred enemy cavalry and infantry equipped with ordnance appeared outside Pradamano. Their captain asked among the peasants if the gates of Udine were guarded and if riots had broken out yet. Many others repeated this intelligence uncritically, but Strumiero survivors always denied any such conspiracy and even accused Antonio of having plotted with the enemy.[17]

To counter the supposed imperialists' threat, Antonio called out the militiamen and his other followers, a combined company of twenty cavalrymen and an estimated fifteen hundred armed infantry who sallied forth from the Aquileia gate to meet the enemy (Figures 6, 7, and 8). The ringing tocsin closed the shops and brought artisans to arms at posts on the outer walls of the city. After wandering about for some three hours and failing to engage anyone, the militias returned to Udine and as they entered the gate chanted, "Savorgnan, Savorgnan."

In the meantime Alvise Della Torre's messenger to Spilimbergo had been captured, and the letter secreted in his boot was brought to Savorgnan, who hurried with this document of insult and possible bad faith to the luogotenente. While the two were conferring they heard a tumult rise up from the city below.[18]

Most of the Strumiero nobles had already gathered at Alvise Della Torre's palace for another banquet or returned there when they heard that the messenger to Spilimbergo had been captured. Nicolò Della Torre joined his uncles Alvise and Isidoro; Teseo Colloredo and Francesco Cergneu, who had debated on strategies the night before, were there together with Giovanni Leonardo Frattina and his nephew Apollonio Gorghi; Giovanni Battista Candido, the cousin of Nicolò Della Torre; Antonio Arcoloniano; Sebastiano Tomasi di Monfalcone and his son Felice; Agostino Partistagno and his four sons Ercole, Girolamo, Francesco, and Alessandro; Francesco Guarienti and his son Troiano; young Bernardino Pavona; and others, mostly youths, boys, and retainers. Outside a pro-Savorgnan crowd of between two and four thousand, consisting mostly of artisans and plebs from Udine but also including about three to eight hundred peasants, surrounded the palace and began a siege that wore on for hours until the defenders escaped. The crowd then plundered and burned the palace; later some twenty-one witnesses would testify that they saw looters take out a large chest full of money and carry it to Savorgnan's house.[19]

Meanwhile in the vicinity of the burning palace a manhunt began for the escaped Strumiero nobles. The leaders of the hunt included several "attendants and dogs of the house of Savorgnan": Giovanni di Leonardo Marangone di Capriglie called Vergon ("lime-twig," a stick smeared with a sticky substance made from holly bark and used to catch small birds, was a nickname applied to a deceitful, predatory person), Bernardino di Narni, Guglielmo di Marco Floriti da Venzone called Tempesta (the storm), Giovanni Pietro Fosca, Zuanetto di Pietro del Pizol called Il Piccolo (shorty), Matana (stingray or in Venetian a migraine headache), Smergon (loon, which was noted for its ability to dive into water to escape hunters, was used as a nickname for a crafty person), Viso (the face), and "the Ferrarese."

The blame for much of what followed fell on the heads of these men because either they served as useful scapegoats or they were act-

FIGURE 6. Drawing of Antonio Savorgnan and his militiamen outside Udine on the morning of Giovedì Grasso, 1511.

ing on their own initiative. Vergon and Narni served as the "principal executioners" of this "dog pack," and the former boasted of personally striking down some of the most important Strumiero nobles. Both would later disappear, leading many to speculate that Antonio Savorgnan had them killed because they knew too much or had held back too much loot; others said they killed each other in a fight over spoils. The ten, however, could not confirm the deaths, and although two unidentifiable bodies turned up in a well, in 1515 the ten banished Vergon, whereabouts unknown. Tempesta, who had precipitated the battle by confronting Nicolò Della Torre earlier in the day, would escape four days later to Feltre, face

FIGURE 7. Udine; Palazzo del Comune (1448–56).

FIGURE 8. Udine; casa Veneziana (fifteenth century) was one of the few palaces that survived the events of 1511.

banishment from the Venetian dominion, and eventually be executed in Rome. Piccolo and Matana would later suffer exile, but of this group only the Ferrarese, a painter who served as Savorgnan's falconer, would be unlucky enough to land in a Venetian jail, where he would languish for four years until he was drawn and quartered in 1515.[20]

Four others who were not actually retainers of Savorgnan also became known as instigators on Giovedì Grasso. Simone Scraiber, a scrivener and procurator from an honorable family, suffered the same fate as the Ferrarese despite an attempt by a group of armed peasants to rescue him as he was being dragged off for confinement. Alvise Spilimbergo and one Antonio, retainer of the gentleman Giovanni Vitturi but also a crony of Tempesta, suffered banishment, and a mysterious Morgante was eventually executed in Cividale. There were also numerous accusations that Antonio Savorgnan's half-brother Pietro and Antonio's bastard son Nicolò both participated personally in the fray.[21]

These men constituted, to use Canetti's apt phrase, the "crowd crystals," that small unified body of men who served to precipitate a crowd. The most ardent in the resulting group hunted down and killed, the less valiant merely watched gang murder. Most would enjoy the safety of anonymity, the collective nature of their actions transforming assassination into an unofficial public execution. The killers saw themselves as the executors of justice, as acting in the name of Venice and the lord Savorgnan to do what the officials wanted but could not do themselves. An apparent confluence of interests, those of Venice which wished to check the philoimperialists, those of Savorgnan who longed to crush his hereditary enemies, and those of the poor who feared that the castellans sought to return them to servility, made massacre possible.[22]

Stimulated by these men, the crowd systematically searched through neighboring houses for the Della Torre and their allies. Isidoro Della Torre, wounded in the flight from the Della Torre palace, found refuge with the Sbroiavacca. When the crowd invaded the house, they found Isidoro lying on a bed and attacked him twice. The second time Girolamo Arlatto, a member of the Udine city council, struck him on the head with a hatchet and left him for dead. Unlike most of the other victims, Isidoro made a final confession and, pardoning his enemies before his death three days later, became a Strumiero martyr: his corpse "filled the room with a most sweet odor to the extreme amazement of those around him and only he among all those killed was buried in the ancient sepulcher of his ancestors."[23]

Isidoro Della Torre's brother, the hearty sixty-year-old Alvise, head of the faction, met a far more miserable fate. He and Apollonio Gorghi hid in the wine vault of the palace of the patriarchal vicar, which is where the Ferrarese and some others discovered them. A shoemaker named Giacomo Vicentino later testified about what happened. Alvise's end was not dignified. He offered a large treasure in exchange for his life, but when Vergon entered the cellar he ignored the proffered ransom and simply slit Alvise's throat. Antonio Savorgnan, who had not known what was going on, came upon the scene and found Vergon torturing Alvise as the latter slowly bled to death; Savorgnan vainly ordered his retainer to stop. The men with Vergon were mostly peasants from Zompicchia, where Alvise had been attacked the year before. They stripped him of four hundred ducats and his clothes and dragged his still half-alive, naked body by the foot into the streets, chanting "here is the traitor." His death was a collective execution in the fullest sense: he was trampled and stoned and his corpse desecrated in the mud.[24]

After dark the looting and burning spread. Next door to the Della Torre, the palace of Francesco Cergneu went up in flames, quickly followed by part of the Guarienti house on the same street. The throng sacked the house of Sebastiano Monfalcone, who had marched the Strumiero *bravi* through the streets of Udine only days before; he found refuge among the nearby Franciscan friars, as did Leonardo Gubertino.

Worse fortune visited Soldoniero Soldonieri. Driven from his house by the flames, he and his two daughters, one a widow and the other a maiden, "among the most beautiful in the city," ran into a band of men who were out searching with lighted torches for refugee nobles. The assailants dispatched several Soldonieri familiars and attacked the already badly wounded old man, but the daughters threw themselves on top of their father to protect him. The younger was herself hurt when the men tore a strand of pearls from her neck. They left the three bathed in the father's blood. The daughters found refuge for their dying father in a neighboring house. Later Simone Scraiber came to find him, and although Soldoniero begged to be allowed to die in peace, Scraiber insisted he had to be moved for his own security; Scraiber's men carried him in a chair followed by the two daughters and a widowed sister. All went well until the little procession reached the cemetery of San Francesco where the captors threatened to cut off Soldoniero's head right there unless given one hundred ducats. One of the women ran to a friend and produced a rich silver belt, but after dividing up the silver pieces from the belt, Scraiber reneged on his promise and whistled for his followers who rushed out and murdered the old man anyway.[25]

Although Antonio certainly permitted, if not encouraged, the extinction of all the adult males in the Della Torre clan, he opposed certain excesses, epitomized by the fate of Soldoniero and his daughters, as can be seen by his actions during Thursday night and the succeeding days when he saved the lives of several Strumiero nobles and sent out trusted servants to contain the spread of violence in the countryside. The crowd and its leaders had their own agenda, which they pursued in the name of Antonio Savorgnan but which went beyond his orders.

Antonio's character manifested many complexities, and his position at the pinnacle of a vast but fragile patronage system necessitated the pursuit of seemingly contradictory actions. For example, Antonio later testified that he himself went to the house of Ascanio Sbroiavacca, in which many nobles had found refuge, and brought to safety in his own palace Francesco Cergneu and his son-in-law Troiano Guarienti, Giovanni Battista Candido, Agostino Partistagno and his three sons, Felice di Sebastiano Monfalcone, and Antonio di Francesco Gorghi. He also personally rescued three of the Brazzacchi from the house of Giovanni Zucco and conducted them to the monastery of San Pietro Martire. Savorgnan's intervention saved some twelve nobles in all. Thus, whatever fate he had desired for the Della Torre, he certainly did not organize a systematic massacre of Strumieri.[26]

However, some of Savorgnan's followers found Tolmezzo's aphorism, "dead men don't fight back," more to their liking than Antonio's apparent caution. When the rioters swarmed into his palace, Federico Colloredo fled to the Roncho gate tower, but a peasant revealed his hiding place. The Ferrarese arrived to talk Colloredo into surrendering by offering a safe conduct to Savorgnan's palace, and after a long resistance Federico saw no alternative and surrendered. Despite their promises his captors killed him and badly mutilated his body as they had the others.[27]

In feeding their own appetite for revenge, the Colloredo family would long remember one particularly shameful detail about the murder. The Ferrarese's gang refused to allow the corpse to be buried, leaving it in the open for a pack of dogs to tear apart and eat. More than fifty years later this particular detail would still be recalled with a shudder, held up and thrown back at the Savorgnan at every opportunity.[28]

The denial of burial to the victims resulted more from systematic choices than from the hazards of chance. Apollonio Gorghi's crying mother had not been allowed to recover his body, Alvise Della Torre was left in the open for three days, and several bodies were abandoned to Udine's roaming pigs and dogs. In late March the stink from a well drew an investigation. Authorities extracted three bodies, one of a strangled woman identified as a servant of the Castello family and two of unidentified men who some speculated were the missing Savorgnan *bravi*, Vergon and Bernardino di Narni, but who were probably Strumiero victims hidden from proper burial. The rioters threw other corpses into caves, wells, and latrines, probably less in an attempt to cover up evidence of killings that had been openly committed in the streets than to deny proper Christian burial to the hated nobles and to condemn their souls to wander among the armies of the dead. During Thursday night a Paduan priest, Bernardino Manzatore, gathered as many bodies from the streets as he could and placed them in a newly built tomb in the façade of the cathedral. Venetian officials came that night to examine the dead; the next morning many filed by to take a look, but the corpses were so badly disfigured they could not be recognized.[29]

The carnival killers revealed a particular *modus operandi*: they murdered, mutilated or dismembered, prevented the burial of their victims, and fed the remains to street scavengers. More than just cruel brutality, this pattern evolved out of carnival itself and reveals the peculiar bond between the body-centered nature of carnival imagery and the style of vendetta murder. In revenge as in carnival, the human body and its parts produced the vocabulary and syntax for symbolic communications.

The luogotenente finally called for outside help from Teodoro Del Borgo, who rushed his one hundred heavy cavalry units from Gradisca to Udine, arriving about three hours after sunset on Friday. As roguish pantomimes displaced murder and fire, more troops marched into Udine, and by Ash Wednesday Antonio Savorgnan's old Venetian friend, Andrea Loredan, then serving as a head of the Council of Ten, arrived and promptly began an investigation.

The Cruel Carnival of Udine consisted of a series of collective murders, mostly by the henchmen of Antonio Savorgnan backed by a large crowd of artisans and peasants, and the victims were exclusively members of the Strumieri. Despite its intensity the looting and violence were confined to specific targets chosen more by the dictates of vendetta than by military necessity. The urban riots had lasted little more than two days, during which some seventeen to twenty-two palaces were sacked or burned, and between twenty-five and fifty of the most influential nobles and their retainers were killed. With the show of force the artisans retreated and the peasants left town, but at the same time the flames of discontent spread into the countryside where more looting and burning put the remaining castellans to flight.[30]

CASTLES BURN

The peasants who wandered out of Udine spread word of their successes. The news encouraged many others across the countryside to take advantage of the castellans' sudden vulnerability that had been created when many of the aristocrats went to Udine to aid the Della Torre, leaving the rural estates occupied only by women, children, and servants. At least in the early stages, the pillagers included others besides local peasants: those forced out of Udine, roaming bands of retainers and clients of Antonio Savorgnan, Udinese artisans, and errant militiamen. But as the disturbances spread, assaults came more often from local peasants acting alone without any outside leaders. The henchmen of the faction yielded to local community leaders. Although the example of Udine stimulated violence elsewhere, each rural community pursued its own particular grievances. Only through a detailed comparison of the locations of peasant turbulence can the geographic distinctions between violent and peaceful villages be explained. In most cases more is known about the objects of attack than about the attackers, and thus grievances and motives can be inferred only from telltale clues found in descriptions of the damage wrought.[31]

The uprising at Sterpo and the promulgation of the Eleven Articles of the Friulan peasants in 1509 disclosed the widespread problems created by the agrarian crisis and the absorption of aggrieved peasants into the military arm of the Zambarlano faction; but in contrast to the vaguely anti-Venetian orientation of the articles, the rural attacks on persons and property in 1511 betray intensely antifeudal and antiimperialist sentiments. Thus, whatever the long-term or immediate causes of discontent, factional identity determined the appropriate objects of violence and gave the attacks their public rationale.

The rural revolt can be divided into four areas of activity. The Tagliamento River created the traditional administrative division between the eastern and western halves of lower Friuli, the halves further subdivided into quadrants by the heavily populated hills to the north and the swampy lowlands near the Adriatic. On the left bank of the Tagliamento, within the broad amphitheater of hills, the most intensely concentrated attacks on noble property took place. In this cluster of villages and castles near Udine, where communal and feudal jurisdictions intertwined and the population density was high, peasants could actually hear the uproar from the villages down the road or across the shallow valleys. There the rebellion spread like wildfire.

Villalta, Moruzzo, and Brazzacco shared a common fate, created by their geographic situation and the personal connections among their castellan families. Here clustered some of the most prominent Strumiero families whose jurisdictional privileges contrasted with the autonomy of a commune, which was nearby, and the paternalistic lordship of Antonio Savorgnan, who also had a large fief in the area. From neighboring mounds each of the castles guarded important roads.

The most important of these fortifications was Villalta, where the Della Torre were lords. Villalta consisted of a pair of towers

FIGURE 9. Villalta; main tower gate of the castle.

and a ring of double walls surrounding a large keep that had been recently transformed into an elegant residence (Figure 9). The buildings overlooked the Udine-Spilimbergo road, but since the Venetian conquest the site had lost its strategic value.

Half of the fortress and its lands and the right to exercise jurisdiction every other year had come to the Della Torre family with the dowry of Giovanna Caporiacco in 1433. After 1473, when Alvise and Isidoro jointly inherited the castle and estate from their father, the two began to buy up lands in the area, the pace of acquisitions quickening during the first decade of the new century. The rapid growth of the Della Torre brothers' land holdings had two important results: first, because Antonio Savorgnan was buying up lands in the same area the struggle between the two families for predominance concentrated here; and second, many of the

Della Torre tenants were relatively new dependents of the family, a fact that made them particularly susceptible to the allurements of the neighboring Zambarlani.[32]

A network of Strumiero alliances bound Villalta to Moruzzo and Brazzacco. Alvise Della Torre's first cousin Cassandra had married Francesco Arcoloniano, consort of Moruzzo along with his brothers Antonio and Troilo, both of whom had been hounded by the carnival killers in Udine. The castellans of Brazzacco were the Cergneu, who looked for leadership to Francesco, the same man who had argued for moderation at the meeting in Alvise Della Torre's palace on the eve of the Giovedì Grasso attack. Moruzzo and Brazzacco formed odd jurisdictional islands in which the lords heard the criminal and civil cases of a tiny area around their castles whereas cases from the villages in the vicinity, even those involving the castellans' tenants, were tried in the town of Fagagna. In Moruzzo, for example, the lords had originally held the castle, lands, and twelve villages in fief, but the jurisdiction went to the Gastaldia of Fagagna. In 1474, however, the Arcoloniano lords received jurisdiction over the castle, but the villages remained under Fagagna. These minuscule islands of feudal privilege aggravated the inequities of local justice, about which the residents frequently complained in the years before the revolt.[33]

No one harmed any of the noble inhabitants of these three castles, and those who forced entry restricted themselves to plundering. A considerable amount of movable goods disappeared, including household furnishings, clothing, foodstuffs, and a chest from Brazzacco containing a rich hoard variously estimated at between one and three thousand ducats. The actual physical destruction of the castles, frequently exaggerated by contemporary partisans of the Strumieri, varied greatly from place to place. Amaseo reported that at Villalta "most of their [the Della Torre] castle was looted and ruined," but by September 1512, if not before, the building had been reoccupied. As at Sterpo peasants quite systematically burned rent-rolls and other seigneurial records. The Della Torre later swore that their inability to document their jurisdiction over two nearby villages stemmed from the fact that most of their papers were burned in 1511.[34]

From the environs of the Della Torre stronghold at Villalta, disturbances spread to the properties of the allied Colloredo clan. Just to the north of the communal jurisdiction of Fagagna and beyond the first range of hills several other great castles clustered. Like Sterpo, three of these (Susans, Mels, and Colloredo di Monte Albano) constituted part of the vast Colloredo-Mels patrimony that was second in size only to that of the Savorgnan. A 1523 Colloredo rent-roll lists tenants in some sixty different locations, many concentrated in the region between Villalta and Mels but others found even within the autonomous Savorgnan jurisdictions at Buia, Belgrado, and Savorgnan.

The number of tenants (and therefore the Colloredos' potential influence) and the kind of contract (*livello* or simple *affittanza*) varied greatly in each location. In Udine the counts had only three *livello* tenants, one of whom did not pay anything in 1509, 1510, or 1511. In Fagagna there were seven manses, in San Daniele only one, and in the Savorgnan stronghold of Buia, nine, some of whom paid *livello* and some *affittanza*. In Susans the Colloredo occupied the newly rebuilt palace and had thirty-four tenants, and although they were rarely in residence at Mels where the castle was probably in poor repair, they had some eleven tenants who tilled about three quarters of the arable land there. The greatest concentration was at Colloredo itself, where the consorts had erected a huge fortified complex; exercised jurisdictional rights of *misto et mero imperio* over the castle and five villages; enjoyed usage rights over pastures, woods, ponds, and streams; collected one third of the income from mills and baking ovens; received rents from forty-two tenants in Colloredo itself and many more in the neighboring villages; and monopolized the Colloredo vote in the parliament of Friuli. Within the jurisdiction there were only two or three other small property holders besides the consorts.[35]

The Colloredo holdings formed an odd hodgepodge created by centuries of acquisitions and losses through dowries, inheritances, sales, and purchases. The family records boast about the influence the consorts enjoyed in the places in which they collected rents from most of the land and had jurisdictional privileges. It was in these areas of concentrated Colloredo power that some of the most intense disturbances broke out: in 1509 in Sterpo and in 1511 in Colloredo di Monte Albano, Susans, and, less forcefully, Mels.

On Friday, February 28, the day after two members of the family had been killed and their property pillaged in Udine, Colloredo

and Susans came under attack. At Colloredo the consort Tommaso
fled with his family; local villagers held Gregorio Colloredo captive for some time, but the other consorts suffered only losses of
household furnishings and supplies of food, much of which was
later returned. The assault seems to have concentrated on the movable property and portions of the castle belonging to Albertino,
the consort whose fortress had been destroyed at Sterpo. His house
at Monte Albano was burned to its foundations. Regarding Susans,
the consorts recorded in a rent-roll for 1513, "we had in the place
where the castle had been a palace or house that was burned at the
time of the looting of 1511 a little after Giovedì Grasso when the
nobles were persecuted by peasants and everything found in that
house was stolen." Vines were also cut and a supply of lumber
burned.[36]

In the same area an episode in defense of the castles of Mels,
Pers, Caporiacco, and Arcano, which fortified positions overlooking a stream named the Corno, generated another of the famous
stories of Giovedì Grasso. Tenants from the nearby villages threatened these four castles with looting and burning, but intervention
by Antonio Savorgnan's agents halted the onslaught, at least temporarily. According to his own account, Nicolò Monticolo went
to Pers to rescue some of his relatives. While in flight, Tommaso
Colloredo met Nicolò at Pers and persuaded him to return to Colloredo di Monte Albano. There Nicolò released Gregorio Colloredo from captivity, restored to the family much of their pillaged
property, including eleven beds (the valuable symbol of aristocratic
comfort), and organized a guard consisting of a knight of the
luogotenente, a priest, and four men from Buia, the nearby collection of hamlets under Savorgnan control. Nicolò later wrote that
had he not intervened the castle would have been leveled to its
foundations.[37]

After returning to Pers, Nicolò met Bernardino Pers, a Strumiero nobleman, and rode toward the smoke rising from Arcano.
There they heard that the castellan's wife, Regina, had fled into the
woods, finding refuge in a cave. More than sixty armed peasants
hunted for her, some watching from hill tops, others, like "dogs
after a scent," searching for her through the dells. The two gentlemen finally found her refuge and brought the distraught woman
and her sister-in-law to safety.

Again Nicolò and Bernardo set off toward distant smoke and at Caporiacco found the humble house of the consort Giovanni Antonio aflame and nearby, crying on the bank of a ditch, his disheveled wife holding an infant. She joined the other refugees in a cart, which headed for the relative security of Pers. Once they had arrived, Regina Arcano asked Nicolò to return to save some of the valuables that she had hidden in a tomb in the Arcano church. When Nicolò arrived there he discovered the chaplain and four peasants dividing up Regina's things. He chased them off and brought back the salvaged property. Nicolò said of himself using the third person that "Monticolo went on to save the castle of Pers and the castle of Mels, which were not touched because he is a very close friend of Antonio Savorgnan and known by everyone as a person of great authority and power, who was nevertheless much loved, and when he was not there anymore, these two castles were not only looted but destroyed."[38]

Monticolo pictured himself as a chivalrous knight saving innocent ladies from house fires, freezing cold, and ruffian rapists. His story has a narrative structure that is almost too pat, and his assessment of the amount of damage to these castles is not entirely sustained by other sources. His tale begins with his intervention at Colloredo di Monte Albano to rescue a prominent noble and to save the property of one of Antonio Savorgnan's most bitter enemies. There follows the remarkable episode of the beautiful lady hiding in a cave from vengeful rustics, and then a maudlin scene of the weeping mother abandoned on the bank of a ditch, and finally the victory over impiety when Nicolò retrieves his lady's treasures from the greedy chaplain and his fellow grave robbers.

There is an element of truth to all of this inasmuch as others reported that Monticolo intervened in some way, but his own version of the events best serves as an example of the transformation of experience into a chivalrous fantasy. In like fashion, most of the indigenous aristocratic sources minimize the autonomy of peasant actions, attributing all *virtù* and leadership to nobles. In contrast to such heroic illusions, the peasants' own materialist values and the absence of a broad reformist, revolutionary, or millenarian ideology limited their objectives and prevented coordinated political action.

In addition to the assaults on castles, the two proper towns in the area, Fagagna and San Daniele, witnessed disturbances during the days after Giovedì Grasso. Most of the inhabitants made their living from tenant farming, making them socially similar to the villagers in the surrounding countryside. The juridical situation in each town juxtaposed communal autonomy with feudal dependence in a conflict-inducing way. The castellan nobles had absolute control over the fortress but no legal privileges in the town itself whereas the commune could not exercise its jurisdictional rights within the castle walls.

Just as in Moruzzo and Brazzacco, rioters in Fagagna limited their looting to the castellan enclaves, especially the houses of the nobles Nicolò and Daniele. However, in San Daniele they caused more extensive damage. The jurisdiction of the town remained in the hands of the patriarch of Aquileia, who exercised his rights through a *gastaldo*. After the townsmen looted and burned the houses of Tommaso di San Daniele and his brothers, the lords of the castle, the patriarch excommunicated the culprits. In both towns, however, the rioters limited themselves to damaging property. Thus, the most intense concentration of peasant disturbances appeared in the morainic hill region in which the contrasts between castellan dominance and communal or Savorgnan jurisdiction were most obvious.[39]

The tide of insurrection in the area stopped at the circuit of hills in the sprawling Savorgnan territories around Buia. After the outbreak in Udine, Antonio Savorgnan wrote to his captain for Pinzano and Buia ordering subjects not to harm any person, to steal any property, or to burn anything. Here Antonio was obeyed. No Savorgnan fief was touched in the aftermath of Giovedì Grasso, although Antonio's orders to his captain imply that he was not so sure himself how far matters would go. Some of his men from Buia went to Colloredo di Monte Albano to guard the castle there, and a group of peasants on their way to sack Gemona got as far as Buia but did not dare defy Savorgnan's men who guarded the road there.[40]

Buia's resistance to the encompassing excitement may be explained by the singularity of its situation. Blessed with exemplary communal statutes, Buia administered itself with considerable autonomy and depended less on its feudal overlord than did other villages in the area, its communal strength giving the Buiesi greater opportunities to pursue grievances through judicial procedures. In comparison with other rural élites, the leaders of Buia had far greater opportunity to play a double game by manipulating judicial procedures and appeals, pitting the Savorgnan lord against the Venetian luogotenente. Although just as dangerously exposed as other villages to the plundering of the Austrians and to the military demands of the Venetians, Buia's greater collective strength, enshrined in local institutions and privileges, exempted it somewhat from the worst feudal excesses. In addition, Antonio Savorgnan's easygoing lordship there served most of all to build a loyal following rather than to exploit the land as fully as possible. Thus, the peasant insurrection limited itself to actions against Strumiero castellans, retained its factional character, and largely exempted Zambarlano nobles and citizens from pillage.[41]

The same general pattern of attacks against the property of Strumiero castellans prevailed among the hills at the eastern edge of the morainic amphitheater. Cergneu may have been the most severely hit. The castle was a possession of the same lords who held Brazzacco and apparently was a simple affair consisting of a tower and two houses on a hilly spire overlooking a valley sealed off by the impassable Mount San Giacomo. Unlike other castles, Cergneu was far from an important road. Apparently the castle's function had degenerated to maintaining symbolic domination over the local tenants and providing a retreat during feuding forays.

Francesco Cergneu's son, Giovanni Battista, chronicled what happened there. The tenants and servants (*massari* and *amici*) of the Cergneu, all of whom were at least five years behind in their rents, joined some men from nearby Nimis who had to pay a *decima* to the Cergneu. Many of these townsmen also owed the lords for small loans that could not be repaid. The assembled crowd sacked and destroyed the castle. Did they want, asked Giovanni Battista rhetorically, to pay their debts with their patrons' lives? After the assault old Francesco arranged a peace with his subjects thanks to the intervention of the luogotenente, but the nobles probably never again occupied the houses and tower in Cergneu.

Nearby at Tarcento the Castello brothers' imposing rectangular fortress with its infamous torture chambers went up in flames. Giacomo Castello, who had been one of the three heads of the castellans of Friuli and had barely escaped from Udine on the morning of Giovedì Grasso, was already safely far away. On the very day that his castle in Tarcento burned, Sanudo saw him at mass in San Marco in Venice.

The castle at Zucco nearly fell after someone inside assisted the rebels, but soldiers from Udine saved it. Some properties of the Della Torre were pillaged at Corglia near Tricesimo, and there was possibly some trouble at Chiasse, Prampero, and Pavona.[42]

In the plain of lower Friuli, Porpetto burned, although the lords there, the consorts of Strassoldo, escaped aboard riverboats from their pursuing tenants. The sources of peasant animus both at Porpetto and Strassoldo toward the Strassoldo family were numerous. Frequently suspected of secret dealings with the Austrian garrison at Gorizia and connected through marriage to the Della Torre, the Strassoldo provided one of the strongest links between the emperor and the Strumieri, and yet imperial mercenaries had recurrently subjected the tenants at Strassoldo to outrages. Located along the strategically vital road between Gorizia and lower Friuli, the castle at Strassoldo fulfilled the same military purpose as would Palmanova later in the century. The various sieges that took place during the war destroyed most of the housing outside the walls and exterminated or dispersed the population. By the time of the carnival riots of 1511, the damage may already have been too extensive to leave the few remaining, long-suffering peasants with much to loot, but something must have happened in Strassoldo because on March 6 the provveditore asked permission to take his men there to put down the peasants and confront the enemy. Permission was denied because the place was deemed too dangerous for soldiers.[43]

Peasants took up arms all across the plain, sacking noble property in Varmo and around Codroipo with its satellite village of Zompicchia, which had been restive for the past year since Alvise Della Torre had jailed those who had assaulted him there. With far fewer castles than in the hill region, the lower plain witnessed more diffused disturbances. As we have seen, two of the most influential Zambarlano leaders came from the lower plain, Asquinio and his nephew Federico Varmo, who organized the assault of Sterpo. Asquinio had been captain of the militias of Varmo since early in 1509, had rounded up three hundred men for duty in December 1510, and would provide some four hundred during the summer of 1511. Federico would later be described the "head of the infantry of the patria," and Amaseo pictured both Varmos as Antonio Savorgnan's devoted followers, who served as the "heads of the popular classes of the city and the peasants from outside." [44]

Many of the peasant bands in Udine on Giovedì Grasso came from the lower plain, and in particular from Fiumicello, Zompicchia, and Pradamano, areas long friendly to the Savorgnan and directly menaced by the enemy, a fact that made the inhabitants all the more enraged by rumors of Strumiero treachery. In this region in which castellan power was weakest and Zambarlano influence strongest, the peasants followed the militia leadership in contrast to the hill country in which the villagers behaved more autonomously. The settlements in the hills had better developed community institutions and greater residential stability than in the lowlands, in which high mortality from disease must have led to frequent changes in tenancy.

In contrast to the short-lived, war-provoked panic found in the eastern lowlands, the disturbances across the Tagliamento came much closer to a revolution, especially in Spilimbergo. The previous December, bravi had been hired to support the citizen faction in Spilimbergo, leading the consorts to bring in retainers as a countermeasure. Exiles also filtered into town during the early winter months while the chief consorts schemed with the Della Torre. Even without Udine's example, Spilimbergo could well have ignited on its own during carnival. On Monday, March 3, the servants and hired guards (famegli e provisionati) of the consorts abandoned the castle, leaving the noble families unprotected and forcing them to flee south to Zoppola, where they found temporary refuge along with many other castellans. While they were gone their subjects and peasants (li popolani et villani loro) set fire to several of the houses in the castle, the smoke from which Nicolò Monticolo saw while on his rescue mission across the river. Damage was extensive but selective, some nobles' buildings remaining intact. However, the looting went beyond the castellan complex to include local merchants. [45]

As was the case in the fifteenth century, Spilimbergo remained a dangerously fissured community in which class conflicts cut across factional affiliations and the consorts themselves were deeply divided. Besides the castellan-commoner split, the Strumiero-

Zambarlano cleavage was perpetuated by successive generations of Spilimbergo nobles, who contributed members to both sides, although most followed the clan's traditional affiliation with the Strumieri and took spouses from among the Della Torre, Colloredo, and Cergneu. Those members attracted to the Zambarlano badge seem to have been disinherited or alienated from their kin in some way.

The Strumiero consorts disagreed about how strong their commitment to friends and allies should be, some supporting Venice, some the empire. When, back in July 1509, Girolamo had sought to go over to the imperial side, other consorts led by Agostino opposed him, and during the same month Viviano was killed while fighting with the Venetians at the siege of Cividale. In contrast, in 1514 Giovanni Leonardo served as chancellor to Count Cristoforo Frangipane, the head of the imperial forces at the siege of Osoppo. Whereas Alvise Spilimbergo was an ardent Zambarlano, one of the leaders during the Giovedì Grasso massacre, and later condemned to death for his involvement in the murder of Alvise Della Torre, his cousin Giovanni Enrico switched allegiances with crude and fickle opportunism.[46]

Because of the clan's numerous branches and highly fecund spouses, the consorts as a body were weakened by a subdivided patrimony, by the competing claims from collateral branches, and by the paucity of resources to satisfy the younger men, many of whom had to seek their own fortunes. Some of these turned to making their livings as bandits. In January 1511, Simone di Francesco di Antonio received a warning from the heads of the Council of Ten that he must cease harboring armed bandits in his quarters in Spilimbergo castle and using them to protect him from the citizens of the town. Other castellans disassociated themselves from him by sending a delegation to the luogotenente.

When Simone failed to follow orders, the ten fined and then banished him. At first he refused to leave; when he finally did depart he only went across the river to San Daniele, where he remained just as troublesome. By the summer of 1511, at least three consorts were under the ban, two of them surviving by robbing peasants. Although the consorts of Spilimbergo would produce one of the most illustrious female painters of the Renaissance, supply a rector of the University of Padua, and host the Emperor

Charles V at their massive complex, several of them lived as thieves and adventurers whose relations with their own family and town were often violent.[47]

Since the revolts there in the 1480s, the townsmen and peasants had been in recurrent conflict with the consorts, reaching levels of violence exceptional even for Friuli. After witnessing the street fights, arson, and looting of 1511, Giovanni Cipernio packed his family up in disgust and moved to Maniago. Later Luogotenente Giorgio Gradenigo wrote that houses in Spilimbergo had become permanent prisons because the hatreds and desire for vendetta which governed the city made the streets so unsafe. Indeed a sturdy dwelling was made even more necessary because of the proclivity of the consorts to vandalize and set fire to the houses of those who did not please them. On several occasions Gradenigo rebuked the consorts about their unseemly and injust behavior, as in 1513 when he wrote that he was amazed to see "gentlemen of a noble family" persist in ruining their own subjects. Citizens found it impossible to receive a fair trial in Spilimbergo. One Rinaldo, a *decano* of Spilimbergo, appealed to the luogotenente in Udine after he had been sentenced in an assault case, complaining that because the judges were his great enemies (*inimicissimi*) he could never obtain impartial justice.[48]

The consorts expressed extreme paranoia about any sort of popular gathering, especially after the 1511 conflagration, and even the flagellant confraternity of San Giovanni could not meet without the senior consort present. There may have been good reason, however, to worry about that confraternity, which had indeed served as a nest of sedition. Certain basic issues reappeared time and time again. Taxation disputes, such as the nobles' right to collect a duty on wine, competed for priority with arguments over access to water from the communal cisterns and water power for mills. The nobles challenged the citizens' right to fish and to use carts when working on houses, demanded *corvées* in paving the square within the castle complex and in maintaining castle walls, and confiscated collateral even when debts were repaid.[49]

Aftershocks from the 1511 carnival radiated from the secondary epicenter at Spilimbergo, threatening castles as far away as Pordenone. The consorts of Spilimbergo and those of the nearby castles fled, in the words of the provveditore of Pordenone Alvise

Bondimier, "screaming to heaven as if mad"; as a puny remedy he sent his chancellor on a tour to threaten the gallows for those who did not desist from violence. The chancellor complained that he could not find any leaders among the crowds to receive the decree and reported that extensive damage had already been done by Monday evening at Spilimbergo, Zoppola, Cusano, and Valvasone. Nobles at Porcìa, Brugnera, and even Pordenone closed their gates to menacing crowds. No more able to take effective action than had the luogotenente in Udine, Bondimier raged in his letters to Venice that the rustic dogs acted more cruelly than Turks.[50]

Because of the strength of its defensive works, Zoppola became a noble refuge center, but even it could not be held for long. Like Spilimbergo, Zoppola consisted of a huge, isolated complex of separate houses that formed a ring around a central piazza (Figures 10 and 11). The Panciera di Zoppola family governed the castle, but many different castellan landlords, including the ubiquitous Colloredo, held the land around it. The peasants who besieged Zoppola committed the only personal atrocity against a noble outside of Udine, but even in this case no one was killed. About twelve hundred peasants attacked the houses with "the fury of rabid dogs," to quote Amaseo's wearisome metaphor, and some few raped Tommaso Panciera's wife, Beatrice de' Freschi da Cucagna, who was later found nude in the courtyard where she had remained with her infirm elderly mother. The assailants also captured and ravished the widow of the consort Alvise.[51]

The castle at Cusano was similar in many respects to those of Spilimbergo and Zoppola. In 1483 Sanudo described Cusano as a "beautiful and strong castle" surrounded by a broad moat, but every trace of the edifice, even its exact site, has long since disappeared. The lords of Cusano, known to be philoimperialists, had strong ties with the Colloredo, who also had properties at Cusano. In 1509 Paolo Cusano, captain of the Venetian garrison at Tolmino, which guarded the passes from Slovenia to Cividale, turned it over to the Austrians, and subsequently Antonio Savorgnan accused Cusano of treachery, pointing to the fact that Paolo's brother Roberto married the granddaughter of Alberto Colloredo, a notorious rebel then serving in the imperial army. At Cusano a local priest led the assault on the castle, in the only known example in Friuli of a cleric's involvement in the Giovedì Grasso violence.[52]

The lords of Valvasone, like those of Spilimbergo, had extensive jurisdictional privileges that soured relations with the small population of the town and ten subject villages. In fact, the citizens of Spilimbergo recurrently reminded their lords of the example of Valvasone, in which matters had reached such an impasse that most of the citizens had left. Enjoying fewer checks to their authority than almost anywhere else, the consorts of Valvasone could legislate, demand *corvées* from subjects, collect an annual rent from anyone who built a house in the town, and name all officials.

The vast complex of fiefs and properties which Simone di Cucagna put together at Valvasone in the thirteenth century had over the centuries been subdivided among four families, the Cucagna, Zucco, Partistagno, and Freschi. The families shared the Valvasone jurisdiction in a four-year cycle: every year all of the privileges of local administration and the rendering of justice changed hands from one family to another. Although the consorts frequently quarreled among themselves, they adhered to the Strumiero faction. The Cucagna, Zucco, and Partistagno houses united in opposition to Antonio Savorgnan; Giacomo Giusto Zucco had been a head of the Strumiero faction during the previous generation; Agostino Partistagno and his three sons barely escaped with their lives on Giovedì Grasso in Udine; and afterwards one of the sons spent a month in Venice as an agent for the survivors of the Della Torre. The Freschi had considerable influence in Udine where two weeks before the Cruel Carnival both Francesco and Giovanni were elected deputies. However, the subjects of the consorts followed the Zambarlani. In the peasants' attack on the castle, they selected three houses within the complex for pillage in a carefully executed operation that distinguished among castellans according to their past behavior toward the subjects of the jurisdiction.[53]

On the lower plain between the Tagliamento and Livenza Rivers, the widely dispersed unrest left many castles untouched. Vague reports came in about disorders in Salvarolo. As Andrea Loredan passed through on his way to Udine, he had Alvise Balbi break up the assault on the castle of Fratta, an extension of the Valvasone patrimony. Balbi also intervened in Cordovado and Portogruaro to prevent significant destruction by the *popolani* who rioted there. San Vito also had similarly inconclusive contention.[54]

Portogruaro witnessed the only openly anti-Venetian demon-

FIGURE 10. Zoppola; the castle.

stration of the entire insurrection. At first the podestà, Bernardo Canal, could not comprehend what was going on and hesitated about what course of action to take. He wrote to the ten saying that inasmuch as he had heard that some rebel castellans had been killed in Udine, he wanted to know whether he should confiscate the property of Giovanni Leonardo and Polidoro Frattina, who had stores of wheat and wine there.

Castellan refugees, however, soon began to pour into the well-fortified town telling a different story. During these same uncertain days a delegation of ten citizens from Portogruaro went to Venice to report on a "sad and dishonest act" that had recently been perpetrated in the town. During the night someone placed horns over the insignia of Saint Mark in the classic symbol of the cuckold. The Council of Ten took this apparently minor indication of anti-Venetian sentiment very seriously, indeed reacting with greater alacrity and decision than it had to other reports of far more damaging and violent civil strife. The council announced an elaborate scale of rewards offering up to two thousand lire and immunity from prosecution to anyone who could provide information about the culprit or culprits, revealing an overwhelming preoccupation with its own security and indifference or at least laxity in providing for the safety of its provincial subjects.[55]

FIGURE II. Zoppola; peasant housing near the castle.

After ten days of fire and tumult, the provveditore of Pordenone finally reported that the peasants had quieted down in his area although the ferment had spread beyond him and still continued as far away as Sacile, Serravalle, Conegliano, and Oderzo. However, the general mood remained uneasy, and flare-ups broke out over the following weeks.

The consorts of Valvasone, Salvarolo, Cusano, Spilimbergo, and others who had sought refuge at Zoppola soon abandoned it and fled to Pordenone, where they found the castle in ruins from the imperialists' recent siege, a fact that obliged them to push on to Porcìa where they formed a council of war. The counts of Porcìa recruited eight hundred peasants from Cordenons and some sixty to seventy knights to hunt down the pillagers. Their reprisals were vicious. They massacred between fifty and one hundred peasants, took many prisoners, and hanged one as an example at Zoppola. The peasant bands fled "like geldings frightened by a wolf," abandoning the field to the castellans. Most of the fighting ceased within a week, but in several places, notably in Spilimbergo, it continued for months.[56]

Deeply disquieted by the news from Friuli, the Council of Ten acted quickly to pacify the region. Choosing expediency over justice, the ten chose one of their own number, none other than Antonio Savorgnan's protector and friend, Andrea Loredan, to go to Udine to stop the violence, arrest the culprits, and restore property. Loredan once again showed himself to be an active partisan rather than an objective arbitrator, offending with his highhanded methods the resident Venetian officials as well as all but the most dedicated partisans of the Savorgnan. Staying for barely two weeks, Loredan left after paving the way for the complete exoneration of Antonio Savorgnan and arresting only two minor figures among the Zambarlani. Very little property was returned. In fact, it was twenty-three years before any serious attempt at compensation for damages was ventured.[57]

When they pictured the peasant crowds, contemporary witnesses imagined only two stark alternatives: either mobs wandering like vagabonds without master, intent solely on plunder, or the opposite situation of gullible rustics manipulated by some treacherous noble. Most observers remarked on the spontaneity and apparent lack of organization in the peasant violence. A noble who later gloried in the brutal crushing of the peasants probably reflected the views of many of his peers in arguing that the peasants went on a rampage "without any cause." Other witnesses confirmed the view that the crowds lacked leaders. One quite frank account states that the peasants "went about without any head at all to guide them in plundering and burning and with the goal of castigating and breaking the rebel castellans, and these were the very subjects of the castellans." Although many of the participants were locals who joined the assault on their own lords' castles, others certainly moved from castle to castle, pillaging where they could, as did those who went on from Spilimbergo to Valvasone, Zoppola, and Cusano. The crowds must have been large otherwise they could not have overwhelmed the castles so easily. Twelve hundred were reported at Zoppola and two thousand at Porcìa, but the assertion that a horde of between four and five thousand wandered from castle to castle is certainly exaggerated.[58]

Many of the anti-Savorgnan sources maintained that Antonio coordinated even these far-flung disquiets. However, even Amaseo had to admit that Nicolò Monticolo succeeded in quieting the peasant Zambarlani, saving lives, and preventing even greater destruction. Monticolo himself asserted that "if Antonio Savorgnan had not had some of his friends ride out, all of the castellans would not only have been plundered and ruined but some of their families would have become extinct. Such was their flight that they abandoned houses, goods, and their own wives with little children in order to save themselves. It was a horrible thing to see."[59]

Although these contrasting opinions create a picture of fragmentation and ambiguity, the rural situation can, in fact, be clarified considerably. In Udine Antonio Savorgnan's agents were visible everywhere and were at the forefront of the attack. It is beyond doubt that they provided the leadership in the streets, identified at least some of the quarry, and did much of the killing themselves. However, the situation in the countryside was quite different. There were very few murders. In fact the only persons killed during the rural outbreak were peasants caught in the castellans' counterattack. The violence of vendetta which predominated in the city almost completely disappeared in favor of highly selective plundering, threats to the dependents of the absent nobles, and vague expressions of long-standing peasant grievances.

The indigenous strengths of the peasant crowd, built around leaders from village councils and the militia, the decade-long experience of collective protest against the parliament, and the memory of the success at Sterpo nineteen months before, collapsed the vertical hierarchy of the Zambarlano faction into localized, fragmentary peasant communities. In the countryside neither nobles nor priests, with one obscure exception, led the rebels, and the known intimates of Antonio Savorgnan protected rather than threatened lives and property.

When Antonio himself attempted to stop the violence, he relied heavily on the indigenous village leadership to do so. He asked two men, Jacomo del Fara and Rosso di Bagnarolla, described as among the "first peasants" in importance from across the Tagliamento, to go home, disperse their people, and stop the pillaging. The starkly popular character of the rural revolt underscores the diverse interests that had been attached to the Zambarlano faction, which was the only effective voice against the castellan-dominated parliament and the only defense against the imperial marauders. Given the limited amount of information available to the peasants and the nature of rumors, such as the one that the Strumiero castellans sought to aid the enemy, the rural rebels need not have had any central directives; they merely seized an opportunity and justified their rampages by labeling their victims as traitors.[60]

During all the violence in Udine and across the countryside attackers exempted women for the most part. As far as can be determined only one woman, a servant of the Castello clan, died in Udine. In another incident, the crowd beat and kicked Angela Gorghi while she was attempting to rescue her son from certain death. In the rural areas assaults on women seem to have been limited to two or three rapes. The general exemption of women from physical harm reflected the theoretical exclusion of women from vengeance killing and confirms the pattern of the careful selection of victims and targets. Although the rapes may have merely been crimes of opportunity, they certainly served to dishonor further the Strumiero lords who proved themselves incapable of defending their own wives. Thus, the violence against women may have been an extension of violence among men.[61]

Selectivity characterized both the Udinese and the rural disturbances in the sense that only aristocrats with close ties to the philo-imperial inner circle of the Strumieri came to grief. The only exceptions were the few merchants of Spilimbergo whose shops were looted. The attacks were most intense in the hill regions that fanned out to the north of Udine and in the arid scrub of Spilimbergo. By contrast, in the lowlands antinoble agitation was less extensive and less successful; nevertheless, several lowland villages contributed bands of armed militiamen who wandered off elsewhere (particularly to Udine) and joined in the fray. The most likely targets of attack, then, were those castellans who had abused jurisdictional rights and who were particularly rich. In fact, the peasant looters were far more successful in obtaining valuable property than the Austrian raiders who had precipitated the conflagration.[62]

Part Three

MENTALITIES
& IDEOLOGIES

CHAPTER SIX

The Problem of Meaning

For those who witnessed and survived the Cruel Carnival or even heard about it after the event, ascribing meaning to the collective killing and pillaging remained an embittering concern. Contemporaries could find an obvious explanation in the long history of the Zambarlano-Strumiero vendetta, but the carnival slaughter seemed so unprecedented in magnitude and involved so many people from outside the narrow ambit of castellans and their familiars that evoking the age-old quarrels between the Savorgnan and Della Torre was inadequate to the task. The meanings attributed to the deaths and destruction came after the fact as persons from various cultural levels with diverse interests and objectives saw very different things in the Cruel Carnival. Just as it had no single cause, the Cruel Carnival had no single meaning, and in the ensuing years the process of imposing meanings on the event became not only a problem of interpretation but the justification for future violence and the substance of political discourse as well.

To understand fully how social position conditioned the assigning of meaning to the Cruel Carnival, the background of the factions should be considered. The language of class distinctions which contrasted peasants and nobles and which was employed by the notaries, chroniclers, and humanists who produced most of the records often masked the fact that the constituent elements of the Zambarlani were usually small communities consisting of internally differentiated groups of neighbors and villagers who had their own abbreviated hierarchy of leaders in the form of *decani* and militia captains.

By 1511, the travails of a decade had drawn the urban poor and rural tenant farmers of these microcommunities into the Zambarlano orbit. The Turkish incursions and the wars between Venice and the Emperor Maximilian escalated Venetian fiscal demands. In addition, changes in the manorial economy led many of the Strumiero landlords to exploit their properties more efficiently by denying tenants compensation for improvements to their leaseholds, by usurping common pastures, and by eliminating many of the guarantees of permanent tenancy which peasants had traditionally enjoyed. Forced by the terms of their leases to pay rents in kind and chronically behind in doing so, peasants could not take advantage of the opportunity for capital accumulation provided by access to the market for agricultural produce in Udine and were, instead, drawn into accepting usurious loans.

Both the artisans and the peasants found solidarity in their neighborhoods or villages and support from the Zambarlani. Such neighborhood and village microcommunities offered the corporate identity and leadership structure necessary for collective action and for incorporation into the larger structure of the faction. Although relations among the communities had historically been competitive, on the eve of and during Giovedì Grasso the communities acted in concert against a common economic and military foe, primarily because of Antonio Savorgnan's patronage and the comradeship of the young men in the militias. The Friulan communities may have been weaker than communities in many other parts of the Mediterranean, but they were still the necessary basis for any larger popular movement.[1]

Particularly characteristic of Friuli was how rural life penetrated deeply into the city and the few towns, making neighborhoods similar to country villages in structure and values. Even in Udine a large portion of the population consisted of peasant cultivators, and artisans often worked as part-time farmers and invested in livestock raising. Thus, the economic concerns of the peasants also motivated many city dwellers.

The smallness and rural nature of the Friulan communities help to account for their limited political expectations, so lacking in radical ideological alternatives or millenarian enthusiasm, unlike even isolated, mountain-bound Belluno, where in 1501 peasant agitators followed a certain mendicant friar who had preached about the common man's God-given rights. When the Friulans went so far as to articulate their desires, the men of the villages and neighborhoods wanted at most local control over their own affairs. To be sure, the Venetian rectors imagined a cataclysmic upheaval, warning the Council of Ten about "the plebs who always want new things" and recalling "the last few days during the revolution of that patria" or the "revolution of the heavens"; and yet the revolution about which they wrote consisted of limited demands for fiscal reform and unity against invaders rather than a transformation of the social system or eschatological expectations of collective salvation. Of course, an endless stream of delegations had made political demands to the parliament and to Venice, but the real revolution in Friuli, rather than a political or religious one, was a moral and cultural one in which the men and women of the villages and *borghi* employed the body metaphors of carnival and vendetta to express their desires for revenge. Giovedì Grasso epitomized the restricted potential of the vendetta-revolt for political change, a potential that could not be expanded until the desire for revenge was channeled into a coherent political movement.[2]

Whatever had been the concerns of the villagers and neighbors of Friuli before Giovedì Grasso, the violence of the day transmogrified their grievances into new representations or ideas that coalesced on at least four different cultural levels. The primary level used traditional motifs of carnival as a form of communication. Significant actions conveyed messages through improvised variations on the accepted forms for the butchery of bodies. Here deeds spontaneously and ritualistically communicated in a form which historians have widely recognized as characteristic of the poor in premodern Europe. These were the immediate messages formulated by the men who did the killing in the streets of Udine.

On a second level participants, survivors, and interested parties in Venice and Udine sought to influence the determination of guilt. Friulans incorporated the Venetian organs of justice into their own struggles, using judicial procedures as an extension of their private and factional quarrels. Although anyone could make a denunciation, serve as a witness, or face charges, the politicized Venetian system of justice, far from being an impartial arbiter, facilitated collective scapegoating in the interests of a powerful few.

The two final levels were the products of hindsight and literacy, attempts to place Friulan events in a cosmological or historical context. Some envisioned Giovedì Grasso and its aftermath apocalyptically, a human vendetta that either fulfilled or precipitated the divine vendetta. Finally, after years of reflection a few humanists and aristocrats wrote up historical narrations of the events, interpreting Giovedì Grasso for outsiders and future generations.

As time passed and individual memories faded, literate sophistication became more important. Time was on the side of those capable of committing their ideas to print although when they did so, they divorced themselves from the catharsis and corporality of the actual Giovedì Grasso, reinterpreting the event to serve a personal or ideological agenda and suppressing entirely the original messages of the participants themselves.

THE CARNIVAL BODY

Carnival has received so much attention from scholars of the Renaissance in recent years because it was so richly complex, subtly interwoven into the fabric of daily life, and therefore resistant to a single or simple interpretation. Relying on a Europe-wide repertoire of images and motifs, carnivals absorbed meanings from the social environment and from certain universal human processes. One of those processes was killing—the killing of animals, the killing of humans. Carnival helped sustain certain beliefs about killing which were shared by both vendetta practices and hunting. (These beliefs will be examined in the next chapter.) Carnival, vendetta, and hunting were distinct activities, but in the act of killing and in talking and writing about killing the boundaries among the three blurred, so that a vendetta could easily become a carnival riot or adopt the cultural trappings of the hunt.

Whatever the local manifestations, carnival images revolved around the paradox that human life sustained itself through death.

Carnival celebrated the necessary deaths: the death of the old season and the birth of a new (carnival as a wake for winter), the killing of animals for meat (carnival as the time for the slaughter of hogs), and the death of Christ soon to be commemorated during Holy Week (carnival as an unloosening of the forces of the underworld). One of the characteristic ways in which carnivals represented the struggle between life and death involved a fight, typically a staged fight between personifications of Carnival and Lent, but the games and mock combats that institutionalized this fight could seldom be controlled entirely by authorities, and carnival festivities often tested the boundaries of order by becoming chaotic.

A related carnivalesque emphasis on gluttony and drunkenness celebrates fat times and recognizes the inevitable recurrence of the opposite condition of lean times; thus, the fight between Carnival and Lent is also a fight between the Fat and the Lean. Given the long history of Savorgnan patronage of the peasants and artisans on the one hand and castellan hostility to agrarian fiscal reform on the other, it is not far-fetched to imagine that in the minds of the poor, the Zambarlani took on the role of the Fat and the Strumieri the Lean. Giovedì Grasso, or Fat Thursday, became the natural, almost inevitable, extension of the local factional struggle when the crowd assimilated popular images of the two factions to carnival archetypes. Actual and mock combat, vendetta and carnival fighting, merged entirely on Giovedì Grasso, and participants stripped away accumulated strictures to concentrate on the central theme of the festival: the act of killing.[3]

While eliminating hated nobles and ransacking their houses on Giovedì Grasso, peasants and artisans also represented their feelings of anger and contempt by employing natural symbols derived from human and animal anatomy. Carnival and vendetta shared a fascination with body imagery because both provided a cultural justification for killing and a formula for disposing of carcasses and corpses. As elsewhere in premodern Europe, Friulans acted out social conflicts in patterned ways that constituted rites of violence, various forms of which came together in a burst of murderous fights on Giovedì Grasso. By exploring contemporary attitudes toward the body and its slaughter, one might better approximate, for that is all we can hope to do, what the Friulan rites of violence meant.[4]

Carnival expressed popular discontent by serving as a means of examining social categories, particularly for the illiterate and weak. The playacting, masking, and satiric mimicry associated with normal, nonviolent carnival helped define social roles and clarify status distinctions because, as Richard Trexler has pointed out, individuals characteristically shaped their identities during the late Middle Ages and Renaissance not so much by following social norms as by imitating others. Carnival commented on imitation by paying homage to the orderliness of personal conformity to group models and also by subverting the order in the process of uncovering it. For example, Rabelais illustrated the power of miming by showing how Panurge's ability to use and interpret hand signs helped him understand and convey meaning better than those whose exclusive reliance on spoken language resulted in a failure to communicate fully. Gestures constituted a universal yet grammatical language because they were derived from the natural movements of the body, and the people closest to nature, peasants, understood these signs better than the élite, whose cultivated speech masked their ignorance of the language of the body, a primary source for the language of carnival.[5]

Animal bodies also contributed to the repertoire of carnival body images. In part because the seasonal chores of hog butchering and making sausages took place at carnival time, the festival was especially concerned with the acts of slaughtering and butchering animals, or as Emmanuel Le Roy Ladurie aptly put it, the language of carnival amounted to saying it with meat. Body parts provided the vocabulary, ritual the syntax.[6]

These corporeal images contributed to the typical carnival process of mimicking established mores and culture. Carnival revelers parodied hierarchic order by transgressing established social distinctions through grotesque juxtapositions including cross-dressing, imitating animals, and torturing or killing animals that symbolized some social group. Transgressions in any area had implications for the others, so that such apparently innocuous activities as men masquerading as women or blacksmiths butchering hogs drew attention to the legitimacy of political authority.[7]

In its lexicon of humorous transgressions, carnival was usually quite conservative, helping sustain the social order by representing and explaining it, and when necessary by reforming or purifying it. Especially in communities in which civic organizations such as guilds, confraternities, and festive clubs were highly developed, transgressions reinforced hierarchy precisely because they were temporary and controlled. In the Schembart carnival of Nuremberg, for example, the vigilance of the city council guaranteed a festival that was, according to Hans Sachs who witnessed it in 1539, a "mirror of a bygone revolt, to remind the common people never to participate in such rebellious madness" as they had when they had assaulted the magistrates in 1348. The Nuremberg carnival, moreover, hosted several kinds of dramas for different cultural levels which transformed social tensions into relatively harmless play.[8]

In Venice between 1521 and 1526, the often pointed carnival comedies by Ruzante served as a form of social protest; but after the playwright went too far by associating himself with dangerous political ridicule, he lost his patrician patrons. The Venetian authorities were particularly adept at containing the subversive potential of carnival, in part by turning aggressions outward as they did with the annual carnival butchery of a bull and twelve pigs sent as tribute, in fact, from Friuli.[9]

However, during times of war or grave social tensions, carnival transgressions could provide a language of protest and a model for violence, especially in feudal Friuli. Without a legitimate prince who transcended factional loyalties, without effective religious institutions that encouraged collective rituals, without a miracle-working shrine that focused the quest for supernatural assistance, the Friulan hierarchy lacked symbolic cohesion, and thus Friulan society was susceptible to having its holidays go wrong.

During the 1511 carnival in Udine, the dominant social organizations of militia companies and factions guided the crowds in their festivity, but the pervasive sense of threat remodeled festivity beyond play and any organization's control. In contrast to the elaborate metaphoric images displayed in the carnivals of more sophisticated areas, carnival in Friuli was hardly subtle: its metaphors of Fat and Lean were the factions themselves, its performances less a substitute for direct action than an incitement to it. The Giovedì Grasso was characterized by a poverty of symbolism and a brutal directness, as when the Savorgnan retainers forced Alvise Della Torre to his knees to beg for his life in an inversion of the normal gesture of respect accorded a man of his rank. After the conflagration the Zambarlani masqueraded in the clothing of their victims and reveled in wearing the hats of the dead aristocrats, the most obvious insignia of rank. These acts of status inversion derived their power from negation and from the lowering of the high born. There were few symbols with which the rioters could identify positively, except perhaps the flag of the Savorgnan. Most powerfully, the Zambarlani gave form to vendetta justice by mimicking the customs of official justice, as Luigi da Porto noted: "I saw the goods taken in that sacking sold at the stands in the piazza of the city, as if such confiscations had been against rebels of Venice and the property sold by commission of the Senate."[10]

The Giovedì Grasso rioters sent their most graphic messages through the disposal of the corpses of their victims, which was performed in ways fraught with symbolic meaning. At least three people were thrown into latrines or wells. The killers left the body of Alvise Della Torre in the streets for three days, and the mother of Apollonio Gorgo had to plead with the Zambarlani to allow her to bury her son's body, which they wanted to leave in the street. Others were systematically dismembered. When Amaseo described Vergon and Bernardino da Narni as "bloody butchers," he was speaking quite literally: they cut up their victims "like beef." Dismemberment deprived the victim of his body, the very source of masculinity and social honor, just as a refusal to bury him denied salvation to his soul.[11]

Dismemberment also had a broader social significance. Mikhail Bakhtin noted that medieval and Renaissance satires typically linked the mutilation of the body with the dissolution of society by adhering to the myth that various social groups originated in the parts of God's body. According to the logic of carnival, hacking up the bodies of dead aristocrats was a way of carving up the body politic.[12]

The lacerating of the bodies of the dead can also be understood as an expression of the widespread belief that corpses retained some sensitivity. Such beliefs were encouraged by religious pictures and sculptures, especially Last Judgment scenes, which explicitly showed the agonized bodies of the dead condemned to Hell. Confirming the theology of corporeal sensation, physicians and legal experts justified many forms of postexecution torture such as drawing and quartering, and they authorized the *jus feretri* whereby the supposed reaction of a dead body in the presence of its murderer would be accepted in a court of law as a valid proof of the identity of the guilty party. In medical schools well into the eighteenth century, dissections continued to produce uneasy emotions about the pain of the dead, which the University of Bologna, for example, respected by relegating public dissections to carnival, when recently executed criminals were available, and the masked audience could watch the procedure as a kind of theatrical performance appropriate to the season. There may also have been a way in which damaging corpses acted as a kind of sympathetic magic, a way of tormenting the victim's soul in the other world and his living relations in this one.[13]

And yet the tortures inflicted on Strumiero corpses did not quite do and say enough to satisfy the Zambarlani. In perhaps the most infamous episode of Giovedì Grasso, the Ferrarese lured Federico Colloredo out of hiding with a promise of a safe conduct but then "killed him and slashed him with so many wounds that one could see all of his insides, which were eaten by dogs; the remains were not allowed to be buried." This most thorough act of revenge drew its evocative power from the horror of dogs and pigs eating humans, a transgression that obsessed the Udinesi. An ordinance of 1490 mentioned a fence built around the public gallows so that "dogs and other animals can not enter in that place to lick up human blood." An edict from 1520 stated that pigs invaded the cathedral of Santa Maria daily and despoiled graves, and reports of animals rooting in cemeteries continued throughout the century. Titian's late sixteenth-century painting of *The Flaying of Marsyas* summoned similar horrors. The image of animals eating human bodies was not only a festive inversion but a perverted fact of life recalled with dramatic effect on Giovedì Grasso. In murdering Federico Colloredo, the Zambarlani degraded him on many levels: by hacking at the corpse, they inflicted additional agony on him; by making him the meat of beasts, they transgressed his status as a man and likened his fate to that of executed criminals; by shaming him in the public streets, they humiliated his surviving relatives; and by disfiguring his body, they destroyed the collective body of castellans he represented. In his death the methods of carnival and vendetta merged completely. More than any other deed, the fate of Federico epitomized for future generations the Cruel Carnival and the cruel revenge of 1511.[14]

The Giovedì Grasso killings, thus, followed certain patterns that generated messages by the forms they took, forms borrowed from vendetta and carnival. Violence in Udine was neither an anarchic expression of "millennial antinomianism" which lacked rules, nor was it entirely planned. The combination of structure and spontaneity discloses the operations of shared beliefs about dying which made it possible for killers to step into defined roles, as if they improvised the lines of stock dramatic characters.[15]

For many Friulans, especially from the peasant classes, death was neither accidental nor natural but was the result of a fight between phantom forces composed of the shades of the dead who enacted revenge among humans by employing living agents. Revenge, in fact, motivated all deaths, even the most apparently innocent ones. Evidence for such beliefs can be found in the Friulan lore about the armies of the dead and the *benandanti*, who fought night battles for the survival of the crops. Parallel beliefs also appear in other feuding cultures such as Corsica, in which all deaths were blamed on the *mazzeri* who went "hunting" at night in dreams or as doubles. As a time of killing, carnival made the living vulnerable to the forces of the dead, and living men with living grievances had little trouble acting as the doubles of the dead.[16]

In the immediacy of the carnival of 1511, I would suggest, something like the above beliefs about bodies and death infiltrated the minds and influenced the behavior of the humble crowd and killer *bravi* who roamed the streets of Udine. In the weeks after the violence and at a slightly higher cultural level, a more extended process of assigning blame began.

ASSIGNING BLAME

On Giovedì Grasso the Zambarlani had scapegoated the Strumieri by describing them as agents of foreign invaders, and after the riots Strumiero survivors sought to reverse the process by attributing the massacres to the will of Antonio Savorgnan. Paralleling these operations were attempts by the Venetian judiciary to determine guilt. However, judicial procedures broke down while investigating Giovedì Grasso, largely because the very act of identifying criminals brought the whole Venetian system of terraferma rule into question. As a result, the indigenous scapegoat mechanisms of the vendetta biased assessments of responsibility.[17]

Within a matter of weeks the Venetian Council of Ten began a general investigation of the Giovedì Grasso disturbances, and in early April the city council of Udine met to elect four delegates to go to Venice to explain what had happened. The chosen four were known Savorgnan associates personally selected by Antonio, who did not allow their formal instructions to be put up for debate in the council. The instructions dismissed all charges of collusion among the attackers of the Strumieri but somewhat inconsistently asserted that the slaughter had been a defensive military action. In their private comments delivered along with their official report, the delegates praised Antonio Savorgnan and emphasized that the common rabble rather than he were responsible for what happened. Subsequently, Antonio Savorgnan himself went to Venice where he testified in secret for more than a week. The investigation finally produced some limited results. The ten issued arrest warrants for Vergon, Tempesta, Mattana, the Ferrarese, Piccolo (the familiars of Savorgnan), Pietro Savorgnan (Antonio's half-brother), Alvise Spilimbergo, Simon Scraiber, and one Antonio, familiar of Giovanni Vittori. A proclamation demanded that all the carnival loot be returned. Only Scraiber and one of the familiars were executed in Venice. The rest were exiled *in absentia*. Most of the Zambarlano élite including seven of the eleven deputies of the council of Udine, chancellor Nicolò Monticolo, and the nine *decani* of the *borghi* of Udine completely escaped blame. Antonio Savorgnan had come under strong suspicion, but as head of the militias and victor over his factional enemies he remained too powerful to be charged with any crime.[18]

For his part, Antonio described himself as in the grips of a kind of madness on Giovedì Grasso. When the luogotenente had asked him to intervene during the riots Antonio had explained away his refusal saying, "I am so angry that I am beside myself and do not know what I am doing." Impelled by his mad blood, Antonio abdicated all responsibility as if his anger had blotted out his reasoning faculties, pushed him beyond the reach of self-restraint, and subjected him to the governance of pure emotion. His words derived their force from the integrity of burning anger, as if authenticity of feeling justified even the most outrageous crimes. His passion replicated Benvenuto Cellini's numerous boastful accounts of violent exploits, petty quarrels, and vicious retaliations told in his *Autobiography* as assertions of his own identity. The artist was saying, it seems, "I hate, therefore I am." By refusing to accept responsibility on the grounds of his mad passion, Antonio had to accuse some of his own men, and when investigators came uncomfortably close to his inner circle, a few of the minor players were sacrificed. Antonio turned over to the Venetian authorities the lowest among his personal retainers and a few lowly peasants but protected the important client brokers of militia captains and *decani* who tied the Savorgnan to the rural villages and neighborhoods of Udine.[19]

In contrast, after the event the Strumieri continued to blame Antonio Savorgnan and his friends, diverting attention from the Strumieri's own potential treason and their own unmanly failure to defend themselves and their dependents despite their considerable military resources. Amaseo wrote that even among the twelve apostles there had been a betrayer and called Savorgnan Antonio Iscariot and Mohammed, a snake charmer whose friends, "hoping for impunity from punishment, attributed all [the violence] to the public anger which proceeded from jealousy of the state, thus calling down the divine vendetta onto the whole city just to free a single Judas." Some Strumieri even extended the blame to Venice itself, which they thought had put Savorgnan up to the task of cleansing the region of its obstinately imperialist aristocracy.[20]

It would take a generation before any serious attempt was made to provide some compensation for damages suffered in 1511. Although the castellans and their heirs continued to clamor, Venice could not risk alienating first Antonio and later Girolamo Savorgnan, who financed his own military efforts on behalf of Venice with the inheritance he received from Antonio's estate. After Girolamo's death in 1529, which coincided with the Peace of Bologna, Doge Andrea Gritti finally began to listen to the Strumiero claimants and decreed in 1530 that some thirty thousand ducats should be paid over a period of fifteen years from the estates of the heirs of Girolamo and Giovanni Savorgnan (Antonio's late brother, whose sons had inherited part of Antonio's patrimony). As soon became obvious, that sum was utterly inadequate, and so a board of arbitrators was set up to examine claims for compensation.[21]

Claimants were required to provide detailed inventories of the damages suffered during the Giovedì Grasso troubles. The amounts they listed probably come as close as one can to determining the extent of the damage in 1511, but the long lapse of time and the obvious incentive to inflate estimates lead one to treat the figures with considerable caution. The final list of fifty-three claimants asked for a total of 158,369 ducats (see Appendix 2). The requests ranged from the twenty-five ducats of Alessandro Spilimbergo's widow to the Della Torre's fifty thousand. After the Della Torre's, the combined claims from Spilimbergo ranked second at 25,648 ducats, the total from Colloredo heirs was third at 18,100, and the Brazzacco's fourth at 10,279. These four alone account for nearly two thirds of the total damages claimed, a fact that suggests a very heavy concentration of the looting and destruction in a few locations: Udine, Villalta, Spilimbergo, Colloredo di Monte Albano, and Brazzacco. After examining all the requests, the arbitrators awarded only 80,114 ducats or about half the total value of the claims and fully honored only four claims. The Della Torre heirs, for example, were allotted just twenty thousand ducats. Moreover, during the fifteen years scheduled for the payment of the reimbursements, the managers of the Savorgnan patrimony made only infrequent outlays.[22]

The Della Torre estimates reveal the kinds of things lost and, incidentally, catalogue the plenitude of castellan riches. The five sons of Alvise reported the complete loss of three houses in Udine and the vandalizing of the castle at Villalta. In addition they produced testimony from twenty-one witnesses who saw some of the henchmen of Antonio Savorgnan remove from the wine cellar of the ruined Della Torre palace in Udine a chest full of money, gold, silver, and jewels valued in all at between three and five thousand ducats. On the day of the riots their uncle, Isidoro, was said to have lost another three thousand ducats that he had hidden in his pockets and up his sleeves, and the potential revenues from the destroyed records of outstanding loans were themselves incalculable. Inventories boasted of books estimated at 620 ducats plus an unvalued shelf of humanistic books; dozens of suits of clothes, cloaks, furs, and jackets including one of double-thick London wool worth fourteen ducats. Lost from the Udine palace were beds, linens, mattresses, blankets, fancy dress shoes, a sword, mirrors, casks of flour, bushels of grain, statues of saints, kitchen knives, crockery, an oven, tools, a barber's basin, two glass windows taken away in their frames, hens, capons, two pigs, and dozens of barrels of wine.[23]

Besides the need to restore property, the cataclysms of 1511 left many things unresolved: the Strumieri would spend a decade avenging their dead, and Venice would seek to break up the factions. But the most pressing need was to provide explanations. Simply put, what had all this violence and destruction meant?

THE APOCALYPTIC

Once justifiable anger had excused the principals and a few expendable henchmen and rustics had suffered punishment, contemporaries indulged themselves in speculations about the deeper causes of their misfortunes. In early sixteenth-century Friuli, everyone believed that deaths were announced by omens, that great events must have great causes, that divine agency influenced natural events, and that clues to divine will could be discovered in astrological conjunctions, miraculous signs, prodigies, and visions. Even Machiavelli and Guicciardini, the most skeptical historians of their time and the most likely to ascribe human causes to human affairs, believed that prodigies signaled future events. Divine vendetta against human sinfulness was adduced by many as the explanation for the difficult years surrounding 1511, and prodigies foretold God's revenge, which would take the form of apocalyptic disasters such as war, civil strife, earthquakes, and plague, each of which might be ameliorated by human acceptance of the suffering they brought and by acts of propitiation. The relationship between God and humanity was cast, thus, as a series of cosmic exchanges in which humans projected onto God their inner fears and hopes.[24]

Aware of the violent consequences of abusive words spoken among humans, authorities throughout northern Italy since the late fifteenth century had concerned themselves with how blasphemy provoked God's ire. One of the first reactions to the events of Giovedì Grasso was a proclamation against blasphemous utterances, which were to be punished by a fifty-lire fine and the cutting out of the profaner's tongue. Venetian authorities had first expressed worries about the consequences of cursing in 1500, when the Council of Ten issued a decree against blasphemers in response to the news of the fall of Modon to the Turks, but during the War of the League of Cambrai, the tendency to see a close relationship between private sins and public retribution intensified. Because communications with the divine were modeled on human patterns, care had to be taken not only to avoid insulting God but also to discern what he was saying in return.[25]

God's intentions had to be read in obscure signs, the meaning of which, indeed the awareness that they had even appeared, only became clear in retrospect. In 1508 during the days when troops were leaving for the battle of Cadore, reports of the moon dripping with blood, lightning striking church towers and killing several people, and wolves attacking children and adults were read as auguries of divine anger to be expiated by "litanies and sacrifices." As Venice's conflict with the papacy and France escalated, some interpreted the mosaic and pavement designs in the basilica of San Marco in a Joachite fashion to prophesy the loss of Venice's empire; although these prognostications may have only been remembered or made up after the disasters at Agnadello, they provided satisfying retrospective explanations of disturbing events. A pamphlet published in Bologna with a backdated publication date of 1511 enumerates the signs and prodigies that announced the imminent punishment of the world and especially of Italy: will-o'-the-wisps appeared above the fields of Agnadello, two angels displayed unsheathed swords over Padua, the heavens spewed forth fire, and a three-headed child was born in Florence. The cataclysm in Friuli became one of many events in a series of portends and disasters which dominated the public imagination during the Italian wars, but Friulans seem to have been particularly open to prophetic interpretations of their affairs. Members of the Amaseo family, Friuli's most prominent humanist dynasty, collected prophecies from numerous sources both by acquiring parchments of old ones and by copying down new ones when they heard them. The notary Antonio Belloni, who wrote an account of the Giovedì Grasso killings, also left a Latin prophecy among his papers.[26]

Reports of astral conjunctions and signs of divine wrath were commonly used to explain Giovedì Grasso. Antonio Savorgnan refused to heed the pleas of the luogotenente because, "more than anything else the evil constellation of that day inclined him in that direction." Accidents to looters signified divine justice and admon-

FIGURE 12. Drawings of Udine. *Upper plate*, pits for the plague dead; *lower plate*, earthquake damage.

ished others; the falling of a lighted torch indicated "how the light of justice must be extinguished"; and a few weeks after the massacre, two angels holding bloody swords hovered above the bell tower of San Francesco, which was next to the Savorgnan palace, "and between them appeared a great pillar of fire in manifest sign of vendetta." Jacopo di Porcìa employed a similar image to describe Antonio Savorgnan's motives: "hatred is a fire, which is extinguished not by water but by great quantities of blood." In April a twelve-year-old peasant girl reported that while collecting firewood she saw the Virgin and an angel, who requested that the girl follow a regimen of fasts and avoid blasphemy. This stock vision, similar to many others recounted in contemporary sources, stimulated her neighbors to organize processions and a Mass in a collective response to the sign of favor bestowed on them in a time of tribulations. In the months after Giovedì Grasso many persons trembled with dire expectations, creating a collective receptivity to, even need for, apparitions.[27]

However, natural catastrophes produced the most telling signs of divine indignation over the killings of Giovedì Grasso. A month after the riots, an earthquake caused extensive damage throughout Friuli and as far away as Venice, where senators rushed from the Ducal Palace when they felt the first tremors, strong enough to shake loose ceiling mosaics in San Marco. In Udine half of the luogotenente's castle collapsed, killing two women, and the many falling buildings produced a cloud of dust so thick that Gradenigo complained he could not see well enough to write his daily dispatch to Venice (Figure 12, *lower plate*). The mountain towns were most gravely damaged, especially Gemona, which was left in ruins. The Venetian patriarch attributed the catastrophe to God's anger with Venice's homosexuals; he was supported by legions of female prostitutes who reported that business had been particularly bad.[28]

In Friuli many were certain that God was furious with them because of the impieties of Giovedì Grasso. "Moreover, the sword of divine justice, which in the heavenly hand moves slowly to avenge, trembled over our land of Friuli." The bishop of Udine organized the clergy, confraternities, luogotenente, and assembled citizens in a sacred procession to the rubble of the Della Torre palace, where he left a piece of the host in an overt linking of the ruin of the Della Torre with divine wrath against the whole city. The breaking of a cross during the procession frightened the crowd almost to the point of riot. The Strumiero survivors portrayed the earthquake and broken cross as an act of divine retribution against Savorgnan and the rebellious peasants, and even the Zambarlani saw God's hand in the disasters, although they imagined them to portend future calamities.[29]

Within weeks of the earthquake, plague infested Udine. Although the deadly disease had briefly appeared the previous au-

tumn, Gregorio Amaseo convinced himself that its reappearance in
the spring of 1511 came from the failure of the Friulans to avenge
the innocent blood spilled on Giovedì Grasso. He examined the
standard naturalistic theories of contagion, corruption, and astrological influence as possible causes and even recognized how bad
weather had produced a poor harvest that elevated mortality rates
over the summer, "but whatever cause was precipitant, by universal judgment it was reputed to have been the result of the divine
scourge" brought on by the actions of Antonio Savorgnan. As
proof, Amaseo reported that when Antonio returned from Venice
on June 15, mortality quadrupled, forcing most of the healthy to
abandon Udine to the dead and dying. Many of the poor perished
in the streets from hunger or disease without the succor of medicines, prayers, last rites, or even a decent burial. As the graves
filled, a terrible odor arose from the putrefying, unburied bodies
(Figure 12, *upper plate*). Only when Antonio Savorgnan finally left
Udine at the end of the summer did the plague abate. Thus, in
the opinion of Amaseo and, by his report, of many others, Friuli's
Iscariot had betrayed the land to the apocalyptic horsemen of war,
sedition, earthquake, pestilence, and famine, who scourged the
land to cleanse it of the pollution brought on by Giovedì Grasso.[30]

For contemporaries these disasters represented a double-edged
sword because they could be both the results of human sins and
portents of additional tribulations soon to befall Friuli. In the many
accounts of those troubled times, Friulans searched to identify the
agents of evil and to recruit cosmic forces in the struggle between
local factions. Projecting their anger with their enemies onto God
and assimilating their own values of vendetta to biblical ideas of
divine justice, many saw the visions and disasters as the measure
of events, the lens through which explanations filtered.

THE WILL TO NARRATE

God's judgment alone did not suffice. The survivors of Giovedì
Grasso sought to enlist the judgment of history as well. For them
the function of history was to preserve a record of past injustices,
creating a peculiar relationship between violence and memory. Perhaps because pain assists recollection, the deepest, most haunting
myths and rituals of many cultures recall bloody sacrifices, cruel
tortures, and the deaths of innocents. Narrations about vendettas

memorialized the travails of ancestors, preserving anguish for years and in so doing establishing a sensitivity to linear time reaching back for generations. The bearing of a grudge may well be one of the wellsprings from which historical consciousness flows, from which the decisions and actions of individuals in the past become for succeeding generations matters of fascination, matters in need of explanation, matters that motivate necessary deeds.[31]

In preliterate feuding societies, various mnemonic devices kept alive the awareness of past slayings that required revenge. The feud sagas of the medieval Icelanders not only recorded the past but, through a stereotypical narrative form, provided a model for the resolution of future disputes. In Somaliland, Southern Greece, Albania, and Corsica, women sang haunting dirges to incite male kin to vengeance, and in some parts of Albania and Corsica a stone cairn erected on the spot of a murder reminded the men of their obligations every time they passed by. In Albania widows preserved vials of their husbands' blood, which they showed to their young sons to teach them to avenge the death of their fathers. Italians usually preserved memories of vendettas through stories told in an oral tradition that has survived in some regions well into the twentieth century.[32]

During his enforced exile in Basilicata during the Fascist period, Carlo Levi heard the stories of ancient murders that ennobled the hatreds still obsessing the principal families; through repeated tellings that were far more common than any act of violence, these stories became the substance of vendettas and, more recently, of politics. If one were to ask where in society vendetta actually exists, how it is preserved, how its rules operate, one might best find the answer in the stories of past deeds, the selective memories that merged into new grievances and new enemies. The roots of vendetta intertwine with a kind of history that is an expression of the will to narrate.[33]

Just as a Florentine merchant might keep a *ricordanza*—a "memory book" designed to inform his sons about the family business, marriage connections, and political alliances—or a Venetian patrician might write a chronicle of his city to instruct his fellows and progeny about the republic's mythic truths, so did Friulan aristocrats write down accounts of their relations with their blood enemies. Besides preserving a memory of events, these narratives justified past deeds, provided a basis for future retaliatory or legal actions, and protected family honor; in short they fashioned a version of events which served the needs of the family. Some of these accounts can be found among the family's private papers and were never intended for publication, but the anguish produced by Giovedì Grasso with its many unpaid debts of blood stimulated a new genre of works variously called *narratives, descriptions, histories, historical letters,* and *chronicles,* circulated as part of a campaign of exculpatory explanation and literary revenge. During the half-century after 1511, narrative assassinations became as much a part of the pursuit of vendetta as actual murders.[34]

Some nine different accounts written after the events constituted the first generation of Giovedì Grasso narrations. In the intensity of its eyewitness descriptions, the *History of the Cruel Fat Thursday* by Gregorio Amaseo has no peer. Much of the attraction of the Friulan Giovedì Grasso for modern historians from Leopold von Ranke to the present author comes from the singular power of Amaseo's little history.[35]

Belonging to a family long involved in the affairs of Udine, Gregorio participated in the events of 1511, a fact that makes his *History* especially valuable as a document of emotions. The Amaseos originated among the *popolo* of Udine, practicing in earlier generations the trades of barber, furrier, and pharmacist. Through the patronage of the Savorgnan, they attained communal office, bought lands, abandoned trade, entered the liberal professions, and by the early sixteenth century adopted a family crest and spurious descent from an ancient Bolognese noble family. Classic parvenus, they maintained a high consciousness of their privileges, worried about slights against their honor, wrote contemptuously about artisans, and tried to act like nobles.

Their attachment to the Savorgnan went back to the patriarchal civil wars, during which Domenico Amaseo saved Tristano Savorgnan from assassination by warning him in the middle of the night of a pending attack, later welcoming him triumphantly into Udine after the success of Venetian arms. "As a result the house of Savorgnan has been more obligated to the house of Amaseo than to all the rest of the patria and most of all has preserved the friendship up to the present because *amicus Socrates, amicus Plato, sed magis amica veritas.*" Even after 1509, when they became alienated from

Antonio Savorgnan, the Amaseos repeatedly tried to reclaim the connection with the Savorgnan on the basis of its antiquity. "I am not one of the new friends," Gregorio reminded Antonio, "ours is an old friendship of more than one hundred years duration."[36]

Three brothers, Leonardo, Gregorio, and Girolamo Amaseo, were among the grandchildren of Domenico and became the leading humanist intellectuals of their generation in Friuli. Leonardo married into the Monticolo family and produced eleven children. By examining the godparents of these children, one can discern the range of Amaseo friendships from the end of the fifteenth century to 1510 when Leonardo died. Three members of the Venetian patriciate stood at the font for Amaseo babies, as did several prominent officials of the Venetian citizen class including a secretary of the procurators, a ducal secretary, a collateral of the signoria, a chancellor of the luogotenente, and a notary of the *auditori nuovi*. After 1502 Antonio, Giovanni, and Girolamo Savorgnan all acted as godparents. Leonardo solidified his alliances within a Zambarlano network consisting of Venetians (especially Venetian professionals who worked in Venice at about the same social level as the Amaseos did in Friuli) and of the leading figures among the Savorgnan. However, these connections began to unravel in 1509 when the council of Udine, fearful that Antonio Savorgnan might be about to transfer his allegiance to the imperialists, elected Leonardo as the head of the city. Thereafter, Antonio considered the Amaseo brothers as traitors to his interests. The next year, Antonio blocked the appointment of Gregorio as a delegate to Venice and openly showed his ill favor to the brothers, who were unable to get even their Monticolo in-laws to help. The brothers' pleas and recollections of ancient friendship with the Savorgnan betrayed their bitterness at being rejected. By the time of Giovedì Grasso, Gregorio found himself in a dangerously ambiguous position, and although he still tried to reclaim Antonio's friendship, in private he was an acerbic critic of the Zambarlano leader.[37]

After Leonardo's death in the summer of 1510, leadership of the family passed to Gregorio. One of the responsibilities he inherited was the continuation of Leonardo's diary, a vast record of the events of the war years begun for motives similar to those of Marin Sanudo, who also thought he was living through momentous times. In addition to recounting episodes in the war, the Amaseo diary chronicled the Friulan vendetta and reported opinions about the conflicts.

The brothers shared in the impulse that was widespread among intellectuals to explain the turmoils provoked by repeated foreign invasions and to capitalize on the confusion by obtaining commissions from governments that needed exculpation. In 1499, after France and Venice occupied Milan and the Venetians proposed to recruit the French for a new crusade against the Turks, the youngest Amaseo, Girolamo, published a book prophesying that the combined Christian powers would finally defeat the infidel, recapture Jerusalem, and impose a universal Christian monarchy that would usher in a new Golden Age. Borrowing the hexameters and rhetorical form of the classical epic, he revived late medieval prophecies and flattered the French king. However, in 1507, when Gregorio formally presented his brother's book to Louis XII in Milan the anticipated commission to write a history of the French conquests failed to materialize. Nevertheless, the brothers continued to keep the diary, which would have served as the source for a proposed Latin history if a patron had ever been found.[38]

Both Gregorio and Girolamo had been students of the famous Friulan humanist Marcantonio Sabellico and struggled to maintain their positions as schoolmasters during the difficult war years. However, Gregorio brought his own personal liabilities to the family struggle for recognition. Frequently reproved for neglect of his duties, he lost his teaching position in Udine in 1489 when arrested after a nun became pregnant with his child. His resulting prison sentence was commuted to a six-month exile. Despite many misadventures including capture by papal troops, Gregorio moved in the highest literary circles of the Veneto and maintained a lively correspondence with other humanists. He eventually became a lecturer in Latin letters in Udine but failed to obtain a similar post in Venice in 1512. In addition to keeping up the family diary and writing his history of the Cruel Carnival he published a commentary on the history of the patriarchate of Aquileia.[39]

Gregorio intended his polemical pamphlet history of Giovedì Grasso for a regional readership inasmuch as he composed it in Venetian rather than in Latin or Tuscan. Written in an unpolished style between March 1513 and February 1514 and giving a recounting of daily events, the *History* merely extended the family diaries in which Gregorio outlined his standards of evidence by noting that he recorded what happened "in large part according to the common gossip of the streets and in part from true information, mostly regarding events that took place in the patria and known positively by us and written down without any ornamentation and with little diligence." The *History* betrays slightly more humanist erudition than the diaries. Its precise beginning recalls the foreign invasions of Italy; a relentless thesis blames Antonio Savorgnan for planning a premeditated and diabolical massacre; and a sweeping conclusion explains all of the misfortunes of Friuli as the result of a divine vendetta provoked by the impieties of the Judas Antonio. The vitriol of Gregorio's language and the sensory immediacy of his descriptions allow the reader to begin to feel what it was like to witness the Cruel Carnival. Amaseo's *History* is reliable in recounting most facts correctly, even agreeing on matters of substance with Nicolò Monticolo's pro-Savorgnan version, but his stated goal not to offend anyone but to write a history motivated solely by a zeal for justice, liberty, the common good, piety, and peace was at best disingenuous. As might have been expected, he offended some people greatly.

Because of his words, Gregorio became as much the object of retribution as those who had actively participated in vendetta murders. During the imperial invasion of 1514, some of the surviving partisans of Antonio Savorgnan proposed to take advantage of the situation to abduct Amaseo secretly, to gouge out his eyes and cut off his tongue and hands "so that," as Gregorio lamented, "I could neither see, nor speak, nor write about my cause." Particularly enraged when he read the *History* in a copy supposedly stolen from Gregorio himself, Antonio's surviving son, Nicolò, threatened to tear the humanist to pieces but missed his chance because, Amaseo thought, God prevented it. "If one still needs another example, then this result fully demonstrates the appearance of the divine vendetta." Gregorio's transition from an ardent Zambarlano to the most adamant literary enemy of Antonio Savorgnan and finally to an open propagandist for the Strumieri was epitomized by the funeral eulogy he gave in 1527 for Giovanni Della Torre, an encomium that led to a series of death threats against Gregorio. Once the memories of the eyewitnesses faded or died with them, Amaseo's *History* became the most important source of the collective memory. Even fifty years later, what Amaseo said had happened justified antagonisms and determined the appropriate forms of revenge.[40]

With the exception of Nicolò Monticolo's pro-Savorgnan version, the other accounts produced in the wake of Giovedì Grasso suggested various combinations of diabolical, providential, and astrological explanations. Giovanni Battista Cergneu and Giovanni Candido emphasized the persuasive power of Antonio Savorgnan's envious, iniquitous, and slanderous tongue among the ignorant. Several authors noted the coincidental revolts against nobles in Dalmatia, Slovenia, Hungary, and southern Germany but offered little to explain the waves of peasant rebellions other than malevolent celestial influences. Whatever the explanations, these narrations provided a literary substitute or postponement for exacting blood revenge. Referring to the Giovedì Grasso murderers, Giovanni Candido vowed, "I will annihilate them like the dust of the earth and crush them like the pieces of brick in the piazze." Of course he did nothing of the sort but contented himself with assaults of the pen.[41]

Friulans could not escape further travails. Although the factions would begin to dissolve after Giovedì Grasso, obligations of revenge remained, especially for the brothers and sons of victims whose honor was hardly restored by the scapegoating of a few lowly thugs. But revenge was not just a matter of keeping score. In retaliation for the 1511 carnival with its systematic butcheries of the Strumieri, avengers had to debase Antonio Savorgnan thoroughly.

CHAPTER SEVEN

Retaliations and Realignments

The events of the Cruel Carnival, continuing pressures of war, and tardy political reforms initiated by Venice eventually broke up the long-standing Friulan factions. Antonio Savorgnan's assassination followed a year of tensions and intrigues during which Venice again lost its hold on Friuli.

The murder was accomplished in a notoriously macabre fashion that reveals the deep cultural connections between vendetta practices and hunting, an activity that created a peculiar identity between killers and hunting dogs and formed a hierarchy for valuing the body parts of animal prey and human victims. A symbolic vocabulary derived from hunting enriched vendetta symbolism and paralleled the body imagery of carnival, which had influenced the forms of killing on Giovedì Grasso. Through a process of multiple projections, killers invested their hunting dogs with their own anger, a process that allowed them to see violent human emotions as being like the madness of a rabid dog or the wildness of a wolf and thus as something beyond human control. In addition, by feeding parts of the bodies of their victims to dogs and treating dead men as the objects of a hunt, avengers dehumanized their enemies, making them quite literally dog meat. As was the case with carni-

val, which emphasized the forms of butchering, vendetta imagery
found its richest source in the processes for transforming bodies
into meat, especially in the hunt.

In the years immediately after the war, factional killings waned
as Girolamo Savorgnan failed to recapture his cousin Antonio's
popular following. As a result of Girolamo's limitations as a leader
and Venice's reforms of the governing institutions of Udine, the
Zambarlano coalition of peasants and artisans collapsed. The course
of Friulan history after the Cruel Carnival reveals how the carnival
killings and the retaliatory assassination of Antonio Savorgnan
produced a deeply resonant catharsis, the memory of which evoked
intense emotions, and so weakened the patronage system that Friuli
underwent fundamental changes.

Assassination of Antonio Savorgnan

During June and July 1511, Venice encountered serious difficulties in its defense of Friuli from the Austrian invasion. Combatants
had become so weakened by famine and plague that the surviving
troops languished in their garrisons, and most of the fighting consisted of minor skirmishes and nocturnal raids. In addition, Venice
found its financial resources drastically depleted. The provveditore
for Friuli, Giovanni Vitturi, had not received regular payments for
his men for months, and Venetian soldiers began to riot and loot
in nearby Treviso. Antonio Savorgnan's repeated pleas for assistance were answered with testimonials of the doge's confidence in
him rather than with troops and money. As a result he was able to
rebuild only a portion of the fortifications at Marano. By the end
of August the entire responsibility for the defense of Friuli had
fallen on his shoulders.[1]

Friuli seemed doomed. The region had been stripped of troops
because the Venetian captains had insisted that the enemy would
find it impossible to ford the Piave after all the available boats
had been destroyed. They were wrong. In September the enemy
crossed with ease. As the traditionally philo-Austrian nobles con-
tacted imperial agents to transfer their allegiance in anticipation of
the collapse of Venetian rule and in hopes of avenging themselves
on Antonio Savorgnan, the Zambarlano townsmen and peasants
tensely waited out events. Short of men and bereft of artillery, Antonio abandoned the fortified town of Sacile, and within hours the

counts of Porcìa and Polcenigo offered their fealty to the empire. In Spilimbergo the exiled castellan Giovanni Enrico Spilimbergo captured the Venetian provveditore Giacomo Boldù and turned him and the town over to the Austrians, who then threatened Antonio's flank as he retreated toward Udine.

Faced with an untenable military situation and the probable sacking of Udine, Savorgnan agreed to receive imperial messengers who offered him extremely generous terms including the retention of all his properties and fiefs and a permanent alliance with the emperor. Antonio accepted, abandoning in a day the Savorgnan allegiance to Venice, which had lasted for more than a century. On September 20, accompanied by the imperial prefects, he entered Udine, hastily abandoned by the Venetian luogotenente, who had left behind all his artillery. With the help of these valuable pieces, Maximilian's captains quickly took the strategic fortress of Gradisca on the Isonzo, thereby completing their surprise conquest. Although none of Antonio's actions was without controversy, least of all this epic treason, most contemporaries agreed that he switched sides to save Udine from the destruction imperial armies had recently visited upon other towns.[2]

All Friuli fell into enemy hands except for the lagoon fortress of Marano and the rock of Osoppo, which held out under Antonio's cousin, Girolamo. Despite his many protestation ɔf loyalty to Venice, even Girolamo contemplated treason, traveling to Austria to negotiate terms with Maximilian. What transpired between them is unknown, but Girolamo returned to Osoppo dissatisfied, possibly because the emperor favored Antonio over him.[3]

The Venetians were finally prompted to decisive political if not military action by the reversal of fortunes in Friuli and the surrender of Antonio in whom they had placed such high trust. The Council of Ten immediately confiscated all of his property and that of his brother Giovanni and Giovanni's sons Francesco and Bernardino, who were considered rebels because they were in imperial territory. Moreover, the ten offered a reward of 5,000 ducats and release from any previous sentence of banishment to anyone who successfully assassinated Antonio. Since its founding in the aftermath of the Querini-Tiepolo conspiracy of 1310, the council had indulged in the occasional political assassination, but the ten recognized that the scheme to kill Savorgnan was special. The assas-

sination contract, signed by three Strumiero lords who desired revenge for the Cruel Carnival, is the only document in the "most
secret" file of the secret archive of the council, which apparently
wanted a quick solution to the Savorgnan threat which could later
be publicly disavowed and blamed on the feuding Friulans, especially if the emperor became overly concerned.[4]

In reaction to Antonio's betrayal, his former supporters in the
Venetian councils suffered political reprisals, none more so than his
most powerful advocate, Andrea Loredan. Despite the fact that on
the day before Antonio's double-cross the citizens of Udine had
sent a delegation to Venice asking that Andrea Loredan command
the city's garrison and despite the fact that on the very day of the
capitulation Loredan had loaned more money than anyone else to
provide for the troops in Padua refusing to leave their barracks
without pay, Loredan bore the brunt of the political backlash
against the Friulan traitor. On September 30 the bid of Loredan
and the other architects of Venice's policy in Friuli to be reelected
to the Senate was rejected, a particularly humiliating defeat inasmuch as established patricians were virtually guaranteed reelection.
In fact, not a single Loredan remained in the Senate. Throughout
the autumn Andrea Loredan and Pietro Cappello lost every office
for which they were nominated; it took nearly a year for Loredan's
career to recover and even longer for Cappello's.[5]

Meanwhile, the enemy experienced its own dreadful problems.
One of the few documents preserved from the imperial side recounts the travails of the army occupying Friuli during the autumn
of 1511. Despite their rapid successes, the troops began to mutiny
because of a lack of pay and food, which could not be expropriated
locally because the region had already been so badly ravaged. Attempts to impose heavy taxes on the inhabitants alienated Maximilian's supporters among the castellans and townsmen, and it
soon became evident that the army could not safely winter there.
With the retreat of the French army under Gaston de Foix in
Lombardy, Venice could concentrate its efforts on recapturing
Friuli. Imperial occupation forces stayed barely three weeks before
they began to withdraw, leaving behind only a token garrison at
Gradisca.

Faced with a debacle, Antonio Savorgnan tried to provoke an
uprising on his behalf in Udine, a desperate measure that failed

and forced him to retire to Gorizia, leaving all of Friuli, except Gradisca, to return peacefully to Venetian authority. Antonio's son Nicolò broke the calm by sacking a few Strumiero castles. Throughout the winter both father and son menaced the borders with small guerrilla armies, but in the end Antonio and his followers faced a complete reversal of their fortunes. The turncoat sent repeated messages to Venice pleading for a safe conduct or a pardon and offering to help Venice capture Gradisca and Gorizia, but the Council of Ten refused to make the slightest concession to him. Girolamo's unbending hostility toward his cousin steeled the resolve of the council, which could not afford to antagonize the new Savorgnan lord, who now possessed all of Antonio's old fiefs and served as Venice's new client prince in Friuli.

During that winter, with the support of Girolamo and the ten, Artico Prampero plotted to lure Antonio into a trap at the mountain fortress of Chiusaforte, and wishful thinking produced recurrent false rumors that Antonio had already been murdered. As the emperor began to rebuild his forces, Venetian politicians were repeatedly gripped by fears that Antonio might return to lead a broad-based revolt. To head off the dangerous prospect of a revival of Antonio's popularity, the Venetians opened negotiations with the emperor in the early spring. On April 6, 1512 Maximilian signed a truce with Venice, an act that now made Savorgnan an unwelcome liability for the emperor, who wanted him to leave Gorizia, where he could cause trouble. Abandoned by all but his son and a few retainers, Antonio made a final retreat through the melting snow across the mountains to find refuge in Austria.[6]

Savorgnan remained in seclusion in Villach, a pleasant town just across the Carnic Alps on the road to Graz and Vienna. There his enemies found him.

A band of Strumiero lords who had signed the assassination contract with the Council of Ten secretly entered the town with the complicity of Maximilian's representative in Villach, an exiled Friulan castellan named Federico Strassoldo. The assassins confessed to a mixture of motives. Girolamo Colloredo, the son of Albertino lord of Sterpo and the brother of Teseo, murdered on Giovedì Grasso, came along just "for revenge" (*per far la vendetta*) whereas Agostino Colloredo sought to reacquire the possessions he had lost the previous year. Peasants had sacked Giovanni Giorgio Zoppola's estate and raped two of the women of the family, and rioters had looted and burned the palace of Giacomo Castello, one of the three ringleaders of the Strumieri in Udine. Giovanni Enrico Spilimbergo had lost a brother on Giovedì Grasso, but for Giovanni Enrico, who had ridden abreast of Antonio Savorgnan when the imperial armies entered Udine in September and was one of the great men of the new imperial coalition, opportunism must have been the strongest motivation. After Antonio's move to the imperial flag had proved foolhardy, Giovanni Enrico again sought to stay on the good side of fortune by negotiating with the ten to assassinate Antonio, receiving in return a revocation of his life sentence of exile.[7]

The Friulans bribed two imperial captains in charge of security to be absent on the morning of May 27 while Antonio attended mass in the gray Gothic cathedral. The attackers concealed themselves at the foot of a stairway leading from the churchyard. After mass, as Antonio descended the stairs, the assassins and some ten *bravi* sprang out and drove their intended victim back into the cemetery. In the fight that followed, Giovanni Enrico Spilimbergo delivered the telling blows (Figure 13). Agostino Colloredo recounted the events:

> It was by divine miracle that Antonio Savorgnan was wounded: his head opened, he fell down, and he never spoke another word. But before he died, a giant dog came there and ate all his brains, and one cannot possibly deny that his brains were eaten. His familiar did nothing about it. . . . Since I am a priest, that is a canon of Aquileia and Cividale, I did not want to participate in that homicide, so I stayed at home.

The macabre detail of a dog eating Antonio's brains became for contemporaries the most revealing point of the whole assassination, one that most subsequent accounts included or embellished. A Spilimbergo family chronicle improved on it by adding a pig:

> It is noted that when Messer Antonio Savorgnan was killed in the square of Villach . . . a pig and a dog came along from which he could not be protected until they had eaten the brains that had fallen on the ground. There are many people who do not believe this, but I have been assured of it by trust-

FIGURE 13. Drawing of the murder of Antonio Savorgnan in 1512
in Villach, Austria.

worthy men, among others by a surgeon, son of an Italian
surgeon from Tolmezzo, who said that his father saw this happen with his own eyes. While this account is widely known, I
do not know from whom it originates, but I know well this
father and his son who, as I said, are faithful and good men.

In his chronicle of the war years, Cergneu further refined the details by alluding to Dante's *Inferno*:

He never arose from that place where by divine will a pig
drank his blood and a dog ate the brains. Such was the just
end to the deeds of the new Judas who was sent to the lowest
circle of Hell in the first place among traitors.[8]

All of the assassins escaped except for Gregorio Colloredo, whom
the Austrian authorities captured when he stayed behind to destroy
a bridge.

The very day on which firm news of Antonio's assassination

arrived in Venice, the ten lifted Spilimbergo's banishment and granted him a safe conduct, valid for one hundred years, to move freely about the patria. When they presented themselves to the heads of the council, the killers tried to put an honorable face on their deeds by refusing the full reward and accepting only enough money to cover their expenses for bribes, hired *bravi*, and lost horses. The ten obligingly and uncharacteristically paid them off immediately and granted them and their relatives the right to bear arms wherever they went as protection from the anticipated retaliations of the Zambarlani. The erstwhile imperial governor in Villach, Federico Strassoldo, spent three years defending himself in Austrian courts against charges of his complicity in the murder, and although never convicted, his involvement ruined his career as an imperial courtier. From the confiscated wealth of Antonio Savorgnan, the ten began to pay a modest annual stipend to the heirs of Alvise Della Torre and to repair frontier fortresses, but the bulk of the estate remained under the control of Girolamo Savorgnan.[9]

Dogs of Revenge

The phenomenon of the dog eating Antonio Savorgnan's brains demonstrates how useful animals can be for understanding human violence. The incorporation of animals into human affairs in Friuli contrasted with the ritual process of incorporation found in Venice with the annual execution of swine during carnival; in the Friulan vendetta animals actually participated in killings when men permitted or encouraged dogs to eat human victims. The Friulan experience might best be understood as an example of what Emmanuel Le Roy Ladurie has called the "spontaneously nominalist" mentality of the Renaissance, a mentality that was "better adapted to handling objects . . . as it saw fit than dealing with abstract concepts such as class struggle, reforms, etc."[10]

In his study of Menocchio, the heretic Friulan miller Carlo Ginsburg observed a similar characteristic. Menocchio treated the many metaphors that he employed in his speech in a "rigorously literal" fashion, thinking through problems by identifying one term of a comparison with the other, a mental process he followed when he envisioned the primal matter of the cosmos as cheese and the first men and angels as worms spontaneously generated from it. The characteristic nominalist logic involved strings of analogies, attaching like to like in an attempt to explain chaotic and violent events. In examining their own violence, even the educated Friulans who wrote the chronicles and histories employed animal metaphors nominalistically; to recapture their meaning, one must begin by trying to appreciate Friulan and Renaissance attitudes toward the animals in question, dogs in particular.[11]

The very lexicon of factionalism identified certain men as dogs. Antonio Savorgnan's principal retainers were the "familiars and dogs of the house" or the "dogs and comrades," an appellation distantly echoed by Shakespeare, who described "a dog of the house of Montague." Although the modern reader might dismiss these appellations as common insults, they seem to have had more substance than that: a subordinate might accept the label by referring to himself as "your dog and slave" when writing to his lord. The term implied that these men obeyed their master with the devotion of hunting hounds and that they were of a lowly condition. For example, when the Zambarlani realized that they could sack the palaces of the enemy nobles, "they became alert like dogs at the chase," and the peasants who attacked the castellans were likened to barking or rabid dogs.[12]

The eating dog more specifically brought out specters of apocalyptic revenge. In the days immediately after Antonio's treason, a defamatory sonnet circulated in Venice which ended with a vision of the traitor hanging by his foot from the gallows while dogs and crows pulled apart his body. Years later Giovanni Candido conjured up a list of horrible fates that he said befell those who had directed the carnival riots of 1511: some were dismembered, others broke their necks, many were thrown into deep wells where they drowned, still more were imprisoned or exiled to live a miserable life in foreign lands, a great many died of starvation, and "many seeking death became like rabid dogs and gave up the ghost." "The others, who were few, remained sick in spirit awaiting God's justice [la divina vendetta], prophesied by David." Few of the events Candido reported ever took place, but the list of imaginary fates provides a useful index of contemporary ideas of revenge.[13]

Friulans also talked about their own offenses by employing animal metaphors, especially comparisons with dogs and pigs, which explained human violence by showing how men had crossed the line into bestiality. In fact, analogies to these animals pervade the dialects of the Veneto, most significantly as blasphemies and insults. Comparing God or the Madonna to a dog or a pig, as in *Dio cane* and *porca Madonna*, juxtaposed the most sacred with the most profane, dragging all that was good and true into the filth, promiscuity, and senseless aggressiveness of these everyday animals. "You were baptized in a pig trough," as the dramatist Ruzante put it, might be the paradigmatic Veneto insult. Pigs and dogs were always in the streets of Udine and Spilimbergo, just as they were in every other European town, and their habits of eating offal and the remains of the unburied dead infested the thoughts of those who witnessed vendetta brutalities. To them the two species became the signs of shame, the contraries of the honorable, socially correct man, whose enemies in a vendetta could most thoroughly dishonor him by making him the food of street scavengers.[14]

The identification of men with dogs had ancient and widespread precedents in which men were said to metamorphose into dogs and dogs became men. Early medieval law considered domestic animals part of the household and subject to the same legal protection accorded to free persons, including *wergild* if killed. The legal personification of animals survived most clearly in the unwritten laws of twentieth-century Montenegro and Albania, in which the regulations of blood feuding made careful provisions for house dogs. Albanians trained and kept attack dogs, which could be handled safely only by the person who fed them; the dogs were unchained at night to guard against intruders. If a house dog killed someone at night, the victim's clan had no rights of revenge inasmuch as the law assumed that any man abroad in the dark was a robber or an enemy. If, on the other hand, a traveler killed a dog near its house in the dark, the dog's owner could seek to take blood from the killer's clan because, according to the laws of the Kanùn, "at night a dog is equivalent to a man." In fact, in some places, clansmen deemed the killing of a dog more serious than the murder of a man, as revealed in the notorious case in which twelve men forfeited their lives in recompense for one dog. In contrast, if a dog attacked a traveler on the public path or during the day, the victim's clan could then seek retribution from the dog's owner because under those conditions the animal was considered an offensive fighter for his clan rather than an exempt house dog deployed for defense.[15]

In a similar fashion in nineteenth-century Corsica, the killing or even criticism of a dog could lead to violent retaliation, so complete was the identification of the owner with his dog. Although we cannot know whether or not Friuli had a similar unwritten law during the Renaissance, many Friulans kept attack dogs for defense, and the language employed to describe feuding families reveals an attitude toward the dogs of a house similar to that of the modern Albanians. In addition, both Turkish and German invaders used dogs as combatants against unarmed civilians.[16]

Some of the habit of personifying dogs survived even in the refined aristocratic regulations governing the duel. Stefano Guazzo reported that most disputes leading to duels arose from quarrels over gambling, women, or dogs; in Ferrara, at the time Ariosto was the poetic luminary of the court, a courtier challenged another to a duel because of the contempt the latter had shown the challenger's dog. The theorists of dueling noted that it would be infamous to attack a fallen duelist who had lost his weapon because even a shameful dog would not bite a prostrate man.[17]

Numerous medieval forms of punishment enlisted dogs to degrade the guilty. The oldest example of a derisory punishment can be found among the laws of the Burgundians according to which robbers were forced to kiss a dog's anus in front of the assembled people. In 1008 the archbishop of Milan promulgated a penalty requiring the guilty to carry a dog while walking barefoot through the streets, and in a French law of 1306 a man accused of slaying his lord had to undergo the ordeal of fighting a dog. In his Roland epic, Boiardo recalled such practices by describing how a king ordered his men to turn over alive his most hated foe so that the king could have the captive fight a dog.[18]

During the Renaissance dogs served as symbols of treason and usury and were feared as carriers of the plague. Their bones and teeth were used as amulets with apotropaic powers; along with pigs, dogs most commonly appeared as the familiars of witches, at least in the imagination of inquisitors who occupied themselves with such matters. The worst fate for a Renaissance duelist was to die like a dog, to be "dragged off by one of his arms or legs, with no more respect than would be shown to a dog or a piece of wood" and thrown in the common pit with other dead animals. Such was the death the Friulan avengers wished for their enemies.[19]

Comparing humans with dogs enabled participants and others

to explain the passionate fury of vendetta killings by distinguishing kinds of anger. The ancient Greeks first isolated two types of anger: the cold-blooded, calculated anger Odysseus betrayed when he systematically killed Penelope's suitors as opposed to the anger that drove Hector on the battlefield, his *lyssa* a wolfish or doglike madness symptomatic of rabies. The most likely stimulus of *lyssa* might be the overwhelming grief that comes from the loss of close kin, the kind that engulfed Hecuba, who, after she lost all of her children, began to bark like a dog. According to the Greeks, men and women in *lyssa* abandoned their humanity and therefore could no longer be subject to the law, and the disease of rabies retains in modern times an association with bestial, uncontrollable violence.[20]

Germanic traditions, which were undoubtedly strong in Friuli, also metamorphosed humans into animals to explain ferocious anger, as can be seen in the sagas about the *berserkirs*, who assumed the forms of wolves or bears to avenge the dead. Friulan folklore assisted in imagining such metamorphoses. In a legend that can be dated from as early as the twelfth century, Attila, the scourge who destroyed ancient Aquileia, had the face and snout of a dog and the body of a man. Instead of speaking his orders he barked them. Indeed the half-dog, half-man became the standard Renaissance astrological image of a degree of Aries labeled as the "quarrelsome and envious man," as can be seen in Pietro d'Abano's *Astrolabium planum* (Figure 14).[21]

Even though they would not have used the same terms as the Greeks or Germans, Friulans understood the different kinds of

FIGURE 14. Drawing of a dog-headed man, astrological emblem for the second degree of Aries, "a quarrelsome and envious man," *right*.

anger when pursuing revenge. Although they most commonly employed the former method of careful planning and efficient execution, as in the murder of Antonio Savorgnan, they were particularly fascinated with the latter form, *lyssa* or going berserk, and they justified even the most cold-blooded killing by arguing that the murderer had been taken over by an uncontrollable rage.

In effect, the dog provided an explanation—to wit, the killers were like rabid dogs, beside themselves in anger, and did not know what they were doing—but the message of the brain-eating dog cannot simply be decoded from a binary distinction between human culture and bestial nature. Neither were humans purely cultural nor dogs exclusively natural. Just like dogs, which were usually tame and obedient, humans usually followed society's rules, but occasionally dogs went rabid and humans berserk. The problem that needed explanation was wildness. Here dogs helped because they provided an observable model for the transformation from domesticity to savagery and not just when they became rabid. There was something in any dog's nature which could go inexplicably wild, something dogs shared with their close relatives the wolves, animals that often preyed on human society. In the two natures of dogs, the servile and the wolfish, humans saw an especially revealing mirror of themselves, of both their need for community and the tendency of some men to tear society apart by murdering others.[22]

In contrast to the ancients, who had such a positive image of the wolf, the mother of Rome, the people of the Middle Ages and Renaissance saw wolves as representing wildness in its most threatening aspect. In describing the earliest settlements of the Venetian lagoon, the *Altine Chronicle* imagined a primordial wilderness occupied by a savage folk who howled like wolves and lived by hunting. Only when they learned the arts of agriculture and civilization did they tame themselves, along with their wilderness habitat.[23]

In Friuli real wolves remained an ever-present threat, recalled by many place names such as Lovària and Lovàries and in numerous accounts of bloody attacks, particularly on children. The howls of wolves could be heard frequently on winter nights when hungry packs descended from the mountains in search of food. Ill protected against these predators, many villagers relied on spike-collared attack dogs which they let loose at night. Dogs best deterred the ravages of wolves precisely because the two species were so similar: a properly equipped and trained mastiff might be the match of a wolf, but he was still vulnerable both to attack and to the temptations of joining the wild pack. In the imagination of contemporaries, the appearance of wolves augured evil events, especially war or tyranny. As Francesco Sacchetti put it in a different context, "more than any other that beast has the desire to kill human nature."[24]

Friulans also believed in wolfmen, but their attitude toward them was contradictory and changing, paralleling the range of attitudes displayed toward the vendetta. Before the advent of inquisitorial procedures in the late sixteenth century, folklore pictured werewolves as benevolent figures who battled devils to save the crops and who served as the hounds of God, tracking down the devil just as good hunting dogs chased foxes. However, under pressure from inquisitors Friulans who were investigated for their alleged magical practices gradually changed their views and began to see werewolves as predators who stole livestock.[25]

In Old German, the word *warg* had the meanings of both *stranger* and *wolf*, an etymologic connection reflected in late medieval statutes that equated the reward for the head of an outlaw with that offered for the head of a wolf. The ominous pronouncement, *caput gerat lupinum*, still in use in England in the thirteenth century, had its origins in a quasi-magical legal formula that transformed a criminal into a werewolf to be hunted down like a dangerous animal, not just because he was outside the law but because he had become, in the words of the law, a wolf.[26]

Friulans also associated wolves with exiles who, as we have seen, became werewolves through a legal metamorphosis. In fact, in reading the Friulan chronicles it is sometimes difficult to determine whether an "attack by wolves" should be understood literally or metaphorically as a reference to a band of outlaws. Faced with roaming bands of outlaws who survived by robbing, Venice frequently added extra bounties and incentives to encourage the killing of these banished wolfmen. Finally, the connection between vendetta and the behavior of wolves becomes most explicit in the term used to describe a formal truce made between feuding parties, the "wolf's peace" (*pace lupina*).[27]

Thus, Friulians connected in several ways the pursuit of revenge with the behavior of dogs, wolves, and wolfmen, connections that envisioned vendetta as a form of wildness. The syllogistic reasoning was simple: avenging men behaved like wolves, wolves were by definition wild, therefore avenging men were wild. Wild animals served as signs of mad impulses found in human nature and as particularly useful receptacles of human vices. Because much modern scholarly work on feuding has emphasized the structural elements of vendetta which make it appear to be a reasonable form of conflict resolution, it might be useful to note the ambivalence that Friulans felt about their own desires for revenge, an ambivalence deriving not only from their mixed legal and ethical traditions but from their very understanding of the nature of humanity and wildness.

References to animal metamorphoses, killings, and wild transformations also recall the vast body of folklore about the armies of the dead. In his largely fictive description of the death in Villach of Gregorio Colloredo, one of Antonio Savorgnan's assassins, Gregorio Amaseo conjured up a diabolic horde rushing to capture the sinner's soul, a reference that imposes a Christian overlay on a deep pagan tradition about phantom armies battling in the sky in clouds and storms:

> [Gregorio Colloredo] was freed from the prison by the anger of the people having been agitated by a terrible cloud within a ferocious storm that struck that town as if the infernal furies with the diabolic hordes raced to abduct that most rotten soul for the eternal torments of the deep abyss; and not satisfied with that, in the following days terrible noises, which turned everything upside down, were heard at night in the cathedral where he [Antonio] was buried, and feeling attacked now here now there, the above mentioned people were so excited in their fury that they pulled the corpse from there and threw him into the Dravo River.[28]

Ottavia Niccoli discusses similar visions seen in storms and clouds near the site of the great battle of Agnadello in which phantom armies composed of the restless souls of dead soldiers transformed themselves into armies of pigs and dogs who rose up in a furious horde that she sees as an expression of beliefs about the wanderings of the dead. Carlo Ginzburg has analyzed a related complex of beliefs about persons who went into battle against evil forces during ecstatic trances or dreams. One of the prime examples of such beliefs comes from the *benandanti* of Friuli, who were set apart at birth by the presence of the caul and who fought as adults to preserve the crops. Ginzburg has found similar beliefs in many areas from Europe to Siberia. All of these groups believed that after a human metamorphosis into an animal, typically a dog or wolf, the changed person fought for good against evil. Ginzburg explains these metamorphoses as symbolizing a temporary death—just as did initiations, rites of passage, and the sentences of exile that transformed men into wolves—and depicts the groups who fought in ecstatic combats as representing the living in a struggle with the dead.[29]

Beliefs about the armies of the dead, which were certainly current in sixteenth-century Friuli, produced numerous homologies to what can be found in descriptions of the assassination of Antonio Savorgnan: the presence of dogs, a combat, and visions of a diabolic horde in a storm. Such homologies enrich the context for understanding beliefs about the dead and the relationship between humans and animals, but they do not explain exactly what happened during the vendetta. After all the assassins of Antonio Savorgnan did not become dogs but brought the animals along to a killing. In the assassination and in the fates of several of the carnival victims, animals were deployed as agents of human retribution. The essential vendetta element seems to be the cooperative relationship between killers and dogs in which the dogs' role is to eat the victim.

The Friulan cases are not isolated examples. A Venetian legend current in the early sixteenth century described the deaths of Doge Pietro Candiano and his son, murdered by a mob in 958. After the people killed them, their bodies were taken to a butcher shop and cut into small pieces, which were thrown to the market dogs. Such a fate continued to be promised to others who violated the trust of the Venetian people, especially to Antonio Grimani who, after his loss of Lepanto in 1499, was the subject of numerous wall posters that threatened to serve him and his sons to dogs. In 1500 the provveditore of Castelmaggiore reported to Venice that some peasants had forcefully boarded a boat on the Po and stolen money from the Milanese ambassador to Spain. The Venetian authorities captured one of the robbers, killed him, and "gave the head to some dogs to eat." Thus, even in cases of summary official justice, the same forms of punishment could be employed as in private acts of revenge, revealing a complex entanglement between public and private notions of justice. Such an interplay can be found in popular lynchings, such as that of Galeazzo Maria Sforza's assassin, who, after he was killed by the crowd, was dragged about the city by children and finally fed to the street swine. And during the wars of religion in France, combatants threatened to and occasionally did feed a victim of the opposite faith to dogs and pigs. Thus, the Friulan examples fit into a broad tradition of feeding an enemy to an animal.[30]

One might begin to look for the meanings conveyed by these acts in the rich religious and literary lore about dogs eating men and women, stories that suggest the possible range of attitudes about the practice. In avenging the death of Patroklas, Achilleus tells the mortally wounded Hektor, in the words of the *Iliad*:

> No more entreating of me, you dog, by knees or parents.
> I wish only that my spirit and fury would drive me to hack
> your meat away and eat it raw for the things that you have
> done to me. So there is no one who can hold the dogs off from
> your head, not if they bring here and set before me ten times
> and twenty times the ransom, and promise more in addition,
> not if Priam son of Dardanos should offer to weigh out your
> bulk in gold; not even so shall the lady your mother who her-
> self bore you lay you on the death-bed and mourn you: no,
> but the dogs and the birds will have you all for their feasting.

In his manic vision, Achilleus identifies himself with the dog, imagining his enemy abandoned to cannibalism and the deserted field of battle.[31]

War was not the only ancient situation that destined a victim to dogs. Jezebel was condemned to be eaten by dogs, "and the carcass of Jezebel shall be as dung upon the face of the field" (2 Kings 9:35–37). For both Greeks and Hebrews the most horrific end conceivable involved turning a corpse over to dogs, whose gluttony made impossible even the most elementary provisions for honorable mourning and burial. The polluting effects of contacts with dogs and pigs permeates the Psalms and can be found in

Christ's commands in the Sermon on the Mount: "give not that which is holy unto the dogs, neither cast ye your pearls before swine, lest they trample them under their feet, and turn again and rend you" (Matthew 7:6). Despite the Christian abandonment of the rigid prohibitions of Leviticus and Hebraic fears of pollution, the medieval penitentials continued to see the eating habits of dogs as especially disgusting. Among the penalties for neglect of the consecrated host was a forty-day penance for those who vomited it up because they had eaten too much beforehand. If they cast it into a fire the penitentials reduced the penance to twenty days, but if they allowed dogs to eat the vomit, the penalty increased to one hundred days.[32]

Renaissance literature continued to associate the hungry dog with fears about dishonorment at death. The most revealing examples from a region near Friuli come from the works of the Paduan dramatist Angelo Beolco, known as Il Ruzante. Working between about 1517 and 1536, Beolco wrote and produced plays that employed peasant characters who commented on contemporary events and mores. The sad-sack character Ruzante, who appears in many of the comedies and was played by Beolco himself, imagined when he felt victimized that he would end up having his starved flesh eaten by dogs and when he felt strong that he could condemn his enemies to the same fate. The image of dogs consuming human flesh appears recurrently in the plays, nearly always as part of an oath or as a vision of perfect revenge.[33]

Similar images can be found elsewhere, especially in Shakespeare. Transforming a man into dog feces denied his very humanity and his chances for proper burial, a result that would have disquieted his survivors and left his soul in torment for eternity. Contemporaries, therefore, understood the presence of a dog feeding on a murdered man as a sign of dehumanization, the most complete form of dishonor.

Many of these examples, from the words of Achilleus to the death of Antonio Savorgnan, emphasize the eating of the head: why is it so often the head rather than the heart, liver, or human tripe? The best clues for an answer might be found in yet another context, that of hunting, from which the forms of revenge killing must have ultimately derived. The division of the bag of a hunt and the servings at a banquet represented and even constructed hierarchies of honor among members of society. The late medieval and Renaissance treatises on hunting, thus, prescribed a rigid code of comportment which divided up the kill according to the social hierarchy: typically, persons of merit or rank received those portions that were large and originated high on the animal's body, cuts from the tenderloin, haunch, thigh, or shoulder. However, the value ascribed to the head was ambiguous inasmuch as, on the one hand, it was not particularly desirable to eat, but, on the other, it was the source of the higher faculties. At medieval royal Irish banquets the head of the prey went to lowly persons such as butchers and stewards. In contrast, in the Veneto and Friuli, the head went to the lord or best hunter; other parts were distributed to lesser men; and the expendable innards of lungs, liver, and entrails were thrown to the hunting dogs. Animals' heads, in fact, had a special significance in feudal homages in the region. In the eleventh century, the doges of Venice received boars' heads to signify feudal dominion over subject towns and decorated the ducal palace with them, probably in imitation of the hunting practice of displaying trophies by hanging parts of the kill in trees. The feeding of a man's head to a dog by Friulans inverted a well-known hunting and feudal practice by giving the most noble part of the kill, the prey's head, to the lowest members of the party, the dog pack. The assassins of Antonio Savorgnan brought down to the lowest possible state the very part that had masterminded so many evils, an act that made his brains no better than the tripes of a boar. Antonio's handsome head literally became offal.[34]

Moreover, the habits of hunters help explain many of the more puzzling events associated with the Cruel Carnival and its aftermath. Several of the members of Antonio Savorgnan's "dog pack" had duties or traits that identified them with hunting. The man known as Ferrarese was Antonio's falconer, the essential expert in the prime aristocratic sport, and the nicknames Vergon (lime-twig) and Smergon (loon), both alluded to the hunting of birds, one of the most popular sports in Friuli, especially in the marshes of the lower plain, in which the Savorgnan had extensive properties. Thus, on Giovedì Grasso Antonio Savorgnan's experts in killing animals served as the experts in killing men. Many of the victims who were systematically dismembered with butcher's knives and fed to the dogs were quite consciously treated as if they were game.[35]

The shared trait of danger links war, revenge, and hunting. An important theme in the hunting literature is of the danger created when boars, bears, and other hunted animals turn on the hunter and attack him. Throughout the Middle Ages hunting represented a necessary exercise for war inasmuch as knights hunted to practice riding and killing and to retain their technical and tactical skills. Following this tradition, Renaissance theorists classified hunting as the "armed peace," a special form of warfare.

Erasmo da Valvasone, a Friulan castellan, wrote a treatise published in 1591 on the history of hunting which makes clear the connection to war by reversing the usual assumptions about historical evolution which supposed that hunting preceded agriculture as a stage of civilization. The first men only killed animals to make sacrifices to the gods, he states, but then after the invention of agriculture goats and boars had to be killed as punishment for destroying crops. Threats to herds and flocks led to the domestication of dogs to serve as guards, and when these animals began to accompany men on their sorties against dangerous wild beasts, the true hunt was born. From the very beginning, according to the Friulan aristocrat Valvasone, the hunt was an aspect of defensive warfare, and over the centuries valiant men continued the practice to facilitate training in the use of arms. By linking the hunt to warfare and by placing the origins of both at an advanced stage in the evolution of civilization, Valvasone tried to remove the taint of primitive wildness from hunting practices and to justify the hunt as a necessary training for aristocratic soldiers.

The similarity between hunting and warfare was so widely accepted that most writers assumed that the eating of meat contributed to the aggressiveness needed in battle. Making an analogous assumption, judges frequently imposed abstinence from meat on violent criminals.[36]

In contrast to the enthusiasm of the nobility, clerical moralists had a strong bias against hunting. True to its urban origins, Christianity evinced a positive horror of the forests and wilds, the domain of pagans and uncivilized brutes, and the place in which the necessary barriers between humans and animals broke down. Early church councils, for example, prohibited bishops, presbyters, and deacons from keeping hunting dogs, and after 826 priests were obliged to refrain from the hunt. John of Salisbury and others wrote harshly about the primitive cruelty of hunters, especially the intolerable exaltation they exhibited when they returned from a successful chase. In a similar vein, an anonymous chronicle of the midfourteenth century described the hunting scenes on the tomb of Mastino II Della Scala as "paganisms." Others, such as a Regensburg monk who said hunters had the qualities of dogs and Thomas More who in *Utopia* pointed out that sportsmen act like dogs pursuing rabbits, thought that hunters rejected God's plan for humanity as his most elevated creation.[37]

Apologists for hunting felt obliged to answer these traditional Christian objections to the practice. The Friulan Jacopo di Porcìa argued that the sweet pleasures of hunting, birding, and fishing must be enjoyed to experience the majesty of divine creation. Did not God create the natural world for our use, he asked? Porcìa explained away the objections of Augustine, Jerome, and Ambrose by arguing that they were only against gladiatorial combats with animals. Moreover, he asserted, hunting could serve ethical purposes because it was better than games of dice and cards, which provoked violence, and considerably better for youths than the alternative pleasures of whoring. Erasmo da Valvasone added that inasmuch as the activities of hunters brought them into contact with witches who lived in the wilds and exposed them to the evil eye, they found Christian piety even more important than those who were devoted to more sedentary pursuits.[38]

Criticisms of hunting suggest a fundamental opposition between the practices of hunting and the Catholic notions of morality and ritual, which derived their power from the liturgical celebration of Christ's singular sacrifice. The relationship or polemical opposition between hunting and religious sacrifice recalls the work of Walter Burkert on the rituals of animal sacrifice in ancient Greece. Burkert linked these practices to Paleolithic hunting. Following anthropological theory, he notes that a transition occurred when humans switched their roles from hunted to hunters and took on the deadly attributes of leopards and wolves, created a culture of weapons, employed fire, differentiated sexual roles markedly, and organized cooperative work by family groups and male hunting bands. "From this perspective, then we can understand man's terrifying violence as deriving from the behavior of the predatory animal, whose characteristics he came to acquire in the course of becoming man." Because the practice of hunting as the principal means of obtaining food distinguishes early humans from other primates and because most of human history comprises the Paleolithic Age of hunting, the hunting experience, Burkert argues, can account for many of the most elemental forms of our culture, especially sacred ritual. In ethnographic accounts, hunters report feelings of guilt about killing animals and describe the ceremonial ways in which they reacquired innocence after a kill. The killing of animals, thus, produced a craving for ritual.[39]

One need not follow Burkert far back into prehistory nor need one accept some notion of a hunting archetype to recognize the power of hunting as a model for killing in Renaissance Italy. All the vendetta killers certainly had years of experience as hunters and knew intimately the little rituals associated with the distribution of the kill. They lived in a culture in which hunting was widespread and yet was understood as antithetical to strict Christian morality. Thus, hunting shared with vendetta an ambivalent position as a practice authorized by custom but criticized by the clergy, and for most people hunting produced the most common experience with killing.

As their comments show, the Christian critics recognized that hunters blurred the distinction between human and animal, most obviously in naming themselves after their prey, particularly their most violent prey, with appellations such as Ursus, Lupus, or Smergon, and in identifying with their canine companions in the chase. From the hunt came weapons and the cooperative society of male hunting bands, so analogous to the wolf pack, so similar to an army. To become effective hunters youths had to learn how to suppress inhibitions to killing; and once they had learned how to kill animals, they knew how to kill men. A final similarity proffers a final hypothesis for understanding vendetta. The game killed in the hunt satiated hunger. The desire for revenge was also often described as a hunger. If hunting provided the model for vendetta and hunters ate their prey, then the great temptation of vendetta killing may have been to eat the victim, to follow the logic of the hunt into cannibalism.[40]

Although Friulans would have recognized that "vengeance is an appetite," as Frank Lestringant has put it, they projected their hunger for revenge onto their dogs, who ate the body parts of their victims. Cannibalism, or more properly anthropophagy, was more often heard as a slur or a threat than enacted as part of the practices of revenge. A defamatory sonnet accused Antonio Savorgnan of drinking human blood, and after a street fight in Orzano the victor threatened to stuff a dying man's brains into the mouth of a woman who attempted to intervene; but the accusation and threat seem to have been unrealized metaphors for uncontrollable anger. Even though nearly contemporary cases of revenge cannibalism can be found in Modena, Florence, Naples, Dalmatia, France, and Holland, avengers in war- and vendetta-ravaged Friuli seem to have employed their dogs to act out cannibalistic hallucinations.[41]

Friulans and others understood the passionate hunger for revenge as a kind of wildness. They might accept the necessity of killing others, even see it as a moral obligation to lost kin, but murder was never normal, never without some taint. Even when they planned their revenge carefully and had authorization from the Venetian overlords, as did the assassins of Antonio Savorgnan, they masked their thirst for blood behind the behavior of canine companions. Dogs helped degrade an enemy completely, and rabid dogs provided a model for explaining human behavior when mad blood stirred or *lyssa* took hold.

Behind political calculations, class pride, obligations to friends and relatives, chivalrous tales, solemn oaths, petty disputes about precedence, and punctilious humanistic discussions about honor, all of which fitted out the vendetta, stalked the self's secret shadow, the beast. Unable to admit his guiding influence in their passions, the revengers of Friuli saw him less often as part of themselves than as some alien, hot-blooded animal that they had become. They transfigured self-delusion through symbols and metaphors and even acted out their bestial metaphors by bringing a hungry dog along to eat their victim's entrails or brains. The incorporation of animals into human events facilitated the projection of disturbing human feelings onto them and provided meaning for a certain kind of murder which was feverish in execution yet cold-blooded in anticipation.

In such habits of thought and action the cultural gap between ourselves and our ancestors is wide indeed, a gap that has tempted many modern scholars to discount or ignore the macabre tales of vendetta violence to search for a more rational, commonplace ex-

planation for seemingly irrational behavior. By trying to bridge
that gap, however, we may recapture a different kind of reasoning
based on a logic of analogies, an alien mental world in which
humanity and nature merged with each other, and we may demys-
tify forms of action which repeated the most primitive human
experiences.

WANING OF THE FACTIONS

Friuli still had much to endure. The war dragged on until 1516,
provoking further atrocities, and the threat or reality of an imperial
invasion reappeared every campaign season. The experience of
prolonged warfare changed Friulan society in several subtle but
significant ways. Girolamo Savorgnan sought to replace his cousin
as a leader; but because of Girolamo's obsession with his own
rights and privileges, he never captured the affection of the common people. Learning the lessons of Antonio's *volte-face* Venetian
politicians trusted Girolamo less, eventually reforming the institutions of Udine and the rural villages to break up the solidarity of
the Zambarlano faction. The final defeat of the empire badly damaged the prestige and autonomy of the Strumiero castellans, who
now had to go into exile or retreat to the safety of their castles.[42]

After his valiant defense of Osoppo in 1514, Girolamo Savorgnan
presented himself as the savior of Venetian dominion. Despite his
success in war, Girolamo had great difficulty in recapturing Antonio's former position of trust with the Venetians and of dominance in Friuli. In a letter written in July 1514, he opined that of all
the ill fortune he had suffered during the war, nothing had angered
him more than the reputation for faithlessness Antonio's defection
had given to "the faction of the house of Savorgnan." Not only
had it been illegal to speak the name and display the insignia of
Savorgnan, but at every rumor or disturbance the Venetian magistrates accused his followers of sedition; even after the courageous
defense of Osoppo the Savorgnan were not considered above suspicion. The arrest of Bartolomeo Brugno da Gemona, "my god-
father" (*mio compadre*), who was Girolamo's agent in the affairs of
the faction, particularly galled the Savorgnan leader. He considered
the charges against Gemona evidence that he and his followers
were not highly esteemed in Venetian councils.[43]

The Janus-faced Girolamo had to look in two directions at once, toward both his Venetian patrons and his Friulan clients. In this difficult task Girolamo contrasted unfavorably with his cousin Antonio, especially in personal style. Girolamo had to maintain his followers' loyalty not only through material rewards but through an effective self-presentation. Unfortunately, he never seemed capable of pulling off the necessary performance because his nervous insecurity, which he tried to mask with a fitful but overweening arrogance, only heightened the distrust endemic to the times. In some ways his personality was almost a parody of the sin of *superbia*, the excessive pride that provokes jealousy rather than admiration.

His early career had been distinguished despite Antonio's superior position. In attempting to outflank his cousin, Girolamo was assisted by marriages that allied him first to the Della Torre and then to the important Venetian noble families of the Tron, Malipiero, and Canal. The able and influential Luca Tron acted as Girolamo's principal patron in the Venetian councils much as had Andrea Loredan for Antonio Savorgnan. Whereas Antonio cultivated Venetian patrons and a vast following of subordinate clients, Girolamo nourished bonds of friendship with formal equals, a strategy that initially gave him an alternative source of power to Antonio's peasant following but which inhibited his ability to take over Antonio's network of clients when the opportunity arose. He also furthered himself by serving in the Venetian army and by cultivating friends in the Venetian Senate. In 1508, after a brilliant military campaign in which he defeated the imperial forces at Cadore, his friends and in-laws in the Venetian Senate tried to obtain for him the castle at Belgrado which went instead to Antonio. In compensation, the Senate supplied him with a modest annual stipend of 120 ducats. Late the same year, the Great Council elected him a member of the *zonta* of the Senate, an unheard of and highly controversial reward inasmuch as non-Venetians' membership in the governing patriciate of the city was generally considered purely honorific. Girolamo scandalized the senators even more when he took the election seriously and actually showed up for Senate deliberations, making himself privy to state secrets about Friulan affairs.

After the signing of the League of Cambrai, senators arranged to get him out of Venice by sending him on a diplomatic mission to the Swiss cantons to negotiate for support in the forthcoming campaign and, when he returned, elected him collateral-general for the operation to retake Vicenza. Wearying of his administrative duties and political isolation, he resigned after a few months and went back home, where he refused the office of collateral when elected again the following spring. Thereafter, he devoted himself to Friulan affairs.[44]

After Antonio's death had conveniently eliminated his principal rival, Girolamo began to act with far less circumspection than before. As his price for helping the Venetians hold onto Friuli, he pressed them for a vast extension of his jurisdictions and privileges. His enemies minced no words in describing these excessive demands. Gregorio Amaseo, who had fawned over Girolamo when he was the leading alternative to Antonio, complained in a passage that becomes almost rabidly incoherent,

> that Messer Girolamo Savorgnan went to Venice where he received the greatest honors and infinite favors, but, as is the case with human weakness which is never contented, these rewards neither satiated his appetites nor was the said Messer Girolamo well satisfied with such dignities. He searched more than ever to subjugate all the rest of the nobility of the patria and especially to put the chain of servitude around the neck and shackles on the feet of the city of Udine. The tyrannical habits of his family wrongfully usurped [the rights of the Udinesi] through the servile patience and cowardice of the city and the injust presumptions of the lords.

Girolamo himself maintained a haughty tone in his correspondence with the Venetian doge, treating him less as his sovereign than as an ally: "I am Girolamo Savorgnan. My family has always been of service to Your Serenity, and as friends rather than nobles, as nobles rather than as subjects." Not above blackmailing the Venetians, he maintained his contacts with imperial agents even as he raged that his faithless cousin had sullied the family honor by switching sides. He reminded his Venetian patrons that if they disappointed him he could get what he wanted from the Germans. In reply Venice granted him the lands of Antonio Savorgnan; the usufruct of the property of Antonio's nephews, Francesco and Bernardino; the additional captured imperial fiefs of Belgrado, Palazzuolo, and Castelnovo; and the title of count of Osoppo. After the lifting of the siege, Girolamo accepted additional lucrative rewards including full title to Osoppo, which eliminated the claims of others in the clan, and the transfer from Gemona to Osoppo of the toll station for German merchants.[45]

However, the Venetians also worked to curtail Girolamo's influence in Udine, once the linchpin of Savorgnan power. They moved to revive a commission to reform the statutes of Udine originally appointed in 1507; under the leadership of Andrea Loredan the commission proposed in 1513 to abolish the civic assembly (*arengo*), which had served as a forum for the artisans and been a creature of the Savorgnan; to reorganize the city council in favor of the nobles (henceforth, there would be 150 noble and 80 artisan members); and to create an executive committee of the council consisting of seven deputies. Through these changes the Venetians intended to create a stable civic oligarchy that might balance the dangerous combination of Savorgnan lord and urban poor.[46]

As long as the war lasted, Venice failed to push home its proposed reduction of Savorgnan power, and Girolamo employed the old family technique of mobilizing popular demonstrations. The ceremonial entrance into Udine in September 1516 of the new luogotenente, Giacomo Corner, best reveals the complex layerings and conflicts of authority: on such occasions the Udinesi affirmed loyalties by the manner in which they welcomed or failed to welcome the new Venetian governor. The evening before the entrance, some thirty lords treated Corner to a sumptuous banquet at Spilimbergo castle. The next day Girolamo Savorgnan met him at the ford of the Tagliamento with a significantly modest entourage of eighteen horses. Along the way some four hundred peasants joined the progress, chanting as they went, "Savorgnan, Savorgnan," instead of the expected Venetian cheer of "Marco, Marco." Sanudo's informant wrote, "you know very well what I want to imply": that is, the count of Osoppo had turned the demonstration of loyalty to Venice into an apparently spontaneous display of his own influence. The entourage finally arrived in Udine amidst a scene of considerable turmoil. Although mercenaries chanted the approved, "Marco, Marco" and "Corner, Corner," the populace only managed, "Viva Savorgnan!" During a reception for the luogotenente, the tumult grew so loud that Girolamo left to quiet his followers and discovered that one of his men was about to lead the multitude in attacking the castellans' palaces just as in 1511. Girolamo killed the man on the spot.[47]

Whereas the formerly rebellious lords of Spilimbergo and other castellans from the right bank of the Tagliamento flattered the representative of Venice, Girolamo's reception was calculatedly austere and highly provocative although stopping short of a direct insult to the luogotenente. In effect, Girolamo employed the ever-ready Savorgnan partisans to put the Venetians on notice that they needed him more than he needed them.

Although Girolamo retained vast wealth and could continue to buy artisan support with bread and wine, his ambitions were eventually checked by the vital group of Udinese notables who had been forging a civic oligarchy since well before the 1513 reforms and whose allegiance he had lost during the war years. Resentful of any attempt to reassert Savorgnan hegemony, they gradually came to see their position in the city as a hereditary right. Despite their many internal divisions, the civic oligarchs eventually succeeded in preventing both the Strumiero hierarchs and the Zambarlano artisans from enjoying anything more than a nominal role in Udine's government, and the latter group lost even that with the elimination of the *arengo*.[48]

Through a series of decisions enacted in 1518 which counterbalanced the old alliance between the Savorgnan lord and the artisans, Venice strengthened the Udinese civic oligarchy. In effect, the Venetians sought to refashion the Udinesi in their own image by introducing into predominantly feudal Friuli electoral procedures that had evolved in republican Venice. Two new laws completed the essential changes begun with the reform of 1513. One defined the civic nobility of Udine by promulgating a list of names of acceptable families and by granting to the city council, already heavily weighted in favor of the nobles, the privilege of judging future applications for citizenship, the necessary prerequisite for communal office. The second new law introduced the Venetian practice of secret ballots into the city council, which the Savorgnan had traditionally controlled through voice voting. The secret ballot in particular damaged Girolamo's ability to distribute patronage jobs and to name his own candidate to the critical position of chancellor of the commune. Contemporaries recognized that these innovations cut into the extrainstitutional authority that had made the Savorgnan comparable to the Medici in Florence and the Bentivoglio in Bologna. Girolamo opposed the changes at every turn, even threatening another violent insurrection:

> Against those new procedures Messer Girolamo Savorgnan repeatedly exercised every power he could, both in Udine and in Venice, by instigating the populace of Udine and the neighborhood chiefs to destroy the very sacred procedures of voting for councillors and officials, seeking thus to return everything to the ancient confusion in order to tyrannize the city again in the interests of his house.

Besides complaining about the loss of the traditional prerogative of the Savorgnan to name important officials, Girolamo encouraged the artisans to push for the reestablishment of the *arengo*, but the Council of Ten stood fast against them. Here perhaps the *popolani* of Udine paid most dearly for the insurrection of 1511.[49]

By 1518 the Zambarlano clientage system in Udine had collapsed. Girolamo continued to exercise great influence, but the dashing Antonio he was not. The new luogotenente refused to tolerate Girolamo's arrogance any more and announced that the last thing Friuli needed was more honors for the count of Osoppo.[50]

In 1526 yet another confrontation with the oligarchs of Udine broke out over Girolamo's bid to have the city pay for a company of soldiers, an act his opponents saw as currying favor with the Venetians and giving him the forces necessary to intimidate his domestic enemies. With their defeat of his plan, Girolamo's support eroded even further. He was obliged to travel with a large escort "because, to tell the truth, I am greatly hated not only by the Germans but by many of my fellow countrymen, and not at all because of any fault of mine but only because of my faithful service" to the Venetians.

By 1528 he retired to Venice, leaving the defense of Friuli to his older sons. After he died intestate the next year, the scavengers circled around. Antonio's nephews Bernardino and Francesco (now the husband of the beautiful Lucina) returned from a long exile and demanded their proper inheritance, much of which Girolamo had usurped, and the castellans injured in 1511 petitioned for compensation from the same sources. Girolamo's sons had to remain vigilant just to retain their inheritance.[51]

The final component of the old Zambarlano coalition had been the peasants. They received little succor from Girolamo Savorgnan, who had disagreed with his cousin's advocacy of their interests. In contrast, the council of Udine, as long as the war lasted, continued to support them, joining the village heads in 1516 in calling for a new list of hearths (*fuochi di lista*) used to make fiscal assessments, for an equitable redistribution of taxes, and for a reduction of the past taxes owed, all of which would help relieve the vast burden caused by the fighting. But after the war the city council and the peasant leaders drifted apart, especially between 1528 and 1540 when widespread famine and epidemics among domestic animals provoked desperate rural protests. Bereft of their traditional allies, the peasants sought and gradually gained their own representative and administrative institutions, collectively labeled the *contadinanza*. Supported by Venice, the *contadinanza* achieved a stable form of organization in a series of laws promulgated between 1537 and 1541, giving Friuli a kind of peasant parliament such as could be found in the Tyrol and Württemberg. However, greater autonomy failed to provide much relief from the persistent rural depression made worse by oppressive labor obligations and public and private impositions that grew to as high as 30 percent of the agricultural yield. The burdens of rural life became so heavy that tens of thousands emigrated to Germany or Venice. By the end of the century, Marc Antonio Memmo, the provveditore at Palmanova, estimated with only slight exaggeration that in the previous thirty years the population of Friuli had dropped by more than half to only ninety-seven thousand.[52]

With the waning of the Zambarlani, factions ceased to matter as they once had. Only a few lone Strumieri carried on personal vendettas against the remnants of Antonio Savorgnan's old circle. Nicolò Savorgnan's success as a vassal of the empire proved no less ephemeral than his father's, and living with a Venetian bounty on his head he became just another scheming exile in Villach, where in 1518 three young Strumieri murdered him while he was attending mass in the church of Saint Mark.[53]

Francesco Janis di Tolmezzo, who had been Antonio's principal advisor and sometime chancellor of Udine, had been arrested and tortured by the Venetians because of his patron's treason. After time in prison and years of house arrest in Venice, he was allowed at the end of the war to return to Udine where he resumed his practice of law. By 1519 he had been rehabilitated enough to serve La Serenissima as an envoy to the new emperor, Charles V. Whereas the Venetians may have been forgiving, the Strumieri were not. In the summer of 1521 Girolamo Colloredo, who had been among the assassins of Antonio and who still blamed Francesco for his father's death on Giovedì Grasso, assaulted the elderly chancellor near one of the gates of Udine. Months later he died from his wounds.

The last to die in direct retaliation for the Cruel Carnival was Giovanni Monticolo, also a close associate of Antonio. In 1522, while serving as the podestà of Monza for the Duke of Milan in whose service Monticolo had eventually found refuge after fleeing Udine, he was killed by the same Nicolò Colloredo who had murdered Nicolò Savorgnan in Villach four years before. After these deaths the Council of Ten finally intervened to stop the violence it had itself encouraged with the contracts on the lives of Antonio and Nicolò Savorgnan. The ten brought to Venice Giovanni Monticolo's surviving brother, Nicolò, and Girolamo Colloredo, who also represented his brother, and imposed on the two sides a pact of peace. The retaliations against the perpetrators of the Cruel Carnival ceased, and for a whole generation the families refrained from killing one another.[54]

Although hardly disappearing, violence became more diffused, more simply criminal and less overtly political in the sense that local rivalries were no longer linked with the greater Venetian and imperial struggle. Defamatory placards put up in Cividale in 1523, for example, ridiculed the Nordiis family without any reference to Venice or Austria, Guelf or Ghibelline, Zambarlano or Strumiero. The Savorgnan youths, who might be expected to carry on fighting and who certainly inherited technical obligations to avenge Antonio and Nicolò, kept relatively quiet. Pagano Savorgnan found himself embroiled in a drawn-out criminal trial, but the issues involved the abduction of a woman and a complicated property dispute. The murder of Constantino Savorgnan in 1534 produced a clamor but no immediate retaliations. For their part, most of the Strumieri in exile concentrated on courting the emperor for favors and withdrew from serious attempts to regain their lost positions through the use of armed force.[55]

The travails of repeated invasions and factional strife exhausted a whole generation. After killing four Zambarlano leaders, the brothers, sons, and nephews of the Cruel Carnival victims worked out a relatively pacific *modus vivendi* with their enemies. Although no one forgot what happened in 1511, obligations to avenge a murdered relative were at least postponed. Once the factional coalitions dissolved, the imperative of vendetta became a less vital part of a family's strategy, probably because the need to appear invincible to clients and retainers became less a measure of power. Young toughs still found themselves in trouble, but their acts of bravado failed to excite others and had few political consequences. Artisans and peasants hardly noticed the blood disputes of lords anymore. When the vendetta finally returned in the 1540s under entirely different stimuli, it quickly evolved into an affair among intensely self-conscious gallants who acted out their animosities on the new stage of the Renaissance courts, where men fought with refined courtesy. As a result, in little more than a generation men whose grandfathers and great uncles had fed their enemies to dogs began to dedicate themselves to a stately pavan of lies given, gauntlets dropped, duels fought.

CHAPTER EIGHT

Toward the Duel

By the middle of the sixteenth century when the vendetta revived, traditional obligations of revenge competed with new attitudes toward honor which were made popular by the spread of courtly manners and the fashion for dueling. Traditional vendetta practices had relied on flexible, implicit rules that encouraged atrocious ambushes and allowed families to devise their own strategies for maintaining their collective honor. In contrast, the new ethos relied on explicit rules codified in books of manners and guides to dueling, publications that portrayed honor as an individual rather than collective trait. Even the most isolated Friulan castellan came into contact with the new values of aristocratic behavior through the proliferation of books on the subject, most of which were printed in Venice, the center of Italian publishing, and through the influence of the many exiled Friulans who found refuge in the north Italian courts. As a result, while old men wondered about how to adapt to the changing times, their sons and nephews self-consciously fashioned themselves as courtiers and duelists.[1]

RESUMPTION OF THE VENDETTA

The most likely reasons for the revival of the vendetta after more
than a generation can be discovered in the declining position of the
Savorgnan clan, which sought an outlet for various pressures in
pursuing old, half-forgotten grievances against the heirs of the
Strumieri. In the first incidents of violence after a twenty-three-
year hiatus the vendetta between the Savorgnan and their enemies
continued to follow the old patterns: one night in 1545 Ercole Della
Rovere was discovered prostrate in the streets of Udine with his
throat slit. Although no one saw Ercole's killer, suspicion immediately fell on Tristano Savorgnan, who found a convenient prostitute to provide him with an alibi for the night of the murder. He
and his brother Giacomo, grandnephews of Girolamo Savorgnan
and members of a minor branch of the clan, were both in their
twenties and, in the fashion of the Savorgnan, had begun to gather
around them a popular following in Udine. Unfortunately for
them, competition for leadership of the traditional Savorgnan clients included the six surviving sons of Girolamo (see Table 7),
much the better equipped to succeed. The struggle among the
Savorgnan for client supporters weakened their influence in the
town, resulting in a loss of the most prized Savorgnan juridical
privileges. Their rights in Udine to transport lumber and collect
rents on watermills were taken away in 1546 when the independent-
minded commune abrogated the clan's jurisdiction over the streams
that ran through the city. With this loss, the three hundred-year-
old ecologic stranglehold of the Savorgnan over Udine loosened.[2]

Having failed to unify themselves or to recreate a large body of
loyal followers, the Savorgnan scattered their energies like shot in
little animosities toward others. In 1547 Germanico Savorgnan, a
son of Girolamo, killed three Corbelli in an ambush he set for them
on the boat route to Venice. A few months after Germanico's banishment, Tristano and a band of *bravi* drew their swords against
three Colloredi, a Strassoldo, and a Caporiacco, leaving several of
the combatants wounded.[3]

The full fury of the contenders was unleashed in yet another
bloody carnival fight in 1549. Girolamo Colloredo and Girolamo
Della Torre on the one side and Giovanni and Tristano Savorgnan
on the other all went to Padua to participate in the scheduled

jousts. The presence of such notorious mutual enemies so worried the rectors of Padua that they required the two groups to swear formal pledges against any trouble. A few days after the pledges, in the labyrinth of blind alleys near the great pilgrimage church of Saint Anthony, a Savorgnan party of eight ran into the Colloredo-Della Torre companions and about twenty of their *bravi*. A desperate fight broke out which left two followers of the Colloredo dead, Giovanni Savorgnan nearly dead, and several others wounded. Tristano barely escaped by finding refuge in a nearby house. In the ensuing investigation, the Council of Ten absolved the Savorgnan from blame and condemned their opponents: Girolamo Colloredo faced perpetual banishment from Venice, Padua, and Friuli; and Girolamo Della Torre was relegated for ten years to Crete, where he had to report on a monthly basis to the local rector. Colloredo could not be released from his banishment under any conditions, and Della Torre might be pardoned only by a unanimous vote of the council.[4]

After the publication of the sentences, Girolamo Della Torre waited in Venice to take passage to Crete. With the intention of seeing him off, several Colloredo and Della Torre relatives journeyed to the lagunar city, choosing a circuitous route to avoid trouble. However, Tristano, whose honor was not satisfied by the sentences of the Council of Ten, had them shadowed and planned an ambush for their arrival in Venice. He hired two spacious Chioggian boats used for transporting fruit: he and his *bravi*, who were heavily armed with harquebuses and swords, hid under reed mats in the bottom of the craft. As the gondola carrying the Della Torre-Colloredo party rowed past the landing at San Marcuola on the Grand Canal, the Chioggian boats pulled along either side. At a signal, Tristano and his men jumped up and let loose a fusillade against the passengers on the gondola. The assailants then boarded the smaller craft and delivered the *coup de grâce* to the survivors. Dead in the attack were old Alvise Della Torre's youngest son, born after his father's murder in 1511 and named in his memory, and the senior Alvise's son-in-law, Giovanni Battista Colloredo. The identities of the victims led contemporaries to remark on the direct link between the events of 1511 in Udine and those of 1549 in Venice. Although the ten immediately arrested other members of the Savorgnan family, Tristano and his men succeeded in escaping to Pinzano, the mountain fortress first granted to Antonio Savorgnan early in the century. Pinzano was so isolated and difficult to approach that the luogotenente complained he could neither surround the refuge nor even determine through his spies if Tristano was still there.[5]

Although the Council of Ten had overlooked Tristano's earlier transgressions, his outrageous ambush in the very heart of Venice could not be ignored. In fact, the ten pronounced the most draconian sentence it had ever emitted against a Friulan criminal, more severe even than the secret condemnation of Antonio Savorgnan in 1511. On August 27, 1549 the council forever banished Tristano from all territories under Venetian jurisdiction, promised to tear down to the foundations his palace in Udine and his other houses and castles, confiscated the lands beneath these buildings so that they would remain forever empty as a perpetual memorial to the crimes (*et Terrenum ipsum si confiscatum super quo nunquem aliquia Fabricari possit ad perpetuam memoriam tanti delicti*), and revoked his and all his descendants' memberships in the Venetian patriciate. If he were ever unlucky enough to be captured, he would be taken to San Marcuola, where the public executioner would read out his sentence and chop off his right hand. He would then be removed to Santa Croce, tied behind a horse, and dragged all the way to San Marco, where he would be beheaded, drawn, and quartered. In the end, only the palace in Udine, the very one from which Antonio Savorgnan had addressed his followers on that fateful carnival morning thirty-eight years before, was torn down. Venetian officials were so thorough in the destruction that they gathered up the remaining rubble and inventoried it to prevent scavenging by Savorgnan partisans. The prohibition against new buildings on the site has remained in force, if only by custom. Today it is used as a municipal parking lot.[6]

Armed with a sword engraved with the boastful motto, MIHI VINDICTAM, Tristano continued to seek revenge from his foes, many of whom were also living abroad under sentences of banishment. The year after the Grand Canal murders, he appeared in Crete and attempted to kill Girolamo Della Torre, still serving his sentence of relegation for his role in the Padua fight. In contrast to Tristano, Girolamo Colloredo wandered to Rome, where after a conversion experience he was admitted into the Society of Jesus.

He wrote letter after letter to his brother Marzio urging him to forget their grievances against the Savorgnan and to accept the mediation offered by Patriarch Giovanni Grimani.[7]

However, Marzio Colloredo showed only contempt for Christian passivity. He became the *de facto* head of the clan and for nearly twenty years devoted himself to avenging the many wrongs visited upon his forefathers. Besides the loss of his father in Tristano's daring Grand Canal ambush, he especially lamented the horrible murder of his maternal grandfather, Alvise Della Torre, who had been thrown to the market dogs in the 1511 slaughter. Marzio soon began to make trouble in Udine. On the feast day of Saint Bernardino in 1551, he and some cousins clashed with a band led by one Marco da Carpi, head of the militia of Portogruaro and partisan of the Savorgnan. Afterward, the luogotenente recommended to the Council of Ten that Marco be removed from the region but also noted that he had been unable to convince the Colloredo to reduce the numbers of their retainers. Each of the Colloredo always had four to eight armed men about him and when traveling expanded the escort to fifteen or twenty. In the opposite camp, the Savorgnan youths shifted their loyalties from the exiled Tristano to Antonio the younger, the grandnephew of the famous Antonio.[8]

Late the following winter Marzio and five others ambushed Antonio in the public streets, killing him and two retainers. News of the attack impelled merchants to close up their shops in anticipation of further street violence, but Luogotenente Francesco Michiel managed to keep the situation under control. In response to these murders the Council of Ten sentenced Marzio, the two Colloredo relatives who accompanied him, and their *bravi* to perpetual exile, confiscated their property, and offered a one thousand-ducat reward for them dead or alive.

Marzio wandered first to Gorizia, then to Milan, and eventually to Florence where he entered the service of Grand Duke Cosimo I. Breaking his ban in 1555, Marzio led a company of armed men back to Udine where they attempted to shoot Antonio Savorgnan's father, Bernardino. They failed to break into the palace room in which he had barricaded himself and had to be content with killing his horses and beating the servants. Another attack on Giacomo Arigone also faltered. In 1559 Marzio was accused of helping some of his relatives murder two men, one a knight of the luogotenente.[9]

During the next two years, Marzio was serving with the Tuscan troops sent to assist Ottavio Farnese in Lombardy and from there renewed his attack on his Savorgnan foes through his son, Ludovico, who fatally wounded Francesco Savorgnan in a nasty street brawl in Udine. In 1561, some Colloredo men and castellan allies ambushed a party of Savorgnan supporters at a crossing of the Tagliamento resulting in a free-for-all among the boulders of the river bank. Only one man survived in the Savorgnan party.

In the most notorious of his attacks, Marzio sent bombs hidden in sealed boxes to Nicolò and Urbano Savorgnan, but the recipients disarmed the devices without injury. There were several subsequent attempts at revenge against the Colloredo for the bombs, culminating in an assault on the steps of the luogotenente's palace, where Federigo Savorgnan hacked down Claudio and Livio Colloredo in broad daylight. After those attacks, the character of vendetta violence began to change.[10]

Marzio himself began to amend his aggressive habits because during his peregrinations he was exposed to a world of courtly refinement, in which men eschewed vendetta and resolved their disputes through duels. Despite his quick temper and fondness for violence, he had considerable success in adapting to his new environment and gradually came to accept the courtly rules of dueling while pursuing his quarrel with the Savorgnan, several of whom were also exiles in other princely courts. We shall return to Marzio Colloredo and the Savorgnan, but first we need to look at the nature of the new manners they learned as courtiers.

The New Manners

During the middle decades of the sixteenth century under the thrall of a renewed courtly ethic, many Italian aristocrats changed their behavior, nowhere more notably than in how they pursued vendetta. The Renaissance revival of courtly values shared with earlier medieval versions of the courtly ethic Cicero's *De Officiis* as the principal source of inspiration, but the sixteenth-century movement, which was made popular by Erasmus's *Manners for Children* and Castiglione's *The Book of the Courtier*, both widely available in numerous printed editions, had a far broader and more lasting influence.

As we have seen, traditional representations of revenge relied on a blurring of the boundaries between humans and animals, pigs and dogs in particular. In contrast, courtliness erected rigid barriers between the human and the animal, condemning all animallike behavior in men and women. Giovanni Della Casa's *Galateo* identified the essential mark of boors as eating like pigs; Della Casa described these ill-bred fellows as "those we sometimes see who, totally oblivious like pigs with their snouts in the swill, never raise their faces nor their eyes, let alone their hands, from the food in front of them." As Norbert Elias pointed out, the new manners reinforced an aversion to animallike traits in men and women by encouraging a repulsion to the bodies of animals themselves, especially in the form of meat. During the sixteenth century feelings among the upper classes changed from those of pleasure in seeing and carving up a dead animal at the table to ones of discomfort with anything that reminded diners that eating meat had something to do with killing. Just by adopting refined table manners, such as using a fork and napkin, courteous men and women distanced themselves from their food, creating a layer of manners which, in separating them from direct contact with bodies and with animals, severed the habitual connections of millennia and produced a new sensitivity. In such an atmosphere the habits of revenge which had mixed the human and the bestial by leaving human corpses to be eaten by dogs became especially repulsive.[11]

The psychological as well as social implications of the new manners can hardly be overemphasized. The courtesy books presented good manners as being similar to a fine cloak, and as Erasmus saw it, clothing revealed much more than a superficial exercise of taste, becoming "in a sense the body of the body," the visible sign by which one discovered the character of the wearer's soul. In addition, other outward signs manifest by bearing, gestures, facial expressions, bodily movements, and above all speech revealed an individual's inner qualities. Such a view was, of course, a neo-Platonic commonplace, but the courtesy books of the sixteenth century translated obscure abstractions into practical rules of behavior which subjected the inner person to an outer tyrant, who demanded conformity to a model of behavior which abhorred excess in any expression of feeling.[12]

Thus good manners repressed emotions. The courteous denied or delayed all impulses, never admitted fear, controlled and channeled anger into the duel, and sublimated sexual appetites through elaborate flirtations. The repression of emotions imposed a kind of lie, a socially salutary lie perhaps, but a lie nevertheless. The courteous man or woman lied to others about their feelings and if truly courteous probably lied to themselves. Yet in the deepest irony of all, every word and deed had to appear to be natural, neither artificial nor false, and avoiding falsehood obsessed the theorists of courtesy, so much so that a reputation for dishonesty became the most serious social fault and calling someone a liar the surest step on the path to a duel. A concern for telling the truth necessarily corrected courtesy's requirements of dissimulation, but the conflict between emotional denial and verbal honesty created by the new manners forced the courteous into fitful inconsistencies of behavior which are characteristic of those who try to live in a double bind.

Giovanni Della Casa's *Galateo*, among Friulans probably the most influential guide to refined manners, best illustrates the conflict. Della Casa spent much of his career in Venice and environs, writing *Galateo* between 1552 and 1555 while in retirement near Treviso. *Galateo* charmed so many because Della Casa chose as his narrator an ignorant old man who brought good manners down from the reconditeness of the learned to the level of the simple gentleman who aspired to emulate those in the highest aristocratic circles. *Galateo* not only refashioned conduct but made unmentionable whole realms of human experience: a polite man never alluded to the wrath, gluttony, lust, avarice, or other unseemly desires of others, "in as much as these appetites are not evident in their manners of behaviour or in their speech, but elsewhere." In other words, those things not manifest through the accepted forms of gentle manners and refined speech should not even register themselves in the mind of the gentleman or lady.

Della Casa also condemned a variety of things which had, in his opinion, the attributes of deceit, those things that consist "in appearances without substance and in words without meaning." Dreams in particular should not be openly discussed because they have no basis in reality and are nearly as deceptive as lies that purposefully contradict reality. When repressed, unpleasant emotions would most likely reveal themselves in dreams and slips of the tongue, those little unintended statements Della Casa correctly understood had to be ignored if courtesy were to be upheld.

Although advocating the adoption of good manners, Della Casa seems to have inadvertently uncovered and tried to resolve the very problem politeness created, the forced distancing of self-expression from uncomfortable realities. By denying even the existence of unpleasant emotions, courtesy encouraged an objectionable artificiality of manners which exemplified mendacity. Although he lamented the unfortunate effects of good manners, in particular the proliferation of empty ceremonies, Della Casa resigned himself to a situation that could not be changed and recommended that readers abide by the customs of the time ameliorated by the principles of moderation. Clients of a prince, especially constrained by courteous formalities, had to cultivate the virtue of honest dissimulation, as it was termed, the trait that required silence or at least great discretion in expressing some thoughts. For them to be caught in a lie did not so much mean a loss of personal dignity as a loss of honor in having failed to manage impressions properly.[13]

Among the principal writers on courtesy, including Baldassare Castiglione, Stefano Guazzo, and Giovanni Della Casa, Annibale Romei best defined the relationship between honor and revenge in his dialogue, *On Honor*. He distinguished between, on the one hand, virtue, which is innate, usually hidden, and rewarded by eternal salvation, and on the other honor, which is acquired, always visible, and rewarded by the esteem of society. Virtue comes from the soul. In contrast, honor comes neither from the soul nor the body but from the proceeds of life, such as riches, political offices, influence, friends, beautiful wives, healthy sons, and titles of nobility. Honor exists in the eyes of other men and disappears when their favor is lost. The most likely way to lose the respect of other men is to fail to avenge an injury. One of the interlocutors in Romei's dialogue points out that previous writers (he is referring primarily to the Thomists) had argued against fighting an injust quarrel or offending God when they avenged; but, he counters, those who truly value the honor of the world will never allow their reputation to die away by failing to redress an insult no matter what its cause. An honorable man must prefer death to dishonor, a short honorable life to a long vituperative one. In addition, an honorable man must avoid resorting to the courts of law when he has received an injury because he might be suspected of lacking valor and courage. Above all he must maintain the appearance of the willingness to defend his honor because once it is lost, no matter what the cause, it can never be regained.[14]

By requiring a gentleman to respond to injuries, the principles of honor placed a courtier in an awkward position in that he needed to sustain his own honor and the honor of his house, but he also had to acquiesce in the restraints on his conduct demanded by the court itself. In accepting the patronage of a prince, the courtier joined a voluntary association that subordinated the needs of its constituent members to those of the prince. Private vendettas could injure the authority of the prince; but also through its etiquette the court incorporated its members into a new body that had its own values, separate and distinct from the traditional family values of the aristocracy. In response to the injured gentleman's dilemma, the princely courts developed compensatory measures that tied up revenge in the elaborate knots of the duel. Although the society of the princely courts needed a mechanism such as the duel, princes themselves had to uphold the law, which meant that at best they winked at what was technically illegal. Absurd as the new behavior of the duel appeared, not just to us but to many contemporaries, it had a civilizing effect, to follow Norbert Elias's famous formula. At least in its early phases in Italy, the duel markedly reduced levels of interpersonal violence and even more importantly replaced the collective aspects of vendetta with a highly individualized concept of honor.[15]

Although historically derived from medieval judicial and chivalric combats, the Renaissance duel can be distinguished by the fact that it was a private affair practiced outside of the official institutions for resolving conflicts. Duelists abandoned armor and usually their mounts, employed simple weapons, and chose isolated spots for fighting. The well-mannered accoutrements of the duel evolved in the Italian courts and were exported elsewhere, especially to Spain, France, and England. The technical literature on dueling developed over two centuries from Giovanni da Legnano's work of 1360 to reach its apogee in the middle third of the sixteenth century. Andrea Alciato codified the circumstances that called for a duel in a work that went through six editions between 1544 and 1552, but the best-known authority became Girolamo Muzio's *The Duel*, first printed in Venice in 1550 and republished in five more editions by 1563, thirteen by the end of the century. The Venetian printing industry issued these and similar dueling manuals for the large market of aristocrats from the terraferma.[16]

The rules for the duel created a script for an extended, almost theatrical, performance that channeled the dangerous anger of the participants into a series of formalities which disarmed opponents until they could meet on the dueling ground. More complicated than the actual rules of combat were the regulations that framed the duel, the formulas for insulting, challenging, arranging, and judging. In theory a precise succession of steps preceded a duel. First, one party insulted or accused the other of something contrary to honor. The second party denied the insult or accusation by giving the lie, saying simply, "You lie" or "You lie in the throat." The original accuser then responded with a formal challenge. Because the gentleman challenged had the choice of weapons, it was advantageous to give the lie first, forcing the other to make the challenge. Each of these three stages depended entirely on words rather than deeds, following an assumption that questions of honor had to be made explicit before they actually existed, which of course made dissimulation an effective defense against involvement in a duel.[17]

The whole dueling script hinged on giving the lie. When a gentleman said, "you lie," he meant "you have unmasked me"; that is, the accuser had uncovered a necessary social fiction, and whatever the truth or falseness of the accusation, the fiction had to be reconstituted.

Definitions of lying and methods of giving the lie harbored immense complexities. Giovanni Battista Possevino defined the lie as, "a statement which nullified something said by another, to the disadvantage of the latter's honor, with intent to free the other party from infamy and to force his opponent to offer his proofs." General definitions, however, did not help much in dealing with the ambiguities of daily conversation, a situation that led theorists to classify the kinds of lies. Muzio suggested five types, and the amendments of others produced a list of thirty-two sorts of lies. After struggling over what was a lie and what was not, potential duelists had to follow the polished formalities of the challenge. A gentleman who slipped up at any step in the process showed himself to be an unworthy combatant and gave his opponent an honorable excuse for backing out of the confrontation.[18]

The challenger sent to the challenged a *pegno*, usually a glove but sometimes a ring, belt, or dagger. If the challenged refused to accept the glove, then the bearer must cast it at his feet in the presence of other worthy witnesses. In the legalistic environment of sixteenth-century Italy, challenges were usually accompanied by a document, which was notarized, witnessed by well-known persons, and sometimes printed up for general circulation around the several courts. Muzio recommended that a document of challenge be as brief as possible, specifying the injurious words spoken and giving precise details such as the time, place, and witnesses. However, many of those that have survived are elaborate treatises, whole pamphlets, or even small books, as excessive in detail as a lawyer's brief. Once all of these stages had been properly executed, the challenged gentleman had three options: to accept the challenge, ignore it, or answer it with objections.[19]

Assuming that the disputants got that far, the forms for the actual combat were relatively simple: the challenger met the challenged on a designated field of battle with designated weapons; seconds backed up each combatant; the seconds took precautions against the use of charms or magic; and before a neutral judge each duelist swore an oath affirming the justice of his cause. The fight sustained the theatricality of the duel by restricting violence to a confined space at a designated time and by requiring the presence of an audience qualified to judge the performance.

After the duel another set of intricate rules came into play, completing the frame of controls around a combat that itself could not be controlled. The seconds and a judge determined the number and character of the wounds inflicted on each duelist, whether dead or alive, ranking each injury by a precise scale that evaluated the parts of the body: they appraised the loss of an eye over a tooth, the right eye over the left, a foot over a hand, a wound on the right hand over the left, one on the head over either hand, and a mark on the front of the body over one on the back, but, not surprisingly, a clean thrust through the body counted more than anything else. After cataloguing the wounds, the judge made two different kinds of determinations: who was the superior fighter and who was correct in the quarrel. Actual duels resulted in various combinations of these two decisions; for example, the loser might recant his accusation but not surrender his person, or he could be mortally wounded but still maintain he was correct. There might not be any decision, but according to the rules it was highly doubtful that a reconciliation taking place on the field would be honorable. Although contrary to statutory law, the duel remained legalistic in its forms. Whatever the result, the findings had to be written up, signed by a judge, and certified by a notary.[20]

However, no matter how punctiliously duelists followed them, the rules themselves neither conferred nor preserved honor, which came from how well a gentleman presented himself and how well others accepted his self-presentation. Some men of high repute could break the rules with impunity; others of tarnished name could never follow them rigorously enough. The transaction of honor came when each man recognized the other as a worthy combatant capable of acting out the drama of honor well.[21]

From the very beginning, the dueling fad in Italy provoked controversy, particularly over its ethical value and its relationship to vendetta. Defenders of the practice argued that the duel derived from the principle of self-defense found in natural law, and some went so far as to say that because the Christian injunction to forgive contradicted this natural principle, the duel represented an ethic superior to religion, an ethic that prevented worse evils such as unregulated fighting and assassinations. According to Paris de Puteo, the duel actually executed divine justice because in private battles God usually favored the just, but Puteo recommended moderate punishments inasmuch as God did not always make His will evident. Fausto da Longiano wrote about the "religion of honor," which reserved the duel for true cavaliers. For several of the sixteenth-century writers, Lombard law provided the ultimate justification for the duel. For example, Muzio found twenty-two reasons for private combats in Lombard law and added seven additional ones of his own, but he distinguished these legitimate situations from the vendetta: "the fields of combat," he insisted, "have been established to realize the truth and not to give anyone a means for carrying on a vendetta." Other writers stressed that the purpose of the duel must neither be revenge, which in any case could be obtained without the risk to life of the duel, nor to acquire honor but only to keep or regain it. Indeed, a gentleman who defended himself from an attack by killing his assailant must not accept a challenge from any of the dead man's relatives because pursuing revenge through dueling was dishonorable. On this point, of course, much of the theory of the duel foundered because distinguishing the motives of others was not a very accurate exercise and because aristocratic avengers became particularly attracted to the duel as a means of pursuing their traditional enmities in the guise of the highest fashion.[22]

Opponents of the duel recognized the problems in determining motives and contended that legal proceedings discovered the truth more accurately than duels and provided ample means for redressing injuries. Antonio Massa's book, *Against the Use of the Duel*, published in 1555, argued on ethical grounds that God reserved revenge for himself and enjoined mortals to forgive their enemies. In the climate of the Counter-Reformation, critics identified the duel with vendetta, both of which valued the private punishment of offenses, and as an alternative to these they advocated clemency, which revealed a greatness of spirit through the generous willingness to pardon wrongs.[23]

Perhaps the most effective polemicist against both vendetta and dueling was Fabio Albergati, who lived as a courtier in Urbino and Rome, where he wrote a series of political and moralistic tracts. His *On the Means of Pacifying Private Enmities* of 1583 built its argument on the fundamental principle that "a person must control himself." In it Albergati discussed five ways of redressing a wrong: restitution, the returning to an owner what is properly his; satisfaction, the receipt of whatever is sufficient for the retention of honor by an offended party; punishment, the product of the judgment of a magistrate or prince; vendetta, an injured party doing something to an offender in recompense for what has been suffered; and chastisement, the penalty a superior administers to an inferior. Although not in principle opposed to restitution and satisfaction, both of which recreated balance in a situation of inequality, and supportive of legitimate punishment, Albergati wanted particularly to undermine vendetta and chastisement, both of which created inequalities. Albergati cleverly employed the very arguments of the apologists of vendetta to connect it to the duel and to undermine both practices. Whereas they thought that honor was best sustained when the offended reoffended the offender in conformity with the ancient law of retaliation, Albergati argued that the principal goal of the offended had to be to remove impediments to retaining his honor, which could be achieved best by demonstrating that he was a man of virtue. Although the vendetta might have brought pleasure, it neither ended the dispute, even if the enemy was killed, nor did it preserve honor inasmuch as a murderer was by definition infamous. Vendetta, therefore, failed to achieve the desired results. Following this essentially pragmatic argument, Albergati added that the duel may have been superior to vendetta because the dispute was ended, and the victor retained his honor; but the duel also had crippling problems. Many believe, he stated, that the duel would become a useful expedient when an offender would obstinately reject both restitution and satisfaction. Their argument came from comparing a duel with a judicial proceeding in which the challenger was the accuser, the challenged the accused, and the fight a means of knowing the truth. But in practice, Albergati argued, the duel failed to render real justice and merely fed the vanity of the combatants. Most seriously, it injured the authority of the prince, whose judgments and punishments had to be heeded. In effect, the duel preserved rather than replaced vendetta and had to be rejected for the same reasons.[24]

As even the apologists for the duel recognized, the law had long been hostile to all forms of private combat. In Italy opposition had come from two primary sources: the church, which prohibited it as early as 855, and the city-republics, which rejected the practice because of its association with the lawlessness of the nobles. The Council of Trent in its first session reaffirmed the ecclesiastical hierarchy's old condemnation of private combat, and as the new dueling fad spread, town after town reenacted old injunctions against it. In Milan it became illegal just to respond to an insult by giving the lie.

Venice's Council of Ten passed laws with penalties more stringent than in other cities. A 1541 decree made it illegal to post written challenges and promised ten years banishment just for drawing one up. A generation later Marco Mantova reported that the council's motive in prohibiting duels had been a religious one although the simple need for maintaining law and order might have been sufficient. The universal legal condemnation of dueling presented combatants with both religious and civil penalties for doing what the preservation of their honor seemed to require.[25]

The Friulans caught up in vendettas found the collective burdens of revenge they shared with other members of their families in-compatible with the new values of individual honor. By the end of the 1550s, castellans throughout Friuli had read and heard a great deal about dueling, and those exiled to foreign courts were con-strained to conform to the new standards if they wished to survive the competition for princely favor. Very quickly, in a matter of a few years, old vendetta practices disappeared in favor of duels.

REVENGE BY COURTESIES

On May Day, the citizens of Udine decorated their houses with boughs and erected the traditional maypole. For the holiday in 1559 they also anticipated watching knights joust in a field of honor marked out for the occasion. Arrangements for the tournament fell to Ugo Candido and Ottavio Zucco, who met to make final plans on the morning of the festival. During their discussions Zucco felt Candido had insulted him in some way and demanded satisfac-tion. Candido angrily yelled, "You lie." Zucco replied, "I accept the challenge." Several nobles rushed in urging a reconciliation, and as a precaution against a murderous engagement, the luogotenente had the tilting bar taken down. Despite numerous attempts at mediation in the ensuing weeks, the luogotenente failed to pacify the two men and finally ordered them to appear in Venice before the Council of Ten, which, upon reviewing the case, requested the in-tervention of the ambassador of the duke of Urbino. After a meeting arranged by the ambassador ended with each disputant throwing down his gage, the ten placed both men under house arrest. It was the end of September before the two cooled off enough to submit to a formal peace administered by the luogotenente.[26]

The Candido-Zucco confrontation took a form entirely new for a dispute in Friuli. Demanding satisfaction, giving the lie, throw-ing down a gage, and accepting a challenge show the first signs that at least some Friulan aristocrats had adopted courtly mores quite different from the traditional ones that promoted vicious am-bushes and theatric degradations. The Council of Ten recognized that it was out of its element in these chivalric formalities and called upon a foreign expert to mediate. The ambassador from Urbino represented, of course, the court most responsible for the propa-gation of the code of aristocratic manners which Candido and Zucco were trying to emulate.

The adoption in Friuli of the new courtly manners, specifically employed to distinguish those endowed with aristocratic virtue from tainted commoners, made final the divorce between the castellans' vendetta and the old factional coalitions that had once bonded upper class disputes with the ambitions of lesser mortals. Clothed in the velvets of good manners, a Savorgnan of the 1560s, for example, would never allow peasant militiamen to do his dirty work for him as had his ancestors half a century before.

Dueling suddenly appeared in Friuli as a by-product of developments in European weaponry and warfare which threatened the status of noble warriors. First, in the midsixteenth century technologic improvements in swordmaking led to the widespread adoption of the needlepoint rapier, which was useless in warfare but extremely deadly in private combat wherein a single well-placed thrust could have fatal consequences. The greater danger of the rapier and the spreading habit of carrying pistols required a code to regulate combat although as critics pointed out, the rules of honor which governed the duel seemed to stimulate rather than inhibit bloodshed. Second, the devastating success of the Swiss pikemen and the use of field artillery during the Italian wars made the infantry triumphant and cavalry largely obsolete, a development that eliminated the rationale for the nobility as the fighting class. The craze for dueling which spread from Italy in the midsixteenth century probably compensated the nobles for the loss of combative purpose which accompanied the military revolution. Thus, Zucco and Candido in their personal transition from a sporting joust to a dismounted duel reflected the general trend of the time.[27]

The influence of exiles quickened the transition among Friulans to the duel as a form of private combat. Marzio Colloredo, who had spent the 1550s avenging the Grand Canal murders, headed up a gathering of Friulan exiles in Florence and Milan while their Savorgnan adversaries found refuge at the Gonzaga court in Mantua. Between 1563 and 1568, the Colloredo and the Savorgnan exchanged a series of manifestos and challenges which reiterated the old quarrels between the two clans and disputed the technicalities of the behavior appropriate to an honorable cavalier. Both sides recomposed the past in light of the explicit rules of courtly honor and the duel, but neither was very consistent in doing so, and neither admitted any contradiction between seeking revenge and behaving as courtiers. In contrast to the unanimity of the dueling apologists, the exiled Friulans envisioned the duel as the potential fulfillment of vendetta.

They printed most of their charges and countercharges, some as pamphlets and others as posters for public display. Each document was addressed to and signed by a specific individual or group, but the intended readership certainly comprised the larger community of gentlemen in the courts of northern Italy in which the exiles from both camps had to maintain their reputations. Urbano Savorgnan defined the desired readership in his mocking response to a printed challenge from Camillo Colloredo, "but I do not believe that it was distributed anywhere except among peasants since no one had heard of it in the courts or the principal cities." Many of the published challenges included a list of witnesses from the most distinguished aristocratic families of northern Italy: signing for the Colloredo were members of the Doria, Pio, Borromeo, Bentivoglio, Malatesta, and Gonzaga families and for the Savorgnan, other members of the Bentivoglio and Gonzaga. The Colloredo boasted the support of Don Pedro de Mendoza, the Spanish viceroy in Milan, and the Savorgnan looked to Duke Alfonso II d'Este of Ferrara and Alfonso Bevilaqua, governor of Modena. The Savorgnan also enjoyed the patronage of the Academy of the Senseless in Bologna, an obscure chivalric debating society devoted to questions of honor.[28]

As late as 1562 Marzio Colloredo employed shameful methods that were incompatible with honorable dueling when he sent package bombs to Nicolò and Urbano Savorgnan. Up until this point Marzio had been quite capable of living in two worlds, fighting against his old Friulan enemies by whatever treachery he could get away with but adapting to the rigors of the duel in his disputes in Milan. In contrast to Marzio's dividedness, the Savorgnan were the first to assimilate completely the new ethic by suggesting that a duel might end the old vendetta.[29]

While visiting the imperial court in 1563, Nicolò Savorgnan widely discussed the situation in Friuli which was almost as troublesome for the empire as for Venice. He was reported to have proposed that to end the enmity between his family and the scions of the old Strumiero families it would be useful to stage a "contest of honor." In Milan Marzio heard about Nicolò's words and on

May 10 sent Savorgnan a formal challenge stating that he was prepared to meet Nicolò in a closed dueling ground without armor,
each with a sword, under the sole condition that the result would
produce a permanent peace: "thus, we cavaliers with a risk to a few
can put an end to the deaths of many." In July Nicolò answered
the challenge. His *Manifesto of the Illustrious Nicolò Savorgnan to the
Readers* appeared on a large sheet suitable for posting and was written in an exquisite Tuscan utterly alien to his native Friuli:

> A hard field of battle is truly that where one finds those who,
> deprived of strength and the secure arms of reason, wounded
> by the very pricking of their own conscience, and hunted by
> fear of the Judgment of the World, resort as an extreme
> remedy of their wretchedness to the insane alchemy of false
> appearances. In such a situation I believe that one truly now
> finds Signor Marzio Colloredo.

An accusation of a lie was, thus, foremost in Nicolò's response
to Marzio. Continuing his mocking tone, Nicolò marveled that
Marzio had suddenly become so fierce after years of failing to
avenge the deaths of so many close relatives, but Nicolò would not
accept a contest of honor with Marzio because he had sent package
bombs to Urbano and Tristano. Moreover, Marzio had shown his
ignorance of chivalric form by proposing the type of weapon in
the challenge, a right reserved for the individual challenged. Instead of a duel, Nicolò perhaps facetiously suggested a "contest of
insults." Marzio replied with the rather fanciful allegation that Nicolò had made the bombs himself and sent them to his relatives in
an attempt to besmirch the honor of the Colloredi. The recrimi-
nations escalated until Nicolò retired from the field of invective,
insisting an honorable gentleman could not deal with someone as
lowly as Marzio. However, during this battle of the pamphlets,
violence between the two sides started to dissipate.[30]

From the autumn of 1563 to the following spring, various individuals from the two sides exchanged challenges and responses in
a war of words which mostly kept the printers happy. At one point
Marzio challenged Nicolò again, offering to submit the dispute to
a neutral judge named by the two sides, a tactical shift that attempted to remove Marzio from the opprobrium of the Nicolò's
Manifesto; Nicolò still refused. Apparently Nicolò's attitude em-

barrassed some of his Savorgnan relations because even before
Marzio issued his second challenge to Nicolò, Federigo Savorgnan
submitted to Marzio a counterchallenge to a duel, saying he supported Nicolò's arguments about the secret bombs but would meet
Marzio anyway. Once arrangements for that duel had been set in
motion, Camillo and Federico Colloredo proposed to Tristano and
Urbano Savorgnan that they also meet on the same field for a final
resolution of all the past conflicts among them, but in an exaggerated display of chivalric form, the two Savorgnan refused.[31]

Thus, only the duel between Federigo Savorgnan and Marzio
Colloredo remained in place. Given the prohibitions of the Council
of Trent, the seconds and judge had to find a secret site for the
combat, a search that prolonged the preparations. Arrangements
for a fight on the banks of the Po had to be aborted on the day of
the duel when soldiers of the duke of Ferrara showed up to arrest
the combatants and witnesses. Finally on June 15, 1564, near the
isolated village of Arenzano on the Ligurian coast, the duel took
place. To prevent any interventions in the fight, the seconds retired
to the ship that had brought the two parties to the shore. Only
some sailors and local men witnessed the opening of the duel, but
their shouts soon brought the seconds back to the beach where
they found the two combatants bloodied with several wounds and
grappling arm to arm. After separating them, the seconds exhorted
them to peace, which the two accepted. Embracing his former
enemy, Marzio declared, "the war between us is now over, and in
the future I intend to be your good brother."[32]

However, the end did not come so easily. After several weeks of
recuperation in Genoa, the two principals could not agree on the
major issue of how to make their friendship public, and they
departed without resolving their quarrel. Letters and rumors began to circulate presenting conflicting details about the duel. An
anonymous pamphlet from the Savorgnan side included the notarized accounts of several eyewitnesses who described Marzio as
having fought like a coward. Colloredo finally replied with his
own pamphlet, published in Brescia in February 1565.[33]

Marzio's tract went far beyond the immediate issues of the duel
to recapitulate the whole history of the vendetta going back to
1511. Opening with a denial that he had anything to do with sending secret bombs, he asserted instead that Nicolò had tried to poi-

son him on three separate occasions. After making this new allegation, Marzio jumped back in time to the atrocities of the Cruel Carnival, emphasizing how the Savorgnan had left the corpses of two of his ancestors in the streets to be eaten by dogs. There followed the long sorry story of the vendetta since that time, complete with details about assaults unknown from other sources. Marzio conceded all the attacks members of the Colloredo had made against the Savorgnan but explained that in each case the Savorgnan had either provoked the fight or deserved to die in retaliation for the murder of a Colloredo. In all he covered some seventeen occasions of conflict between the two families, insisting that his family had never resorted to any of the horrible, dishonorable deeds of the other side, whose crimes included burning corpses, killing old men and priests, and administering poison.

Colloredo's tract is a history, albeit a highly biased one, complete with specific citations of sources and evaluations of conflicting evidence. Although he asserted that he had based his version of the Cruel Carnival on the account with the most prestige, the humanist history of the Venetian wars by Pietro Bembo, he in fact ransacked the Amaseo diary and Colloredo family papers for details that slandered the Savorgnan. To Marzio the complete history outweighed any individual event, such as his recent duel, but he had to rewrite that history to make it conform to the new principles of honor. The character of past deeds became of paramount importance because in little details of behavior and speech one discovered the honor of true gentlemen.

In these waning years of the vendetta, reinterpreting the history of the previous half-century became the dominant weapon, more useful than any sword. In an odd twist, the duel's emphasis on verbal formalities and conformity to a rigid code of honor helped convert violence into a debate about history from which the proof of honor and shame could be truly found.

The duel for a perpetual peace had obviously failed. On August 5, 1565, in answer to the allegations made in Marzio's tract, Tristano Savorgnan challenged him to another duel. By then, however, Marzio had joined Don García de Toledo's expedition to relieve Malta from the Turkish siege. Marzio's brother Camillo presented himself as a substitute duelist, but Tristano refused to accept the substitution, accusing Marzio of having fled to Malta to escape the

Savorgnan. The affair degenerated into a petty squabble although on technical grounds Tristano had a point. Theorists of dueling emphasized that honor must be seen as the attribute of an individual, a trait that could not be transferred even from brother to brother. In the exchange of communications that followed Tristano's challenge, two contrasting notions of honor were clarified, the Colloredo insisting on a more old-fashioned concept that honor based on lineage could be defended by any member of the family and the Savorgnan adopting the more contemporary idea of the individuality of honor.[34]

Once he returned to Italy, Marzio renewed his pamphlet war on the Savorgnan, repeating many of the old allegations and inventing new facts to support them. Although back in 1545 no one had noted such an important clue, in 1566 Marzio reported that on his deathbed Ercole Della Rovere had named Tristano as his murderer, and in discussing Giovanni Battista Colloredo's assassination on the Grand Canal, Marzio raised his father's age by ten years from the last time he had discussed it, apparently to make the assassination of an elderly man appear more dishonorable. Just as critical as the shameful episodes of the past, however, were new issues such as the ability to write correct Tuscan and to employ the proper jargon of a cavalier.[35]

The three principal Savorgnan (Federigo of the duel, Tristano of the Grand Canal murders, and Nicolò the intended victim of the bombs) responded in a joint defense published in Ferrara at the end of April 1566. Besides offering his version of what had happened at the duel, Federigo noted that although Marzio had not personally offended him before the combat, all the Savorgnan considered Marzio an enemy because of his filthy scheme of sending bombs to Urbano and Nicolò. Tristano, who had previously rejected a duel with a substitute because honor was a purely individual trait, now switched tactics and characterized his past actions as a response to the collective shame of the Colloredo. "When I murdered your father on the Grand Canal," he taunted Marzio, "it was because of your threats to murder me. As the blood that gave him life flowed from his veins, your father forgot the inscription on my sword, MIHI VINDICTAM. Now you do not want a test of arms because you do not adhere to the 'rules of knighthood.' "

In Tristano's view, Marzio faced two choices: if he thought the murders of his father, uncle, and others had been sufficiently avenged, he should make peace, but if not, he should fulfill his debt, just as Tristano had done for his side. The most extensive defense of the three came from Nicolò, who carefully went over all of Marzio's published allegations point by point. Showing how Marzio had misquoted the history of Bembo and the chronicle of Candido, Nicolò set out his own historical argument that countered Marzio's alleged errors by relying heavily on the citation of original documents and eyewitness accounts. Several of Marzio's sources for the events of 1511, Nicolò wrote, were madmen who died in the hospital, one was six years old at the time, and another lived outside of Udine during the troubles. In assigning responsibility for the 1511 confrontation, Nicolò reprinted the old letter from Alvise Della Torre to the lords of Spilimbergo which Antonio Savorgnan had used to blame the Strumieri for the breakdown of the peace pact on the morning of Giovedì Grasso. On the basis of that letter, Nicolò refused to accept Savorgnan culpability for any of the notorious deeds of the day. The fact that dogs ate Federico Colloredo's corpse during the carnival riots, Nicolò reasoned, could hardly be blamed on the Savorgnan, who had killed him for legitimate reasons, but must be accepted as the fault of his Colloredo relatives who failed to bury him for three days.

In listing the retaliatory assaults and deaths since 1511, Nicolò agreed with Marzio in most cases about who killed whom—only the murder of Ercole Della Rovere produced a major controversy—but in every case Nicolò had a different view of the circumstances and motive behind the incident. Appended to the three Savorgnan defenses were copies of official documents, usually Venetian ones, which put the Colloredo in a bad light. Those condemning Savorgnan outlaws, of course, were left out.[36]

Marzio took nearly two years to reply to the three Savorgnan. Part of the delay, he asserted, came from the fact that when he went to Malta he had entrusted his files of legal documents proving his accusations against the Savorgnan with someone who betrayed him by turning the files over to his enemies; but also it must not have been an easy matter for Marzio to contradict the apparent historical erudition of the Savorgnan defense. Although he had not been loath to make up evidence in the past, an effective rejoinder would have required research that an exile could pursue only with difficulty.

In his *Response*, Colloredo retraced in tiresome detail much of the same ground he had covered before, adding his own interpretation of the past events, but when confronted with facts inconvenient to his case, he changed his method of argument and recalled the long-standing social distinction of his clan. In answering the allegation that in 1511 the Colloredo had merely been followers of the Della Torre, an assertion that was certainly in part true, Marzio reached back four hundred years into the period of the patriarchs to point out that the Colloredo had been prominent in Friuli for longer than the Della Torre and had always been a mainstay of the castellan faction whereas the Savorgnan had relied on the support of mere commoners. Although irrelevant to the immediate issues, this new argument provided the Colloredo with a more noble lineage than the Savorgnan could claim. Faced with Tristano's taunts about how the Savorgnan had been more valiant than the Colloredo in paying debts of revenge, Marzio composed paeans to all the murders his family had committed during the previous sixty years and reckoned up the deaths. With the precision of a banker he demonstrated how each Colloredo victim had been fully repaid by a specific Savorgnan death. Of course, he had not achieved all this mayhem alone, conceding that his own contribution had been slight, and he could not resist boasting that because his relatives had accomplished so much he felt obliged to drop from his calculations the deeds of those outside his particular branch of the family.[37]

While Marzio was still composing his elaborate response, Troiano Arcano, an in-law of the Colloredo, challenged Federigo Savorgnan to duel. Federigo accepted. After unusually tedious negotiations over the choice of weapons and the field of combat, they met in a secluded spot between Mantua and Cremona on April 14, 1568, for what really became the final duel. The result made all the petty details of the combat irrelevant. Both duelists died. Experts called the decision a draw, and in a Latin epigram Francesco Amulio celebrated the equality of their deaths.[38]

The parity in deaths now made peace likely. The intervention of Venice made it inevitable. A truce signed in 1567 between Sultan

Selim II and Emperor Maximilian II freed the two great empires to attack the republic. As a defensive measure, Venice sought to secure the Friulan border by eliminating the potential for trouble from the feuding families. The Council of Ten authorized the future doge Alvise Mocenigo to negotiate a peace among the Friulans. Mocenigo did not negotiate exactly; he imposed peace by forbidding them to speak ever again about the dispute.

Throughout August 1568 all of the Colloredo, Della Torre, Caporiacco, Strassoldo, Arcano, Dal Torso, Arigoni, and Savorgnan, including even those in exile, signed notarized proxies that authorized the heads of their respective families to act in their name. These heads pledged themselves and all their relatives to the peace, agreeing that if any member of their family broke it, the property of all would be confiscated. Mocenigo, thus, relied on the ancient principle of collective familial responsibility to maintain respect for the agreement. In his final declaration, Mocenigo spoke on the matter of the pamphlet war. He had read the many hate-filled writings that had been exchanged between the two sides and in particular reviewed the Savorgnan response to Marzio Colloredo's last essay, finding the Savorgnan argument quite credible, "but for the greater confirmation and establishment of this holy peace, we wish and we declare that these writings shall not be published any more." He explained why.

> Because, one can truly say that when the writing of such material began, it quickened the passions and the spread of hatreds more than anything else. However, all these noble families, the names of which are too numerous to repeat, must now follow peace and reconciliation. We attest and declare by the authority conceded to us that both sides must desire that everything said or written be nullified, as if nothing had ever been written on this subject. And as a sign of a good and true peace, everyone, one by one, shall embrace the others in a friendly fashion, obliterating all the hatreds and passions of the past, promising in the future with truthfulness of heart in word and deed to use all those gestures of love and benevolence that are usually used among true and faithful friends.

Mocenigo's perspective on the vendetta was too limited for him to assess correctly the provocative effects of print, which had in fact provoked more additional print than violence. The two duels during the five-year period of the pamphlet war revealingly contrast with the numerous atrocities of the previous two decades.[39]

After hearing Mass, the family heads and many others embraced one another and kissed on the mouth. Although neither did sinners become saints nor did hatred change to love through such a ceremony, thus ended the vendetta. It did not really matter whether those who embraced the murderers of their fathers and brothers were sincere in their professions of friendship, but it did matter that they publicly staked their honor and their fortunes on accepting the peace. The whole ceremony was founded on yet another socially useful fiction that ignored inner motivations but demanded conformity in speech and act. This peace worked because for Friulan aristocrats a local reputation for ferocity was by then becoming less essential than their standing as honorable gentlemen in the larger world wherein it was most important to have appearances respected. For many years to come, violence certainly continued to be a way of life in Friuli. But when mad blood stirred, men no longer fed on their enemies like wolves but showed that revenge is a dish best eaten cold.

Conclusion

The vendetta that pitted the Savorgnan against other castellan families, most notably the Della Torre and the Colloredo, began amid the civil wars of the late fourteenth and early fifteenth centuries when the expanding commercial and military power of the Venetian republic defeated the enervated feudal regime of the patriarchs. From the beginning, local rivalries and debts of blood among the Friulan castellans connected to the interests of competing foreign powers and those of other classes in Friulan society. These connections became crucial during periods of crisis provoked by war, especially the Turkish raids of the late fifteenth century and the imperial invasions of the early sixteenth. After the War of the League of Cambrai ended in 1517 the vendetta families in Friuli began to lose their ability to attract others to their private quarrels, the factions faded, and the implications of local controversies for foreign affairs became less vital. Even after the revival of blood vendetta in 1545 the factions were never effectively reconstituted, and the Venetians saw the violence more a criminal matter than a breach of state security. Only when the rapprochement between the emperor and the sultan again made an invasion possible did Venice see the need to bring the contending clans into a lasting pact of peace, ending for the Savorgnan and Della Torre a vendetta that had lasted more than ten generations.

Before these sixteenth-century changes, deep structural discontinuities had long branded Friulan history with anarchic vendettas that survived in the interstices between official institutions of justice. The incompatibility of Venetian and Friulan judicial systems; the feebleness of parliament and the Venetian luogotenente; the contradictory operations of government on the village level; the corruption of decisions made by castellan judges; the incommensurability of language and standards of justice at different cultural levels; and the seeming impossibility of understanding, of consensus, of impartiality, of lawfulness all thrust Friulans into a fear-provoking labyrinth. Among these windings and turnings Friulans at all social levels sought security, the most reliable sources of which were family and clan, community and faction. Family and clan formed the core of all social groupings that had any consistency or cohesion. Before 1511 the most important of these were the factions whose character may be best illustrated by the fact that the two were socially asymmetric; that is the Zambarlano faction headed by the Savorgnan consisted of a vertical formation that cut across class lines linking thousands of peasants and artisans to a castellan clan and in turn to the dominant city of Venice whereas the Strumiero faction led by the Della Torre created a horizontal grouping of castellans united in opposition to the Savorgnan, the peasants, and Venice. One faction incorporated individuals from various classes and disparate communities, the other represented most of the members of a single class.

The characteristic tribal feuds of the Mediterranean and Middle East tend to establish some form of stratification among contenders who are at least nominal social equals. By revealing differences in power, these feuds form the basis of local and sometimes regional politics. In Friuli the struggle of the Savorgnan to rise above other castellans certainly disrupted the class's social equilibrium, if an equilibrium ever existed, and the Savorgnan's transitory success made possible the creation of factional coalitions. Particularly during the time of Antonio Savorgnan when whole villages of peasants and the artisans of Udine and Spilimbergo joined the Zambarlani against the aristocratic Strumieri, vendetta represented far more than feuding among formal social equals. Through it communities of commoners sought to redress a variety of economic grievances. Only partially masters of their followers and of events, the aristocratic leaders never achieved the "deliberate social engineering" imagined by many modern scholars of feuding. In 1511 artisans and peasants within the Zambarlano faction acted semiautonomously, transforming an aristocratic feud into a vendetta-revolt, following the logic of violence more than the leadership of men. In Friuli vendetta fed on other conflicts, especially those of the countryside against the city, community against community, class against class, and the disaffected against the state. The vendetta provided a model for resolving many social discontents, but it was never the only model, and by the middle of the sixteenth century alternatives had begun to supplant it.[1]

As was the case with many other peripheral regions of Europe in which feuding was common, places such as highland Scotland, Iceland, or Corsica, Friuli found itself enmeshed in the politics of a distant regime which expressed its nominal dominion by trying to alter balances between the contending sides in local and private disputes, actions that favored one group over another, eliminated potential combatants, and established political rewards and punishments. Feuds in these areas were never self-regulating but were instead the point at which local and state politics met and the means for providing justice, which the dominant regime had failed to supply. Vendetta murders were, thus, akin to and a substitute for judicial punishments, murders that conveyed a judgment that the shamed victim was also the guilty party.[2]

If one set up a spectrum of European feuding types, at one end might be medieval England, where royal justice stamped out blood feuds earlier than in any other kingdom, and at the other modern Albania, where governments have hardly touched the endemic tribal feuds in the mountains. Although a feudal and not a tribal society, Friuli in the Renaissance came closer to the Albanian than the English end of the spectrum. After the Venetian conquest in 1420 it fell under the influence of a regime that had succeeded in abolishing the scourge of vendetta among its own patriciate earlier than any other Italian city. In the absence of an efficient policing system, as in England, or the willingness to incorporate provincial nobles into the ruling hierarchy, as in Grand Ducal Tuscany, Venetian magistrates could not hope to inculcate in the Friulans their own habits of restraining violent urges. Although the factions of Zambarlani and Strumieri had become memories by the 1520s and the vendetta between the Savorgnan and their enemies died out after 1568, neither can Venetian policies be given credit for the changes nor did they have any particular success in reducing overall criminal violence in the region after the old vendetta ended. In fact, generally high levels of violence continued and probably increased during the late sixteenth century.[3]

How then did the Cruel Carnival violence of 1511 create the conditions for structural changes, specifically for the demise of the factions and the end of vendetta? The several invasions by Turks and Austrians and the agrarian crisis of the first decade of the sixteenth century pushed Friuli to the brink of a civil war that severely threatened Venice's wobbling dominion already debilitated by other foreign onslaughts. Motivated by serious deprivations and raw fear, the struggling villagers and the poor of Udine accepted the protection offered by Antonio Savorgnan's Zambarlani. At the same time the Venetians placed all their hopes for retaining Friuli in Antonio, whom they sustained with loans, favors, and arms.

The career of Antonio Savorgnan, more than anything else, demonstrates how individual leadership could matter, even in as remote and backward a place as Friuli, bound up as it was by conservative social traditions and an immobile economy. Leadership mattered, not so much because Antonio could control events—he could not—but because the whole social system hinged on him and people like him, the great patrons. Antonio offered villagers and tenants the opportunity to choose a new loyalty, the substance of which was not blood ties or feudal obligation but a patronage system that rested on the double foundations of paternalism and the militia. His paternalism took the form of loans, the repayment of which, it seemed, could be delayed indefinitely. The militia offered men better weapons than would otherwise be available, the solidarity of mutual defense, and a kind of liminal release from the obligations of daily work. Antonio Savorgnan's Zambarlani made social homicide possible by transforming class conflict into vendetta conflict. His service in connecting the Zambarlano villagers to the patriciate of Venice further illustrates how critical were the patrons who served as the intermediaries between intersecting patronage systems, a role the village *decani* performed at a lower social level and on the local stage. Nevertheless, while compensating for the weakness of formal institutions, the highly personal nature of the system created significant hazards.[4]

The Cruel Carnival brought the whole system to the point of fissure because it was so violent and because of the forms that the violence took. Serving as crystals for a murderous crowd, the Savorgnan henchmen co-opted popular grievances for the service of the clan's vendetta, and the fortuitous occasion of the carnival celebration, which allegorized a struggle between the forces of the Fat and Lean, reinforced the vendetta preoccupation with the dismemberment and desecration of the victims' bodies. The horrors of the day remained in the minds of survivors as a poisonous residue that afflicted their judgments for decades, forming a morbid memory against which all future events were measured.

The Cruel Carnival drastically upset the rough balance between the Zambarlani and the Strumieri and made Antonio Savorgnan the unchallenged arbiter of Friulan affairs, a success that made his future missteps all the more a calamity. Antonio acted with the expertise of a brilliant tactician who had honed his skills in many little battles for regional supremacy but seemed to lack the strategic vision his position demanded. When in September of 1511 he thought Fortune had begun to smile on the Austrians and he switched sides, his mistake sealed his own doom, eviscerated his faction, and finally revealed to the Venetians the folly of their reliance on a local lord as the guarantee of their dominion. Antonio's treason inverted the traditional alliances of the Friulan factions, obliging the Venetians to rely on the formerly hostile Strumieri to hunt him down, thus breaking up the established Venetian system of interlocking patronage networks.

Antonio's successor Girolamo Savorgnan, much to his displeasure, never enjoyed the same privileges Antonio had coerced from the Venetians who after 1513 tried to inhibit opportunities for Savorgnan patronage by reforming the communal government of Udine and by allowing the establishment of a peasant parliament, the *contadinanza*. At the same time, the Venetian reforms made marginal the dangerous classes by eliminating the *arengo* of Udine, once the voice of the urban artisans, and by limiting the powers of the peasant assembly. When the vendetta revived in midcentury, none of the major participants could call upon the vast retinue of clients which had empowered Antonio and made the old factions the centerpiece of Friulan life and politics.

Because Antonio's assassination is so amply documented, it serves as the most revealing example of the traditional mores of vendetta killing, which borrowed heavily from the hierarchic values of the hunt. Nourished in innumerable expeditions when lords and their retainers rode out together into the forests in search of game and sport, the hunting ethic with its emphasis on comradeship, cooperation, the acceptance of authority, and the proper forms for killing was easily transferred to the hunting of men. In particular, avengers relied on two practices derived from hunting: the butchering of the victim according to a hierarchy of body parts and the incorporation of dogs into the act of killing. By inverting the normal hierarchic evaluation of body parts, as when Antonio's assassins fed his head to dogs, avengers employed a vocabulary of shame to represent the degradation they hoped to inflict on their enemy.

Dogs became the object of multiple projections through which men imitated the *lyssa* or rabid madness of the dog, thereby transforming themselves into wildmen who lived outside the rules of civilization. Enthralled by the stirrings of mad blood, such men asserted that they were not responsible for their own actions. The hunting ethic provided a psychologically safe and culturally authorized way to express maddening anger, and the connections between hunting and revenge killing help explain the macabre emphasis on the forms of assault and the dismemberment of victims. Thus, the goriest murder became the most socially acceptable murder.

Although functionalist anthropology and structuralism have now allowed us to see how feuding is, in part, a rational and systematic means of resolving conflicts and of maintaining balances in traditional societies, there was in the Renaissance a deep ambivalence about the practice, best expressed in the need to represent revenge murders as somehow the act of madmen. The problem of revenge in the Renaissance was understood less in social than in psychological and cultural terms as a problem created by violent human emotions. The traditional mores of vendetta fighting acknowledged the reality and legitimacy of anger, managing it through carnival and hunting motifs that focused on human and animal bodies. The eclipse of a culture that had accepted the naturalness of the human body, its processes, and its emotions was the necessary prerequisite for delegitimizing revenge, a change that eliminated some of the ambivalence about vendetta but created new problems, the modern problems that come from the repression of emotions.

To think about and represent abstract ideas such as justice and villainy or honor and shame, traditional Friulans had employed analogies, especially analogies with animals, and sometimes acted out the analogies in violent deeds, as if anger had pushed killers across the barrier between the human and the beast. By ceasing to think with animal metaphors, Friulan nobles gave up one major tie that had bound them to the common culture shared by all the classes, urban and rural, literate and ignorant, aristocratic and peasant. For aristocrats the courtly ideology of their class supplanted the once widely accepted mentality of revenge which survived only in a few isolated pockets impervious to outside influences.

As Gabriel Maugain noted long ago, revenge violence began to fade away in much of northern Italy during the last half of the sixteenth century. For him Counter-Reformation piety and the reinvigoration of official justice made the change possible, a view that is undoubtedly correct in some cases but incomplete, especially in explaining the situation in Friuli and other Venetian territories.[5]

In studying the Friulan avengers as individuals, I have found only one member of a vendetta family who had a religious conversion experience and little indication that the administration of justice improved in any marked way. The end of revenge among Friulan aristocrats came with the adoption of refined manners learned during sojourns, often as exiles, in the courts of northern Italy and from reading fashionable books about courtly manners such as Castiglione's *The Book of the Courtier* and Della Casa's *Galateo*, books that also tutored these provincials in the standardized Tuscan that was bringing linguistic unity to the ruling classes of Italy.

In the 1560s as Friulan combatants began to accept duels with their enemies, they abandoned the old vendetta values for a new definition of honor, one that supplemented the collective, hereditary honor of aristocratic birth with individual conformity to an explicit code of behavior. Personal comportment began to change

from what might be called the traditional style of defensive du-
plicity to attempts at conveying trust, a style that betrayed an ob-
sessive concern with the lie. After all, duelists could not fight for
motives of revenge but only over allegations of a lie.

The influence of books on courtly manners represents only a part
of the effect of the spread of print in a vendetta society. The transformation of revenge narratives from oral legends to published
dueling manifestos cooled the enthusiasm for blood as much as
anything else. Printed words stirred passions less than spoken
words simply because they were communicated at a distance, and
print was most often answered with print. In the published versions of the revenge narratives, Friulans went public on a stage
very different from the intimate *fogolar* of a castle or the scruffy
streets in which they took revenge, a stage on which documentary
evidence, the rhetoric of persuasion, and good Tuscan determined
the victor in the game of honor. Even after some Friulans began to
duel, the accounts of what supposedly happened carried the day
better than any deed on the field of honor, especially if the deed
was challenged in print. As in theology and science where movable
type liberated thought by fixing texts, print drove at least a few
Friulan aristocrats out of their provincial isolation into a wider
world of relationships in which the private control of anger proved
more rewarding than the public display of it.

In accepting a new standard of behavior, Friulan aristocrats
formed or reformed their identities through a process that was
based less on the imitation of elders in the family and the display
of the symbols of clan and faction than on the conscious cultivation
of acquired behaviors: the courtesies of speech and comportment,
the refinements of dress and manners, a disdain for coarse and rustic ways, the hiding of bodily functions, and the sublimation of
dangerous emotions. In the older process youths assimilated themselves to the group through provoking hereditary enemies. In such
a culture, aggression helped form and confirm identities for males.
The new process shifted the emphasis from aggressive action to
the measured response to a provocation, the ability to extricate
oneself from a dangerous situation with a cool head and one's
honor unblemished. The change was more one of emphasis than
of kind, but it foretold a new world that placed great value on
deflecting or channeling interpersonal violence with a view to sta-

bilizing the ruling class. Those who made the transition successfully found themselves in possession of far greater authority than
their forefathers could have ever imagined for they helped create
the modern states with all their enormous coercive powers. Thus,
in the microcosm of Friuli one can trace how the acceptance of an
ideology of civility stimulated an important transformation in human behavior, one that first took place among the patricians in the
successful Italian city-republics centuries earlier and which has yet
to take hold in parts of the globe still plagued with internecine
violence.[6]

What have been missing from this masculine picture, and conspicuously missing, are women. The sources reveal their presence
in the conflicts through only a few illusive clues: the mother of
Apollonio Gorghi pleading to save her son's life in the streets of
Udine, the abandoned ladies of the castle at Zoppola assaulted by
peasant rapists, the village women masquerading in looted dresses
as they left Udine, the mutilated corpse of a servant woman found
in a polluted well weeks after the great massacre, the depositions of
female eyewitnesses to the Cruel Carnival. The women were there,
but the exclusively male chroniclers treat them as a mere backdrop
to the grand struggle among men. They were certainly there in
encouraging their men to remember their obligations, in teaching
sons to avenge dead fathers, in shaming husbands into countering
insults. They were certainly there as the sources of rivalry among
men, as the audience for what men thought were brave deeds, as
the bonds between rival clans brought together through marriages.
Women managed the estates while the men fought; they supplied
the militias, nursed the wounded, told the stories around the *fogolar*
on winter nights, and adopted the feminine versions of the new
manners. By inference from later periods when criminal records
are more complete, one can assume that Friulan women had a share
in the fighting as did Corsican women in the nineteenth century.[7]

It is revealing that we know so little about women in the Friulan
vendettas. In the eyes of men, vendettas could only be a matter
among men, a belief that created in their relationships with women
an island of repose in which women lived safe from the world of
masculine violence. The exemption of women from violent attack
was in large part a myth, but the myth was necessary for a culture
that sustained itself in the anthropophagy of revenge.

The last and perhaps deepest irony of the story told here has been that the wars of the early sixteenth century, which finally destroyed the power of the patriciates in most Italian cities to act independently of a foreign sovereign, also finally helped to bring to the countryside the manners of self-restraint characteristic of the cities. The wars made the pursuit of a career as a soldier and courtier the most likely alternative for many displaced and ambitious men, and in making their careers the courtiers had to conform to the mores of a highly self-conscious and reflexive group. Despite a century and a half of rule, the patricians of Venice had found it impossible to educate, persuade, or force the aristocrats of Friuli to change their violent ways and to act more like the good citizens and businessmen of the maritime republic; but the princely courts of Ferrara, Mantua, and Milan worked the desired miracle in a matter of a few years. The civic values proved to be untransferable to the countryside because they were too closely tied to the experience of citizenship in specific cities, to being a Florentine or a Venetian. A gentleman courtier, on the other hand, did not need to be a Ferrarese, a Mantuan, or a Milanese; he merely had to speak and behave properly, to be an individual of a certain stamp. Although historians of the Renaissance in Italy have long devoted themselves to uncovering how the experience of citizenship related to the development of civility, the civic Renaissance had its limits, especially in ripening a culture that could also nourish the countryside. The final burden of this book has been to uncover the nature of those limits.

Strumieri and Zambarlani during Giovedì Grasso, 1511

The following names and their factional affiliations have been compiled from the sources cited in Chapter 5 and then correlated with the list in BCU, MS Joppi 592. Evidence for inclusion in the lists comes from overt statements of affiliation; from signatures on petitions; and from records of adherents to the truce on the eve of Giovedì Grasso, guests at the Della Torre or the Savorgnan banquets on the eve of Giovedì Grasso, loyalists at either palace the next day, participants in an act of violence against a member of the opposing faction, participants in the looting or burning of property of a member of the other faction, victims of violence by the opposing faction, victims of looting or burning by the opposing faction, recipients of Antonio Savorgnan's pardon during the violence, and claimants for damages after the event. Where not specified, relationships among individuals with the same surname are unknown.

Legend:
m = murdered
s = property sacked or looted
b = house or castle burned

STRUMIERI

Leaders

DELLA TORRE, Alvise, m, s, b (married to Tadea Strassoldo); his brother, Isidoro, m, s, b; their nephew, Nicolò, m (married to Giacoma Brazzacco)

Followers

AMASEO, Gregorio (originally a Zambarlano but in opposition to Antonio Savorgnan on Giovedì Grasso; he was not, however, a victim of violence)
ARCANO, Giovanni and Nicolò, s
ARCOLONIANO, Antonio, m; his brothers, Francesco, m (married to Cassandra Della Torre, first cousin of Alvise) and Troilo, s; Daniele; Dario; Martino, s attempted; Pietro, s attempted
ATTIMIS, Guariento; Odorico
BERTOLINO, Bertolino; his brother, Battista, m, s
BOCCASTORTA, Andrea, m
BRAZZACCO (BRAZZÀ), Antonio, s; his son, Corado; Antonio's brother, Nicolò, s; their sister, Giacoma (married to Nicolò Della Torre)
CANDIDO, Giovanni, s (brother-in-law of Giovanni Enrico Spilimbergo); his cousin, Giovanni Battista, s; Francesco (wounded before Giovedì Grasso, later murdered Nicolò Savorgnan); Aloisa (married to Giacomo Spilimbergo)
CASTELLO, Giacomo, s, b; Pietro Urbano, s; Giovanni Battista, s; Doimo, s
CAPORIACCO (CAVORIACO), Giovanni Giacomo (later murdered Nicolò Savorgnan); Giovanni Nicolò; Nicolò Maria, m on January 1, 1511
CERGNEU (CERGNEO), Francesco, s (married to Antonia Frattina; their son-in-law was Troiano Guarienti)
COLLOREDO, Albertino, s; his sons, Leandro, Nicolò (later murdered Nicolò Savorgnan and Giovanni Monticolo), Girolamo, and Gregorio (both later murdered Antonio Savorgnan, Girolamo murdered Francesco Janis di Tolmezzo); Odorico; from a different branch, Teseo, m, s; from yet another branch, Federico, m, s
? COLOMBATTI, Francesco (gave refuge to Teseo Colloredo, Nicolò Della Torre, and Giovanni Leonardo Frattina, but it is questionable whether this act makes him a Strumiero)
CUCCAGNA, whole clan, individual names unknown
FRATTINA, Frattinate; Giovanni Leonardo, m, s; his brother, Polidoro, m?, s; Giovanni Leonardo and Polidoro's sisters, Angela (married to Apollonio Gorghi) and Antonia (married to Francesco Cergneu)
GORGHI (GORGO), Apollonio, m (married to Angela Frattina); Troilo, s; Antonio di Francesco

GUARIENTI (PERCOTO, PIRCUT, PORTO), Francesco; his son, Troiano, s (son-in-law of Francesco Cergneu); Troiano's son-in-law, Giovanni Francesco (surname unknown); Jaca, s; Guareto, s; Gotardo

GUBERTINO, Leonardo, s; Agostino (canon of Cividale)

MELS (MELSO, METZ), a branch of the Colloredo, individual names unknown

MONFALCONE, Sebastiano, s; his son, Felice

MONTORIO, Francesco (probably a *bravo* of Giovanni Candido)

MOZENINI (MAZAVINO), Francesco, s; his brother, Hironimo, s

PARTISTAGNO (PARTENSTEIN), Agostino, s (married to Tranquilla Della Torre; their son-in-law was Francesco Pavona); their sons, Alessandro, Ercole, Francesco, Girolamo; Agostino's brothers, Francesco, Alvise, and Isidoro

PASSERINO, Pietro

PAVONA, Francesco, s attempted (son-in-law of Agostino Partistagno); his son, Bernardino; Gerolamo

PERS (PERSO, PARSO), Antonio; Bernardino; Gerolamo (son-in-law of Soldoniero Soldonieri)

POLCENICO, Francesco; Giacomo Antonio

PORCÌA (PORCIGLIE, PURCIGLIE, PURZIGLIE), Bartolomeo; Federico; Giulio; Prosdocimo

PRAMPERO (PRAMPERGO), Andrea

SBRUGLI, the whole clan, individual names unknown

SOLDONIERI, Soldoniero, m, s; his daughter, Lucrezia (married to Gerolamo Pers)

SPILIMBERGO, Alberto; Barnaba; Giacomo (cousin of Alvise Della Torre); Girolamo; Troilus; Nicolò; Giovanni Enrico (brother-in-law of Giovanni Candido, later murdered Antonio Savorgnan); Urbano, m

STRASSOLDO, Ettore (married to Smirelda Della Torre); Tadea (married to Alvise Della Torre); Giovanni (exempted from Antonio Savorgnan's blanket condemnation of the clan)

? SUSANNA, Beltrame (canon of Aquileia who helped Giovanni Candido escape); his brother, Marco; Cristoforo

? TERZAGO, Antonio, s; Nicolò, s

TINGO, Nicolò

TOMASI DI MONFALCONE (MONTEFALCONE), Sebastiano, s; his son, Felice

VALENTINIS (VALENTINO), Enrico; Giovanni Guberto; Martino, s attempted

VALVASONE, Bertoldo, s; Modesto, s; Valenzio, s; Francesco (married to Tadea di Raimondo Della Torre, a first cousin of Alvise Della Torre)

VEGIA, Andrea

ZOPPOLA, Battista; Giovanni Giorgio (later murdered Antonio Savorgnan)

? ZUANE, Soldoniero, m

ZUCCO, Giovanni

Zambarlani

Leaders

SAVORGNAN DELLA TORRE DEL ZUINO, Antonio (later murdered); his illegitimate son, Nicolò, called Il Cheribino (later murdered); Antonio's
nephews, Francesco and Bernardino; Antonio's illegitimate brother, Pie-
tro, called Il Cargenello; Antonio's sister, Lisabetta (mother of Luigi
da Porto); Antonio's "familiars and dogs of the house," Bernardino da
Narni, Matana, Zuanetto di Pietro del Pizol called Piccolo, Smergon,
Guglielmo di Marco Floriti da Venzone called Tempesta, Giovanni di
Leonardo Marangone di Capriglie called Vergon, Viso, Il Ferrarese, and
Giovanni Pietro Fosca
SAVORGNAN DEL MONTE D'OSOPPO, Girolamo (not directly involved in the
Giovedì Grasso events)

Followers

ARLATTO, Girolamo
ARRIGONI, Simone di Francesco di Antonio Parto
BRUGNO DA GEMONA, Bartolomeo (son-in-law of Mario Frattina)
CAINER, Nicolò (artisan and *decano* of a *borgo* of Udine)
CARNEVAL, Uccello
CORBELLO, Pietro (citizen of Udine)
? CORTONA, Francesco
DELLA ROVERE, Battista
DURISSINO, Pietro
FAGAGNA, Giovanni (artisan)
FILITINO, Alessandro (doctor)
FONTANABUONA, Rizzardo
JANIS DI TOLMEZZO, Francesco (doctor, supposedly responsible for a num-
ber of Giovedì Grasso deaths, later murdered by Girolamo Colloredo)
JUSTO, Pietro
LANCILLOTTO (notary)
LODRON, Antonio (count)
LUCADELLO, Giovanni
MELS (METZ), Girolamo (not one of the consorts of Colloredo-Mels but
the son-in-law of a notary from Udine)
MONTICOLO, Giovanni (later murdered by Nicolò Colloredo); his brother,
Nicolò (chancellor of Udine)
? MORIPOTE, Federico
PORTO, Luigi (Alvise) da (nephew of Antonio Savorgnan)
POZZO, Vincenzo
PROSDOCIMO, Raimondo

Rosso, Giacomo
Sbroiavacca, Ascanio (doctor); Girolamo
Scraiber, Odorico (doctor); Simone (executed by Council of Ten)
Spilimbergo, Alvise (condemned by Council of Ten); Tomaso (married to
Beatrice de' Freschi de Cucagna)
Susanna, Odorico
Torso, Battista; Giovanni Francesco
Valvasone, Ippolito
Varmo, Asquinio; Federico
Vitturi, Antonio (retainer of Giovanni Vitturi and condemned by Council of Ten)
Zanni da cortona, Nicolò

Claims for Losses and Damages from Rioting in 1511

Source: BCU, MS Joppi 592, copied from the "Sentenze" of the *Atti* of Antonio Belloni, notary of Udine, June 30, 1534. Arbitrators in the evaluation of the claims were Pietro, Daniele, and Dario Arcoloniani.

Claimants	Claimed	Awarded
1. Ser Gio. Battista q. Ser Francesco Cergnoco	2,000	400
2. Heirs of Ser Troian de Percoto	3,000	600
3. Antonio Brazacco	10,279	8,000
4. Ser Tomaso di Castello di S. Daniele	2,000	1,500
5. Heirs of Ser Jancolao di Tricano	1,300	1,300
6. Heirs of Ser Francesco Mozenini	600	300
7. Ser Gio. Ant. Caporiacco	1,000	600
8. The hospital as heir of Ser Troilo Arcoloniano	160	100
9. D. Bertoldo di Valvasone	3,500	2,500
10. Gregorio Bertolino	1,060	900
11. D. Gerolamo de Colloredo	16,660	7,589
12. D. Valentio di Valvasone	5,106	4,000

13. Signori Torriani	50,000	20,000
14. Padre Giacomo Faidut	60	30
15. Sebastian di Porcìa servant of D. Albertino di Colloredo	30	
16. M.o Francesco di Vevo in Graga	365	200
17. M.o Bidin del Nievo	400	250
18. D. Perina, wife of Ser Paolo di Sanctis	559	300
19. D. Polidoro Frattina	3,081	2,000
20. Bernardino Pavone	566	200
21. Ser Mario Colloreto	1,500	1,000
22. Mario q. D. Leonardo Guberto	775	350
23. Ser Zuanne Soldoniero	9,991	5,000
24. Ser Hector de Zoppola	400	200
25. Ser Albertino Cusano	100	100
26. Hector q. Ser Battista Candido	1,000	900
27. Messer Modesto di Valvasone	1,063	800
28. Ser Zuanbattista q. Ser Simon di Zoppola	100	50
29. Brothers of Castello q. Ser Doino	423	350
30. Sons of D. Agostino Partistagno	900	700
31. Ser Girardo del Gorgo	150	100
32. D. Manfredo di Castello, brother and cousin	2,071	1,600
33. D. Paolo di Cusan, Guberto, Agilino, and Elia	1,200	700
34. Gerolamo and brothers q. Ser Martino de Valentinis	1,051	800
35. D. Federico and Gio. di Strassoldo	538	500
36. Ser Cristoforo Strassoldo	85	70
37. D. Odoardo di Spilimbergo	2,600	2,600
38. D. Pomponio di Spilimbergo	4,800	2,000
39. D. Fabio di Spilimbergo	2,750	2,000
40. D. Gio. Antonio di Spilimbergo	2,081	900
41. Heirs of q. Ser Gio. Francesco di Percuto	503	200
42. Nicolò di Zoppola q. Ser Gio. Battista	681	250
43. D. Marcantonio di Spilimbergo	7,000	3,000
44. Heirs of D. Enrico di Spilimbergo	2,500	1,000
45. Sons of Pietro Stringaro di Spilimbergo	472	300
46. D. Pertoldo di Toppo, inhabitant in Spilimbergo	50	50

47. Sons of Ser Orfeo di Crema, inhabitant in Spilimbergo	1,100	900
48. Sons of Ser Giorgio di Crema, inhabitant in Spilimbergo	800	600
49. Lugia, widow of nob. Giacomo di Spilimbergo	1,000	900
50. Lugia, widow of nob. Alessandro di Spilimbergo	25	25
51. Ser Bertoldo Cisternino di Spilimbergo	470	370
52. Mattio di Cordignan di Udine	60	40
Totals	158,369	80,114

Note at bottom: *In tutto ridotto a ducati 81,000—Inmittendo ducati 1,000 all'anno, trova per ducato Lire di piccoli 610/27, cioè circa un terza di bagattiro per ducato.*

Notes

Introduction

1. The treatment of sources as dialogues has multiple origins, perhaps most importantly through the influence of the "dialogism" of Mikhail Bakhtin, *Rabelais and His World*. See Katerina Clark and Michael Holquist, *Mikhail Bakhtin* (Cambridge: The Belknap Press of Harvard University Press, 1984) and Tzvetan Todorov, *Mikhail Bakhtin: The Dialogical Principle* (Minneapolis: University of Minnesota Press, 1984). Carlo Ginzburg developed independently a historical method for treating inquisitorial records as dialogues. See his *Night Battles: Witchcraft and Agrarian Cults in the Sixteenth and Seventeenth Centuries*; *The Cheese and the Worms: The Cosmos of a Sixteenth-Century Miller*; and the essay "The Inquisitor as Anthropologist," in *Clues, Myths, and the Historical Method*, 156–64. Also see his postscript to Natalie Zemon Davis, *Il ritorno di Martin Guerre: Un caso di doppia identità nella Francia del Cinquecento* (Turin: Giulio Einaudi, 1984), 129–54. For a general discussion of the approach with regard to the study of feuding, see Osvaldo Raggio, "Etnografia e storia politica: La faida e il caso della Corsica," *QS* 75 (1990): 937–54.

On the poststructuralist interest in narration, see Lawrence Stone, "The Revival of Narrative: Reflections on a New Old History," *Past and Present* 85 (1979): 3–24; E. J. Hobsbawm, "The Revival of Narrative: Some Comments," *Past and Present* 86 (1980): 308; Mark Phillips, "The Revival of Narrative: Thoughts on a Current Historiographical Debate," *University of Toronto Quarterly* 53 (1983–84): 149–65; and Hans Kellner, "Narrativity in History: Post-Structuralism and Since," 1–29.

2. On the microhistorical method, see Carlo Ginzburg and Carlo Poni, "Il nome e il come: Scambio ineguale e mercato storiografico," *QS* 40 (1979): 181–90, translated as "The Name and the Game: Unequal Exchange and the Historiographic Marketplace," in *Microhistory and the Lost Peoples of Europe*, ed. Edward Muir and Guido Ruggiero, 1–10; Ginzburg, *The Cheese and the Worms*, especially 155n; Giovanni Levi, *Inheriting Power: The Story of an Exorcist*, xiii–xviii; and my introduction to *Microhistory and the Lost Peoples of Europe*, vii–xxviii. A parallel method has developed in sociology; see Thomas J. Scheff, "Micro-linguistics and Social Structure: A Theory of Social Action," 71–83. On the influence of social theory on Renaissance studies, see Ronald F. E. Weissman, "Reconstructing Renaissance Sociology: The 'Chicago School' and the Study of Renaissance Society."

3. For the classic statement on the anthropology of feuding, see Max Gluckman, "The Peace in the Feud." For a critique of Gluckman's theory, see Renato Rosaldo, *Illongot Headhunting, 1883–1974: A Study in Society and History*, 273–74. Also see idem, "From the Door of His Tent: The Fieldworker and the Inquisitor," in *Writing Culture: The Poetics and Politics of Ethnography*, ed. James Clifford and George E. Marcus, 77–97. Comparisons with other studies of vendetta and feuding will be made in the chapters that follow. Some of the more important recent anthropological studies for comparison include Keith F. Otterbein and Charlotte Swanson Otterbein, "An Eye for an Eye, a Tooth for a Tooth: A Cross-Cultural Study of Feuding"; Jacob Black-Michaud, *Cohesive Force: Feud in the Mediterranean and the Middle East*; Elisabeth Claverie and Pierre Lamaison, *L'impossible mariage: Violence et parenté en Gévaudan XVIIe, XVIIIe, et XIXe siècles*; Christopher Boehm, *Blood Revenge: The Anthropology of Feuding in Montenegro and Other Tribal Societies*; Stephen Wilson, *Feuding, Conflict, and Banditry in Nineteenth-Century Corsica*; David D. Gilmore, *Aggression and Community: Paradoxes of Andalusian Culture*; Kirsten Hastrup, *Culture and History in Medieval Iceland: An Anthropological Analysis of Structure and Change*. Also see Jesse Byock, *Feud in the Icelandic Saga*.

From a historical point of view see John Larner, "Order and Disorder in Romagna, 1450–1500"; Angelo Torre, "Faide, fazioni e partiti, ovvero la ridefinizione della politica nei feudi imperiali della Longhe tra Sei e Settecento;" Osvaldo Raggio, *Faide e parentele: Lo stato genovese visto dalla Fontanabuona*; Jenny Wormald, "The Blood Feud in Early Modern Scotland"; Keith M. Brown, *Bloodfeud in Scotland, 1573–1625: Violence, Justice and Politics in an Early Modern Society*; David Nicholas, *The Van Arteveldes of Ghent: The Varieties of Vendetta and the Hero in History*; and Altina L. Waller, *Feud: Hatfields, McCoys, and Social Change in Appalachia, 1860–1900*. On the settlement of disputes, see Sarah R. Blanshei, "Criminal Law and Politics in Medieval Bologna"; John Bossy, ed., *Disputes and Settlements: Law and Human Relations in the West*; and Wendy Davies and Paul Fouracre, eds., *The Settlement of Disputes in Early Medieval Europe*.

4. On the traditional distinction between vendetta and feud, see Boehm, *Blood Revenge*, 198–99. Boehm himself does not accept this distinction.

5. Cf. Weissman, "Reconstructing Renaissance Sociology," 40–45.

6. Lucien Febvre made the now-famous initial plea for a history of emotions, "Comment reconstituer la vie affective d'autrefois? La sensibilité e l'histoire," in *Combats pour l'histoire* (Paris: Armand Colin, 1953), 221–38, especially 238. For a

more recent plea, see Peter N. Stearns with Carol Z. Stearns, "Emotionology: Clarifying the History of Emotions and Emotional Standards," *American Historical Review* 90 (1985): 813–36. On Renaissance notions of anger, see J. R. Hale, "Sixteenth Century Explanations of War and Violence," *Past and Present* 50 (1971): 13; Lawrence Stone, "Interpersonal Violence in English Society 1300–1980," *Past and Present* 101 (1983): 22–33; Natalie Zemon Davis, *Fiction in the Archives: Pardon Tales and Their Tellers in Sixteenth-Century France*, 11, 37, and passim; and René Girard, "Hamlet's Dull Revenge," in *Literary Theory/Renaissance Texts*, ed. Patricia Parker and David Quint (Baltimore: Johns Hopkins University Press, 1986), 280–302. On the history of anger, see James R. Averill, *Anger and Aggression: An Essay on Emotion*, Springer Series on Social Psychology, ed. Robert F. Kidd (New York: Springer-Verlag, 1982), 73–102; and Carol Z. Stearns and Peter N. Stearns, *Anger: The Struggle for Emotional Control in America's History*, 14–35. On the sociology of revenge, see Thomas J. Scheff, "Shame and Conformity: The Deference-Emotion System," 395–406; and Jonathan Rieder, "The Social Organization of Vengeance," in *Toward a General Theory of Social Control*, ed. Donald Black, vol. 1: *Fundamentals* (Orlando, Fla.: Academic Press, 1984), 131–62. For a view similar to mine which emphasizes the affective basis for behavior and the influence of negative emotions on social structures, see Gilmore, *Aggression and Community*. For a persuasive argument from the point of view of the biological sciences declaring aggression as much a cultural as a biological phenomenon, see Henri Laborit, *La colombe assassinée* (Paris: Editions Grosset and Fasquelle, 1983).

7. Gabriel Maugain, *Moeurs italiennes de la Renaissance: La vengeance*.

8. Lauro Martines, ed., *Violence and Civil Disorder in Italian Cities, 1200–1500*; Guido Ruggiero, *Violence in Early Renaissance Venice*; and idem, *The Boundaries of Eros: Sex Crime and Sexuality in Renaissance Venice*.

9. On the importance of legends and rational calculations in feuds, see Boehm, *Blood Revenge*, 143–44.

10. On pardon tales, see Davis, *Fiction in the Archives*. On the social role of language, see Peter Burke, *The Historical Anthropology of Early Modern Italy: Essays on Perception and Communication*, 79–94. A now-outdated anthropological theory emphasized the atemporality of feuds. Black-Michaud, *Cohesive Force*, 74 and passim. Cf. Brown, *Bloodfeud in Scotland*, 2.

Prologue

1. *DU, GAH*, 516.

2. Ibid., 509.

3. For all the above quotes, see ibid., 510–13. For Gregorio's briefer account of the same events, see *DU, GA*, 227. Others, far more distant from the actual event, depicted Savorgnan as playing an even more active role in the attack on the Della Torre palace than even had Amaseo. Agostino Colloredo asserts that Antonio encouraged his men by telling them that the Venetian signoria had given him a free hand with the traitors. Yet another alleged that Savorgnan had distributed a list with a code letter written beside each victim's name indicating whether the house was to be burned or sacked or the inhabitants killed. Antonio defended himself by

pointing out that he went unarmed the whole day and could not stop his followers; on his own initiative he twice put out the fire at Alvise Della Torre's palace but in the end was unable to prevent it from going up in flames. Although Savorgnan's precise responsibility for the events will require further examination, he could by no means predetermine every action and, as his subsequent activities demonstrated, was himself faced with a crowd that had taken on its own direction and had its own objectives. For Agostino Colloredo, see Colloredo, "Croniche friulane 1508–18," 5. For list, see MCV, MS Correr 963, pezzo 3, fol. 24v. For Savorgnan's defense, see "Autentiche testimonianze intorno alla famiglia Savorgnan," 304.

4. For quote, see *DU*, GAH, 513–14. On the Giovedì Grasso dance, see Dionisio Tassini, "La rivolta del Friuli nel 1511 durante la guerra contro i tedeschi," 146.

5. *DU*, GAH, 516–17.

6. Ibid., 519–20. On the career of Janis, see *DU*, GA, 229n, 257, 268; *DU*, GAH, 498n, 499, 516; Giovanni Battista di Cergneu, *Cronaca delle guerre friulane*, 47; Marino Sanuto, *I diarii*, 10: 376–77; 12: 109, 618; BCU, ACU, Annali, reg. 41, fol. 204r; Fabia Savini, "Antonio Savorgnan," 293; Marino Sanuto, "Viaggio in Spagna di Francesco Janis da Tolmezzo," 63–64.

7. For quote, see Colloredo, "Croniche friulane," 5.

8. For the escape story, see *DU*, GAH, 521–23. It is confirmed in its general outline by Colloredo, "Croniche friulane," 6, and Nicolò Monticolo, *Descrittione del sacco*, 17. A mention can be found in Sanuto, *I diarii*, 12:15. Antonio Savorgnan takes credit for saving the baby in a document from the Cormons archive published in Savini, "Antonio Savorgnan," 304, but in a letter to the Council of Ten Andrea Loredan and Luogotenente Gradenigo wrote that they saved the boy. ASV, CCD, Lettere rettori, Udine, busta 169, fol. 70r. Cf. *DU*, GAH, 522–23; da Porto, *Lettere storiche*, no. 64, 279.

9. For the first quote, see Colloredo, "Croniche friulane," 6. For the second quote, see *DU*, GAH, 523.

Chapter 1: The Friulan Enigma

1. For an account of the war and conquest, see Gian Carlo Menis, *Storia del Friuli dalle origini alla caduta dello stato patriarcale (1420)*, 225–50; Pier Silverio Leicht, "La rivolta feudale contro il Patriarca Bertando," *MSF* 41 (1954–55): 1–94; Tito Miotti, "Udinesi e friulani ribelli," 121–23; Roberto Cessi, "Venezia e la preparazione della guerra friulana (1381–5)," 431–73; Michele Zacchigna, "I Savorgnano di Udine. L'espansione fondiaria (sec. XIII–XIV)," 43–56; Amelio Tagliaferri, "Idee nuove per un vecchio problema: La caduta dello stato patriarcale," 211–12; Liliana Cargnelutti, "Tristano Savorgnan (1377–1440) nella crisi del Patriarcato," in *I Savorgnan e la Patria del Friuli dal XIII al XVIII secolo*, 113; Pio Paschini, *Storia del Friuli*, 2: 239–41, 324–32; Pier Silverio Leicht, "L'esilio di Tristano di Savorgnano," 37–68; idem, "Il tramonto dello stato patriarcale e la lotta delle parti in Friuli durante le tregue del 1413–1418," 83–108; G. Cogo, "La sottomissione del Friuli alla signoria di Venezia," 95–146; Carlo Guido Mor, "Problemi organizzativi e politica veneziana nei riguardi dei nuovi acquisti di terraferma," 1–10; and

M. E. Mallett and J. R. Hale, *The Military Organization of a Renaissance State: Venice c. 1400 to 1617*, 26–31.

2. On Venice's spiritual connections to the patriarchate, see Edward Muir, *Civic Ritual in Renaissance Venice*, 77, 79–80, 83. On the lack of institutional change, see Mallett and Hale, *Military Organization*, 7–8, 16.

3. On the absence of full sovereignty, see John Easton Law, "Venice and the Problem of Sovereignty in the *Patria del Friuli*, 1421," in *Florence and Italy: Renaissance Studies in Honour of Nicolai Rubenstein*, ed. Peter Denley and Caroline Elam (London: Westfield College, University of London, Committee for Medieval Studies, 1988), 135–47. I wish to thank Dr. Law for supplying me with a copy of his article.

The centuries of Venetian rule constitute the most controversial period in Friulan historiography, dividing historians into pro- and anti-Venetian schools. For the definitive statement of the pro-Venetian school, see Leicht, "Il tramonto dello stato patriarcale," 108. Cf. a sixteenth-century view in "Anatomia della Patria del Friuli," ONV, Cod. 6415 (N.s.n.), 154v–155r, and the seventeenth-century historian, Gio. Francesco Palladio degli Olivi, *Historie della provincia del Friuli*, 494–95. An early nationalistic assault on the philo-Venetian position came from Vincenzo Marchesi, "Le relazioni dei luogotenenti della Patria del Friuli al senato veneziano," *Annali dell' Istituto Tecnico di Udine*, ser. 2, vol. 2 (1893). Defending Venetian rule, Pompeo Molmenti criticized Marchesi in "Il dominio Veneto nel Friuli," *NAV* 6 (1893): 87–110. For Marchesi's response, "Il dominio veneto nel Friuli (risposta al prof. Molmenti)," *Atti della Accademia di Udine*, ser. 3, vol. 1 (1893–94): 7–26. Also see idem, "Le condizioni del Friuli alla fine del '500," *Pagine friulane* 7 (1895): 171–73; idem, "Le relazioni dei provveditori e sindici inquisitori della terraferma al senato veneziano," *Annali dell' Istituto Tecnico di Udine*, ser. 2, vol. 14 (1896); and idem, "Il Friuli al tempo della Lega di Cambrai," 501–37.

For more recent attempts to define the Friulan "national consciousness" that came from the patriarchal period and survived the cultural influences of Venice, see Amelio Tagliaferri, ed., *Venezia e il Friuli*, 11; Miotti, "Udinesi e friulani ribelli," 119; and G. C. Menis, *Storia del Friuli*, 228–29. Elsewhere, however, Menis points out that only in 1482 after sixty-two years of Venetian rule can one find the first reflections about the meaning of a unified Friuli and that literature in Friulan flourished during the sixteenth and seventeenth centuries when Venetian dominion became solidified. "La dominazione Veneta e la reazione culturale friulana," in *Atti del convegno: Venezia e la terraferma attraverso le relazioni dei rettori, Trieste, 23–24 ottobre 1980*, 41–44. An early version of the history of *mentalités* that integrated historical and anthropological approaches for the study of a peasant society first appeared in the work of Josef Marchet (Giuseppe Marchetti), who published his masterwork in Friulan as *Cuintristorie dal Friûl*, ed. 2 (Udine: "Risultive," 1975). Since the earthquake in 1976, a new historiography has dominated regional scholarship by emphasizing the singularity of Friulan history but also enthusiastically adopting the methods of *Annales: E.S.C.* For a survey of Friulan historiography, see Gian Carlo Menis, *Storiografie furlane dal nestri timp 1970–1980*, Serie didatiche, no. 1 (Udine: Societât Filologjche Furlane, 1982).

Figures published in 1985 by the Istituto Centrale di Statistica demonstrate that

Friuli is still a highly distinctive region. In the basic categories measuring consumption habits, social mores, and demographic patterns, Friuli ranked, more often than any other region, either in first or last place or at least among the highest or the lowest. Friulans had the lowest marriage rate, spent the most for health and for education, had the smallest families, were the most likely to separate and to divorce, had the highest suicide rate, and died at a younger age than in any other region. Claudia Giannini, "Triveneto allo specchio: I vizi, le virtù, i consumi e le malattie," *Gazzettino*, 7 October 1985.

4. Quote from *The Castle of Fratta*, trans. Lovett F. Edwards (London: Oxford University Press, 1957), 12. On the popularity in the Veneto of chivalric given names, especially of Tristan, see Linda L. Carroll, *Language and Dialect in Ruzante and Goldoni*, 17.

5. On "total scarcity," see Jacob Black-Michaud, *Cohesive Force: Feud in the Mediterranean and the Middle East*, 160. Stephen Wilson shows that in Corsica feuding thrived not just on scarcity per se but on a variety of conflicts over limited resources. *Feuding, Conflict and Banditry in Nineteenth-Century Corsica*, 61–90.

6. For the quote by the anonymous local, see "Dell'imperio venetiano in Italia," BMV, It. VII, 225 (8512), fol. 8v.

7. For his account of the mainland tour, see Marino Sanuto, *Itinerario per la terraferma veneziana nell'anno 1483*, 143 for Aquileia. On the nature of the trip, see Rinaldo Fulin's introduction to a second edition titled, "Frammento inedito dell'itinerario," 3. The first edition is based on a manuscript, corrected and completed by the author, found in the Biblioteca of the Università degli Studi, Padua. The second edition is based on an uncorrected holograph manuscript in the BMV, a version more candid and complete in the views expressed about persons and places and with a multiplicity of particulars cut out of the corrected version. The second version, unfortunately, does not include Friuli. For the quote from the formal description, see idem, *Descrizione della Patria del Friuli (1502–3)*, 16.

8. The tradition of formal humanist descriptions of Friuli began with Marc' Antonio Sabellico, *De vetustate Aquileiensis patriae* (Venice, ca. 1482–84).

9. For the organic description, see "Anatomia della Patria del Friuli," ONV, Cod. 6415 (N.s.n.), 147r–93r, for quotes 152r–57r. On the emblem of Friuli, see *Leggi per la Patria*, in prefatory material under heading, "Insegna della Patria del Friuli."

10. For Luigi da Porto's description, see *Lettere storiche dall'anno 1509 al 1528*, 178–82.

11. On the luogotenenti's reports, see *Relazioni dei rettori veneti in terraferma*, vol. 1, *La Patria del Friuli (Luogotenenza di Udine)*, for Mocenigo, 90; for Morosini, 122; for Erizzo, xliii. Cf. Jacobus Stainer, *Patria del Friuli restaurata*, 18. On the open door theme, see Amelio Tagliaferri, "Castelli, giurisdizioni, economie," 7; idem, introduction to *Relazioni*, 1: xvii.

12. The description of Friulan geography is based on the classic guides, M. Gortani, *Guida geologica del Friuli* (Tolmezzo: Carnia, 1926) and idem, *Caratteristiche generale e fisiche del Friuli* (Udine: Pellegrino, 1956). There is an excellent short summary of Gortani's work in *Enciclopedia monografica Friuli-Venezia-Giulia*, vol. 1

(Udine: Istituto per l'Enciclopedia del Friuli-Venezia-Giulia, 1971), s.v. "Geologia generale e geomorfologia," by Bruno Martinis.

13. On the number of villages, see Amelio Tagliaferri, "I caratteri dell'habitat rurale ed il trend demografico," 236. Some recognized the need for irrigation projects in the area as early as the fourteenth century when schemes were drawn up, but no action was taken. Nicolò Maniago had two canals dug on the right bank of the Tagliamento in 1445 and 1453, but he intended them to transport lumber, and their use as a water source for irrigation was at best surreptitious. In 1457 he proposed a canal between the Tagliamento and the upper reaches of the Ledra to bring water to the wide flat fields of Osoppo, but the council of Udine opposed him on the grounds that any change would abuse the city's privileges. Work began, nevertheless, near Osoppo in 1487 but was interrupted and restarted only in 1592. On irrigation projects, see S. Ciriacono, "Irrigazione e produttività agraria nella terraferma veneta tra Cinque e Seicento," 131–35.

14. On the Spilimbergo protest, see *Chronicon Spilimbergense*, in Pognici, *Guida Spilimbergo e suo distretto*, 200.

15. Quotes on bread are cited in Antonio Measso, "Il pane quotidiano a Udine nel 1500: Note d'archivio," *Atti dell'Accademia di Udine*, ser. 2, 7 (1887): 10, 14. On wines, see Sanuto, *Itinerario*, 139.

16. On shipbuilding demands, see Alberto Tenenti, *Piracy and the Decline of Venice, 1580–1615*, trans. with introduction and glossary by Janet and Brian Pullan (Berkeley and Los Angeles: University of California Press, 1967), 89–149 and passim. For an example of an official tour to survey timber resources, see Marino Sanuto, *I diarii*, 3: 1097–98. The products of Friuli in the midsixteenth century are described in Girolamo di Porcìa, *Descrizione della Patria del Friuli con l'utile che cava il serenissimo principe e con le spese che fa*, 15–17.

17. On industrial activities, see Amelio Tagliaferri, *Udine nella storia economica*, 70–76, 116–17. On the fame of Friulan scythes, see da Porto, *Lettere storiche*, 178–82.

18. On the sites of castles, see Tagliaferri, "Castelli," 7-9. On Girolamo di Porcìa's count of castles, see *Descrizione del Friuli*, 16; a complete survey of Friulan castles may be found in Tito Miotti, *Castelli del Friuli*; on Palmanova, E. Concina, *La macchina territoriale*; cf. Carlo Guido Mor, "L'ambiente agrario friulano dall'XI alla metà del XIV secolo," 215–16.

19. For example, Ligurian feuding was typically isolated in the mountain valleys above the coastal towns; see Osvaldo Raggio, *Faide e parentele: Lo stato genovese visto dalla Fontanabuona*, 68, 176, and passim.

20. On Venetian interest in the passes, see *Relazioni*, 1: xxvii.

21. On Roman use of passes, see Fernand Braudel, *The Mediterranean and the Mediterranean World in the Age of Philip II*, 41. On Gemona and Venzone, see Sanuto, *Descrizione*, 32–33.

22. On the routes of the mountain roads, see Sanuto, *Itinerario*, 134; BMV, It. VII, 225 (8512), fols. 52v–53r.

23. On the Venetian use of passes for defense, see Piero Pieri, *Il Rinascimento e la crisi militare italiana* (Turin: Einaudi, 1952), 450–51; and Mallett and Hale, *Mili-*

tary Organization, 461–84. For quote, see Niccolò Machiavelli, *Discourses on the First Decade of Titus Livius*, in *Machiavelli: The Chief Works and Others*, 1: 250 (book 1, chap. 23). Cf. comments by Luogotenente Antonio Loredan in Sanuto, *I diarii*, 3: 189.

24. On Chiusaforte, see Miotti, *Castelli del Friuli*, 1: 70–76 and BMV It. VII 225 (8512), fols. 48v–49r. Quote from the *relazione* of Luogotenente Stefano Viaro, presented 4 November 1599, is in *Relazioni*, 1: 114; cf. 12, 137–38, 183; and BMV, It. VII, 225 (8512), fol. 53v.

25. On the routes to Gorizia, see BMV, It. VII, 225 (8512), fols. 9r, 98v.

26. On the defenses in general, see Mallett and Hale, *Military Organization*, 91–93, 96; and Francesco Micelli, "I Savorgnan e la difesa della Patria," 135.

27. Savorgnan's letter is in Sanuto, *I diarii*, 10: 352–53; cf. descriptions in BMV, It. VII, 225 (8512), fols. 49r–50v, 51v–52r. I assume here that Savorgnan was using the Udinese system of linear measurements in which one *passo* equaled 1.7 meters. In the Venetian system one *passo* equaled 1.75 meters. See Joppi's notes in Girolamo Savorgnano, "Lettere, risposte, documenti sulla vita 1499–1528, Atti e memorie," BCU, MS Joppi 689d, vol. 4, unpaginated.

28. For quote, see Porcìa, *Descrizione del Friuli*, 12. For total population figures, *Relazioni*, 1: xvii, 83. On the problems of calculating populations for Friuli, see Giovanni Ferrari, *Il Friuli: La popolazione dalla conquista veneta ad oggi*, 9–26. On city populations for the Veneto, see "Milizie Venete, 1462–1557," BMV, It. VII, 1213 (8656), fols. 62r, 63. Cf. figures in Amelio Tagliaferri, "Ordinamento amministrativo dello Stato di Terraferma," 43 and idem, *Udine nella storia economica*, 54–58. On the city populations for Friuli, see "Summario delle città, castelli, ville, et anime che sono in Terra ferma sotto L'Illustrissima Signoria di Venetia," BMV, It. VII, 924 (8874), fol. 159v.

29. On German customs, da Porto, *Lettere storiche*, 180. On evidence of Italian identity in the sixteenth century, "Canzone in laude dei Venzonesi," published in Pier Silverio Leicht, "La difesa del Friuli nel 1509, con appendice di documenti," 115.

30. Giuseppe Francescato and Fulvio Salimbeni, "Per un'analisi della situazione linguistica e culturale del Friuli nel '500," 112–13. Idem, *Storia, lingua e società in Friuli*, 144–50, quote on 150. On the peasant's request for interpretation, see Carlo Ginzburg, *The Night Battles: Witchcraft and Agrarian Cults in the Sixteenth and Seventeenth Centuries*, 117. On Menocchio, see idem, *The Cheese and the Worms: The Cosmos of a Sixteenth-Century Miller*.

31. On the Slovenian speakers, see BMV, It. VII, 225 (8512), fol. 54v; Gogo Grafenauer, "La vita economica e il problema dell'autonomia locale della Slavia Veneta nel periodo della repubblica," *Atti del Convegno*, 183. On the German speakers, see Giorgio Marcuzzi, "Demaecologia delle isole linguistiche tedesche delle alpi e prealpi orientali (Sauris, Timau e Sappada)," 207–209.

32. On the singular position of Friuli, see Angelo Ventura, "Il dominio di Venezia," 184; Carlo Guido Mor, "Aristocrazia veneziana e nobiltà di terraferma," 358–59; *Relazioni*, 1: xxxi; Giuseppe Gullino, "Un problema aperto: Venezia e il tardo feudalismo," *SV*, n.s., 7 (1983): 183–93.

33. On the need for maps, see Mallett and Hale, *Military Organization*, 409, 414.

34. Antonio Battistella, "Udine nel secolo XVI: L'edilizia, l'igiene e la polizia urbana," 27–28.

35. For an assessment of Venetian rectors, see Battistella, "Udine nel secolo XVI: L'ordinamento interno della città," 161–62; and Giovanni Scarabello, "Nelle relazioni dei rettori veneti in terraferma: Aspetti di una loro attività di mediazione tra governanti delle città suddite e governo della dominante," 485–89.

36. Tagliaferri, "Ordinamento amministrativo," 15–17. *Relazioni*, 1: xxxvi–xxxviii. The luogotenente had a vicario, two provvisori, a cancelliere, two giudici, a camerlengo, and a maresciallo as assistants. Idem, *Udine nella storia economica*, 45–46.

37. *Relazioni*, 1: xxxv–xxxvi; for opinions of luogotenenti on problems of multiple jurisdictions, 21, 48, 62. Tagliaferri, "Ordinamento amministrativo," 15–21. On Prata and Toppo, see idem, *Udine nella storia economica*, 45. On Soffumbergo, see Gaetano Perusini, "L'amministrazione della giustizia in una giurisdizione friulana del Cinquecento," 205–6. On La Motta, see Sanuto, *Itinerario*, 128. The quotation from Francesco Sanuto is cited in Gaetano Cozzi, *Repubblica di Venezia*, 112n. Also see Claudio Povolo, "Aspetti e problemi," 176–92.

38. On Valvasone, see Tarcisio Venuti, "I 32 capitoli della sentenza arbitraria tra i consorti e il popolo di Valvasone nel 1580," 22. On a claim that the Strassoldo lords were exempt from arrest within their jurisdiction, see Niccolò Maria di Strassoldo, *Cronaca: Anni 1469–1509*, 13. On Latisana, see Michele Gottardi, "La struttura politico-amministrativa del Friuli occidentale nel XVI secolo," 77–78. On Buia, see Gian Paolo Gri, "Giurisdizione e vicinia nell'età moderna: Il caso di Buia," 177–97. On Aviano, see Pier Silverio Leicht in the preface to Gian Lodovico Bertolini and Umberto Rinaldi, eds., *Carta politico-amministrativa della Patria del Friuli al cadere della repubblica veneta*, 8.

39. *Relazioni*, 1: xxxi–xxxiii. Amelio Tagliaferri, "Rettori veneti e castellani nella Patria del Friuli," 195. Pier Silverio Leicht, "La riforma delle costituzioni friulane nel primo secolo della dominazione veneziana," 73–78.

40. On the church in general, see Francescato and Salimbeni, *Storia, lingua e società*, 133–34. For a copy of the agreement limiting the temporal domain of the patriarch, see BSU, Archivio Capitolare di Udine, Raccolta Bini, Miscellanea, 19: 109. On San Daniele, see Giuseppe Trebbi, *Francesco Barbaro, patrizio veneto e Patriarca di Aquileia*, 346–81, 441–69.

41. On rural magic, see Ginzburg, *Night Battles*; and idem, *The Cheese and the Worms*.

42. On Udine, see Antonio Battistella, "Udine nel secolo XVI: La religione e i provvedimenti economico-sociali," 1–40, quote on 9–10.

43. Wilson notes that in nineteenth-century Corsica priests also failed as peacemakers. *Feuding*, 230–31.

44. Tagliaferri, *Udine nella storia economica*, 45–49. Andreina Stefanutti, "Giureconsulti friulani, tra giurisdizionalismo veneziano e tradizione feudale," 75–79.

45. On red flags, see Pompeo Molmenti, "I bandi e i banditi della repubblica veneta," 139. On the contribution of patrilocality to feuding, see Keith F. Otterbein and Charlotte Swanson Otterbein, "An Eye for an Eye, a Tooth for a Tooth: A Cross-Cultural Study of Feuding," 1472–73; and Christopher Boehm, *Blood*

Revenge: The Anthropology of Feuding in Montenegro and Other Tribal Societies, 223–24.

46. On the enfeoffing of condottieri in border areas, see Mallett and Hale, *Military Organization,* 187–88. For formal definitions of the four types of fiefs granted in Friuli, see Daniele Fabrizio, "Informazione intorno la qualità de feudi nel Friuli," BMV, It. II, 8 (4903), fols. 18r–19v. A register of feudal investitures made in Friuli by the luogotenenti between 1420 and 1551 can be found in ASV, Secreta, Materie miste notabili, reg. 117. For later periods, see ASV, Provveditori sopra feudi. On the Villalta example, see ASU, AT, busta 39, doc. dated 24 April 1476.

47. On family and private law, see Leicht, "La riforma delle costituzioni friulane," 79–83. For an example of the division of the holdings among the members of a fraternal *societas,* see MCV, MS P.D. 755/6, pergamena dated 17 February 1570.

48. For an excellent discussion of property rights, see James S. Grubb, "Il mondo di Lisiera nel Quattrocento," in *Lisiera: Immagini, documenti per la storia e cultura di una comunità veneta—strutture, congiunture, episodi,* 2 vols. (Lisiera: Edizioni parrocchia di Lisiera, 1981), 1: 84–85.

49. On the Strassoldo, see Paolo Cammarosano, ed., *Le campagne friulane nel tardo medioevo: Un'analisi dei registri di censi dei grandi proprietari fondiari,* 34–35, 40–41, 88–90.

50. Ibid., 71–75. Gottardi, "La struttura politico-amministrativa," 85–86. Gaetano Perusini, "Le condizioni di vita in un paese della pianura friulana nel secolo XVI," 169.

51. Recent years have seen a dramatic debate about the history of Friulan rural settlement patterns in which many of the issues are both methodological and ideological. The traditional method relied principally on an interpretation of legal terms employed in written documents and emphasized the relative immobility of agrarian structures throughout the later Middle Ages and a predominant settlement pattern of houses concentrated in centralized nuclear villages. See, in particular, the distinguished work by Carlo Guido Mor, *L'età feudale,* 2 vols. (Milan: F. Vallardi, 1952–53); "'Universitas Vallis': Un problema da studiare relativo alla storia del comune rurale," in *Miscellanea in onore di Roberto Cessi* (Rome: Edizioni di storia e letteratura, 1958), 1: 103–9; "'Campo friulano': Una chiarificazione della storia dei Longobardi in Italia," *MSF* 46 (1965): 145–53; "Nuove vedute metodologiche sulla storia friulana," *MSF* 56 (1976): 15–27; *Scritti di storia giuridica altomedievale* (Pisa: Pacini, 1977); and especially, "L'ambiente agrario friulano," in which Mor modifies his view to emphasize greater dynamism in late medieval Friulan agriculture.

A new view, which relies heavily on the interpretation of maps and aerial photographs but is marred by elementary mistakes in the use of technical terms, argues that the agrarian past was markedly unstable, and settlements followed a variety of patterns including ones in which houses were dispersed rather than concentrated in villages. See Alessandro Guaitoli, *Comunità rurale e territorio: Per una storia delle forme del popolamento in Friuli;* idem, "Beni comunali e istituti di compascuo nel Friuli agli inizi del secolo XVII: Con particolari riferimenti alla montagna e alta pianura della destra Tagliamento," 33–55. For criticisms of Guaitoli, see Carlo Guido Mor, "Comunità rurali e territorio: Un po' di metodologia storica," *CF* 60 (1984): 7–19.

Perhaps the most promising new work, the outlines of which have been followed here, has been by the équipe at the University of Trieste headed by Paolo Cammarosano. They have systematically compared the extant rent-rolls (*rotuli*) of the large landed proprietors mostly on the left bank of the Tagliamento. See Cammarosano, "Il paesaggio agrario del tardo medioevo;" "Strutture d'insediamento e società nel Friuli dell'età patriarchina;" and, especially, *Le campagne friulane*. Also see Donata Degrassi, "La zona collinare di Faedis," in *Contributi per la storia del paesaggio rurale nel Friuli-Venezia Giulia* (Pordenone: Grafiche Editoriali Artistiche Pordenonesi, 1980), 145–52. Idem, "Fonti per lo studio del paesaggio agrario in Friuli nei secoli XII–XV: I registri censuari," in *Fonti per lo studio del paesaggio agrario*, Atti del terzo convegno di storia urbanistica. Lucca, 3–5 ottobre, 1979 (Lucca, 1981), 227–34. Idem, "Il registro del notaio Giacomo di Faedis: Una ricerca sulla vita rurale in Friuli nel secolo XIV," *Studi medievali* 22 (1981): 183–223. Idem, "La piccola proprietà nel Friuli del tardo medioevo attraverso gli inventari," *Metodi e ricerche*, n.s., 1 (1982): 23–53. Students of Giorgio Politi at the University of Venice have pursued similar methods. For an example in Friuli, see Cinzia Borghese, "Castellani e contadini del Friuli orientale negli anni della rivolta: Le proprietà dei Colloredo e dei Savorgnan (Feudo di Buia)."

52. The extreme heterogeneity of Friulan villages contrasts with the pattern Raggio found in the Ligurian area of Fontanabuona, in which there was a strong correspondence between clan identity (*parentela*) and residence, which meant that legal, social, and property rights were closely interlinked. *Faide*, 80. On Orzano, see Perusini, "Le condizioni di vita," 165–66.

53. On Buia, Pietro Menis, *Buia e il suo duomo: Origine e vicende* (Gemona: n.p., 1942); and idem, *Cenni storici sul castello di Buia* (Udine: n.p., 1931).

54. On serfdom, see Antonio Battistella, "La servitù di masnada in Friuli, con documenti e regesti," *NAV*, n.s., 6 (1906): 3–62, 169–91, 320–21; and Gino di Caporiacco, "Il dominio veneziano e la mancata formazione di una classe dirigente friulana," 31–33 in Tagliaferri, ed., *Venezia e il Friuli: Problemi storiografici*.

55. On the structure of rural villages, see Perusini, "Le condizioni di vita," 170; and Cammarosano, *Le campagne friulane*, 79–85.

56. On peasant obligations, see Mor, "Ambiente agrario," 214; and Tagliaferri, *Udine nella storia economica*, 67. On Venetian attempts to protect the peasants from creditors, see Gaetano Perusini, *Vita di popolo in Friuli: Patti agrari e consuetudini tradizionali*, xxii. Perusini's book is a remarkable early example of a combination of historical and anthropological methods written long before it became fashionable. For example, see his discussion on 223–27 of the customs of property division among peasant families; it is based on both the legal history of contracts and a survey made in 1948 of forty-two communes in the province of Udine.

57. Stefanutti, "Giureconsulti friulani," 80. On the early history of Udine, see Amelio Tagliaferri, *Struttura e politica sociale in una comunità veneta del '500 (Udine)*, 15–18; Guido Barbina, "La centralità di Udine nel sistema insediativo friulano:

Analisi di un processo," 43–49; and Carlo Guido Mor, "Nascita di una capitale," 79–90.

58. Sanuto, *Descrizione*, 17–18; idem, *Itinerario*, 133–34.

59. Battistella, "Udine nel secolo XVI: L'edilizia," 2–7.

60. Battistella, "Udine nel secolo XVI: L'ordinamento interno," 149–51; Tagliaferri, *Struttura e politica sociale*, 34–41, 51–63; idem, *Udine nella storia economica*, 70–76.

61. R. Romano, F. C. Spooner, and U. Tucci, "Le finanze di Udine e della Patria del Friuli all'epoca della dominazione veneziana," 235–40. For a list of Udine's communal properties, see "Catastico di beni fiscali in Friuli 1506," BCU, MS 999, pp. 1–13 (catastico of 1506-7), 73–88 (catastico of 1515).

62. Vincenzo Joppi and Alessandro Wolf, eds., *Statuti e ordinamenti del commune di Udine*, xxx–xxxix, liv–lvi, lxiv–lxv, lxx–lxxvii.

63. Romanello Manin, "Dialoghi tra cittadino e castellano," BCP, MS, CM 44.

64. Giovanni Levi, introduction to special issue titled, "Villaggi: Studi di antropologia storica," QS 46 (1981): 7–10. Cf. idem, "I pericoli del Geertzismo," QS 58 (1985): 269–77; and Ronald F. E. Weissman, "Reconstructing Renaissance Sociology: The 'Chicago School' and the Study of Renaissance Society."

65. The discussion here closely parallels some of the findings in Giovanni Levi, *L'eredità immateriale: Carriera di un esorcista nel Piemonte del Seicento* (Turin: Giulio Einaudi, 1985), 51–53, 67, 74–78, 144n, 148–49, 159, 167–69, now in English as *Inheriting Power: The Story of an Exorcist*; and Edoardo Grendi, "Il sistema politico di una comunità ligure: Cervo fra Cinquecento e Seicento," 92–93, 124, in English as "The Political System of a Community in Liguria: Cervo in the Late Sixteenth and Early Seventeenth Centuries," in *Microhistory and the Lost Peoples of Europe: Selections from Quaderni Storici*, ed. Edward Muir and Guido Ruggiero.

Chapter 2: Regulating Conflicts

1. Jacob Burckhardt, *The Civilization of the Renaissance in Italy*, trans. S. G. C. Middlemore (New York: Harper and Row, 1958), 21–142. P. J. Jones argues that institutional diversity and oligarchic hegemony characterized all Italian city-states and that the idea of a distinctive Renaissance state is a crude fiction. "Communes and Despots: The City State in Late-Medieval Italy," *Transactions of the Royal Historical Society*, ser. 5, 15 (1965): 71–96 and "Economia e società nell'Italia medievale: La leggenda della borghesia," in *Storia d'Italia, Annali*, vol. 1, *Dal feudalismo al capitalismo* (Turin: Einaudi, 1978), 187–372. Also see John Easton Law, "Un confronto fra due stati 'rinascimentali': Venezia e il dominio sforzesco," in *Gli Sforza a Milano e in Lombardia e i loro rapporti con gli stati italiani ed europei (1450–1535)* (Milan: Cisalpino-Goliardica, 1982), 401-2. There is an excellent general discussion of the historiography of the Renaissance state in James S. Grubb, *Firstborn of Venice: Vicenza in the Early Renaissance State*, ix–xvi. However, Grubb wants to retain the term *Renaissance state* because he sees the fifteenth century as a period of significant change and the Roman heritage as formative for that change.

2. Federico Chabod, *Scritti sul Rinascimento* (Turin: Giulio Einaudi, 1981); idem,

Lo Stato e la vita religiosa a Milano nell'epoca di Carlo V (Turin: Giulio Einaudi, 1977). On the regional state, see Giorgio Chittolini, *La formazione dello Stato regionale e le istituzioni del contado* (Turin: Giulio Einaudi, 1979); idem, "Stati padani, 'Stati del Rinascimento': Problemi di ricerca," in *Persistenze feudali e autonomie communitative in stati padani fra Cinque e Seicento,* ed. G. Tocci (Bologna: Il Mulino, 1988), 9–29; and Elena Fasano Guarini, ed., *Potere e società negli Stati regionali italiani del '500 e '600* (Bologna: Il Mulino, 1978).

On the Venetian state, see Marino Berengo, *La società veneta alla fine del Settecento: Ricerche storiche* (Florence: Sansoni, 1956). For the idea of "diarchy," see Angelo Ventura, *Nobiltà e popolo nella società veneta del '400 e '500.* On cultural differences, see Gaetano Cozzi, "Ambiente veneziano, ambiente veneto"; idem, "Considerazioni sull'amministrazione della giustizia nella Repubblica di Venezia (secc. XV–XVI)," in *Florence and Venice: Comparisons and Relations,* ed. Sergio Bertelli, Nicolai Rubinstein, and Craig Hugh Smyth, vol. 1, *Quattrocento* (Florence: La Nuova Italia, 1979), 101–33; idem, "La politica del diritto," in *Stato, società e giustizia nella Repubblica Veneta (sec. XV–XVIII),* ed. Gaetano Cozzi, 1: 17–152; and idem, "Politica, società, istituzioni," in *Storia della Repubblica di Venezia,* ed. Gaetano Cozzi and Michael Knapton, 3–252.

On "indirect government" in the Genoese state, Osvaldo Raggio, *Faide e parentele: Lo stato genovese visto dalla Fontanabuona,* xiv. Cf. Maurice Aymard, "La transizione dal feudalismo al capitalismo," in *Storia d'Italia, Annali,* vol. 1, *Dal feudalismo al capitalismo* (Turin: Einaudi, 1978), 1131–92.

3. For the Genoese state, Raggio argues that the pacification of local feuds and the mediation of disputes in the courts became the principal mechanism of government and the major source of its legitimation. *Faide,* xvii–xviii, 197.

4. For an excellent survey of the historiography of Venice, see James S. Grubb, "When Myths Lose Power: Four Decades of Venetian Historiography," 43–94.

5. On the early doges, see Pompeo Molmenti, "I bandi e i banditi della repubblica veneta," 126–29.

6. On the conflict between Dandolo and Tiepolo and on the hegemony of Rialto, see Giorgio Cracco, *Società e stato nel medioevo veneziano (secoli XII–XIV),* 89–173; Frederic C. Lane, *Venice: A Maritime Republic,* 91–95; and Carlo Guido Mor, "Aristocrazia veneziana e nobiltà di terraferma," 355–56. On street images, see Edward Muir, "The Virgin on the Street Corner: The Place of the Sacred in Italian Cities." On Lorenzo Tiepolo, see Martin da Canal, *Les estoires de Venise: Cronaca veneziana in lingua francese dalle origini al 1275,* 282.

7. On the criminalization of vendetta in Venice, see Guido Ruggiero, *Violence in Early Renaissance Venice,* 125–55; idem, *The Boundaries of Eros: Sex Crime and Sexuality in Renaissance Venice,* 89–108; Jacques Heers, *Family Clans in the Middle Ages: A Study of Political and Social Structures in Urban Areas,* 103; Donald E. Queller, *The Venetian Patriciate: Reality versus Myth,* 75–84, 234–39; Stanley Chojnacki, "Crime, Punishment, and the Trecento Venetian State," and J. K. Hyde, "Contemporary Views on Faction and Civil Strife in Thirteenth- and Fourteenth-Century Italy," in *Violence and Civil Disorder in Italian Cities, 1200–1500,* ed. Lauro Martines, 184–228 and 273–307, respectively; and Elisabeth Crouzet-Pavan, "Vio-

lence, société et pouvoir à Venise (XIVe–XVe siècles): Forme et évolution de rituels urbains," *Mélanges de l'École française de Rome: Moyen Age–temps modernes* 96 (1984): 903–36.

8. On the 1272 joust, see Canal, *Les estoires*, 126–30, 328–32; on the decline of retribution, see Ruggiero, *Violence*, 43–44.

9. On humanism, see Margaret L. King, *Venetian Humanism in an Age of Patrician Dominance*, 92 (first quote), 150–57 (second quote from 151 is her translation), 333–35.

10. Gasparo Contarini, *The Commonwealth and Government of Venice*, trans. Lewes Lewkenor (London, 1599), 125–49, quotes on 129–30. The original Latin edition is *De magistratibus et republica Venetorum libri quinque* (Venice, 1551). On the inadequacy of these views for explaining Venice's terraferma dominion, see Grubb, "When Myths Lose Power." On the theoretical problems presented by the terraferma dominion, see Innocenzo Cervelli, *Machiavelli e la crisi dello stato veneziano*, 165–217.

11. The two most important native critics of the Venetian system who were contemporaries of Machiavelli, Girolamo Priuli and Domenico Morosini, went unheard during their own lifetimes. Girolamo Priuli, *I diarii*, ed. Arturo Segre et al., Rerum Italicarum Scriptores, vol. 24, ed. 2 (Città di Castello and Bologna: 1912–33) and Gaetano Cozzi, "Domenico Morosini e il *De bene instituta republica*," *SV* 12 (1970): 405–58.

12. On Venice's "most sacred laws," see Aldo Mazzacane, "Lo stato e il dominio nei giuristi Veneti durante il 'secolo della terraferma,' " 581–82; and Angelo Ventura, "Il dominio di Venezia nel Quattrocento," 176–77. On concessions of citizenship, see James S. Grubb, "Alla ricerca delle prerogative locali: La cittadinanza a Vicenza, 1404–1509," in *Dentro lo "Stado Italico*," ed. Giorgio Cracco and M. Knapton, 177–91. On the contractual basis for rule, see Ventura, *Nobiltà e popolo*, 33–36 and passim. Carlo Guido Mor argues that Venetian policies threatened the local oligarchies, especially those in Friuli. "Aristocrazia veneziana," 353–58. John Easton Law emphasizes the hesitant character of Venetian rule in Verona; see "Verona and the Venetian State in the Fifteenth Century." In contrast, Giorgio Borelli, who is the source of the idea of two family systems, emphasizes the compatibility between the Venetian patriciate and the Veronese elites; see *Un patriziato della terraferma veneta tra XVII e XVIII secolo: Ricerche sulla nobiltà veronese* (Milan: Giuffrè, 1974), 83, 92–95. For similarities to Liguria, see Raggio, *Faide*, 3. Grubb emphasizes the balance between Venice and Vicenza and the moderation of Venetian councils in dealing with mainland subjects; see *Firstborn of Venice*.

As the references in the rest of this chapter will make clear, Jacques Heers's lament that "the social structure of Venetian country districts seems very little known" is no longer true. *Family Clans in the Middle Ages*, 43. The grants of Venetian noble status to terraferma nobles which took place in the seventeenth and eighteenth centuries were attempts to arrest the demographic decline of the Venetian nobility rather than to incorporate provincial elites into a unified state. James C. Davis, *The Decline of the Venetian Nobility as a Ruling Class*, Johns Hopkins University Studies in Historical and Political Science, ser. 80, no. 2 (Baltimore: Johns Hopkins University Press, 1962).

13. On the theory of an alliance between Venice and the rural lower classes, see Cervelli, *Machiavelli*, 393. On the Venetian army and failure to protect subject populations, see M. E. Mallett and J. R. Hale, *Military Organization of a Renaissance State: Venice c. 1400 to 1617*, 217 (for quote, "the Venetian patriciate's"), 410–13. For a beautifully concise summary of Venetian influence on the terraferma, see Cozzi, "Ambiente veneziano, ambiente veneto," 93–146.

14. On the legal disharmonies, see Giovanni Scarabello, "Nelle relazioni dei rettori veneti in terraferma: Aspetti di una loro attività di mediazione tra governanti delle città suddite e governo della dominante," 491; Gaetano Cozzi, "La politica del diritto nella Repubblica di Venezia," in *Stato, società e giustizia nella Repubblica Veneta (sec. XV–XVIII)*, ed. Gaetano Cozzi, 1: 79–121, quote on 95–96; and Grubb, *Firstborn of Venice*, passim.

15. On the reformed statutes of Friuli, see Pier Silverio Leicht, "La riforma delle costituzioni friulane nel primo secolo della dominazione veneziana," 73–84; idem, "Lo stato veneziano e il diritto comune," 204–7; and Andreina Stefanutti, "Giureconsulti friulani tra giurisdizionalismo veneziano e tradizione feudale," 80–83.

16. On provincial oligarchs, see Ventura, *Nobiltà e popolo*, 39–52; and idem, "Dominio di Venezia," 182.

17. On the Council of Ten, see Michael Knapton, "Il Consiglio dei Dieci nel governo della terraferma: Un'ipotesi interpretativa per il secondo '400," in *Atti del convegno*, 237–60. Knapton places the expansion of the powers of the Council of Ten in the last half of the fifteenth century in contrast to Gaetano Cozzi, who dates the principal changes after 1509. "Authority and the Law in Renaissance Venice," in *Renaissance Venice*, ed. J. R. Hale, 293–345. On the council's protection of local privileges, see Grubb, *Firstborn of Venice*, 10–13. On the limits of the closed patriciate, see Ventura, "Il dominio di Venezia," 187. New offices included Tre Savi alle Acque (1501), Collegio alle Acque (1505), Cinque Savi alla Mercanzia (1506), Tre Esecutori contro la Bestemmia (1537), Tre Inquisitori di Stato (1539), Tre Provveditori sopra Beni Inculti (1556), Tre Provveditori sopra Monasteri (1521–28), Tre Provveditori sopra Beni Comunali (1574), and Provveditori e Sovraprovveditori alla Legna e Boschi (1532–1677). Giorgio Borelli, *Un patriziato della terraferma veneta*, 84.

18. Claudio Povolo, "Aspetti e problemi dell'amministrazione della giustizia penale nella repubblica di Venezia, secoli XVI–XVII," 155–66, 177, 192–99. R. Giummolè, "I poteri del luogotenente della Patria del Friuli nel primo cinquentenario: 1420–70," 57–124. Amelio Tagliaferri, "L'amministrazione veneziana in terraferma: Deroghe e limitazioni al potere giudiziario dei settori," 111–16.

19. For quote, Povolo, "Aspetti e problemi," 207n citing Tommaso Garzoni, *La piazza universale di tutte le professioni* (Venice, 1585), 929–30. Translation is mine.

20. The above discussion has relied primarily on Povolo, "Aspetti e problemi," 207–58. Also see Tagliaferri, "L'amministrazione veneziana," 122–31. The views of Cozzi can be found in *Repubblica di Venezia*, 217–318, and his students in the two volumes of idem, ed., *Stato, società e giustizia*. On surgeons as sources for judicial accusations, see Guido Ruggiero, "The Cooperation of Physicians and the State in the Control of Violence in Renaissance Venice," *Journal of the History of*

Medicine and Allied Sciences 33 (1978): 156–66. On Venetian prisons, see Giovanni Scarabello, *Carcerati e carceri a Venezia nell'età moderna* (Rome: Istituto della Enciclopedia Italiana, 1979); and idem, "La pena del carcere, aspetti della condizione carceraria a Venezia nei secoli XVI–XVIII: L'assistenza e l'associazionismo," in *Stato società e giustizia*, ed. Gaetano Cozzi, 1: 317–76. On the rise of banditry in the Veneto, see Claudio Povolo, "Nella spirale della violenza: Cronologia, intensità e diffusione del banditismo nella terraferma veneta (1550–1610)"; James S. Grubb, "Catalysts for Organized Violence in the Early Venetian Territorial State"; Nicholas S. Davidson, "An Armed Band and the Local Community on the Venetian Terraferma in the Sixteenth Century"; and Enrico Basaglia, "Il banditismo nei rapporti di Venezia con gli stati confinanti," in *Bande armate, banditi, banditismo e repressione di giustizia negli stati europei di antico regime*, ed. Gherardo Ortalli, 21–52, 383–400, 401–22, 423–40, respectively.

21. On the appeals process, see Ceferino Caro Lopez, "Gli auditori nuovi e il dominio di terraferma," in *Stato, società e giustizia*, ed. Gaetano Cozzi, 1: 259–316; Povolo, "Aspetti e problemi," 200–203; Cozzi, *Repubblica di Venezia*, 114–21; Law, "Verona and the Venetian State," 17–20; and Grubb, *Firstborn of Venice*, xix and passim. Grubb is particularly effective in showing the failures of the *auditori* to perform as intended.

22. On the fiscal system, see the articles in G. Borelli, P. Lanaro, and F. Vecchiato, eds., *Il sistema fiscale veneto, problemi e aspetti, XV–XVIII secolo*, Atti della prima giornata di studio sulla terraferma veneta (Lazise, 29 marzo 1981) (Verona: Libreria Universitaria Editrice, 1982). On general budgets, see *Bilanci generali della repubblica di Venezia*, vol. 1, pt. 1, pp. 148–50. Total figures reported here vary slightly from the document because the figures for the terraferma cities were added incorrectly in the original. On the *dazi* of Udine, see Tagliaferri, *Udine nella storia economica*, 98. On shortfalls in quotas, see Grubb, *Firstborn of Venice*, 123.

23. On the demography of Verona, see David Herlihy, "The Population of Verona in the First Century of Venetian Rule," in *Renaissance Venice*, ed. J. R. Hale, 91–120.

24. On Ruzzini, see Amelio Tagliaferri, "Ordinamento amministrativo della terraferma," 31.

25. On the relationship between the two systems of justice, cf. Raggio, *Faide*, 239; and Stephen Wilson, *Feuding, Conflict, and Banditry in Nineteenth-Century Corsica*, 265–93, 416. On attempts to isolate the implicit rules of revenge, see Raymond Verdier, "De l'une a l'autre vengeance," in *La vengeance: Études d'ethnologie, d'histoire et de philosophie*, vol. 2, *Vengeance et pouvoir dans quelques sociétés extraoccidentales*, ed. Raymond Verdier (Paris: Éditions Cujas, 1980), 7–13; Patrick J. Geary, "Vivre en conflict dans une France sans état: Typologie des mécanismes de règlement des conflicts (1050–1200)," *Annales: E.S.C.* 41 (1986): 1118; Robin Fox, *The Tory Islanders: A People of the Celtic Fringe* (Cambridge, United Kingdom: Cambridge University Press, 1978), 186–88; idem, "The Inherent Rules of Violence," in *Social Rules and Social Behavior*, ed. Peter Collett (Totowa, N.J.: Rowan and Littlefield, 1977), 132–49; and Margaret Hasluck, *The Unwritten Law in Albania*, 219–37. For an attempt to catalogue the rules of vendetta in Renaissance Italy, see Anna Maria Enriques, "La vendetta nella vita e nella legislazione fioren-

tina," *ASI* ser. 7, vol. 19 (1933): 87–117. Cf. Pierre Bourdieu, *Outline of a Theory of Practice*, 1–27, 182–95.

26. David D. Gilmore, *Manhood in the Making: Cultural Concepts of Masculinity*, 30–55. Cf. idem, *Aggression and Community: Paradoxes of Andalusian Culture*. On the meanings of *vendetta*, see Carlo Battisti and Giovanni Alessio, *Dizionario etimologico italiano* (Florence: G. Barbera, 1957), s.v. "vendetta." Dante Olivieri, *Dizionario etimologico italiano* (Milan: Ceschina, 1961), s.v. "vendicare." Giacomo Devoto, *Avviamento alla etimologia italiana: Dizionario etimologico* (Florence: Felice Le Monnier, 1967), s.v. "vendetta." P. G. W. Glare, *Oxford Latin Dictionary* (Oxford: Clarendon Press, 1982), s.v. "vindicta," "uindex," and "uis."

The dialect variants of *vendetta* and *vendicare* in Friulan employ an *s* prefix, which, in contrast to its negating function in Tuscan, acts as an intensifier in Veneto dialects and in Friulan. The specific emotional correlate of the *s* prefix is one of menace because the sound produced resembles a growl. One might conclude, therefore, that these words in Friulan were even more highly charged with anger than in other Italian dialects that did not introduce the *s* prefix. On Friulan, see Giulio Andrea Pirona, Ercole Carletti, and Giovanni Battista Corgnali, *Il nuovo Pirona: Vocabolario friulano* (Udine: Società Filologica Friulana, 1983), s.v. "svindìc" and "svindicâsi." The *s* prefix also appears as a variant usage in the related dialect of Bisiàc; see Silvio Domini, Aldo Fulizio, Aldo Miniussi, and Giordano Vittori, *Vocabolario fraseologico del dialetto "Bisiàc"* (Bologna: Cappelli Editore, 1985), s.v. "svendegar." On the *s* prefix as an intensifier in Veneto dialects, see Edward F. Tuttle, *"Snaturalitè* in Ruzante and the Venetian Prefix *s-*," in *Proceedings of the Eighth Annual Meeting of the Berkeley Linguistics Society, 13–15 February 1982*, ed. Monica Maccaulay, et al. (Berkeley: Berkeley Linguistics Society, 1982), 117–26. On the emotional correlates of the *s* prefix, see Linda L. Carroll, "Linguistic Correlates of Emotion in Ruzante," in *The Eleventh LACUS Forum 1984*, ed. Robert A. Hall, Jr. (Columbia, S.C.: Hornbeam Press, 1985), 380–81 and passim.

27. On the transactional nature of feuding, see Jacob Black-Michaud, *Cohesive Force: Feud in the Mediterranean and the Middle East*, 80–85. Cf. Edward C. Banfield, *The Moral Basis of a Backward Society*. Keith M. Brown describes a similarly broad range of meanings for the word *feud* in Scotland; see *Bloodfeud in Scotland, 1573–1625: Violence, Justice and Politics in an Early Modern Society*, 4. On *contrappasso*, see Anna Maria Enriques, "La vendetta nella vita," 97. Jacques Heers apparently takes this prescriptive formulation as an accurate description of behavior; see *Family Clans*, 108–9. I find little evidence that avengers took at all seriously the obligation not to increase excessively the level of insult; in fact, they typically thrilled in the large number and the gravity of the wounds delivered. See, in particular, the many descriptions of attacks in Niccolò Maria di Strassoldo, *Cronaca: Anni 1469–1509* and Soldoniero di Strassoldo, *Cronaca dal 1509 al 1603*.

28. Pasquale Del Giudice, "La vendetta nel diritto longobardo," 217–52. Joppi and Wolf, eds., *Statuti di Udine*, lxxxviii, 46n, and rubrics 89, 90, 91. Cf. J. M. Wallace-Hadrill, "The Bloodfeud of the Franks."

29. On the double tradition, see Gabriel Maugain, *Moeurs italiennes de la Renaissance: La vengeance*, 3–16; and Curtis Brown Watson, *Shakespeare and the Re-*

naissance Concept of Honor, 124–27. Citations from Aquinas, *Summa Theologiae*, part 2, 2, question 108.

30. On vendetta di Dio, see Anna Maria Enriques, "La vendetta nella vita," 143. On Panzano, see Luca di Totto da Panzano, "Memoria, che io andai a Prato per uccidere Carlo di Baldovinetto Gherardini . . . ," *Giornale storico degli archivi toscani* 5 (1961): 62; and Philip J. Jones, "Florentine Families and Florentine Diaries in the Fourteenth Century," in *Studies in Italian Medieval History Presented to Miss E. M. Jamison*, ed. Philip Grierson and John Ward Perkins, Papers of the British School at Rome, vol. 24, n.s., vol. 11 (London: British School at Rome, 1956), 183n.

31. For criticism and bibliography on *Inferno*, canto 29, see Gaetano Mariani in *Lectura Dantis Scaliger: Inferno* (Florence: F. Le Monnier, 1967), 1029–56. Cf. the excellent discussion of similar issues in John Larner, *The Lords of Romagna: Romagnol Society and the Origins of the Signorie* (Ithaca: Cornell University Press, 1965), 58–74; and idem, "Order and Disorder in Romagna, 1450–1500," 50, 54–56, 63–65.

32. On Bruni, see Hans Baron, "Das Erwachen des historischen Denkens im Humanismus des Quattrocento," *Historische Zeitschrift* 147 (1933): 5–20; and idem, *In Search of Florentine Civic Humanism: Essays on the Transition from Medieval to Modern Thought* (Princeton: Princeton University Press, 1988), 1: 134–57.

33. For examples of revenge humanism, see Maugain, *Moeures italiennes*, 83–108. In discussing the Elizabethan Renaissance Curtis Brown Watson states, "The duality of Renaissance ethics is striking in any discussion of revenge. . . . Here Christian teaching is completely clear and dogmatic, so here the divided soul of the Renaissance most clearly reveals itself. The law of the land of course accorded with the teachings of the church. But the powerful hold of the pagan-humanist ethics, and of the code of honor which resulted from it, led to a sharp cleavage between religious theory and the civil law on the one hand and actual Elizabethan practice on the other." *Shakespeare*, 127. This view of Christian and humanist ethics misstates the situation. The Christian view was far more equivocal than Watson admits even though he cites both Aquinas and Dante, who both exhibited a divided opinion, and there were other medieval and popular sources of honor probably far more potent and deeply rooted in society than those introduced by humanism.

34. The first quote is from Carlo Ginzburg, *The Cheese and the Worms: The Cosmos of a Sixteenth-Century Miller*, 81. The second quote is from Luigi da Porto, *Alcune lettere inedite scritte dall'anno MDIX al MDXIII*, 80. Gregory Hanlon also emphasizes the role of the passions in "Les rituels de l'agression en Aquitaine au XVIIe siécle," 265. Carol Z. Stearns and Peter N. Stearns argue "there were no real standards for anger restraint" before the modern period, an observation that ignores the popularity at various times of Stoicism and the elaborate social restraints of Christian monasticism. *Anger: The Struggle for Emotional Control in America's History*, 23. A document that is particularly revealing of the complex attitudes about revenge in the Renaissance is Benvenuto Cellini's *Autobiography*, which has not been fully analyzed from this point of view. Cf. Sir John Pope-Hennesy, *Cellini* (New York: Abbeville Press, 1985).

35. On outrages to reputation, see Maugain, *Moeurs italiennes*, 50–69. On laws, see Antonio Pertile, *Storia del diritto italiano dalla caduta dell'Impero Romano alla codificazione*, 5: 343–55, 622–34; and Joppi and Wolf, eds., *Statuti di Udine*, lxxxvii–lxxxix, 50n. Similar concerns with insults have been observed in seventeenth-century France, see Hanlon, "Rituels de l'agression," 245; modern Albania, see Christopher Boehm, *Blood Revenge: The Anthropology of Feuding in Montenegro and Other Tribal Societies*, 15–17, 55–57, where informants defined blood feud as an insult, blow, or killing returned in kind; and Corsica, see Wilson, *Feuding*, 91–93.

36. On restricted codes, see Basil Bernstein, *Class, Codes and Concord*, vol. 2: *Theoretical Studies toward a Sociology of Language* (London: Routledge and Kegan Paul, 1971), 175–78. Also on insults, see Peter Burke, *The Historical Anthropology of Early Modern Italy: Essays on Perception and Communication*, 95–109; Samuel Y. Edgerton, Jr., *Pictures and Punishment: Art and Criminal Prosecution during the Florentine Renaissance*, 59–63; and David Parkin, "The Creativity of Abuse," *Man* 15 (1980): 45–64. On the relationship between fighting and talking, see Simon Roberts, "The Study of Dispute: Anthropological Perspectives," 8–10. On the power of curses, see Keith Thomas, *Religion and the Decline of Magic* (New York: Charles Scribner's Sons, 1971), 510–11, 522–24.

37. For the outlaw as a member of the "living dead," see Hans-Peter Hasenfratz, *Die Toten Lebenden: Eine religionsphänomenologische Studie zum sozialen Tod in archaischen Gesellschaften: Zugleich ein kritischer Beitrag zur sogenannten Strafopfertheorie*, Zeitschrift für Religions- und Geistesgeschichte, *Beiheft* 24 (Leiden: E. J. Brill, 1982). On the scapegoat mechanism, see René Girard, *Violence and the Sacred*; idem, "An Interview with René Girard," *Diacritics* 8 (1978): 31–54, republished in *"To Double Business Bound": Essays on Literature, Mimesis, and Anthropology*, 199–229; idem, "Generative Scapegoating"; and idem, *Job: The Victim of His People*.

38. On outlawing in ancient Athens, see Michael Gagarin, *Drakon and Early Athenian Homicide Law* (New Haven: Yale University Press, 1981), 119–21; and Eberhard Ruschenbusch, *Untersuchungen zur Geschichte des Athenischen Strabrechts* (Cologne: Böhlau Verlag, 1968), 16–21. On Rome, see Brent D. Shaw, "Bandits in the Roman Empire," *Past and Present* 105 (1984): 3–52 and Pertile, *Storia del diritto italiano*, 5: 302–11. On Germanic law, see Hermann Nehlsen, "Der Grabfrevel in den germanischen Rechtsaufzeichnungen," in *Zum Grabfrevel in vor- und frühgeschichtlicher Zeit: Untersuchungen zu Grabraub und "haugbrot" in Mittel- und Nordeurope*, ed. Herbert Jankuhn, Hermann Nehlsen, and Helmut Roth, Bericht über ein Kolloquium der Kommission für die Altertumskunde Mittel- und Nordeuropas vom 14. bis 16. Februar 1977 (Göttingen: Vandenhoeck und Ruprecht, 1978), 108–109; and Del Giudice, "La vendetta," 372. Especially useful on these issues is Randolph Starn, *The Contrary Commonwealth: The Theme of Exile in Medieval and Renaissance Italy*, 20–21.

39. On bandits, see Eric J. Hobsbawm, *Primitive Rebels: Studies in Archaic Forms of Social Movement in the Nineteenth and Twentieth Centuries* (New York: W. W. Norton, 1965), 13–29; idem, *Bandits*, rev. ed. (New York: Pantheon Books, 1981), 41–57; and J. C. Holt, *Robin Hood* (London: Thames and Hudson, 1982), 15–39.

The notion of social banditry has been criticized for the modern period; see Wilson, *Feuding*, 334, 347. On exile bands in general, see Starn, *Contrary Commonwealth*, 32–40, 86–96, 119–20. Cf. Giovanni Cherubini, "La tipologia del bandito nel tardo Medioevo" and Enrico Basaglia, "Il banditismo nei rapporti di Venezia con gli stati confinanti," in *Bande armate, banditi, banditismo*, ed. Gherardo Ortalli, 353–56 and 423–40, respectively.

40. On exiles in the Veneto and Friuli, see Enrico Basaglia, "Il controllo della criminalità nella repubblica di Venezia. Il secolo XVI: Un momento di passaggio," 71–74; and Mallett and Hale, *Military Organization*, 218–20. In the Vicentino in 1426, exiles made up more than 1 percent of the entire population; see Grubb, *Firstborn of Venice*, 104. I can find no evidence that the motive behind the practice of exiling was a fear that if the guilty were executed, authorities would face the revenge of the condemned person's relatives. Venice, in fact, did execute persons guilty of particularly vicious crimes. On the fear of revenge, see Boehm, *Blood Feud*, 111–12, 249n.

41. On Venetian exile policy, see Grubb, *Firstborn of Venice*, 106–7; and Gaetano Cozzi, "Authority and the Law in Renaissance Venice," 322–23, 338–39.

42. For the laws, see Joppi and Wolf, eds., *Statuti di Udine*, lxxxv–lxxxviii, 49–50; *Novissimum statutorum ac Venetarum legum volumen, duabus in partibus divisum, Aloysio Mocenico Venetiarum Principi dicatum*, pt. 2, fols. 1r–82v; Pertile, *Storia del diritto italiano*, 311–43; Basaglia, "Il controllo della criminalità," 74–76; and Molmenti, "I bandi," 146–49. For the original ducal decree directed to Friulan castellans prohibiting them from harboring persons wanted for homicides, see "Ducali sulla giurisdizione in Friuli," BCU, MS 977, fol. 2v.

Chapter 3: Factions in the Fifteenth Century

1. On the Ligurian *parentele*, see Osvaldo Raggio, *Faide e parentele: Lo stato genovese visto dalla Fontanabuona*, 152–58. Mobility between factions was rare in Liguria but relatively common in Friuli. Cf. ibid., 176–77. Stephen Wilson also sees feuding in Corsica as "part of a wider complex of conflict, which occurred with some frequency between communities and within families as well as between families." *Feuding, Conflict, and Banditry in Nineteenth-Century Corsica*, 415.

2. Antonio De Cillia and Emilia Mirmina, "Udine e il Torre, un rapporto vitale," in *Udin: Mil agn tal cûr da Friûl*, ed. Gian Carlo Menis, 51–73.

3. On Savorgnan investments, see Liliana Cargnelutti, "I Savorgnan: Note sull'origine e sulla storia della famiglia"; idem, "I Savorgnan e la città di Udine: Il patrimonio fondiario"; and Michele Zacchigna, "L'espansione fondiaria (sec. XIII–XIV): Aspetti dell'economia agricola friulana fra i secoli XIV e XV," in *I Savorgnan e la Patria del Friuli dal XIII al XVIII secolo*, 41–56, 57–70, and 95–110, respectively. Idem, "I Savorgnano di Udine. L'espansione fondiaria (sec. XIII–XIV)," 46–48. For a detailed listing of the locations of Savorgnan properties, see Paolo Cammarosano, *Le campagne friulane nel tardo medioevo: Un'analisi dei registri di censi dei grandi proprietari fondiari*, 35–37. For titles to and formal descriptions of the actual properties, see ASU, AS, busta 72, pergamene 102–12, 115, 118, 120, 123, 127, 128, and 130. These properties are also summarized in busta 39 of the

same archive. For the Tuscans in Friuli, see Antonio Battistella, *I Toscani in Friuli e un episodio della Guerra degli Otto Santi: Memoria storica documentata* (Bologna, 1898); and G. Loschi, *Documenti storici sui Fiorentini nel Friuli* (Udine, 1893).

4. On loans as a reflection of patronage ties, see Ronald F. E. Weissman, "The Importance of Being Ambiguous: Social Relations, Individualism, and Identity in Renaissance Florence." On the Savorgnan and the Jews, see Michele Zacchigna, "I Savorgnan," 52. Amelio Tagliaferri, *Udine nella storia economica*, 113-17. Pier Cesare Ioly Zorattini, "Aspetti e problemi dei nuclei ebraici in Friuli durante la dominazione veneziana," in *Atti del convegno*, 227-36. Brian Pullan, *Rich and Poor in Renaissance Venice: The Social Institutions of a Catholic State, to 1620*, 526, 540-41, 544, 595, 619-20. Until the midsixteenth century, Jews were frequently subject to harassment but suffered from few official restrictions except for those instituted by the Venetians. In 1511, for example, Luogotenente Alvise Gradenigo ordered that the Jews of Udine be forced to wear yellow hats because it would not be good to permit the disorder that proceeded from the lack of clear public identification of their status. ASV, LPF, busta 133, "Extraordinarior. Liber primus," dated 31 August 1511. In a fashion similar to the Savorgnan reliance on Jews, the Medici grand dukes in Tuscany used the capital of the Monte di Pietà as a source of loans to clients. Carol Bresnahan Menning, "Loans and Favors, Kin and Clients: Cosimo de' Medici and the Monte di Pietà," *The Journal of Modern History* 61 (1989): 487-511. In Liguria the connection between urban patrons and peasant cultivators often took the form of loans. Raggio, *Faide*, 175.

5. On the right to appoint the *camerarius*, see BCU, ACU, reg. 41, fol. 186v. For lists of deputies, see BCU, ACU, Annali series. On the Savorgnan blazon, see "Blasone Veneto," BMV, It. VII, 720 (7901), fols. 159r-165r. For Venice's confirmation of Savorgnan jurisdictions, see ASV, Secreta, Materia Miste Notabili, reg. 117, fol. 27v. On Savorgnan jurisdictions, see Michele Gottardi, "Struttura politico-amministrativa del Friuli occidentale nel XVI secolo," 90-91 and Fulvio Bonati Savorgnan d'Osoppo, "Di una famiglia storica del Friuli: I Savorgnano," 15-16, which gives a useful summary of Savorgnan rights.

6. For quote, see M. E. Mallett and J. R. Hale, *Military Organization*, 343.

7. Cf. Wilson, *Feuding*, 25, 129, 142-43; Raggio, *Faide*, 113.

8. On divisions in the clan, see Niccolò Monticelli, "Cronaca di famiglie nobili della Patria del Friul (1526)," BMV, It. VII, 59 (6031), fols. 5v-6r. The standard Venetian genealogies need to be corrected for the Savorgnan: Marco Barbaro, "Genealogie delle famiglie patrizio venete," BMV, It. VII 928 (8597), fol. 97r; and Girolamo Cappellari, "Il campidoglio veneto," BMV, It. VII, 18 (8307), fols. 68r-69r. Cf. Bonati Savorgnan d'Osoppo, "Di una famiglia," 9-13. Also see BCU, MS 1247 for several genealogies. I have profited from the genealogy prepared for the superb museum show, "I Savorgnan e la Patria del Friuli dal XIII al XVIII secolo," Museo della Città, Udine, 1984-85.

9. On the origins of the family and its patriarchs, see Pompeo Molmenti, "I bandi e i banditi della repubblica veneta," 317-24; Gian Carlo Menis, *Storia del Friuli dalle origini alla caduta dello stato patriarcale (1420)*, 230-33; and Giacomo Valvasone di Maniaco, "Compendio delle vite de Patriarchi, serie delli Logotenenti," MCV, MS Correr 963/1, fols. 43r-110r. On Della Torre membership in the Vene-

tian Great Council, see Cappellari, "Il campidoglio veneto," BMV, It. VII, 18 (8307), fols. 123v–124v.

10. On the acquisition of Villalta, see ASU, AT, busta 24, doc. dated 26 April 1398; on other properties, see busta 7, pacco 18, doc. 10; on imperial privileges and patronage of Della Torre, see busta 7, pacchi 12 and 25 (22 April 1435), pacco 1 (26 May 1533), and pacco 14 (docs. of 1579, 1583, 1585, 1600).

11. For a summary of the theory, Jacob Black-Michaud, *Cohesive Force: Feud in the Mediterranean and the Middle East*, 228. The Corsican example does not entirely support the theory either; see Wilson, *Feuding*, 263.

12. On the social composition of the factions, see Nicolò Monticolo, *Descrittione del sacco MDXI seguito in Udine il giovedì XXVII febbraio*, 11. Cf. Giovanni Battista di Cergneu, *Cronaca delle guerre friulane coi Germani dal 1507 al 1524*, 6.

13. For Savorgnan marriages, I have cautiously followed Marco Barbaro, "Genealogie delle famiglie patrizie venete," BMV, It. VII, 928 (8597), fol. 97r and Girolamo Cappellari, "Il campidoglio veneto," BMV, It. VII, 18 (8307). fols. 68r–69r. I was able to correct these sources with information and documents on display at the Savorgnan museum show cited above. The Savorgnan married into the following castellan families: Cuccagna, Porcìa, Collalto, Della Torre, Colloredo, Zucco, Valvasone, and Strassoldo. The Venetian families they wedded included the Tron, Malipiero, Canal, Mocenigo, Giustinian, Priuli, Venier, and Tiepolo. There were three exceptions to the rule that Savorgnan did not marry other Zambarlani, but all of these marriages were between the Torre di Zuino and Monte d'Osoppo sub-branches of the Savorgnan dello Scaglione, and all took place after 1511. I have considered these as examples of clan rather than factional endogamy and as special cases inasmuch as they were apparently attempts to reunify the clan after a series of catastrophes.

14. For Della Torre marriages, see ASU, AT, busta 22, doc. titled, "Doti uscite dalla famiglia Della Torre, 1260–1565," and busta 24, doc. titled, "Elenco degli instrumenti delle doti entrate nella famiglia dei NN. SS. Conti Della Torre."

15. Stanley Chojnacki, "Marriage Legislation and Patrician Society in Fifteenth-Century Venice," 163–84.

16. On Savorgnan-Della Torre marriages, see Alvise Savorgnan di Brazzà, *"Maledetti Savorgnan": Mille anni di simbiosi con Udine*, 40. For copies of the wedding contract between Girolamo Savorgnan and Maddalena Della Torre, see BCU, MS Joppi 689d, fol. IV, dated 13 July 1491; and ASU, AT, busta 22, "Elenco degli instrumenti delle doti uscite dalla famiglia dei NN. SS. Conti Della Torre." Maddalena's first cousins, Isidoro and Alvise, acted as her guardians and signed the contract for a dowry of fifteen hundred ducats plus two hundred from her mother. A morganatic instrument attached to the contract prohibited the offspring of the marriage from receiving more than eighty ducats from the Della Torre estate. Witnesses to the contract signed in the Franciscan friary in Udine included a broad cross-section of Strumiero and Zambarlano figures, some of whom twenty years later would murder others present at the signing.

17. Cf. Jacques Heers, *Family Clans in the Middle Ages: A Study of Political and Social Structures in Urban Areas*, 226–28, in which he emphasizes only the cohesive aspects of clan gatherings.

18. Max Gluckman, "The Peace in the Feud," 1–14. On bilateral kinship and vengeance groups, see Marc Bloch, *Feudal Society*, vol. 1: *The Growth of Ties of Dependence* (Chicago: University of Chicago Press, 1961), 137–41.

19. On the pervasiveness of kinship terms for defining individuals, see Edward C. Banfield, *The Moral Basis of a Backward Society*, 103–11. Ad hoc vengeance groups also characterized feuds among the Franks (see J. M. Wallace-Hadrill, "The Bloodfeud of the Franks"), the Scots (see Jenny Wormald, "The Blood Feud in Early Modern Scotland"), the Turks (see Arthur Paul Stirling, *Turkish Village* [London: Weidenfeld and Nicolson, 1965], 251–52), and the Corsicans (see Wilson, *Feuding*, 177–89). On the relationship between dependence and the obligation to avenge, see Black-Michaud, *Cohesive Force*, 39–41.

Gregorio Amaseo describes one Cecho, son of Tomaso de Cecho de Ragognia, as a "fameglio de miser Nicolà Savorgnan lo cavalier in zoventù." In describing the members of a *compagnia*, Amaseo distinguishes between a *fameio* and two *servitori* of the leader. *DU, GA*, 259, 269.

20. Possible etymologies for the names of the factions are discussed in Ernesto Degani, *I partiti in Friuli nel 1500 e la storia di un famoso duello*, 4–5 and Giovanni Battista Romano, "Strumieri e Zamberlani," 5, in which it is argued that Zambarlani meant the "decorated ones" and Strumiero came from *sdrumà*, a Friulan word meaning a multitude of people. Miotti rejects this derivation of Strumiero as "a little stupid" inasmuch as it would better apply to the Zambarlani, most of whom were *popolani*. "Udinesi e friulani ribelli," 127n. The contemporary Giovanni Battista de Cergneu derived Strumiero from the German *turm*, meaning tower or *torre*, which became in local dialect *strum*, a war cry of the partisans of the Della Torre. *Cronaca delle guerre friulane coi germani dal 1507 al 1524*, 6. In reporting on events in France, Marino Sanuto used the word *zamberlani* to mean the chamberlains of the French court, a usage that may explain the origins of the label in Friuli inasmuch as the Savorgnan had served as the chamberlains of the patriarchs of Aquileia. *I diarii*, 7: 695, dated 13–14 December 1508. For Amaseo's use of the terms *Guelf* and *Ghibelline*, see *DU*, xxxii, li and *DU, GAH*, 494–95. On yells and insignia, see Cergneu, *Cronaca delle guerre friulane*, 6–7 and *DU, GAH*, 495.

21. A model proclamation against displays of factional identity can be found in ASV, CD, Misto, reg. 20, fols. 136v–137r, dated 29 December 1481. On prohibitions in Cividale and San Daniele, see BCU, MS Joppi 592, fol. 8v, which is a copy from the Archivio di San Daniele, "Tanse e Campatico"; and Aurelia de Savorgnani, "Antonio Savorgnano e l'insurrezione Friulana del 1511," 28.

22. On the Cividale-Udine war, see Pier Silverio Leicht, "La rivolta feudale contro il Patriarca Bertrando," *MSF* 41 (1954–55): 38–47.

23. G. C. Menis, *Storia del Friuli*, 225–50.

24. On the phases of feuds, see Wilson, *Feuding*, 53–56.

25. On the Colloredo-Savorgnan disputes, see Prospero Antonini, *I baroni di Waldsee o Walse, i visconti di Mels, i signori di Prodolone e di Colloredo: Accenni genealogici e note storiche*, 84. On the attack on the Della Torre, see ASU, AT, cartella 19, colto 26, fascicolo 3. The document is dated 1480 and refers to the attack as having taken place ten years previously. For Marino Sanuto's observation, see *Itinerario per la terraferma veneziana nell'anno MCCCCLXXXIII*, 133.

26. G. Gortani, "I Turchi in Friuli," 111–12. Francesco Musoni, "Le ultime incursioni dei Turchi in Friuli," 101–5. Paolo Preto, *Venezia e i Turchi*, 32–33. Mallett and Hale, *Military Organization*, 49–50. For correspondence by Nicolò Savorgnan concerning the Turkish invasion of 1478, see BCU, MS Joppi 592.

27. Venice made Nicolò Savorgnan permanent head of the *cernide* in 1487; see Pier Silverio Leicht, *Parlamento friulano*, 1: lxxvi, 48, 89, 104.

28. The above account comes from ASU, AT, cartella 19, colto 26, fascicolo 7, which includes seventy-seven unnumbered pages, variously dated 1478 and 1479. Cf. Liliana Cargnelutti, "Antonio Savorgnan e l'insurrezione del 1511," 121–22.

29. On the attack, see ASU, AT, cartella 19, colto 26, fascicolo 3.

30. E. E. Evans-Pritchard, *The Nuer: A Description of the Modes of Livelihood and Political Institutions of a Nilotic People*, 156. On Corsica, see Wilson, *Feuding*, 235–46.

31. For other examples of factions in Friulan communities, see Girolamo Sini, *Cronaca di S. Daniele dai primi tempi all'anno 1515*, 44–45; and Pier Silverio Leicht, "Un programma di parte democratica in Friuli nel Cinquecento," 108–21.

32. Girolamo di Porcìa listed the population of Spilimbergo in 1548 as consisting of 244 able-bodied men with 1,041 dependents for a total of 1,285. *Descrizione del Friuli*, 40. On the poverty of the area, see Gottardi, "Struttura politico-amministrativa," 83. For a list of products paid as rent to the consorts, see APS, MS IV, 3. On the pasturage system, see Alessandro Guaitoli, "Beni comunali e istituti di compascuo nel Friuli agli inizi del secolo XVII: Con particolari riferimenti alla montagna e alta pianura del destra Tagliamento," 50; and Giancarlo Zannier, "L'amministrazione del feudo spilimberghese fino al 1509," 183–85. The center of agitation over pasturage rights was usually Barbeano. The parish priest of Barbeano informed me in 1985 that there were ambushes over the use of pastures as recently as the 1960s.

33. On the castle, see Tito Miotti, *Castelli del Friuli*, 384–401.

34. On the jurisdiction, see Gottardi, "Struttura politico-amministrativa," 91; and Zannier, "L'amministrazione," 115–17, 130–39, 164. For various divisions of the jurisdiction and properties among the consorts, see Archivio Eredi Irene di Spilimbergo Spanio (private archive in possession of Dr. Clotilde Spanio, Venice, with microfilm copies in the Biblioteca Comunale, Spilimbergo), pergamene dated 1332, 1366, 1367, 1390, 1522. The 1522 document lists nine consorts by name.

35. APS, MS IX, A, docs. 5 (3 August 1443), 5bis (13 September 1443), 27 (22 June 1443), and a doc. dated 12 October 1443, which I have not been able to locate in APS, published in Ferruccio Carlo Carreri, "La rivolta di Spilimbergo nel 1443," *Scintilla*, no. 17 (8 May 1887). Cf. Tito Miotti, "Udinesi e Friulani ribelli: Dal patriarcato d'Alençon alle lotte fra Zambarlani e Strumieri," 124–25.

36. Every hearth had to pay twelve *denari per annum* to maintain the twelve guards of the city, even after the lords abolished the office; indirect taxes (*dazi*) on wine, salt, oil, and meat, the most important single source of income for the lords, were usually farmed out to Jewish contractors, which removed all vestige of communal control and led to abuses by the collectors. All merchants had to have a license from the lords and to collect a tax on every measure they sold. Travelers using the ferry across the Tagliamento had to pay a special tariff. Most tillers of

allodial lands paid an *affittanza* or *livello* in kind to the lords. On administration, see Zannier, "L'amministrazione," 47, 62–69, 76–87, 119–21. On agreements between consorts and citizens, see APS, MS XI, A, docs. 1 (15 May 1423), 2 and 11 (1 September 1445), 8 (10 January, 10 March, 30 March, 26 April, and 20 May 1446); on elections, see 12–15 (3 February 1446). On lords' complaints and militias, see Archivio Eredi Irene di Spilimbergo Spanio, pergamene dated 6 November 1478, 26 February 1481, and 8 December 1499.

37. Ferruccio Carlo Carreri, ed., *Convenzione tra i giusdicenti ed il popolo di Spilimbergo*, published under the cover title *Pergamena della fabbriceria di S. Maria di Spilimbergo* for the nozze Onaro-Spilimbergo (Spilimbergo?, 1885). Cf. Zannier, "L'amministrazione," 50–59. A later undated accord shows that the consorts were not adhering to the obligations made in the 1445 aggreement. APS, MS XI, A, doc. 23.

38. An Italian translation of the anonymous *Chronicon Spilimbergense* is in L. Pognici, *Guida Spilimbergo e suo distretto* (Pordenone, 1872), 196–234. Although the standard bibliographies list them together, the *Chronicon* published by Pognici is not the same as the *Chronicon Spilimbergense* (Udine, 1856), which is far more schematic and does not mention political events. Pognici was working from a Latin manuscript in the BCU discussed in G. Bianchi, "*Chronicon Spegnimbergense* – copia manoscr. B.C.U.," *ASI* 3 (1856): 213–16. Unfortunately, I have been unable to locate the original Latin manuscript in the BCU to check Pognici's translation against it. Pognici's florid style, uncharacteristic of fifteenth-century Latin chronicles, raises doubts about its accuracy, and the translation has been employed here with considerable caution. The chronicler was clearly biased in favor of the consorts, but evidence supporting the citizens' complaints is apparent as well.

39. On the final raid, Ferruccio Carlo Carreri, "Come si chiudesse il dicembre 1485 per Spilimbergo," *Scintilla* no. 24 (26 June 1887).

40. For quote, see *DU*, GAH, 499.

Chapter 4: Approaching Thunder

1. For the first quote, see Luigi da Porto, *Lettere storiche dall'anno 1509 al 1528*, 276–77. For the second quote, see ASV, CCD, Lettere di condottieri (Savorgnan), busta 308, quoted in Forgiarini, "Quattro lettere storiche," 302. In his highly laudatory history of the Savorgnan family, Francesco Caro found Antonio such a difficult figure that he ignored his career completely and mentioned him only once when quoting a ducal decree. *Istoria de'signori Savorgnani detti del Monte, Conti di Belgrado, Castel Nuovo, etc.* (Udine, 1771), 51–56.

2. For quote, see *DU*, GAH, 497.

3. Information on Antonio's early career comes from Fabia Savini, "Antonio Savorgnan," 266–70. For quote on his rhetorical skills, see *DU*, GAH, 503–504.

4. For quote from Antonio, see ASU, AS, busta 7, doc. 1, "Memoriale di Urbano a Niccolò Savorgnan," 59r–v, as cited in Liliana Cargnelluti, "Antonio Savorgnan e l'insurrezione del 1511," 125n.

5. On Capello, see *Dizionario biografico degli Italiani*, s.v. "Capello, Pietro" and Manfredo Tafuri, *Venezia e il Rinascimento: Religione, scienza, architettura*, 34n.

6. Andrea Loredan and Doge Leonardo Loredan were distant cousins with the closest ancestor in common going back six generations from Andrea and four from Leonardo to Marchesino q. Alberto Loredan, who lived in the thirteenth century. Girolamo Capellari, "Il campidoglio Veneto," BMV, MS It. VII 16 (8305), fols. 228v, 234r–37v. The Barbaro genealogy is unclear on their relationship. BMV, MS It. VII, 926 (8595), fols. 238v–239r. On Andrea's early career, see MCV, MS P.D. 819, fascicolo 8; and Michael Hirst, *Sebastiano del Piombo* (Oxford: Clarendon Press, 1981), 20. On his reputation in Friuli, see Giovanni Partenopeo, *La guerra del Friuli contro i tedeschi (1508–13)*, 7. On the loan to Udine to pay troops, see *DU*, GA, 41. On the arbitration of Savorgnan differences and on the 1511 request for his return, see Marino Sanuto, *I diarii*, 7: 184 and 12: 534.

7. On the political events around Andrea's deportation, see Sanuto, *I diarii*, 9: 5, 42–43, 54, 70, 77, 96–97, 368, 417–27; 10: 26–27; 11: 483. On the function of provveditors, see M. E. Mallett and J. R. Hale, *Military Organization*, 262–83.

8. Sanuto, *I diarii*, 11: 613–14.

9. On Andrea's marriage to Maria Badoer in 1483, see BMV, MS It. VII 926 (8495), fol. 246r. On his patronage of Codussi, see Vittorino Meneghin, *San Michele in Isola di Venezia* (Venice: Stamperia di Venezia, 1962), 296–97, 313, 316–18; Maria Luxoro, *Il Palazzo Vendramin-Calergi* (Florence: Leo S. Olschki, 1957), 15–17; Loredana Olivato Puppi and Lionello Puppi, *Mauro Codussi* (Turin: ERI, 1977), 58, 93, 221–26 and passim; and Tafuri, *Venezia e il Rinascimento*, 10, 53. Loredan's palace also contained two pictures by Giovanni Bellini and some figures by Titian; see Oliver Logan, *Culture and Society in Venice 1470–1790: The Renaissance and Its Heritage* (London: B. T. Batsford, 1972), 313. He was probably the patron of Sebastiano del Piombo's *Judgement of Solomon*; see Michael Hirst, *Sebastiano del Piombo*, 19–21. Loredan died a hero in 1513 while serving near Padua. For his final speech to the troops, "Orazione ai soldati per esortarli a seguitare il nemico nei contorni di Padova nel 1513," BMV, It. VII, 783 (7291), fols. 290r–291r.

10. On votes in parliament, see BCU, MS 927, 1: 82r. On his career in Padua, Archivio della Curia Vescovile, Padua, "Diversorum," 40: 34v and 42: 98r. On council of Udine, BCU, ACU, Annali, reg. 41, passim and BCU, Acta publica, reg. 3, fol. 178v.

11. On Monticolo and reform of statutes, see Savini, "Antonio Savorgnan," 269.

12. *DU*, GAH, 498–99. On Nicolò Chiribin, see Savini, "Antonio Savorgnan," 267. Cardinal Grimani obtained a benefice in Friuli for Nicolò, and the doge personally presented the *bolla* for the benefice to Nicolò in the college of the Senate. Sanuto, *I diarii*, 10: 790. On the Varmo, see ASU, Archivio Varmo, busta 25, doc. titled "Certificati relativi alli vantaggi recati alle pubbliche armi contro i Tedeschi (anno 1510 e sequenti) dalli consorti di Varmo."

13. On Antonio's support of the poor, see BCU, ACU, Annali, reg. 38, fols. 24r (26 September 1490), 184v (27 July 1494); reg. 39, fols. 18v (5 January 1495), 92v–93r (29 September 1496), 95v (6 April 1496); reg. 40, fol. 190v (24 September 1504); reg. 41, fols. 18r (27 September 1505), 57v–58r (29 September 1506), 64r (18 October 1506), 186r (29 September 1510). Also on bread

supply, see BCU, MS Joppi 592, fol. 5r and Antonio Measso, "Il pane quotidiano a Udine nel 1500: Note d'archivio," *Atti dell'Accademia di Udine*, ser. 2, 7 (1887): 5–6.

14. On Antonio's defense of peasant interests, see Andreina Stefanutti, "Udine e la contadinanza: Solidarietà e tensioni sociali nel Friuli del '500 e '600," 111.

15. On Tristano, see Ernesto Degani, *I partiti in Friuli nel 1500 e la storia di un famoso duello*, 10–13.

16. On Buia, see ASU, AS, busta 42, rotuli 1499–1508.

17. Cf. the parallel investigation and comparison with Colloredo rent-rolls for the same period by Cinzia Borghese, "Castellani e contadini del Friuli orientale negli anni della rivolta: Le proprietà dei Colloredo e dei Savorgnan (Feudo di Buia)," 141-82. On the social implications of uncollected loans, see Ronald F. E. Weissman, "The Importance of Being Ambiguous: Social Relations, Individualism, and Identity in Renaissance Florence."

18. For the law enabling the formation of militias, see *Leggi per la Patria*, 418–19. On Nicolò Savorgnan, see Cargnelutti, "Antonio Savorgnan," 121.

19. On changes in military practice, see Luciano Pezzolo, "Milizie e contadini nelle campagne vicentine (Lisiera nel '500 e '600)," in *Lisiera: Immagini, documenti e problemi per la storia e cultura di una comunità veneta, strutture—congiunture–episodi*, ed. Claudio Povolo, 419–34.

20. On the Friulan militia, see Mallett and Hale, *Military Organization*, 350–52, 362. Cf. for later in the century, Peter January, "War, Defence and Society in the Venetian Terraferma, 1560–1630" (Ph.D. diss., University of London, 1983; copy for consultation available at the Institute for Historical Research), 31–37, 41–46, 57–58, 66–67, 113, 120, 168–69.

21. On estimates of the size of Savorgnan's militias, see Sanuto, *I diarii*, 11: 90, 99, 137; da Porto, *Lettere storiche*, 188; and G. Baldissera, *Il contegno del famigerato Antonio Savorgnan all'espugnazione de'castelli di Vipulzano e S. Martino di Quisca nel 1510: Rimostranze della comunità di Cividale alla Veneta Repubblica* (Venice: Istituto Veneto di Arti Grafiche, 1913), 8n. On loans, see ASU, AS, busta 42, rotulo for 1508, dated 20 April. On Udine, see *DU*, LA, 101. On Cormons, see ASV, CCD, Lettere di condottieri (Savorgnan), busta 308, letter from syndics and deputies of Cividale, dated 23 March 1510. For complaints from the 1530s about the unreliability of the militiamen, see *Relazione*, 1: 22.

22. The concept of the liminal was introduced by Victor W. Turner, *The Ritual Process: Structure and Anti-Structure* (Chicago: Aldine Publishing, 1969). For its application to Renaissance society and literature, see Linda L. Carroll, "Authorial Defense in Boccaccio and Ruzante: From Liminal to Liminoid," 103–16. On the connection between military and festive companies, see Natalie Zemon Davis, "The Reasons of Misrule," 109.

23. On opinions of the two and quotation, see Pier Silverio Leicht, "La figura di Girolamo Savorgnan," 77. On Giacomo Janis di Tolmezzo and the granting of Castelnovo, see BCU, MS Joppi 689d, vol. 4, letters dated 16 June 1508 and 15 October 1509, respectively. On Girolamo's captaincy of militias, see Sanuto, *I diarii*, 9: 92. On complaints about Antonio, see Girolamo Savorgnan, "Lettere sulla guerra combattuta nel Friuli dal 1510 al 1528 scritte alla signoria di Venezia," vol. 2, pt. 2, pp. 16–20, dated 4 March 1510 and p. 22, dated 25 June 1510.

24. On the distribution of imperial and Gorizian fiefs, see Pier Silverio Leicht in *Carta politico-amministrativa*, ed. Gian Lodovico Bertolini and Umberto Rinaldi, 6–7, 16. On 12 April 1500, the date of the death of the last count of Gorizia, the county had sixteen districts: Pletz, Tolmino (Tolmin), Gorizia, Cormons, Gradisca, Vipacco, Postoina, Reifenberg, Schwarzenegg, Duino, Aquileia, Porpetto, Marano, Latisana, Belgrado, and Pordenone; see Francesco di Manzano, *Annali del Friuli ossia raccolta delle cose storiche appartenenti a questa regione*, 7: 101.

25. On Strumiero links to Gorizia, see Prospero Antonini, *I baroni di Waldsee o Walsee, i visconti di Mels, i signori di Prodolone e di Colloredo: Accenni genealogici e note storiche*, 66–67.

26. On the bandit problem in Pordenone, see Gio. Francesco Palladio degli Olivi, *Historie della provincia del Friuli*, pt. 2, 44; and Andrea Benedetti, *Storia di Pordenone*, 101–6. On Austrian and Venetian Friuli in general, see Tommaso Fanfani, "Friuli Austriaco e Friuli Veneto: Differenze e contraddizioni," in *Venezia e il Friuli: Problemi storiografici*, ed. Amelio Tagliaferri, 25–29. On the similar role in Liguria of border fiefs as havens for bandits, see Osvaldo Raggio, *Faide e parentele: Lo stato genovese visto dalla Fontanabuona*, 17–18.

27. Sanuto, *I diarii*, 1: 539, 611–12, 685, 999; 3:231. On the Venetian investiture of the count of Gorizia, see ASV, Collegio, Cerimoniale, 1: 15r. Also see Antonini, *I baroni di Waldsee*, 66–67; and idem, *Il Friuli orientale: Studi*, 262–71.

28. The invasion can be followed practically step by step in Sanuto, *I diarii*, 2: 1103, 1139–40, 1325–26, 1348–52, 1355, 1360, 1362, 1364–68, 1373, 1380–81; 3: 6–9, 19–20, 22–23, 26, 35, 73, 77–78, 129–30, 181; 4: 325, 327. Cf. Niccolò M. di Strassoldo, *Cronaca: Anni 1469–1509*, 20–21. On the Aviano area, see A. De Pellegrini, "Danni recati dai turchi nel 1499 ai villaggi di S. Martino e S. Leonardo nel territorio di Aviano," *MSF* 8 (1912): 193–96. On Valvasone, see Ferruccio Carlo Carreri, *Breve storia di Valvasone e dei suoi signori dagli inizi al 1806*, 46. The most important secondary sources are Francesco Musoni, "Le ultime incursioni dei Turchi in Friuli," 107–17; G. Gortani, "I Turchi in Friuli," 112; and Paolo Preto, *Venezia e i Turchi*, 32–34. The damaged Friulan villages received exemptions from *gravezze*, in some cases for twelve years, until a new generation could come of age. ASV, Senato, Terra, reg. 13, fol. 170r; reg. 19, fol. 52; and ASV, LPF, Processi e investure, filza 114, fols. 36–37, 53–54.

29. On Porcìa, see Aldo Mazzacane, "Lo stato e il dominio nei giuristi veneti durante il 'secolo della terraferma,' " 607–11.

30. On Maximilian in Friuli, see Antonini, *Il Friuli orientale*, 264, 271–72. On rumors of Turkish invasion in 1500, see Sanuto, *I diarii*, 3: passim; on Gorizian factions, 3: 250; on Savorgnan's analysis, 3: 1333–34; on rumors of an invasion in 1506, 5: passim.

31. On the campaign, see Sanuto, *I diarii*, 7: 186, 252, 261, 273, 295–96, 309, 312, 324, 357, 400–402, 406, 410, 419–20, 524–26, 552; DU, LA, 1–4, 10–12, 14, 17–38, 40, 49–50, 55, 57–58; Girolamo Colletti, "Giornali dal 1507 a 1510," BCU, MS 715; ASV, CD, Misto, reg. 32 (1508–9), fol. 125v; Partenopeo, *La guerra del Friuli*, 5–15; Pier Silverio Leicht, "La difesa del Friuli nel 1509, con appendice di documenti," 97–98; and Mallett and Hale, *Military Organization*, 63–64 (for bibliography on campaign, see 64n), 85, 131 (for budget). In general, see Piero Pieri,

Il rinascimento e la crisi militare italiana (Turin: Giulio Einaudi, 1952), 448–55. On Savorgnan and Loredan, see *DU*, LA, 41.

32. On the treaty, see Mallett and Hale, *Military Organization*, 221; and Antonini, *Il Friuli orientale*, 277–78. On Girolamo Savorgnan's mission to enlist Swiss support after the treaty, see Fulvio Bonati Savorgnan d'Osoppo, "Gerolamo Savorgnan ambasciatore agli Svizzeri," *MSF* 48 (1967–68): 143–52.

33. On Agnadello, see Pieri, *Il rinascimento*, 455–69.

34. On strategic withdrawal, see da Porto, *Lettere storiche*, 64–65; Partenopeo, *La guerra del Friuli*, 28–29; Mallett and Hale, *Military Organization*, 177, in which the Venetian policy of strategic withdrawal is analyzed. On the power of the Council of Ten, see Robert Finlay, *Politics in Renaissance Venice*, 188–89.

35. On Udine, see BCU, MS Joppi, 689d, vol. 4, fol. 55r–v; Sanuto, *Il diarii*, 8: 375, 446–47 (for luogotenente's decree); *DU*, LA, 88, 100, 101 (for quote about Spilimbergo), 103–4; Angelo Ventura, *Nobiltà e popolo nella società veneta del '400 e '500*, 177n; Innocenzo Cervelli, *Machiavelli e la crisi dello stato veneziano*, 42–43n.

36. For the list, see *DU*, GAH, 499. For Girolamo Savorgnan's evidence, see ASV, CCD, Lettere di condottieri (Savorgnan), busta 308, letter from Udine dated 5 September 1509. Cf. Dionisio Tassini, "La rivolta del Friuli nel 1511 durante la guerra contro i tedeschi," 142–43 and Vincenzo Marchesi, "Il Friuli al tempo della Lega di Cambrai," *NAV*, n.s., 6 (1903): 513–14.

37. On rumors about Savorgnan, see *DU*, LA, 93; and Partenopeo, *La guerra del Friuli*, 34–35. Letters to Gradenigo, see ASV, CD, Misto, reg. 32 (1508–9), fols. 175 (13 July), 179r (27 July).

38. On Priuli, see Felix Gilbert, "Venice in the Crisis of the League of Cambrai," in *Renaissance Venice*, ed. J. R. Hale, 274–75. On da Porto, see *Lettere*, 26–30; and Cervelli, *Machiavelli*, 143–63. On mainland historians, see Eric Cochrane, *Historians and Historiography in the Italian Renaissance* (Chicago: University of Chicago Press, 1981), 181–87. On Venetian financial strategies during the war, see Felix Gilbert, *The Pope, His Banker, and Venice* (Cambridge: Harvard University Press, 1980).

39. On *ad meliorandum* clauses, see Carlo Guido Mor, "L'ambiente agrario friulano dall'XI alla metà del XIV secolo," 205-9. On acts of parliament, see "Parlamento del Friuli," BCU, MS 927, 1: 42r–43r (18 October 1501), 47 (1 November 1505), 56v–57r (30 May 1502), 65v–66r (22 November 1502), 67v–68r (22 November 1502), 70 (14 February 1503), 74 (19 March 1503), 75r–81v (20 March 1503). On billeting troops, see Mallett and Hale, *Military Organization*, 134.

40. On castellan complaints about peasants, see "Parlamento del Friuli," BCU, MS 927, 1: 84r–87r (84v for quote); on peasants' appeal to parliament, see 93r–95v (93r for quote). The quote about the castellans' complaints also appears with the incorrect date of 1508 in Gaetano Perusini, *I contratti agrari nel Friuli durante il dominio veneto*, 7 and Carlo Ginzburg, *The Cheese and the Worms: The Cosmos of a Sixteenth-Century Miller*, 13–14.

41. On peasants' appeal to Udine, see BCU, Acta publica, 3: 178v–179r.

42. On Loredan's response, see Sanuto, *I diarii*, 5: 632.

43. Quote about Monfalcone, see Sanuto, *I diarii*, 7: 360; on mutual reprisals between groups of peasants and foreign soldiers, see 9: 92, 96, 105, 158–59, 316;

on peasant refugees in Venice, see 154, 161, 164, 173. On Venetian retaliation and the sacking of Cormons, see Partenopeo, *La guerra del Friuli*, 12–13, 31–32 (for quote about 1509); Giovanni Battista di Cergneu, *Cronaca delle guerre friulane coi Germani dal 1507 al 1524*, 13–16; and *DU*, LA, 20–23, 27 (23 for quote about 1508). For a poem by an anonymous Friulan who recounts the atrocities perpetuated by the Germans in 1509, see Vincenzo Joppi, *Canzone popolare contemporanea sulle guerre dei Tedeschi in Friuli nel 1509* (Udine, 1884).

44. On the loyalty of the peasants, see Cervelli, *Machiavelli*, 346–52, 363–69; and Mallett and Hale, *Military Organization*, 344–46. For a more skeptical view, see Gino Benzoni, "Venezia ai tempi di Giorgione," *Critica storica* 17 (1980): 411.

45. On Colloredo properties, see Paolo Cammarosano, *Le campagne friulane nel tardo medioevo: Un'analisi dei registri di censi dei grandi proprietari fondiari*, 37–38. On Colloredo jurisdictions, see *Leggi per la Patria*, in preface under Colloredo-Mels; and Borghese, "Castellani e contadini," 55. On Sterpo, see ASU, AC-M, parte 1, busta 5, vacchetta 1497, fol. 5v; and Antonini, *I baroni di Waldsee*, 73–74. On Albertino and Odorico in the imperial camp, see ASV, Lettere di condottieri (Savorgnan), busta 308, letter dated 5 September 1509, published in Giovanni Forgiarini, ed., "Quattro lettere storiche di Antonio Savorgnano (1457–1512)," 305. On Odorico's death, see *DU*, LA, 151.

46. The 1502 document is published in Tito Miotti, *Castelli del Friuli*, 2: 307–11.

47. The opinion about the Colloredos' intentions for Sterpo is from Borghese, "Castellani e contadini," 74–75, 85. For price statistics, see Tagliaferri, *Udine nella storia economica*, 71 (table 2), 82–83.

48. The sources for the Colloredo estates are the rent-rolls in ASU, AC-M, parte 1, busta 5, vacchetta degli affitti di 1497 (missing at least 131 pages); parte 1, busta 6, no. 37, vacchetta degli affitti di 1502; parte 1, busta 6, no. 40, vacchetta degli affitti di 1509–1510; parte 1, busta 6, no. 41, vacchetta degli affitti di 1512; parte 1, busta 3bis, rotolo dell'entrate 1513 (and 1514 in part); parte 3, busta 24, vacchetta di 1515. The holdings are described in the 1502 volume, 4v: "Nuij havemo el logo de sterp cu(m) lo Dominio ac miro et misto Imper(er)io nec cu(m) terenj Campi pindi boschi paludi aque Comugne et teritorio ch(e) li ap(ertie)ne nec il q(u)al logo havessimo del mag(nifi)co m. phebus Junior delatore n(ost)ro barba et(iam) in p(resen)te d(e)li lervj a parte aparte Come apare p(er) li n(ostr)i Ind."

In these rent-rolls the Colloredo proprietors registered the annual payments in kind and in specie made by tenants, village by village. The forms of the books had been standardized since the end of the fourteenth century, recording for each tenant the rent required by contract and the amount actually paid. Sometimes the type of contract is noted, as are special considerations such as changes in the tenants, loans, and agreements between proprietor and tenant. These books include only those tenants of the Colloredo lords in each of these villages and, therefore, reveal nothing about peasants who may have been tenants of another landlord or about the small independent proprietors who were usually quite numerous in Friulan villages. They also do not include any information about other economic activities of the Colloredo family.

On agrarian contracts in general, Perusini, *I contratti agrari*; Mor, "Ambiente agrario," 205–9; Michele Zacchigna, "Alcuni aspetti dell'economia Pordenonese alla fine del Quattrocento," in *Società e cultura*, ed. Andrea Del Col, 107–10; and Borghese, "Castellani e contadini," 31.

49. For study of other estates between 1371 and 1453, see Cammarosano, *Le campagne friulane*, 103–7, and graph 1 from which I have calculated the average percentages of grain payments cited. I have not been able to calculate similar aggregate figures for the Colloredo properties because of extensive damage to the rolls, which sometimes makes it impossible to determine anything other than the number of tenants entered in the book. My method, therefore, has been to trace the readable names of individual tenants and to compare their ability to pay from one year to the next.

50. On crop rotation, see Cammarosano, *Le campagne friulane*, 60–61. On Jacomo's rent, see ASU, AC-M, parte 3, busta 24, vacchetta 1515. I have been unable to determine which system of measurement was employed in Sterpo. The *staio* (*starium*) was a measurement of volume for dry goods, and the *conzo* was a cask for wine, but the sizes of these units varied from place to place. In Friuli there were nineteen different measurements called a *staio* which varied from 61.5 to 101 liters. See Cammarosano, *Le campagne friulane*, 101–2.

51. On indebtedness at Sterpo, cf. Borghese, "Castellani e contadini," 84–99. Because of damage to the rolls which makes some payment entries illegible, the percentages of Colloredo tenants who paid no, partial, or full rent payments are based on the following: for 1497, seven legible entries out of nine known tenants; for 1502, twenty-six out of twenty-six; for 1509, twenty-eight out of twenty-nine; for 1510, thirteen out of thirteen; for 1512, eight out of thirteen; and for 1513, six out of six.

52. On Savorgnan loans in Buia, see ASU, AS, busta 42, rotulo 1508.

53. On payment of rents, see ASU, AC-M, parte 1, busta 6, vacchetta 1509.

54. On Valvasone, see Carreri, *Breve storia di Valvasone*, 48; and Miotti, *Castelli del Friuli*, 4: 442. On munitions in Sterpo, see *DU, LA*, 114; *DU, GAH*, 500 (for quote); and Baldissera, *Il contegno del famigerato Antonio Savorgnan*, 6. Leonardo Amaseo reported that Varmo brought six hundred peasants to Sterpo (*DU, LA*, 114), but on other, better documented, occasions they mustered between three and four hundred. Federico was later described as the "capo de fanti della ordinanza della Patria," who recruited under the authority of the luogotenente. He could threaten to hang men who refused to join. ASU, Archivio di Varmo, busta 25, doc. titled "Artificati relativi alli vantaggi recati alle pubbliche armi contro i tedeschi (anno 1510 e sequenti) dalli consorti di Varmo." For a description of the attack, see Cergneu, *Cronaca delle guerre friulane*, 31–33.

55. For quote, see ASU, AC-M, parte 2, busta 3bis, fol. 136v. The date given is 1511, but it is evident from the other rent-rolls that most of the damage took place in 1509. The 1511 date is also given in the 1530 estimate of damages, but the claims made then were specifically to compensate for the 1511 revolt, and if they hoped to obtain anything, the Colloredo heirs had to fix the date for the destruction of Sterpo at 1511. BCU, MS Joppi 592, doc. dated 10 October 1530. Also see Agostino di Colloredo, "Chroniche friulane, 1508–1518," 5–6.

56. On the investigation, see *DU, LA*, 126. For the Colloredos' legal actions,

see ASV, LPF, filza 132, fol. 201r, dated 6 December 1510. For Strumiero opinion that Sterpo began the civil war, see *DU*, GAH, 500. For a similar Zambarlano opinion, see Nicolò Monticolo, *Descrittione del sacco MDXI seguito in Udine il giovedì XXVII febbraio*, 11.

57. ASV, LPF, filza 132, fol. 239. On the *gravezze* and other imposts the peasants had to pay, see Luciana Morassi, "Sistema fiscale e diritti giurisdizionali," in *Savorgnan e la Patria del Friuli dal XIII al XVIII secolo* (Udine: Provincia di Udine, Assessorato di Cultura, 1984), 215-24.

58. For the Articles of Merano produced during the South Tyrol rebellion, see Manuela Acler, ed., "La completa versione in volgare italiano degli articoli di Merano," *Studi trentini di scienze storiche* 56 (1977): 225-53. For the German revolts in general, see Peter Blickle, *The Revolution of 1525: The German Peasants' War from a New Perspective*, trans. Thomas A. Brady and H. C. Erik Midelfort (Baltimore: Johns Hopkins University Press, 1981). On the absence of class consciousness among Friulan peasants, see Ginzburg, *Cheese and the Worms*, 16. Quote from Gregorio Amaseo cited in Savini, "Antonio Savorgnan," 275.

Chapter 5: The Tempest of 1511

1. On castellan delegations to Venice, see *DU*, LA, 143-47 (144 for first quote); *DU*, GAH, 500-501; Marino Sanuto, *I diarii*, 9: 486. For the Zompicchia attack and Amaseo quote, see *DU*, GAH, 502; Amaseo misdates the Zompicchia attack to May. Cf. Giovanni Battista di Cergneu, *Cronaca delle guerre friulane coi Germani dal 1507 al 1524*, 33-34; ASV, CCD, Lettere di condottieri, busta 308 (Savorgnan), letters dated 3 March, 5 March, and 16 April 1510. The 5 March letter is published in Giovanni Forgiarini, ed., "Quattro lettere storiche di Antonio Savorgnano (1457-1512)," 304-6. Cf. Fabia Savini, "Antonio Savorgnan," 275-77. The events of the spring 1510 can be traced in ASV, CD, Misto, reg. 33 (1510), fols. 68v-69r (6 March), 76 (19 March), 76v-77r (22 March), 77v (26 March), 78r (3 April); ASV, CCD, Lettere di condottieri (Savorgnan), busta 308, letters from Antonio Justo dated 9 March and 16 April (for third quote); ASV, LPF, filza 132, fols. 144v (15 April), 243v-244r (22 March and 4 April); and Sanuto, *I diarii*, 10: 33, 52, 53.

2. For quote on the turbulent past and election of new luogotenente, see ASV, Senato, Terra, reg. 17, fols. 55 and 66v dated 10, 12 October and 11, 12 December 1510. The politics behind the decisions can be traced in Sanuto, *I diarii*, 11: 507, 569, 576, 577-78, 719. As was the case with other burdensome offices, taking up the position of luogotenente of Friuli was frequently evaded or put off by those elected; see Donald E. Queller, *The Venetian Patriciate: Reality versus Myth*, 113-71.

3. For quote on cannon incident, see *DU*, GAH, 504. On New Year's decree, see ASV, LPF, busta 133, under title "Extraordinar. liber primus," dated 11 January 1511. Cf. decree for 1512 in ASV, LPF, busta 134.

4. On the salt bribe, see Luigi da Porto, *Lettere storiche dall'anno 1509 al 1528*, 227-28. On the enemy raids, see Sanuto, *I diarii*, 11: 756-57, 781, 789-90. On peasant losses to raiders and on kidnappings for ransom, see ASV, LPF, busta 133, under title "Extraordinarior. liber primus," dated 18 January and 9 February

1511. On Vitturi's appointment, see Marcantonio Michiel, "Diarii," MCV, Cod. Cicogna 2848, fol. 6r. On the Udine city council decision, see BCU, ACU, Annali, reg. 41, fol. 204r.

5. For quote, see DU, GA, 224; for an account of these events, see DU, GAH, 504. On forged safe conducts, see ASV, LPF, busta 132, fols. 259v, 260r, 261v. On Nicolò di Albertino Colloredo and Francesco Candido, see DU, GA, 232n, 234n, 269–70; DU, GAH, 542n; and Cergneu, Cronaca delle guerre friulane, 77.

6. Savorgnan's request is in ASV, Lettere di condottieri (Savorgnan), busta 308, published in Forgiarini, "Quattro lettere storiche di Antonio Savorgnano," 307. For the Council of Ten's reply and request of Antonio, see ASV, CD, Misto, reg. 33, fols. 181v–182r, dated 4 February.

7. For Strumiero views, see DU, GAH, 504-5. On Antonio's claims, see "Autentiche testimonianze intorno alla famiglia Savorgnan," 300–305.

8. On Chiavris, see Paolo Cammarosano, Le campagne friulane nel tardo medioevo:- Un'analisi dei registri di censi dei grandi proprietari fondiari, 36n. For other locations of Savorgnan support, see Nicolò Monticolo, Descrittione del sacco MDXI seguito in Udine il giovedì XXVII febbraio, 11. The editor, Gian Giuseppe Liruti, makes the attribution to Monticolo, but Dionisio Tassini expresses doubts about the authorship, see "La rivolta del Friuli nel 1511 durante la guerra contro i tedeschi," 146. For the luogotenente's edict, see ASV, LPF, busta 133, under the title "Extraordinarior. liber primus." DU, GAH, 505 indicates that the prohibition was announced on Monday the 24th.

9. The dangers of major festival days such as carnival had long been a matter for official concern. The parliament of Friuli prohibited peasants from carrying arms on feast days as early as 1458. Pier Silverio Leicht, Parlamento friulano, 72–73. Venice had forbidden weapons and masks during carnival the previous year; ASV, CD, Proclami, filza 1, fol. 87. Cf. Sergio Gobet, "1511: Agitazioni contadine nelle campagne del Friuli," 1: 158.

10. On the brigades, see DU, GAH, 505. For quotes and Antonio Savorgnan's purported thoughts, see "Autentiche testimonianze," 301-2. On the Strumiero buildup during Antonio's absence, see Sanuto, I diarii, 12: 17.

11. On the peace pact, see Monticolo, Descrittione del sacco, 12; Cergneu, Cronaca delle guerre friulane, 36–37; Antonio Belloni, De clade Turriana, 152. Antonio Badoer, the Venetian treasurer posted to Udine, reported that Savorgnan opposed the peace; Sanuto, I diarii, 12: 17. On Florence, see Isidoro Del Lungo, "Una vendetta in Firenze il giorno di San Giovanni 1295," 373–74; Richard C. Trexler, Public Life in Renaissance Florence, 116n; and Samuel Y. Edgerton, Jr., Pictures and Punishment, 40. For Bologna, see Sarah R. Blanshei, "Criminal Law and Politics in Medieval Bologna."

12. On Sebastiano Vicentino, see BCU, MS Joppi 592, "Esame di testimoni di Sebastiano Vicentino." On Antonio's message, see "Autentiche testimonianze," 302.

13. On the dance, see Sanuto, I diarii, 12: 17. On Luigi's military career, see M. E. Mallett and J. R. Hale, Military Organization, 342. On the love affair between Pietro Bembo and Maria Savorgnan, see their Carteggio d'amore 1500-1501,

ed. Carlo Dionisotti (Florence: F. Le Monnier, 1950); and Gildo Meneghetti, *La vita avventurosa di Pietro Bembo: Umanista, poeta, cortigiano (documenti inediti)* (Venice: Tip. Commerciale, 1961), 20–36.

Professor Cecil H. Clough kindly allowed me to see his paper, "La verità dietro la novella di Giulietta e Romeo" before publication. Also see his "The True Story of 'Romeo and Juliet,'" *Renaissance Papers, 1962* (Durham, N.C.: Duke University Press, 1963), 45–51; "Pietro Bembo, Luigi Da Porto, and the Court of Urbino in the Early Sixteenth Century," *AV,* ser. 5, 81 (1967): 71–87, especially 71, 79, and 81, reprinted in his *The Duchy of Urbino in the Renaissance* (London: Variorum Reprints, 1981); and "Le 'Lettere Storiche' di Luigi da Porto fonte della 'Istoria Viniziana' di Pietro Bembo," *AV,* ser. 5, 73 (1963): 5–15. Cf. da Porto, *Lettere storiche,* 13 for the dedication to Lucina. Clough's forthcoming new edition of the *Lettere storiche* will add more information to this topic. On Francesco Savorgnan, see ASU, AT, cartella 19, colto 26, fascicolo 3, dated 3 April 1530; Savini, "Antonio Savorgnan," 302; and Sanuto, *I diarii,* 18: 30.

The history of the Romeo and Juliet story is, of course, a complex one, and da Porto by no means should be given sole credit for it. Perhaps the earliest version is in a Sienese legend, written down by Masuccio Salernitano, *Il Novellino,* ed. Alfredo Mauro (Bari: Laterza, 1940), no. 22, in which the principals are called Mariotto and Ganozza. The story also appears in Matteo Bandello, *Tutte le opere,* ed. F. Flora (Milan: A. Mondadori, 1935), 2: 263–64. Shakespeare probably relied on the Bandello version. The idea that da Porto wrote the story after his own unhappy love affair first appears in studies that Giuseppe Todeschini appended to his edition of the *Lettere storiche.* Todeschini thought da Porto's beloved was a Monticolo of Udine, a family descended from the Montecchi of Verona. Because the soldiers in da Porto's unit were called *cappelletti* after their practice of wearing hats rather than helmets, Todeschini surmised that Luigi pictured himself as Romeo Capulet. Others who accept a connection between Luigi's experiences in Udine and the *novella* include C. Foligno, "Appunti su Luigi da Porto e la sua novella," *NAV,* n.s., 12 (1912): 430; and Gioachino Brognoligo, *Studi di storia letteraria* (Rome: Società editrice Dante Alighieri, 1903), 74. G. Chiarini has tried to demolish any connection between the *novella* and actual historical events. "Romeo e Giulietta: Le fonti," in his *Studi Shakespeariani* (Leghorn, 1897), 223–307. Also see his *Romeo e Giulietta* (Florence: Sansoni, 1906), 42. Olin H. Moore traces the antecedents to da Porto's version of the story but badly misunderstands the nature of his involvement in Friuli, saying he served in the "imperial Venetian army against Udine" when in fact he served in the Venetian army in defense of Udine against the imperial forces. *The Legend of Romeo and Juliet* (Columbus: Ohio State University Press, 1950), 52. For recent literary criticisms that analyze the feuding aspects of the play, see Coppélia Kahn, *Man's Estate: Masculine Identity in Shakespeare* (Berkeley and Los Angeles: University of California Press, 1981) and Richard Levin, "Feminist Thematics and Shakespearean Tragedy," *PMLA* 103 (1988): 125–38.

14. On the meeting, see *DU,* GAH, 506 and Cergneu, *Cronaca delle guerre friulane,* 39. On Francesco Cergneu's career, see Pier Silverio Leicht, "La difesa del Friuli nel 1509, con appendice di documenti," 101; and *DU,* GAH, 500, 502–3,

508. The quote is from Savini, "Antonio Savorgnan," 276. On Teseo Colloredo, see *DU, GAH,* 504.

15. Copies of the letter with insignificant variations can be found in many sources. The text of the possible holograph is published in Savini, "Antonio Savorgnan," 296–97.

16. Cergneu, *Cronaca delle guerre friulane,* 39; for predictions, see "Autentiche testimonianze," 303. For participants in the events, see Appendix 1.

17. Savorgnan's account is in "Autentiche testimonianze," 302-3. The provveditor stated in a letter to the Council of Ten that the Austrians came as close as Pradamano; ASV, CD, Misto, reg. 34, fol. 54r. The Austrian threat is also cited by Giovanni Partenopeo, *La guerra del Friuli contro i tedeschi (1508–13),* 74; by Sebastiano Decio, "Notitia de clade Utinensi et de terraemotu anno 1511," BCU, MS Joppi 66; by Belloni, *De clade Turriani,* 152; by Monticolo, *Descrittione del sacco,* 14–15; by all three of the Venetian eyewitnesses whose letters appear in Sanuto, *I diarii,* 12: 5, 18, 26–29; and by the delegation of *decani* who came to see the head of the Council of Ten, Andrea Loredan, after he arrived in Udine. ASV, CCD, Lettere rettori (Udine), busta 169, fol. 67r, dated 6 March. Antonio's enemies protested that he concocted the reports of the Austrian threat as an elaborate trick, which he made credible by sending his nephew Luigi da Porto and fifty cavalrymen out to masquerade as an invading band of Austrians; one antagonist even asserted that Savorgnan himself left town to treat with the enemy. For views that reports were part of a trick, see *DU, GA,* 226; *DU, GAH,* 507-8; Cergneu, *Cronaca delle guerre friulane,* 40; Giovan Candido, *Commentarii de i fatti d'Aquileja,* 174; and Gio. Francesco Palladio degli Olivi, *Historie della provincia del Friuli,* 105.

18. The sources for the account of Giovedì Grasso here and in the following paragraphs are as follows. Savorgnan's version is in "Autentiche testimonianze," 303-5. The fullest descriptions are *DU, GA,* 224-29; *DU, GAH,* 507-21; and Monticolo, *Descrittione del sacco,* 14–16. The principal Strumiero versions are Agostino di Colloredo, "Chroniche friulane, 1508-18," 5–6; and Cergneu, *Cronaca delle guerre friulane,* 39–47. Also see Belloni, *De clade Turriana,* 152; Decio, "Notitia de clade utinensi," BCU, MS Joppi 66; and "Udine saccheggiata l'anno 1511," MCV, MS Correr 963, pezzo 3, fols. 24r–31r. Three letters from Venetians on the scene can be found in Sanuto, *I diarii,* 12: 5–6, 17–19, and 26–30. Except where otherwise indicated the narrative below is based on *DU, GAH.*

19. On the chest from the Della Torre palace, see BCU, MS Joppi 592, fol. xlvii (recto).

20. On Vergon, Narni, and Tempesta, see *DU, GA,* 227; *DU, GAH,* 509, 513–14, 516, 519, 531n; Cergneu, *Cronaca delle guerre friulane,* 41, 49–50; and Monticolo, *Descrittione del sacco,* 15, 21.

21. *DU, GAH,* 513, 531n; Monticolo, *Descrittione del sacco,* 15, 20; BCU, MS Joppi 592, dated 13 June 1511; and Sanuto, *I diarii,* 20: 477, 505. Of all those named here, only Nicolò Savorgnan was not ordered arrested on 30 May 1511; ASV, CD, Parti criminali, reg. 1 (1502–11), fol. 168v. Several other intimates of Savorgnan were said to have been deeply involved in the Giovedì Grasso killings, but they escaped punishment entirely and are not implicated in the later official investigation. These included Vicenzo Pozzo, Girolamo Arlati, Battista Torso, Pietro Du-

rissino, Pietro Justo, Sebastiano Cornetto, Uccello Carneval, Rosetto and Pietro Stringaro, and Giovanni Bianchino; *DU*, GAH, 500, 509, 512–14, 515, 517, 521. Bianchino later followed Savorgnan into exile. Savini, "Antonio Savorgnan," 291.

22. On crowd crystals, see Elias Canetti, *Crowds and Power*, 73–75. I wish to thank Frederick Marquardt for this reference. Natalie Davis notes that rites of violence are "likely to occur when it is believed that religious and/or political authorities are failing in their duties or need help in fulfilling them"; "Rites of Violence," 169.

23. On Arlatto, see BCU, ACU, Annali, reg. 41, fol. 204r. On the death of Isidoro and other attacks on his close allies, see *DU*, GAH, 510, 514–15 (514 for quote), 518; Savini, "Antonio Savorgnan," 301, 304; Sanuto, *I diarii*, 12: 28; Belloni, *De clade Turriana*, 154; and Monticolo, *Descrittione del sacco*, 16.

24. On the murder of Alvise Della Torre, see *DU*, GAH, 514; Cergneu, *Cronaca delle guerre friulane*, 45; Monticolo, *Descrittione del sacco*, 16; BCU, MS Joppi 592, "Esame di testimoni di Giacomo Vicentino calzolaio."

25. On the Soldonieri story, see *DU*, GAH, 515; Cergneu, *Cronaca delle guerre friulane*, 46; Sanuto, *I diarii*, 12: 28.

26. On the rescues, see "Autentiche testimonianze," 304; and Sanuto, *I diarii*, 12: 28. On Brazzacco, see *DU*, GAH, 517–18.

27. Gregorio Amaseo was precise about how he found out about Janis's aphoristic advice. Amaseo cited two indirect sources. His nephew Giacomo heard about it at a dinner in July 1520 from the priest Giovanni di Basaldella. At another dinner Tricesimo di Battista di Federicis recounted the statement to Gregorio, his wife, and brother Girolamo; *DU*, GA, 257. I have taken certain liberties in the translation of Janis's statement, which was "homo morto non fa guerra" (literally, "a dead man does not make war") *DU*, GAH, 516. From the context, however, it is clear that Janis implied more than keeping the Strumieri from siding with the enemy in the current war. The aphorism, in fact, was a Venetian commonplace. To justify their warlike efforts, the Venetians sent letters to Maximilian and to several towns in Flanders saying, "huomo morto non fa piu guerra." Jean Lemaire de Belges, *La légende des Vénitiens*, 377.

28. On Colloredo: "Fo morto et manzato da cani quella notte, quasi tutto, sier Federigo da Coloreto." Anonymous letter dated 2 March in Sanuto, *I diarii*, 12: 28. Also Cergneu, *Cronaca delle guerre friulane*, 46; BCU, MS Joppi 67, no. 15, Pompeo Litta, "Il Giovedì Grasso di Udine," 218r.

29. On bodies abandoned to animals, see *DU*, GA, 227–28; *DU*, GAH, 514, 518–19; BCU, MS Joppi 67, no. 15, fol. 218r. On the bodies in the well, see *DU*, GA, 228; and *DU*, GAH, 518–19; Tassini, "La rivolta del Friuli," 154; Monticolo, *Descrittione del sacco*, 21; and Cergneu, *Cronaca delle guerre friulane*, 49–50.

30. Monticolo lists seventeen houses; *Descrittione del sacco*, 16. Francesco Portis says twenty-one houses were sacked or burned; BCU, MS Joppi 66. Colloredo says both twenty and twenty-one; "Croniche friulane," 5–6. Sanuto lists twenty-one houses; *I diarii*, 12: 28–29. Belloni counted twenty-two; *De clade Turriana*, 153. Marchesi accepts the figure twenty-two; Vincenzo Marchesi, "Il Friuli al tempo della Lega di Cambrai," 525. Decio reports twenty-five to twenty-eight killed; BCU, MS Joppi 66. The number of dead is fifty in MCV, MS Correr 963, fol. 24v,

but this figure is probably an exaggeration as certainly is the figure of two hundred in ASMn, Archivio Gonzaga, busta 1445, fol. 34.

31. On those forced out of Udine, see BCU, MS Joppi 67, no. 15, Pompeo Litta, "Il giovedì grasso di Udine," 218r. On the social composition of these bands, see Monticolo, *Descrittione del sacco*, 20.

32. On the marriage of Alvise Della Torre to Tadea Strassoldo in 1500, see ASU, AT, busta 18, "Prove genealogiche della famiglia Della Torre," 246–49. On the history of the Della Torre acquisition of Villalta, see ASU, AT, busta 33, "Informazione de' feudi e giurisdizioni acquistati dalla famiglia dei Signori Conti Della Torre di Valsassine, etc." and Tito Miotti, *Castelli del Friuli*, 2: 399–407. On 3 November 1467 the Della Torre received an extra one quarter of the castle, its lands, and jurisdictional rights from the non-Della Torre consorts. On 10 March 1490 Odorico di Villalta protested that Alvise and Isidoro had erected a building on land that did not belong to them. Land purchases were made on 4 February 1500 (*m.v.*), 2 March 1500 (*m.v.*), 9 April 1502, 14 October 1506, 6 March 1507, and 16 May 1508. See the original parchment deeds for the above dates and the "Nota delle investiture e compere fatte dai Signori di Villalta," ASU, AT, busta 33.

33. On Moruzzo and Brazzacco, Miotti, *Castelli del Friuli*, 2: 59–67, 221–25; Francesco di Manzano, *Annali del Friuli ossia raccolta delle cose storiche appartenenti a questa regione*, 7: 92; and *DU*, GAH, 523.

34. Quote about Villalta, see *DU*, GAH, 522. On 9 September 1512, Tadea, widow of Alvise Della Torre, signed a contract with Jacopo q. Paulo Michele di Fagagna in the "sala magna castri Villaltae"; ASU, AT, busta 33. On the loss of records at Villalta, see doc. dated 1535, "Informazione de' feudi e giurisdizione acquistati dalla famiglia dei Signori Conti Della Torre di Valsassine etc.," 4–5. For a similar declaration that records were destroyed at Colloredo di Monte Albano, see ASU, AC-M, parte 3, busta 73, ca. 1581.

Alvise Della Torre left five surviving sons and one daughter; Colloredo, "Croniche friulane," 6. The Della Torre would never regain the influence enjoyed by the older generation snuffed out on Giovedì Grasso, and the young survivors and their offspring altered the family's strategy of building a castellan power base in Friuli. Raimondo, the eldest, later became a Knight of Malta and disappeared from family history. His place as head of the family fell to Girolamo, who judiciously ended the family's animosity to the Venetian overlords by marrying the daughter of a senator, Matteo Bembo. Nevertheless, the Della Torre also maintained the traditional Strumiero alliances through Ginevra's marriage to Giovanni Battista Colloredo, who served in the armies of Emperor Charles V. Giovanni Della Torre left little mark; but Michele pursued a brilliant career in Rome as an advisor to Pope Paul III. He became bishop of the lucrative diocese of Ceneda in 1546, attended the Council of Trent, was twice papal nuncio to France, served as governor of Umbria, and received a cardinal's hat in 1583. A fifth son, named Alvise for the father he never knew, was born after the Giovedì Grasso massacres. He seems to have bumped along through life in some minor ecclesiastical posts, probably obtained through Michele's influence, until his murder in 1549 at the hands of the Savorgnan. On Girolamo Della Torre, see ASU, AT, busta 18, "Prove genealogiche," 144; on Michele and Alvise, see 251–52, 297–301 and cartella 19, colto 26, fascicoli 1, 2, 3. On Giovanni Battista Colloredo, see Prospero Antonini, *I baroni di Waldsee o Walsee, i visconti di Mels, i signori di Prodolone e di Colloredo: Accenni genealogici e note storiche*, 89.

35. On Colloredo holdings, see ASU, AC-M, parte 1, busta 6, no. 41, dated 1512, fols. 4v–11v, 23v–26r, 34v, 35v–39r, 42v–44r, 54v–55r; parte 2, busta 3bis, fol. 24v; parte 3, scatolone 9, busta 24, "Estratto di Conti di Colloredo," dated 1523; and parte 3, busta 73, dated 1503, fols. 1r–2v, 19r. A later inventory in busta 24 lists fifty-four locations: "Libro dei fitti della signoria di Colloredo," dated 1545. Also Degani, *Partiti in Friuli*, 32. The basic study of the family is Antonini, *I baroni di Waldsee*. On the castles, see Miotti, *Castelli del Friuli*, 2: 129, 209–13, 321–25.

36. An overall assessment of the consorts' holdings and jurisdictions can be found in ASU, AC-M, parte 3, busta 73, dated ca. 1581; and for quote, see parte 2, busta 3bis, rotulo dated 1513, fol. 62v. For losses, see *DU, GAH*, 523; Miotti, *Castelli del Friuli*, 2: 129, 322. Other damage is reported in BCU, MS Joppi 592, doc. dated 10 October 1530.

37. On the geographic position of the castles, see Miotti, *Castelli del Friuli*, 2: 38–46, 79–86, 209–31, 247–51. On Antonio's agents, see doc. in Cormons archive, published in Savini, "Antonio Savorgnan," 305. Nicolò and his brother Giovanni had become two of the closest associates of Antonio Savorgnan and had been rewarded with lucrative posts in Udine city government including the chancellorship of the commune, Giovanni gaining the office only after Antonio Savorgnan pushed his nomination through over the objections of the Udinese notaries. Nicolò Monticolo was appointed podestà of Pordenone by Bartolomeo d'Alviano in 1508; in 1511 he was serving as a deputy of the Udine city council and as chancellor. Giovanni, who had been accused of being the principal instigator of the uprising at Sterpo, followed Savorgnan's every step on Giovedì Grasso and had acted as guardian for Antonio's nephews. On Giovanni Monticolo, see Monticolo, *Descrittione del sacco*, 11; *DU, GA*, 258, 269; *DU, GAH*, 498n, 499, 507, 512, 529, 540; and Savini, "Antonio Savorgnan," 269, 293, 302. On Nicolò Monticolo, see *DU, LA*, 53, 59; *DU, GA*, 238, 270; *DU, GAH*, 498, 523; preface by E. del Torso in Nicolò Monticolo, *Cronaca delle famiglie udinesi*, especially 5–6; and for his election as deputy of Udine on 11 February 1511, BCU, ACU, Annali, reg. 41, fol. 204r.

38. Stories and quote are from Monticolo, *Descrittione del sacco*, 18–19. On Bernardino Pers signing a Strumiero petition against Antonio Savorgnan on 1 January 1510, see *DU, GAH*, 500. An anonymous letter in Sanuto, *I diarii*, 12: 29, reports that at Caporiacco two houses and much of the castle were pillaged. The fates of the castles at Pers and Mels are uncertain. In contrast to Monticolo's assertion that after his departure they were sacked and destroyed, Amaseo merely states that Monticolo defended them and does not list them among the looted castles; *DU, GAH*, 523. A statement in a Colloredo record from later in the century complicates the picture further by implying the structure at Mels had burned sometime before the 1511 lootings. "Si ha anco da sapere che anticamente ne fu abrusciato Mels che e il nostro luogo antico poi del 1509 ne fu abrusciato il castello di sterp et del 1511 fussino sachigiati et abrusciati le case et in udine et

in Colloredo insieme con le scritture"; ASU, AC-M, parte 3, busta 73, dated ca. 1581.

39. On the general jurisdictional problem, see Miotti, *Castelli del Friuli*, 2: 141–46, 279–92; and 4: 7–22. On damage, see *DU*, GAH, 523; Monticolo, *Descrittione del sacco*, 19; Girolama Sini, *Cronaca della terra di S. Daniele dai primi tempi all'anno 1515*, 53; and Archivio di San Daniele, "Tanse e campatico," MS copied in BCU, MS Joppi 592, fol. 8r.

40. On peasants stopping at Buia, see doc. in the Cormons archive published in Savini, "Antonio Savorgnan," 305; Sebastiano Mulioni di Gemona, *Chronicon glemonense dal 1300 al 1517*, 13.

41. On Buia's special juridical situation, see Gian Paolo Gri, "Giurisdizione e vicinia nell'età moderna. Il caso di Buia."

Claims that Zambarlano nobles were also attacked can be found in three sources: Savini, "Antonio Savorgnan," 305; Sanuto, *I diarii*, 12: 28; and Monticolo, *Descrittione del sacco*, 17. However, these claims are not very convincing. Savini lists places in which Antonio sent men to stop the rioting, but a careful examination of each of these locations indicates that in every case Strumiero property alone was damaged or lost. Likewise, the passage in Sanudo is not supported by other evidence: a check of each of the names of persons attacked indicates that all can be identified with Strumiero activities, such as anti-Savorgnan petitions, with the exceptions of Zuan Francesco and Gotardo Parceto, Antonio Andecanis, and two da Portos. The affiliations of these men cannot be determined. Despite the general statements that Monticolo makes, he provides no specific examples of Zambarlani coming under attack.

42. On the castles, see Miotti, *Castelli del Friuli*, 2: 329–36, 3: 113–20. For descriptions of the sackings, see Cergneu, *Cronaca delle guerre friulane*, 4, 47–49; *DU*, GAH, 523; Sanuto, *I diarii*, 12: 29; and Monticolo, *Descrittione del sacco*, 19. On the *decima* of Nimis, see Manzano, *Annali del Friuli*, 7: 84. P. Bertolla discusses the pacification of Cergneu but says that the Udinesi did the pillaging, which seems doubtful given the contemporary reports that locals did it. "Il castello di Cergneu," 150. On Giacomo Castello's position, see *DU*, LA, 157; and *DU*, GAH, 499, 500, 502, 508, 517, 525; Cergneu, *Cronaca delle guerre friulane*, 37, 40–41; Sanuto, *I diarii*, 8: 510, 9: 13, 10: 53, 12: 15; ASV, CD, Misto, reg. 33, fols. 68v–69r; and ASV, Lettere dei condottieri (Savorgnan), busta 308, published in Forgiarini, "Quattro lettere storiche di Antonio Savorgnano," 305, 307. On Chiasse, see Savini, "Antonio Savorgnan," 305; there is no contemporary mention of Prampero, but it is listed among the locations of disturbances in Angelo de Benvenuti, *Inchiesta sugli archivi del Friuli: Archivi comunali*, 37.

43. Sanuto, *I diarii*, 12: 15, 29 (on Porpetto), 5: 632 (on Francesco Strassoldo's defense of castellan prerogatives). The consorts of Strassoldo had been the greatest losers among the castellans when Venice defeated the empire in 1508 because they had held in fief from Maximilian the very castles of Belgrado and Castelnovo which went to Antonio Savorgnan as his reward for service to Venice. On events in Strassoldo and marriage alliances, see *DU*, GAH, 521, 523. On suspicions about Piero Strassoldo, see *DU*, LA, 109. On Federico's Strumiero activities, see *DU*, 232n and BCU, MS 1247. On the castle of Strassoldo, see Miotti, *Castelli del Friuli*,

2: 312–19. On the provveditore's request, see ASV, CCD, Lettere rettori, Udine, busta 169, fol. 67r.

44. On the sacking in Varmo, see Monticolo, *Descrittione del sacco*, 19. On Codroipo, see Sanuto, *I diarii*, 12:31. On Asquinio and Federico Varmo, see ASU, Archivio di Varmo, busta 25, "Artificati relativi alli vantaggi recati alle pubbliche armi contro i tedeschi (anno 1510 e sequenti) dalli consorti di Varmo"; and *DU*, GAH, 499–500.

45. On events, see *DU*, GAH, 499, 524; Monticolo, *Descrittione del sacco*, 19; Roberto de' Signori di Spilimbergo, *Cronaca de' suoi tempi dal 1499 al 1540*, 11. Members of the Spilimbergo consortium made eight separate requests, ranging from 158 to 7,000 ducats, for compensation for damages. Giovanni Antonio said that his father, Tommaso, lost a house in the fire at the castle. Giacomo's widow asked for compensation for loss of a house, furnishings, and food stores. One deposition collected in 1534 came from Francesco Bremasco who was only eleven years old at the time of the troubles. His paternal grandfather, a merchant from Crema, lived in Spilimbergo, and during the night his grandfather, father, and uncle escaped in their nightshirts across the roof tiles. From their shop they lost all their merchandise, grain, wines, furniture, and money. Unlike all other localities, where even Jews were spared, in Spilimbergo merchants suffered alongside the castellans. The total Spilimbergo claim of 22,756 ducats was less than half that of the Della Torre family, but the Della Torre account included the totally destroyed palace in Udine as well as the looting of Villalta. On losses, see Appendix 2; but for some differences in figures, see BCU, MS 693, filze 1, 7, 10, 12, 27, 28, 29, 35, 41. The Bremasco deposition is in filza 18. For the rebuilding of Spilimbergo castle, see Archivio Eredi Irene di Spilimbergo-Spanio, pergamena dated 29 March 1512.

46. Giacomo Spilimbergo was Alvise Della Torre's cousin and the brother-in-law of Giovanni Candido. On Girolamo, Agostino, and Giovanni Leonardo, see *DU*, LA, 101, 116; *DU*, GAH, 500, 502, 505–6, 522, 524, 531n, 535, 541; Sanuto, *I diarii*, 18: 169–70; Leicht, "La difesa del Friuli," 107. On Giovanni Enrico, see Sanuto, *I diarii*, 14: 282; BCU, MS 1247; ASV, CD, Misto, reg. 35, fol. 87v.

47. On Simone, see ASV, LPF, busta 133, entries dated 12 and 18 January 1511 and under the title "Litterarum mandatorum et appelationum, liber primus," 28 February 1511; APS, MS I, 59, dated 21 January 1511. On other exiles, see ASV, Lettere condottieri (Savorgnan), busta 308, published in Forgiarini, "Quattro lettere storiche di Antonio Savorgnano," 308, dated 20 August 1511. On the cultural accomplishments of the clan, see Anne Jacobson Schutte, "Irene di Spilimbergo: The Image of a Creative Woman in Late Renaissance Italy," *Renaissance Quarterly* 44 (1991): 42–61.

48. On Cipernio, see BCU, MS 1530, busta 1. On Giorgio Gradenigo's letter, see Armida Sacchetti, "Un entusiasta di Cividale (Giorgio Gradenigo)," 79n. On the tearing down of houses, see ASV, LPF, busta 134, doc. dated 12 March 1512; for quote, see busta 135, undated doc. after 16 November 1513 and doc. dated 12 June 1512.

49. On the confraternity, see F. C. Carreri, "Del buon governo spilimberghese," *AV* 36 (1888): 329–30. The defense of the citizens' interests against

such exploitation fell largely to immigrants, who characteristically retained their connections with their home communities, had some surplus capital, and owned shops in Spilimbergo, a group that constituted the citizen élite. After the 1511 revolt during which several of these families saw their property looted, they came to monopolize the deputyships and eventually succeeded in partially transforming the violent struggle of the fifteenth and early sixteenth century into one based on negotiation and adjudication. On the citizen élite, see Andreina Stefanutti, "Consorti feudali, 'cittadini' e 'popolani' a Spilimbergo: Spunti per la storia di una società tra XVI e XVII secolo," 95–103.

50. ASV, CCD, Lettere rettori, Pordenone, busta 189, fols. 335r–36r, dated 3 and 4 March 1511.

51. On the castle, see Miotti, *Castelli del Friuli*, 4: 463–73. On Colloredo properties in Zoppola, see ASU, AC-M, parte 1, busta 6, no. 40, fol. 94v. On Panciera and events, see *DU*, GAH, 500, 524, 541 confirmed by ASV, CCD, Lettere rettori, Pordenone, busta 189, fol. 335r. On estimates of losses, see ASV, CD, Misto, reg. 35, fol. 22v; Cergneu, *Cronaca delle guerre friulane*, 59; and BCU, MS 693, filze 2, fol. 42.

52. For castle, see Marino Sanuto, *Itinerario per la terraferma veneziana nell'anno MCCCCLXXXIII*, 131; and Miotti, *Castelli del Friuli*, 4: 115–17. On the Colloredo properties, see ASU, AC-M, parte 1, busta 6, no. 40, fols. 105v–106v, 206v–208r (1509 and 1510, respectively); no. 41, fols. 145v–147r (1512). On the career of Paolo Cusano, see Partenopeo, *La guerra del Friuli*, 48; and ASV, Lettere di condottieri (Savorgnan), busta 308, published in Forgiarini, "Quattro lettere storiche di Antonio Savorgnano," 304. The evidence for the priest's involvement comes from the following story. Several months after the carnival rioting, some of Roberto Cusano's men accosted a knight and notary who had come to the church at Pescincanna, a village just across a little stream from Cusano, to post a decree from the luogotenente about a dispute over the investiture of the presbyter. The *bravi* were about to kill the two officials when Roberto himself intervened and discovered their identities. He excused himself saying, "Pardon me that I did not know who you were or that you had a decree from the signoria. I thought that you were that traitor Father Giacomo who wanted to have them burn my castle." The priest in question, Giacomo di Monselice, officiated at the time in the village of Gruaro and apparently had led the local peasants in the assault on Cusano during the carnival riots. ASV, LPF, busta 133, under the title "Extraordinariorum liber primus," doc. dated 14 June 1511.

53. On Valvasone in general, see Monticolo, *Cronaca delle famiglie udinesi*; Ernesto Degani, "Un comune friulano sotto il Veneto dominio," 193; Vincenzo Joppi, *I signori ed il comune di Valvasone nel secolo XVI: Documenti e note*, 10–12; and Miotti, *Castelli del Friuli*, 4: 441–54. On commitments to Strumieri, see *DU*, GAH, 498–500, 515; ASU, AT, colto 19, pacco 26, fascicolo 7, doc. dated 1479; Sanuto, *I diarii*, 10: 91–92 (on Ippolito Valvasone), 12: 28; Belloni, *De clade Turriana*, 154; Savini, "Antonio Savorgnan," 304; and BCU, MS 693, filza 36. On the Freschi election, see BCU, ACU, Annali, reg. 41, fol. 41, dated 11 February 1511. The most notable commoner, Dr. Ippolito Valvasone, moved among the closest associates of Antonio Savorgnan and, it was said, knew all of his secrets. At Sterpo he

had been one of the leaders of the assault, on a mission to Venice he represented the Savorgnan clique in an attempt to reform the government of Udine, the luogo-tenente arrested him when searching for someone to blame for Giovedì Grasso, and after his release from prison he became involved in a brawl with Agostino Colloredo whose brother had been murdered on Giovedì Grasso. In addition, Dr. Ippolito still maintained contacts and influence in his home town. On Ippolito, see BCU, MS Joppi 592, doc. dated 18 June 1512; and ASV, CCD, Lettere rettori, Udine, busta 169, fol. 104r. The damaged houses were those of Bertoldo, Modesto, and Valentino; Monticolo, *Descrittione del sacco*, 19; and Carreri, *Breve storia di Valvasone*, 48–49. These men or their heirs later made large claims for reparation payments, in Modesto's case for 1,063 ducats and in Valentino's 8,507; BCU, MS 693, filza 2. For the historical opinion, see Degani, "Un comune friulano," 193. On the escape of the consort Valentino, see ASV, CCD, Lettere rettori, Porto-gruaro, busta 190, fol. 9, dated 3 March 1511.

54. On the Valvasone possession of Fratta, see ASU, AT, busta 25, various docs. dated 1503 and 1524; Carreri, *Breve storia di Valvasone*, 20; and Miotti, *Castelli del Friuli*, 4: 131–38. On disturbances in the area, see BCU, MS Joppi 592, fol. xxxvii; Sanuto, *I diarii*, 12: 31; ASV, CCD, Lettere rettori, Udine, busta 169, fol. 66r, dated 5 March 1511.

55. On Canal's information and queries, see ASV, CCD, Lettere rettori, Porto-gruaro, busta 190, fols. 9–10, letters dated 3 and 4 March 1511. On the insult to Venice, see Sanuto, *I diarii*, 12: 14–15, dated 2 March; ASV, CD, Misto (1511), filza 27, fol. 8, letters dated 6 and 7 March; and reg. 34, fol. 4r. The delegates were Dr. Nicolò Monfalcone, Bernardo da Pangai, Marquado Della Frattina, Dario Sbroiavacca, Giacomo dal Torre (cittadino), Giacomo q. Francesco, Dr. Girolamo Salore, Girolamo Vida, ser Boretto, and ser Paolo q. Gasparino (del popolo); BCU, MS Joppi 592, fol. xxxiv (verso).

56. On the castellans and for quote, see *DU*, GAH, 524–25. On the castellan flight, see Sanuto, *I diarii*, 12: 15; and Monticolo, *Descrittione del sacco*, 19–20. On the counts of Porcìa (Porciglie), see *DU*, GAH, 500, 502; and for characterization of their enmity to Antonio Savorgnan, see Sanuto, *I diarii*, 13: 78–79. For additional estimates on the size of forces and number killed, see Cergneu, *Cronaca delle guerre friulane*, 48. For an eyewitness account of the slaughter by one of the castellans, see ASMn, Archivio Gonzaga, busta 1445, fol. 34, dated 12 April 1511. On the return of the consorts of Spilimbergo, see BCU, MS Joppi 592, fol. xxxv.

57. The controversy over Loredan's role failed to abate, and in a June election for the provveditore generale for Friuli, he lost to Alvise Mocenigo. On Loredan's selection and orders, see reg. 34 (1511), fol. 53r and 54v; Sanuto, *I diarii*, 12: 8 and 141. Also see ASV, CCD, Lettere rettori, Udine, busta 169, fol. 66r–67r, 68r, dated 7 March; fol. 69r, dated 8 March; fol. 70r, dated 10 March; and fols. 71r–72r, dated 13 and 15 March. ASV, CD, Misto, filza 27, fols. 20r and 36r; reg. 34, fols. 59v–60r. *DU*, GAH, 526–27. Cf. *DU*, GA, 229; Monticolo, *Descrittione del sacco*, 19; and Sanuto, *I diarii*, 12: 31.

58. For the first quote, see "Se levorno absolerte et senza cause alcuna," Zaccaria Canecini to the Marquis of Mantua, ASMn, Archivio Gonzaga, busta 1445, fol. 34, dated 12 April 1511. The figure of four to five thousand is also in Canecini's

letter. For the second quote, see Monticolo, *Descrittione del sacco*, 17. The view that there were no leaders is repeated by Belloni, *De clade Turriana*, 153 and implied in *DU*, GAH, 523–24. The account of rioters moving from place to place and the estimate for Zoppola come from the provveditore of Pordenone, ASV, CCD, Lettere rettori, Pordenone, busta 189, fol. 335r, dated 3 March 1511; in a similar fashion Valentino da Valvasone came to Portogruaro seeking refuge from the "furia de vilani i quali sono susitati et vano vagabundi per questa patria," ASV, CCD, Lettere rettori, Portogruaro, busta 190, fol. 9. On Porcìa, see Cergneu, *Cronaca delle guerre friulane*, 48.

59. Monticolo, *Descrittione del sacco*, 19–20.

60. On Antonio's orders to peasant leaders, see doc. from Cormons archive published in Savini, "Antonio Savorgnan," 305. Gobet considers the issue of rural leadership in "1511," 140–42. On crowds, see George Rudé, *The Crowd in History: A Study of Popular Disturbances in France and England* (New York: John Wiley and Sons, 1964) and E. P. Thompson "The Moral Economy of the English Crowd in the Eighteenth Century," *Past and Present* 50 (1971): 76–136.

61. On Angela Gorghi, see ASV, LPF, busta 133, under the title "Testes examinati pro requisitione M.ci D. advocatus con Troyanus de Archoloneanis pro morte q. Ser Apolonii del Gorgo Vincentini"; and Sanuto, *I diarii*, 12: 28.

62. During the rebellions in Germany in 1525, peasants also avoided atrocities against persons. Peter Blickle, *The Revolution of 1525: The German Peasants' War from a New Perspective*, trans. Thomas A. Brady and H. C. Erik Midelfort (Baltimore: Johns Hopkins University Press, 1981), 136 and 165.

Chapter 6: The Problem of Meaning

1. For discussions of causes of the disturbances, see Pier Silverio Leicht, "Un movimento agrario nel Cinquecento"; Dionisio Tassini, "La rivolta del Friuli nel 1511 durante la guerra contro i tedeschi," 145–46; Angelo Ventura, *Nobiltà e popolo nella società veneta del '400 e '500*, 172–209; Andreina Stefanutti, "Maniago nell'età moderna e contemporanea: Linee e tempi di una ricerca storica," 76; Sergio Gobet, "1511: Agitazioni contadine nelle campagne del Friuli," 89–90; idem, "La rivolta contadina del 1511 in Friuli: Le cause e gli avvenimenti"; and Luisa Accati, "La rivolta contadina del 1511: Una possible lettura." Accati emphasizes the importance of community over class identity and pursues a systematic comparison of the violence in Udine with the findings in Emmanuel Le Roy Ladurie, *Carnival in Romans*. Petitions for exemptions from *gravezze* and the payments of debts escalated in January 1511, testifying to the dramatic fiscal crisis that immediately preceded the Giovedì Grasso uprising. Because of crop damage from storms and plunderings, the inhabitants of Muscletto near Belgrado, Madrisio, Canussio, S. Leonardo, Ontegnano, and Pavia were allowed a reprieve on the collection of private debts, usually for six months; ASV, LPF, busta 133, under the title "Extraordinariorum liber primus," dated 5, 10, 11, 14, 18, and 21 January. For examples of individuals receiving debt relief after the sackings, see docs. dated 14 March and 8, 11, and 12 April.

The theme of a class-based revolt, which even had overtones of a socialist revolution, is strongest in the writings of Ernesto Degani, *I partiti in Friuli nel 1500 e la storia di un famoso duello*; and V. Marchese, "Il Friuli al tempo della Lega di Cambrai," especially 525. The inspiration for envisioning premodern society in terms of communities comes from Yves-Marie Bercé, *Histoire des Croquants: Étude des soulèvements populaires dans le Sud-Ouest de la France*, 2 vols. (Geneva: Droz, 1974) and (Paris: Seuil, 1986); idem, *Fêtes et révolte: Des mentalités populaires du XVIe au XVIIIe siécle* (Paris: Hachette, 1976); and René Pillorget, *Les mouvements insurrectionnels de Provence entre 1596 et 1715* (Paris: A. Pedone, 1975). For Italy, see Giovanni Levi, introduction to "Villaggi: Studi di antropologia storica," *QS* 46 (1981): 7–10; and idem, *Inheriting Power: The Story of an Exorcist*. Local solidarity rather than patronage networks among communities characterized the feuding in a Ligurian coastal area. See Edoardo Grendi, "The Political System of a Community in Liguria: Cervo in the Late Sixteenth and Early Seventeenth Centuries," in *Microhistory and the Lost Peoples of Europe*, ed. Edward Muir and Guido Ruggiero, 119–58; originally published as "Il sistema politico di una comunità ligure: Cervo fra Cinquecento e Seicento," *QS* 46 (1981): 92–129. Community solidarity was likewise important in nineteenth-century Corsica. See Stephen Wilson, *Feuding, Conflict, and Banditry in Nineteenth-Century Corsica*, 164–65. Cf. Accati, "La rivolta contadina del 1511," 131–32. Even in a city with a highly articulated civic ethos such as Florence, neighborhoods remained an important if not the most important source of collective identity; see Gene Brucker, *The Civic World of Early Renaissance Florence* (Princeton: Princeton University Press, 1977), 311; Dale Kent, *The Rise of the Medici: Faction in Florence, 1426–34* (Oxford: Oxford University Press, 1978), 62; Ronald F. E. Weissman, *Ritual Brotherhood in Renaissance Florence* (New York: Academic Press, 1982), 20–21; and Samuel Kline Cohn, Jr., *The Laboring Classes in Renaissance Florence* (New York: Academic Press, 1980), 87–88, 198–99 and passim. Le Roy Ladurie notes that in early modern towns "in the vast middle ground of cases a simple conflict between two powerful clans degenerated into a combat between the ruling oligarchy and sections of the masses, each supporting one of the rival clans." *Carnival in Romans*, 189–90.

2. On Belluno, see P. S. Leicht, "Un movimento agrario nel Cinquecento," 7–8. The absence of religious content was also noticed by Gaetano Perusini, *Vita di popolo in Friuli: Patti agrari e consuetudini tradizionali*, xx (note). Statements about a revolution include, "la plebe che sempre desiderano cose novitatis," in a letter from Andrea Loredan in ASV, CCD, Lettere rettori, Portogruaro, busta 190, fol. 11; "nele revolution de quella Patria," in a letter from Piero Boldù, ASV, LPF, busta 134, under the title "Litterarum liber primus"; "revolution di cieli," in ASV, Senato, Terra, reg. 18, fol. 166v; and "per la Revolution di tempi," reg. 19, fol. 18r.

3. The literature on carnival in Renaissance Europe is now quite vast. The best recent guide to the issues raised by carnival studies is Samuel Kinser, *Rabelais's Carnival: Text, Context, Metatext*; on the fight between the Fat and the Lean, see 50–53.

4. On rites of violence, see Natalie Zemon Davis, "The Rites of Violence," 186–87; and Michael D. Bristol, *Carnival and Theater: Plebeian Culture and the*

Structure of Authority in Renaissance England, 34. On crowd behavior, see E. P. Thompson, "Time, Work-Discipline, and Industrial Capitalism," *Past and Present* 38 (1967): 56–97; idem, "The Moral Economy of the English Crowd in the Eighteenth Century"; Mark Harrison, "Time, Work, and the Occurrence of Crowds 1790–1835," *Past and Present* 110 (1986): 134–68; and the Bologna Seminar coordinated by Carlo Ginzburg, "Ritual Pillages: A Preface to Research in Progress," in *Microhistory and the Lost Peoples of Europe*, ed. Muir and Ruggiero, 20–41; originally published as "Saccheggi rituali: Premesse a una ricerca in corso," *QS* 65 (1987): 615–36.

5. On miming and identity, see Richard C. Trexler, ed., "Introduction," in *Persons in Groups: Social Behavior as Identity Formation in Medieval and Renaissance Europe*, 16. On hand signs, see François Rabelais, *The Histories of Gargantua and Pantagruel*, trans. J. M. Cohen (New York: Penguin, 1955), 2.7, 2.9, 2.10-13, 2.18-19, and 3.19-20.

6. On the symbolic grammar of meat, see Le Roy Ladurie, *Carnival in Romans*, 301-2, 317–18.

7. Mikhail Bakhtin, *Rabelais and His World*, passim, but especially 278–302. Among the many commentaries on Bakhtin, particularly useful is Peter Stallybrass and Allon White, *The Poetics and Politics of Transgression*, 1–19. Following the reasoning of Bakhtin, Michael Bristol argues that "the most intangible 'semiotic material' of Carnival is the organization of the festive crowd itself"; *Carnival and Theater*, 57–58.

8. On the problem of the social function of carnival in general, see Peter Burke, *Popular Culture in Early Modern Europe*, 199–204. On Nuremberg, see Samuel Leslie Sumberg, *The Nuremberg Schembart Carnival* (New York: Columbia University Press, 1941), 26–33 (31 for quote), a study now replaced by Samuel Kinser, "Presentation and Representation: Carnival at Nuremberg, 1450–1550."

9. On Ruzante, see Linda L. Carroll, "Carnival Rites as Vehicles of Protest in Renaissance Venice," *Sixteenth Century Journal* 16 (1985): 487–502.

10. Cf. René Girard, *Violence and the Sacred*, 37, 125, 306. On the importance of shrines, see Lionel Rothkrug, "Holy Shrines, Religious Dissonance and Satan in the Origins of the German Reformation," *Historical Reflections* 14 (1987): 143–286; and idem, "German Holiness and Western Sanctity in Medieval and Modern History," *Historical Reflections* 15 (1988): 161–249. On hats as insignia, see Samuel Y. Edgerton, Jr., *Pictures and Punishment: Art and Criminal Prosecution during the Florentine Renaissance*, 65n. On flags, see Richard C. Trexler, "Follow the Flag: The Ciompi Revolt Seen from the Streets," *Bibliothèque d'Humanisme et Renaissance* 46 (1984): 357–92; and on insults, see idem, "Correre la terra: Collective Insults in the Late Middle Ages." For quote, see Luigi da Porto, *Lettere storiche dall'anno 1509 al 1528*, 279. On traditions of popular participation in official justice which made the imitation of official procedures seem quite natural, see Orest Ranum, "The French Ritual of Tyrannicide in the Late Sixteenth Century." Elias Canetti links public executions themselves with earlier forms of collective killing. *Crowds and Power*, 50.

11. For specific examples of the disposition of corpses, see *DU, LA*, 227–28; *DU, GAH*, 514, 516–20; Nicolò Monticolo, *Descrittione del sacco MDXI seguito in*

Udine il giovedì XXVII febbraio, 21. On the denial of burial in general, see Gabriel Maugain, *Moeurs italiennes de la Renaissance: La vengeance*, 136–37. On the body as the source of honor, see Pierre Bourdieu, *Outline of a Theory of Practice*, 14–15.

12. On the linking of bodily dismemberment and the dissolution of society, see Bakhtin, *Rabelais and His World*, 351. Cf. Leonard Barkan, *Nature's Work of Art: The Human Body as Image of the World* (New Haven: Yale University Press, 1975).

13. E. A. R. Brown, "Death and the Human Body in the Later Middle Ages: The Legislation of Boniface VIII on the Division of the Corpse," *Viator: Medieval and Renaissance Studies* 12 (1981): 221–70; Giovanna Ferrari, "Public Anatomy Lessons and the Carnival: The Anatomy Theatre of Bologna," *Past and Present* 117 (1987): 50–106. The torture of the corpse of a murderer appears as a frequent theme in Renaissance *novelle*. See Dominic Peter Rotunda, *Motif-Index of the Italian Novella in Prose*, motif no. Q491.6, entry nos. 4, 18, and 28. In the deposition ritual of King Henry IV of Castile at a time when the actual body was unavailable, an effigy was degraded in place of the corpse. See Angus MacKay, "Ritual and Propaganda in Fifteenth-Century Castile," *Past and Present* 107 (1985): 3–43. In Scotland feudists mutilated the bodies of the dead, and as a reminder of the need to avenge the death relatives might not bury the dead man. Keith M. Brown, *Bloodfeud in Scotland, 1573–1625: Violence, Justice and Politics in an Early Modern Society*, 30–32. Natalie Zemon Davis notes that desecration of corpses was more characteristic of Catholic than of Protestant crowds; see "Rites of Violence," 179. In the American South during the colonial period combatants usually tried to sever some of the body parts of the opponent. Elliott J. Gorn, "'Gouge and Bite, Pull Hair and Scratch': The Social Significance of Fighting in the Southern Backcountry." In nineteenth-century Corsican feuding, dismemberment and mutilation of victims were common; see Wilson, *Feuding*, 32, 35, 36, 47, 405–9. Disfigurement of enemies remained common in the Balkans well into this century. Christopher Boehm, *Blood Revenge: The Anthropology of Feuding in Montenegro and Other Tribal Societies*, 80. In Bologna in 1926 Fascist *squadristi* lynched and dismembered the body of a sixteen-year-old boy alleged to have attempted to assassinate Mussolini; see Denis Mack Smith, *Mussolini: A Biography* (New York: Knopf, 1982), 144.

14. For the first quote, "Qual di fatto tolto de mezzo, fo morto e strazzato da piu ferite per tal che se li vedeva tutti l'anteriori, che li sono manzati da cani, non permettendo il fosse sepulto"; see *DU, GA*, 517. "Et miseramente la notte mangiato da' cani," see Monticolo, *Descrittione del sacco*, 16. "La mattina seguente in Porta di Ronco fu morto Federico di Colloreto, e tanto ivi ignudo lassato, che li cani e porci ne magnò, alcuno darli sepoltura non audendo," see Giovanni Battista di Cergneu, *Cronaca delle guerre friulane coi germani dal 1507 al 1524*, 46. "Et fo morto et manzato da' cani quella notte, quasi tutto, sier Federigo da Coloreto," see Marino Sanuto, *I diarii*, 12: 28. "I capi dei nobili non furono sepolti, ma si lasciarono pasto ai cani ed ai porci," see Pompeo Litta, "Il giovedì grasso di Udine . . . ," BCU, MS Joppi 67, no. 15, fol. 218r. For the quote from the 1490 ordinance, "Canes et alia animalia non possint intrare in eo loco ad comedendum sanguinem humanum," see Antonio Battistella, "Udine nel secolo XVI: L'ordinamento interno della città," 184; on the 1520 edict, see idem, "Udine nel secolo XVI: L'edilizia, l'igiene e la polizia urbana," 26–28.

15. On "millennial antinomianism," see Bruce Lincoln, *Discourse and the Construction of Society: Comparative Studies of Myth, Ritual, and Classification* (New York: Oxford University Press, 1989), 114–17.

16. On the *benandanti*, see Carlo Ginzburg, *The Night Battles: Witchcraft and Agrarian Cults in the Sixteenth and Seventeenth Centuries*. On the Corsican *mazzeri* and the specific connection between such beliefs about the dead and vengeance, I am indebted to Wilson, *Feuding*, 377–414.

17. On the scapegoat mechanism, see René Girard, "Generative Scapegoating," 91. Also see idem, "Violence and Representation," in *"To Double Business Bound"*; idem, *Violence and the Sacred*; and idem, *Job: The Victim of His People*. The killers of Giovedì Grasso formed a collectivity that made them similar to Canetti's "baiting crowd"; *Crowds and Power*, 48–50. On the problem of criminal behavior as a form of self-help, see Donald Black, "Crime as Social Control," *American Sociological Review* 48 (1983): 34–45 and James C. Scott, *Weapons of the Weak: Everyday Forms of Peasant Resistance*.

18. On the delegation consisting of Francesco Janis di Tolmezzo, Pietro Corbello, Nicolò Cainer, and Giovanni Fagagna, see *DU*, GAH, 528–31 and BCU, ACU, Annali, reg. 41, fols. 214r–215v. On reports about the delegation's presentation in Venice, see Sanuto, *I diarii*, 12: 104, 109. On the investigation and arrest warrants, see ASV, CCD, Lettere, filza 14, fol. 95r, dated 14 May and filza 13, fol. 112r, dated 30 May; ASV, CD, Parti criminali, reg. 1, fol. 168v, dated 30 May and fol. 172v, dated 8 June, warrants repeated in reg. 2, fols. 151r, dated 9 August 1515 and 163r, dated 25 February 1515 (*m.v.*); ASV, LPF, busta 133, under the title "Extraordinariorum liber primus" dated 13 and 14 June; ASU, Archivio consorti di Spilimbergo, dispensa dated 13 June; APS, MS I, 61, dated 13 June. Witnesses kept in Venice were let go on 16 June; ASV, CD, Misto, reg. 35, fol. 90v and ASV, CCD, Lettere, filza 14, fol. 144r. On imprisonments, see ASV, LPF, Processi ed investiture, filza 133, under the title "Carceratorum liber," entries dated 14, 17, 24 March, 29 April, 18 May, 1 June, and 14 June. After four years in prison, Simone Scraiber and the Ferrarese were executed on 9 August 1515; Sanuto, *I diarii*, 20: 477.

Unfortunately, none of the records of the preliminary investigations or the trials themselves has survived. Only the sentences are extant. Gobet searched the ASV, ASU, and BSU and found only the fragmentary evidence cited above and copies of the sentences in ASU, AT. He did discover records of two inquests related to the sacking of Udine, one on the murder of Apollonio del Gorgo Vicentino (ASV, LPF, busta 133, "Testes examinati pro requisitione m.ci d. advocati contra Troyanum de Archoloneanis pro morte q. ser Apolonii del Gorgo Vincentini," dated 30 May, 12 and 13 June 1511) and the other on the theft of money from Leonardo Guberti (ASV, LPF, busta 133, n.p., "Testes m. Leonardi Guberti medici pro pecuniis sibi acceptis," dated 13–21 March 1511). There are also contradictory clues about the fate of the Savorgnan familiar, Tempesta, one of those exiled *in absentia*. One source states that he was arrested and drawn and quartered in Feltre (Cergneu, *Cronaca delle guerre friulane*, 50), and another says that he was executed in Rome (*DU*, GAH, 531, repeated in Marzio Colloredo, *Risposta del Sig. Martio Colloreto, a tre manifesti de' signori Savorgnani*, 265, 271–72). However, I was unable to find any record of a trial or execution in Rome. On Gobet's efforts, "1511," 1: 102, 105–6, 116–18n, 267–68.

19. *DU, GAH*, 512 (for quote about Antonio's anger), 528–29 (for partisanship of the deputies). On the role of client-brokers, see Eduardo Grendi, "Microanalisi e storia sociale," *QS* 35 (1977): 512–13.

20. On slurs against Savorgnan, see *DU, GAH*, 505, 507, 523, 527, and 529 for quote. Cf. Cergneu, *Cronaca delle guerre friulane*, 36. On the charge that Venice encouraged Savorgnan, see Agostino di Colloredo, "Chroniche friulane, 1508–18," 5–6. The evidence for this accusation is analyzed and partially accepted in V. Marchesi, "Friuli al tempo della Lega di Cambrai," *NAV*, n.s., 6 (1903): 521–24. For more balanced views that generally absolve Savorgnan of major responsibility, see Fabia Savini, "Antonio Savorgnan," *MSF* 27–29 (1931–33): 284–85; Liliana Cargnelluti, "Antonio Savorgnan e l'insurrezione del 1511," 123n, 125n; and Amelio Tagliaferri, *Udine nella storia economica*, 51.

21. On the compensation issue, see Cargnelluti, "Antonio Savorgnan," 123–25. Cf. ASU, AT, cartella 19, colto 26, fascicolo 3, docs. dated 30 April and 5 May 1530. I have used the following estimates and inventories of damages, all apparently prepared between 1530 and 1534: an undated single page summary in BCU, MS 693, filza 2, and related documents in filze 1, 3, 9, 25, 30, 31, and 42; a comprehensive list of claimants giving the amount requested and the amount awarded in a manuscript copied from the "Sentenze" in the *Atti* of Antonio Belloni, notary of Udine, 30 June 1534 (see Appendix 2) and numerous related docs. in BCU, MS Joppi 592; ASU, AT, buste 19 and 33; and ASU, Archivio della Porta, busta 8, fasc. 9, doc. titled, "Danni subiti dai Torriani nel Giovedì Grasso 1511."

22. On complaints about Savorgnan failures to pay, see BCU, MS 1247, doc. dated 13 January 1532. Some payments were made in 1546 and 1547; see ASU, AS, busta 7, fascicolo 4, docs. dated 10 and 14 January 1546 and 17 January 1547. Della Torre heirs were complaining about the inadequacy of their compensation as late as 1556; see ASU, AT, cartella 19, colto 26, fascicolo 3.

23. ASU, AT, cartella 19, colto 26, fascicoli 3 and 6; ASU, Archivio della Porta, busta 8, fascicolo 9.

24. On Machiavelli and Guicciardini, see Ottavia Niccoli, *Prophecy and People in Renaissance Italy*, xiii–xiv, originally published as *Profeti e popolo nell'Italia del Rinascimento* (Bari: Laterza, 1987). On apparitions as projections see Chapter 3; and idem, "The Kings of the Dead on the Battlefield of Agnadello," in *Microhistory and the Lost Peoples of Europe*, ed. Muir and Ruggiero, 72, originally published as "Il re dei morti sul campo di Agnadello." Also see Ottavia Niccoli, "The End of Prophecy."

25. On the proclamation, see ASV, LPF, filza 133, "Extraordinarium liber primus," dated 29 March 1511. On Venetian concerns in general, see Renzo Derosas, "Moralità e giustizia a Venezia nel '500-'600: Gli Esecutori contro la Bestemmia," in *Stato, società e giustizi a nella Repubblica Veneta (sec. XV–XVIII)*, ed. Gaetano Cozzi, 1: 431–528. The increase in antiblasphemy decrees during the war years can be traced in ASV, CD, Proclami, filza 1. Worries about blasphemy appear in apparitions from this period. Niccoli, "The End of Prophecy," 669, 672.

26. On prodigies of 1508, Giovanni Partenopeo, *La guerra del Friuli contro i te-*

deschi (1508–13), 5–6. For prognostications about 1509, see Linda L. Carroll, "Giorgione's *Tempest*: Astrology is in the Eyes of the Beholder." On prophecies in Venice, see Sanuto, *I diarii*, 8: 326; and Jean Lemaire de Belges, *La légende des Vénitiens*, 361–64. For the 1511 Bologna pamphlet, see *Memoria delli novi segni e spaventevoli prodigii comparsi in più loci de Italia et in varie parte del mondo lanno mille cinquecento undese* (Bologna, 1511?). Cf. Niccoli, *Prophecy and People*, 23–25; on Friulan collectors of prophecies, 10-11.

27. *DU, GAH*, 513 (quote on constellation), 518, 522 (quote on justice), and 527 (quote on pillar of fire). The apparition of angels is also reported in Sanuto, *I diarii*, 12: 105; as is the peasant girl's vision, 107-9. Also see Niccoli, "The End of Prophecy," 669–70. Quote from Porcìa is cited in Marchesi, "Friuli al tempo della Lega di Cambrai," 520n.

For evil portents on the eve of the siege of Osoppo in 1514, see Sebastiano Mantica, *Diario di Pordenone febbraio MDXIV*, ed. Giuseppe Valentinelli (Venice, 1862). For Friulan interpretations of the famous astrologic predictions of disaster in 1524, see Cergneu, *Cronaca delle guerre friulane*, 74–75; and Niccoli, *Prophecy and People*, 152–59.

28. For firsthand reports on damage, see Sanuto, *I diarii*, 12: 79–86 (on sodomy explanation), 90–91 (on bishop's procession), 108; and Monticolo, *Descrittione del sacco*, 20; BCU, ACU, Annali, reg. 41, fol. 212v; and BCU, MS 715, pezzo 5, "Memoria estratta dal protocollo del notaio Roberto da Latisana esistente nell'Archivio Notarile di Udine."

29. For quote, see Cergneu, *Cronaca delle guerre friulane*, 51. For similar opinions, see Partenopeo, *La guerra del Friuli*, 76–77 and *DU, GAH*, 528, 533. For Zambarlano views, see da Porto, *Lettere storiche*, 283.

30. On the course of the plague, see BCU, ACU, Annali, reg. 41, fols. 183, 187, 189, 193v, 213v, 219v, 220r; ASV, LPF, busta 133, under the title "Extraordinarior. Liber primus," entry dated 7 August 1511; BCU, MS Joppi 689d, vol. 4, filza 8, doc. dated 17 August 1511; Sanuto, *I diarii*, 12: 242, 243, 263, 293, 347; and *DU*, xxv–xxvi. On interpretations of plague, see *DU, GAH*, 532–34 (533 for quote and 543 for list of scourges). There is some evidence that Jews were also blamed. See Pier Cesare Ioly Zorattini, "Aspetti e problemi dei nuclei ebraici in Friuli durante la dominazione veneziana," in *Atti del Convegno*, 230. On the social interpretations of plague, see Giulia Calvi, "Una metafora degli scambi sociali: La peste fiorentina del 1630," *QS* 55 (1984): 35–64; idem, *Histories of a Plague Year: The Social and the Imaginary in Baroque Florence*, trans. Dario Biocca and Bryant T. Ragin (Berkeley and Los Angeles: University of California Press, 1989); and Ann G. Carmichael, *Plague and the Poor in Renaissance Florence*, Cambridge History of Medicine (Cambridge, United Kingdom: Cambridge University Press, 1986), 108–26.

31. Cf. Northrop Frye, *A Natural Perspective: The Development of Shakespearean Comedy and Romance* (New York: Columbia University Press, 1965), 361; Susan Jacoby, *Wild Justice: The Evolutions of Revenge*, 1; and Renato Rosaldo, *Ilongot Headhunting, 1883–1974: A Study in Society and History*, passim.

32. On Icelandic feud sagas, see Jesse Bycock, *Feud in the Icelandic Saga*, 25–28, 47–62, and passim. On mnemonic devices, see Jacob Black-Michaud, *Cohesive*

Force: Feud in the Mediterranean and the Middle East, 78–80; Boehm, *Blood Revenge*, 60–63; and Wilson, *Feuding*, 42, 400–402.

33. On stories in Basilicata, see Carlo Levi, *Christ Stopped at Eboli* (New York: Farrar, Straus and Giroux, 1982), 24–27. Although I am not employing his terminology, I accept the distinctions made by Mark Phillips: "It is basic to a number of critical programmes that we should distinguish between 'story' and 'discourse,' where 'story' is the underlying or pre-existing set of events, as distinct from the order of the telling, which is 'discourse.' In many cases, of course, especially in traditional narratives, the two orders will lie parallel and the order of telling will mime the order of the story. But there is no necessity that this be so and the tension between the two may well be a major feature of a given narrative." "The Revival of Narrative: Thoughts on a Current Historiographical Debate," *University of Toronto Quarterly* 53 (1983–84): 149–65.

34. For a general discussion of family records, see Peter Burke, *The Historical Anthropology of Early Modern Italy*, 116–20. On Florentine *ricordanze*, see Philip J. Jones, "Florentine Families and Florentine Diaries in the Fourteenth Century," in *Studies in Italian Medieval History Presented to Miss E. M. Jamison*, ed. Philip Grierson and John Ward Perkins, Papers of the British School at Rome, no. 24, n.s., vol. 11 (London: The British School, 1956); David Herlihy and Christiane Klapisch-Zuber, *Les Toscans et leurs familles: Une étude du catasto florentine de 1427* (Paris: Press de la fondation nationale des sciences politiques, 1978), passim. For the English translation, which is somewhat abridged, see *Tuscans and their Families: A Study of the Florentine Catasto of 1427* (New Haven: Yale University Press, 1985). Also see, Christiane Klapisch-Zuber, *Women, Family, and Ritual in Renaissance Italy*, trans. Lydia Cochrane (Chicago: The University of Chicago Press, 1985), 69–93 and passim. On vendetta obligations in Florentine *ricordanze*, see Marvin B. Becker, *Civility and Society in Western Europe, 1300–1600*, xvii–xix, 13, 94, 96. Cf. idem, "Changing Patterns of Violence and Justice in Fourteenth- and Fifteenth-Century Florence," *Comparative Studies in Society and History* 18 (1976): 281–96. For an example of a Friulan rent-roll that is similar to a Florentine *ricordanza*, see Pamphilo Valvasone, "Rotolo de li fitti," BSU, Archivio Capitolare, Raccolta Bini, Misc., 19: 133–50.

35. The nine narrations are Amaseo, *Historia della crudel Zobia Grassa* (see abbreviations, *DU*, *GAH*); Cergneu, *Cronaca delle guerre friulane*; Partenopeo, *La guerra del Friuli*; Antonio Belloni, *De clade Turriana*; Monticolo, *Descrittione del sacco*; Sebastiano Decio and Roberto da Latisana, BCU, MS Joppi 66; Sanuto, *I diarii*, 12: 5–6, 17–19, and passim; and da Porto, *Lettere storiche*. Based primarily on the letters sent to Venetian councils, the entries in Sanudo's *I diarii* comprise the best version of the episode from the Venetian point of view. Sanudo himself never wrote a separate account, but he did turn his diaries over to Pietro Bembo to be used as a source for his official history of the war period. Bembo's protégé, Luigi da Porto, recalled various things he had witnessed in Udine in 1511 in his *Lettere storiche* and carried the emotional burdens of his memories into his *novella* of *Giulietta e Romeo*. Leopold von Ranke had a manuscript copy of the Amaseo history in his private collection, which is now in the Syracuse University Library, Syracuse, New York, Leopold von Ranke Collection, MS 368. See Edward Muir, *The*

Leopold von Ranke Manuscript Collection of Syracuse University: The Complete Catalogue (Syracuse: Syracuse University Press, 1983), 234.

36. On the Amaseo family, see Ventura, *Nobiltà e popolo*, 200–203; *DU*, xxxv (note), lxxx–lxxxi (note), *DU*, GAH, 511 (for second quote), 526 (for first quote).

37. On godparents, see *DU*, xiv–xxv. On the break, see *DU*, LA, 178–81. On Gregorio's blocked election as delegate, see BCU, ACU, Annali, reg. 41, fols. 176v–177r.

38. Girolamo's book is the *Vaticinium quo praedicitur universum orbem terrarum christianae religionis imperium subiturum* (Venice: Aldo Manuzio, 1499). See *Dizionari biografico degli Italiani*, s.v. "Amaseo, Girolamo." On his teaching career, see BCU, ACU, Annali, reg. 41, fol. 64r; and Carlo Ginzburg, *The Cheese and the Worms: The Cosmos of a Sixteenth-Century Miller*, 31.

39. On Gregorio's career, see *Dizionario biografico degli Italiani*, s.v., "Amaseo, Gregorio"; and *DU*, xxvii, xliii. On his capture, see *DU*, LA, 75–76. On his appointment as lecturer in Udine, see MCV, Cod. Cicogna 2848, fol. 4r. On his competition for the post in Venice, see Sanuto, *I diarii*, 13: 406, 486. His commentary was coauthored with Giovanni Candido, *Commentariorum Aquileiansium libri octo* (Venice: Allesandro Bindoni, 1521). Cf. Italian version, Candido, *Commentari dei fatti d'Aquileja*.

40. On date of writing of the *History*, see Ventura, *Nobiltà e popolo*, 204n. On reactions to it, see *DU*, GA, 235 (for quote, "in large part"), 257–58, and 269 (for quotes, "so that I could" and "if ever one needs"). On the Della Torre eulogy, see *DU*, li–lii. Gregorio also reported threats to his life from his own nephew, Leonardo's son, who wanted to inherit the property Gregorio had retained from the patrimony shared with his dead brother. *DU*, GA, 250–51, 266–69. There is no way of knowing how accurate these self-serving reports of threats to his life are, but Gregorio is always careful to detail how he heard about them. Although I was unable to make a direct comparison between the two documents, the anonymous "Historia de Guelfi e Ghibellini" in the BSU, Archivio Capitolare, Raccolta Bini, Miscellanea, 5: 139–256 appears to be a polished, Tuscanized version of Amaseo's *Historia*. Gabriel Maugain discusses how humanist studies could inspire and help justify revenge; see *Moeurs italiennes de la Renaissance: La vengeance*, 83–108.

41. Cergneu, *Cronaca delle guerre friulane*, 48–50; Emilio Candido, *Commentarii de i fatti d'Aquileja*, 93v and 96v (for quote); *DU*, GA, 228; and Andrea Mocenigo, *La guerra di Cambrai fatta a'tempi nostri in Italia*, 87v.

Chapter 7: Retaliations and Realignments

1. On the military situation, Marino Sanuto, *I diarii*, 12: 245, 261–62, 347, 395–96; ASMn, Archivio Gonzaga, busta 1445, fol. 11, dated 19 June, and fol. 14, dated 23 June; Andrea Ziliolo, "Cronaca," BMV, It. VII, 328 (8513), fol. 81v; and ASV, Senato, Terra, reg. 17, fol. 102v, dated 28 August. During one of the skirmishes, Luigi da Porto received a severe neck wound that left him an invalid for life; see Luigi da Porto, *Lettere storiche dall'anno 1509 al 1528*, 243–46, dated 15 July. On Antonio Savorgnan, ASU, AS, busta 203, doc. dated 13 August; BCU, MS Joppi 689c, docs. dated 11 and 30 August published in Fabia Savini, "Antonio

Savorgnan," *MSF* 27–29 (1931–33): 297–300; BCU, MS Joppi 592, vol. 29, p. 389, dated 17 September; and ASV, CCD, Lettere, filza 13, fol. 316.

2. For the course of events, see Sanuto, *I diarii*, 12: 452, 455, 457, 459, 467, 488–90, 495, 500–506, 516–20, 522, 523, 525, 528, 530, 534–35, 544, 548, 551–52, 554–60, 565–66, 572, 578, 581–83, 587, 594, 616–18, 622–23; 13: 6, 11–13, 70, 236–37; *DU*, GAH, 535–38; Andrea Ziliolo, "Cronaca," BMV, It. VII, 328 (8513), fols. 85v–87r; ASV, CCD, Lettere, filza 13, fol. 395r, letter to Antonio Savorgnan dated 19 September; ASV, CD, Criminali, reg. 1, fol. 178v, dated 22 September; ASV, CD, Misto, reg. 34, fol. 153r, dated 3 November; and Savini, "Antonio Savorgnan," 286–88. On the dilemmas that the Friulans faced during the invasion, see A. Benedetti, "Le turbinose giornate dell'autunno 1511 a San Vito al Tagliamento," *MSF* 43 (1958–59): 193–213. On motives of castellans in capitulating, see Giovanni Battista di Cergneu, *Cronaca delle guerre friulane coi germani dal 1507 al 1524*, 53–54. On the capture of Spilimbergo by exiles, see ASV, CCD, Lettere di condottieri (Savorgnan), busta 308, letter from Antonio Savorgnan dated 20 August in Fagagna; ASV, CCD, Lettere rettori, Provveditore generale in terraferma, busta 297, letters dated 7, 12, 27 July and 20 August; ASV, CD, Misto, 1511, filza 27, fol. 163 and reg. 34, fol. 100. For the reward Maximilian offered Antonio for his defection, see ASU, AS, busta 72, pergamena 133, dated 15 October. For explanations of Antonio's capitulation, see da Porto, *Lettere storiche*, 271–83; Giovanni Partenopeo, *La guerra del Friuli contro i tedeschi (1508–13)*, 72–74; Pier Silverio Leicht, "Aneddoti sul Friuli al tempo della Lega di Cambray," 184; and Liliana Cargnelluti, "Antonio Savorgnan e l'insurrezione del 1511," 123. For a list of those who cooperated with Antonio in his surrendering of Udine, see BCU, MS Joppi 592, fols. xxix–xxx.

3. ASV, CCD, Lettere, filza 13, fol. 396r, letter to Girolamo Savorgnan dated 19 September and his letters to the Council of Ten in Girolamo Savorgnan, "Lettere sulla guerra combattuta nel Friuli dal 1510 al 1528 scritte alla signoria di Venizia," 13–14, 17–18, 25–26; Partenopeo, *La guerra del Friuli*, 78–79; and Sanuto, *I diarii*, 12: 572, 576–77. The Amaseo brothers had taken refuge from the plague at Osoppo and witnessed Girolamo's activities during these critical days; *DU*, GA, 230; and *DU*, GAH, 538–39.

4. On provisions to punish Antonio Savorgnan, see ASV, CD, Parti criminali, reg. 1, fols. 168v, 178v, 213v–214r; for the assassination contract, see ASV, CD, Secreta, Secretissima, 1r. On the Council of Ten and assassinations, see Dennis Romano, "The Aftermath of the Querini-Tiepolo Conspiracy in Venice." For the names of those who adhered to the contract, see *DU*, GA, 231–32n.

5. On the political fallout in Venice, see Sanuto, *I diarii*, 12: 534, 550, 565, 607, 610; 13: 75, 199, 227, 248, 360, 486; 15: 144. Cf. Robert Finlay, *Politics in Renaissance Venice*, 62–63.

6. On the conditions for imperial armies in Friuli, Haus-, Hof- und Staats Archiv, Vienna, Maximiliana, fasc. 19b, dated 18 October, published in Attilo Tamaro, "Documenti inediti di storia triestina (1298–1544)," *Archeografo triestino* 43 (1929–30): 75–76. On attempts at taxation, see Cergneu, *Cronaca delle guerre friulane*, 54–55. On the German withdrawal and Antonio's attempts to return, see *DU*, GAH, 539–41; Sanuto, *I diarii*, 13: 120, 165, 170, 179, 187, 193, 197, 208,

210–11, 217–19, 223, 227–28, 231–32, 360, 380, 386, 388, 395–96, and 416; ASV, CCD, Lettere, filza 13, fols. 502r (5 December), 512r (12 December), 522r (19 December); ASV, CD, Criminali, reg. 1, fols. 185v, 220v; ASV, CD, Misto, reg. 34, fol. 161v; ASV, Senato, Terra, reg. 17, fol. 120v–21r. For inventory of confiscated Savorgnan properties, see BCU, MS Joppi 2, "Atti e memorie Savorgnane," 1: 5v–6r, 12v–13r, 93r; 2: 3r, 45r, 174r–76v. On evidence of continuing support for Antonio, see ASV, CCD, Lettere, filza 13, fol. 579r, dated 17 January 1511 (m.v.); ASV, CCD, Lettere rettori, Udine, busta 169, fol. 249r, dated 12 March 1512 and fol. 78r, dated 19 March. On Artico di Prampero, see ASV, CCD, Lettere, filza 14, fol. 20r, dated 16 March 1512. He later claimed to have been one of the assassins; ASV, CCD, Lettere rettori, Udine, busta 169, fol. 157r, dated 8 January 1517. Cf. Savini, "Antonio Savorgnan," 293–94 and V. Marchesi, "Friuli al tempo della Lega di Cambrai," *NAV*, n.s., 6 (1903): 527–28n. On rumors of Antonio's death, see Sanuto, *I diarii*, 14: 5–6, 15, 21. For a list of exiles considered traitors, see ASV, CCD, Lettere, filza 14, fols. 2r, 2bisr, dated 2 March 1512.

7. Degani includes a Giorgio Colloredo and leaves out Agostino Colloredo in the group of assassins, but he is contradicted by the primary sources; see Ernesto Degani, *I partiti in Friuli nel 1500 e la storia di un famoso duello*, 63. On the Colloredo participants, which also included Gregorio, and for source of quotes, see Agostino di Colloredo, "Chroniche friulane, 1508–18," 6. On Zoppola, see Cergneu, *Cronaca delle guerre friulane*, 59. On Castello and Spilimbergo, see Sanuto, *I diarii*, 10: 53; 12: 15; 13: 236–37; 14: 282, 284; *DU*, GAH, 500, 517, 535, 541; ASV, CD, Misto, reg. 35, fol. 87v; APS, MS VI, 165, dated 24 January 1511 (m.v.). On Spilimbergo's presence at the entrance into Udine, see Prospero Antonini, *Il Friuli orientali: Studi*, 282.

8. For quotes, see Colloredo, "Chroniche friulane," 6; Roberto de' Signori de Spilimbergo, *Cronaca de'suoi tempi dal 1499 al 1540*, 23–24; Cergneu, *Cronaca delle guerre friulane*, 59–60. There is considerable disagreement about the date of the murder, but I follow Sanudo's date of May 27 because his diary was written closest to the actual time of the event. His account leaves out any mention of a dog or pig: "e cussì li dete su la testa sì gran bota che il cervello li cazete zoso, e li taiò la man *adeo* morite." *I diarii*, 14: 282. Gregorio Amaseo includes only the dog: "de mane de magnanimo conte Zuanne Henrico de Spilimbergo per la qual botta li cazette parte dele cervelle in terra, le quale subito fu manzate d'un cane"; *DU*, GA, 233 and *DU*, GAH, 541. Amaseo also quotes (259) an eyewitness whom he met in 1521 who said, "et un can li manzò le cervelle." Savorgnan family accounts leave out the animals entirely and emphasize the treachery of the imperial captains who were bribed by the killers. "Famiglia Savorgnan," BCU, MS 1247, fascicolo titled "Memorie sopra la famiglia Savorgnan," doc. titled "Narrazione della morte di Antonio Savorgnano nel 1512 in Villacco." Cf. MCV, Correr 963, pezzo 3, fols. 30v–31r. Without citing his source, Antonini reports that Antonio was found murdered in his own bed; Prospero Antonini, *I baroni di Waldsee o Walsee, i visconti di Mels, i signori di Prodolone e di Colloredo: Accenni genealogici e note storiche*, 82.

9. On the actions of the Council of Ten, see ASV, CD, Misto, reg. 35, fols. 87v, 89v–90v, 134v, 140, 147v–148r; ASV, CCD, Lettere, filza 14, fols. 141r,

184r, 185r, 353r. On Federico Strassoldo, see Soldoniero di Strassoldo, *Cronaca dal 1509 al 1603*, 81–82.

10. Emmanuel Le Roy Ladurie, *Carnival in Romans*, 318.

11. Carlo Ginzburg, *The Cheese and the Worms: The Cosmos of a Sixteenth-Century Miller*, 62.

12. *DU, GAH*, 513 ("famegli et cani de casa"), 508 ("donde li erano eretti come cani ala cazza"), 517 (Giovanni di Leonardo Marangone di Capriglie described as a rabid dog), 524 ("furia di rabiati cani"). For "cani et compagni," see ASMn, Archivio Gonzaga, busta 1445, fol. 34, dated 12 April 1511. For Shakespeare quote, see *Romeo and Juliet*, 5.1.10–12. For letter closing "vostro cane e schiavo" from Filippo da Pietrasanta to Duke Galeazzo Maria Sforza, dated 20 July 1473, see Archivio di Stato, Milan, Archivio Sforzesco, Carteggio interno, cartella 914. I wish to thank Gregory Lubkin for providing me with this last reference. For "cani brachi," see Nicolò Monticolo, *Descrittione del sacco MDXI seguito in Udine il giovedi XXVII febbraio*, 18. Cf. Colloredo, "Chroniche friulane," 6. In a summary of depositions collected after a riot in Buia against Girolamo Savorgnan, the investigating magistrate attributed to the leaders of the riot the following call to arms: "Cane, cane rabiosi instigati dal diavolo, dalì dalì, amaza, amaza"; BCU, MS 1042, busta 1, filza 3, fol. 11r; also see fol. 13r. An alleged wolfman tried in Livonia in 1692 described the wolfmen as "the dogs of God," who fought the devil; Carlo Ginzburg, *Storia notturna: Una decifrazione del Sabba*, 130. For a comparison of the plebs of Naples with Cerberus, see Peter Burke, *The Historical Anthropology of Early Modern Italy: Essays on Perception and Communication*, 195. In the backwoods of the American South where in frontier times physical insecurity was the rule, men often asserted they were wild animals to create a fearsome image. See Elliott J. Gorn, "'Gouge and Bite, Pull Hair and Scratch': The Social Significance of Fighting in the Southern Backcountry," 28–29.

13. For the anti-Savorgnan sonnet, see Sanuto, *I diarii*, 12: 577. For the apocalyptic vision of revenge, see Candido, *Commentarii d'Aquileja*, 96.

14. For the quote, see Ruzante, *La Moscheta*, act 4, scene 3, in Ruzante, *Teatro*, 651. Everyday experience with Veneto dialects can confirm the observation about insults, but also see Giuliano Averna, "Italian and Venetian Profanity," *Maledicta* 1 (1977): 63–64.

15. On the early medieval legal treatment of animals, see Edward P. Evans, *The Criminal Prosecution and Capital Punishment of Animals*, 10–11. On Albania, see Margaret Hasluck, *The Unwritten Law in Albania*, 73–78; and Christopher Boehm, *Blood Revenge: The Anthropology of Feuding in Montenegro and Other Tribal Societies*, 110–11.

16. On Corsica, see Stephen Wilson, *Feuding, Conflict, and Banditry in Nineteenth-Century Corsica*, 51, 78–79. On the Turkish use of attack dogs, see Sanuto, *I diarii*, 2: 1365. On the German use, Andrea Mocenigo, *La guerra di Cambrai fatta a'tempi nostri in Italia*, 23r. Cf. John Grier Varner and Jeannette Johnson Varner, *Dogs of the Conquest* (Norman, Oklahoma: University of Oklahoma Press, 1983).

17. Frederick Bryson, *The Sixteenth Century Italian Duel: A Study in Renaissance Social History*, 26, 59, 94, and 116.

18. On Burgundians and Milan, see Antonio Pertile, *Storia del diritto italiano*

dalla caduta dell'Impero Romano alla codificazione, 5: 343-44n. On France and for quote, see Bryson, *Sixteenth Century Italian Duel,* xvi, 179n. On the Roland story, Matteo Maria Boiardo, *Orlando innamorato: Amorum libri,* ed. Aldo Scaglione (2 vols., Turin: Unione tipografico-editrice Torinese, 1963), 1: 260 (canto 4, stanza 30).

19. On treason, see Ruzante, *Reduce* in idem, *Teatro,* 525; and Brian Pullan, *Jews of Europe,* 76. On usury, see Ruzante, *Dialogo facetissimo* in idem, *Teatro,* 694. On dogs as carriers of the plague, see Ann G. Carmichael, *Plague and the Poor in Renaissance Florence,* 105. On dog amulets, see Michelangelo Biondo, *De canibus et venatione libellus,* 247–51; and Hannalore Zug Tucci, "La caccia, da bene commune a privilegio," 432. On witches' use of dog bones, see ASV, Sant' Ufficio, busta 55, Dalle Vergole, Felicita, Stregheria, 31 May 1585. I wish to thank Guido Ruggiero for this last reference. On dogs as diabolic familiars, see Carlo Ginzburg, *The Night Battles: Witchcraft and Agrarian Cults in the Sixteenth and Seventeenth Centuries,* 87.

20. On rabies, see Kathleen Kete, "La Rage and the Bourgeoisie: The Cultural Context of Rabies in the French Nineteenth Century," *Representations* 22 (1988): 89–107.

21. On *berserkir,* see Carlo Ginzburg, "Mitologia germanica e Nazismo: Su un vecchio libro di Georges Dumézil," in *Miti, emblemi, spie: Morfologia e storia,* 210–38, especially, 212–24, originally published in *QS,* n.s., 57 (1984): 857–82. On the Attila legend, see V. Ostermann, *Illustrazione della comune di Udine* (Udine, 1886), 173; and *Enciclopedia monografica del Friuli-Venezia-Giulia,* vol. 3, part 3 (Udine: Istituto del Enciclopedia del Friuli-Venezia-Giulia, 1980), s.v. "Miti e leggende in Friuli," by Novella Cantarutti. On Renaissance astrologic images, see Linda L. Carroll, "Giorgione's *Tempest:* Astrology is in the Eyes of the Beholder."

22. Cf. Hayden White, "The Forms of Wildness: Archaeology of an Idea," especially 7, 13.

23. On the *Altine Chronicle,* see Zug Tucci, "Caccia," 399, 401.

24. On wolves in Friuli, see Pier Cesare Ioly Zorattini, "*Preenti* contro il lupo negli atti del S. Uffizio di Aquileia e Concordia," *CF* 52 (1976): 131–46; Andrea Benedetti, "Il trattato della caccia, uccellagione e pesca del Conte Jacopo di Porcìa," 49–50; and *DU, GA,* 344, 449, 452, 459, 464. For quotation from Sacchetti, see Zug Tucci, "Caccia," 401.

25. On sixteenth-century werewolf beliefs in Friuli, see Ginzburg, *Night Battles,* 29–32. Cf. idem, "Freud, l'uomo dei lupi e i lupi mannari," in *Miti, emblemi, spie,* 239–51, trans. into English in *Clues, Myth and the Historical Method;* and idem, *Storia notturna,* 134–36. On modern Friulan werewolf beliefs, see *Enciclopedia monografica del Friuli-Venezia-Giulia,* vol. 1, part 1 (Udine: Istituto dell'Enciclopedia del Friuli-Venezia-Giulia, 1971), s.v. "Leggende e tradizioni delle grotte," by Pier Carlo Caracci.

26. On *warg,* see Mary R. Gerstein, "Germanic Warg: The Outlaw as Werwolf," in *Myth in Indo-European Antiquity,* ed. Gerald James Larson, coeditors C. Scott Littleton and Jaan Puhvel (Berkeley and Los Angeles: University of California Press, 1974), 131–56. On English law, see Sir Frederick Pollack and Frederic Maitland, *The History of English Law Before the Time of Edward I,* ed. 2 (Cambridge, 1898), 449, 476. I wish to thank Barbara Hanawalt and Robert Gottfried for references and advice on English law.

27. On *pace lupina*, see *DU*, GAH, 501. On the process of dehumanizing people by classifying them as animals, see Keith Thomas, *Man and the Natural World: A History of the Modern Sensibility*, 47–48.

28. *DU*, GAH, 542. On the actual fate of Gregorio Colloredo who "fu pigliato . . . et appiccato per la gola," see "Famiglia Savorgnan," BCU, MS 1247; and *DU*, GA, 232–34n.

29. On Agnadello visions, see Ottavia Niccoli, "Il re dei morti," 929–58, trans. into English in *Microhistory and the Lost Peoples of Europe*, ed. Muir and Ruggiero. Her interpretation has been modified slightly in her *Prophecy and People in Renaissance Italy*, 66–71. Ginzburg first discussed the *benandanti* of Friuli and suggested their connection to armies of the dead in *Night Battles*. Also see his "Charivari, associazioni giovanili, caccia selvaggia," *QS* 49 (1982): 164–77 and "Présomptions sur le Sabbat," *Annales: E.S.C.* 39 (1984): 341–54. His most complete examination of the theme of ecstatic combats is in *Storia notturna*, 130–51.

30. On Candiano, see Jean Lemaire de Belges, *La légende des Vénitiens*, 367. On threats to Grimani and robbers, see Sanuto, *I diarii*, 2: 1377; 3: 5, 272. The threats to Grimani reappeared when he was a candidate in a ducal conclave; see Edward Muir, *Civic Ritual in Renaissance Venice*, 270n. On Sforza, see Eugenio Casanova, "L'uccisione di Galeazzo Maria Sforza e alcuni documenti fiorentini," *Archivio storico lombardo*, ser. 2, 11 (1899): 306. Boiardo describes the father of a Saracen killed by a French knight vowing that if he does not avenge his son's death, he should be drawn, quartered, and eaten by a dog. *Orlando innamorato*, canto 19, stanze 37–38. On France, see Michel de Montaigne, "Des cannibales," in *Essais*, ed. Pierre Michel (Paris: Gallimard, 1973), 1: 303–19. During one particularly vicious charivari in the village of Chêne, the couple being attacked was threatened with burning, after which every dog in the village was to be let loose to eat them; Natalie Zemon Davis, "Charivari, Honor, and Community in Seventeenth-Century Lyon and Geneva," 49. The Mackenzies cut up one Donald Mackmarock Roy and left his torso to be eaten by dogs and wild animals; Keith M. Brown, *Bloodfeud in Scotland, 1573–1625: Violence, Justice and Politics in an Early Modern Society*, 32.

31. Homer, *Iliad*, trans. Richard Lattimore (Chicago: University of Chicago Press, 1951), 22.345–54.

32. On the Jezebel theme, see Natalie Zemon Davis, "Rites of Violence," 153. On penitential articles, see *The Irish Penitentials*, trans. and ed. Ludwig Bieler (Dublin: The Dublin Institute for Advanced Studies, reprint 1975), 113, 115 quoted in William R. Cook and Ronald B. Herzman, *The Medieval World View* (New York: Oxford University Press, 1983), 137–38.

33. Ruzante, *La Moscheta*, act 3, scene 6, par. 47; act 4, scene 2, par. 8; *La Pastoral*, scene 15, lines 39–42; *La Piovana*, act 3, scene 2, par. 34; *Fiorina*, act 1, scene 1, par. 10. For the plays, see Ruzante, *Teatro*. These references and my understanding of Beolco come from Linda L. Carroll. See her *Language and Dialect in Ruzante and Goldoni*, "Linguistic Variation and Social Protest in the Plays of Ruzante," "Carnival Rites as Vehicles of Protest in Renaissance Venice," "Authorial Defense in Boccaccio and Ruzante: From Liminal to Liminoid," and *Angelo Beolco (Il Ruzante)*. Another recurring theme in Italian literature depicts the disposing of an unwanted illegitimate child by giving it to dogs to eat. Boccaccio, *Decameron*,

day 5, stories 7 and 8; Bandello, *Novelle*, part 3, novella 52; and Sperone Speroni, *Canace e scritti in sua difesa*, ed. Christina Roaf (Bologna: Commissione per i testi di lingua, 1982). For crows eating a dead man, see François Rabelais, *Pantagruel*, book 4, chap. 13. For dogs eating men, see Shakespeare, *Merry Wives of Windsor*, 3. 5. 3-9 and *Henry IV, Part 2*, 1. 3. 93–100. Some of the inspiration for these themes may have come from Ovid and Seneca.

34. On the relationship between the parts of game and hierarchy and for the Irish example, see Bruce Lincoln, *Discourse and the Construction of Society: Comparative Studies of Myth, Ritual, and Classification*, 75–80. On the symbolism of game in Venice and Tuscany, see Zug Tucci, "Caccia," 425–34. On the practice of hanging trophies in trees, see Maurizio Bertolotti, "Le ossa e la pelle dei buoi: Un mito popolare tra agiografia e stregoneria," *QS* 41 (1979): 483, trans. into English in *Microhistory and the Lost Peoples of Europe*, ed. Muir and Ruggiero.

35. On falconers and aristocratic privileges, ibid., especially 441. Friuli became a famous hunting preserve during the Renaissance. Jacopo di Porcìa, the great propagandist of Friulan hunting and author of one of the principal Renaissance treatises on the sport, boasted about the region's variety of quarry such as boars, bears, mountain goats, and deer. By the early sixteenth century, the right to hunt in Friuli had become an aristocratic privilege that limited hunting, at least legally, to the lords and their specialist retainers. On hunting in Friuli in general, see Jacopo di Porcìa, *Tractatus de venatione, aucupatione et piscationibus Jacobi comitis Purliliarum*, in Benedetti, "Trattato della caccia," 49, 76–78.

36. Zug Tucci, "Caccia," 408–9, 435. Erasmo da Valvasone, *Della caccia: Poema del Signor Erasmo di Valvasone all'Ill. Signor Cesare di Valvasone suo nepote. Con gli argomenti a ciascun canto del Sig. Gio. Domenico de gli Alessandri* (Bergamo, 1591), republished in *Arte della caccia*, ed. Giuliano Innamorati (Milan: Polifilo, 1965), 2: 273–312.

37. Zug Tucci, "Caccia," 399–411.

38. For Porcìa, see Benedetti, "Trattato della caccia," 56–57. Valvasone, *Della Caccia*, 273–312.

39. Walter Burkert, *Homo Necans: The Anthropology of Ancient Greek Sacrificial Ritual and Myth*, 1–79, 296–97, quote on 17; idem, *Structure and History in Greek Mythology and Ritual*, 1–57. Burkert modified his views in "The Problem of Ritual Killing," in *Violent Origins*, ed. Robert G. Hamerton-Kelly, 149–90. For criticisms of Burkert's theory, see Ginzburg, *Storia notturna*, xxxi. On the theme of hunting, cf. Robert Ardrey, *The Hunting Hypothesis: A Personal Conclusion Concerning the Evolutionary Nature of Man*; J. K. Anderson, *Hunting in the Ancient World*; H. L. Savage, "Hunting in the Middle Ages"; and J. B. Russell, *Witchcraft in the Middle Ages* (Ithaca: Cornell University Press, 1972), 50, 51, 56, 58.

40. On Lombard practices of naming hunters after their prey, see Zug Tucci, "Caccia," 400. On the similarities between hunting and killing humans, cf. Burkert, *Homo Necans*, 12–20.

41. Frank Lestringant, "Le cannibale et ses paradoxes: Images du cannibalisme au temps des guerres de religion," *Mentalities* 1 (1983): 7. For the sonnet, see *DU*, *GAH*, 548. On threat to woman, see Gaetano Perusini, "Le condizioni di vita in un paese della pianura friulana nel secolo XVI," 172. For the cannibalism case in

Modena, see Ludovico Antonio Muratori, *Delle antichità estensi ed italiane* (Modena, 1740), 2: 179–81. On Florence and Naples, see my "Cannibals of Renaissance Italy." For Dalmatian examples, see Sanuto, *I diarii*, 15: 153 and M. E. Mallett and J. R. Hale, *The Military Organization of a Renaissance State: Venice c. 1400 to 1617*, 243. On France, see Davis, "Rites of Violence," 181; Emmanuel Le Roy Ladurie, *Les paysans de Languedoc* (2 vols., Paris: SEVPEN, 1966), 1: 398n; idem, *Carnival in Romans*, 208, 312–20; and Orest Ranum, "The French Ritual of Tyrannicide in the Late Sixteenth Century," 72, 79. On Holland, see Herbert Rowen, *John De Witt* (Princeton: Princeton University Press, 1978), 878–84.

42. On the war in general, see Mallett and Hale, *Military Organization*, 222-23 and Marchesi, "Friuli al tempo della Lega di Cambrai," 531-35. On specific events in Friuli, see Sanuto, *I diarii*, 16: 448, 638, 654; 17: 41–42, 52, 98, 118, 268, 389, 456, 561, 574; 18: 25, 30, 37–38, 44–45, 47–48, 66, 81–82, 87, 92, 105, 168; 19: 218. On treaties, see Dionisio Tassini, *Il Friuli dopo la guerra contro i tedeschi (1508–13)* (Udine: n.p., 1917).

43. Between 1505 and autumn 1514, Gemona held eleven important civic offices in Udine, including three terms as a deputy. After the defection and death of Antonio, it was rumored that Gemona hid in his own house some of the traitor's property to prevent it from being confiscated. For Gemona's offices, see BCU, ACU, Annali, reg. 41 and 42. For his delegations to Venice, see Sanuto, *I diarii*, 11: 460; 19: 243. ASV, CCD, Lettere di condottieri (Savorgnan), busta 308, letter from Jacobo de Castello dated 9 December 1513 (on Bartolomeo Brugno da Gemona hiding Savorgnan property); letter from Girolamo Savorgnan, dated 23 July 1514 (for complaints about abuse of his faction); letter from Girolamo, dated 15 March 1515 (on the murder of his supporter). For the Council of Ten's response to Girolamo's letter of complaints, see ASV, CD, Misto, reg. 37, fol. 108, dated 28 July 1514.

44. On Girolamo's early career, see Sanuto, *I diarii*, 7: 309, 574, 627, 643, 645, 683; 8: 16, 73, 142, 179; 9: 319-21; 10: 29, 462, 599; Bonati Savorgnan D'Osoppo, "Aspetti della personalità di Gerolamo Savorgnan," 81–83; and Mallett and Hale, *Military Organization*, 343. The marriage to Maddalena Della Torre lasted from 1491 to 1495 and produced four children. He was married to Felicità Tron, widow of Matteo Tiepolo, from 1496 to 1501 and fathered three offspring. His third wife, Bianca Malipiero, the widow of Mario Tiepolo, married Girolamo in 1502 and gave birth to five more children before her death in 1507. The following year he married Orsina Canal, widow of Marcantonio Marcello. She outlived Girolamo, giving him eleven children for a total of twenty-three legitimate offspring, fifteen of whom survived to adulthood. There was also one known illegitimate son named Turco. See BCU, MS Joppi 689d, vol. 4. On the politics behind relieving the siege in 1514 and Luca Tron's efforts on behalf of Girolamo, see Finlay, *Politics in Renaissance Venice*, 236-37.

45. For the first quote, see *DU*, GA, 241. Cf. a similar view in Cergneu, *Cronaca delle guerre friulane*, 69. The quote from Girolamo is as cited and translated by Mallett and Hale, *Military Organization*, 344. The negotiations for rewards present a complicated picture. For Girolamo's requests, see G. Savorgnan, "Lettere sulla guerra," vol. 2, part 2, 26–27, dated 14 October 1513; vol. 3, part 1, p. 5, dated

23 April 1514; and ASV, CCD, Lettere di condottieri (Savorgnan), busta 308, letters dated 12 July 1514 and 7 August 1515. For Venice's rewards to him, see ASV, CD, Misto, reg. 36, fols. 88r–89r, 93r–94r, 126v–127r, 187r–188r, and ASV, Provveditori sopra feudi, busta 544, doc. dated 19 April 1514.

46. Nicolò Monticolo, *Cronaca delle famiglie udinesi*, 9–10. Antonio Battistella, "Udine nel secolo XVI: l'ordinamento interno della città," 151–61. Marchese, "Friuli al tempo della Lega di Cambrai," 526. Ventura, *Nobiltà e popolo*, 187–214.

47. The entrance is recounted in a description by Zuan di Strassoldo which appears in Sanuto, *I diarii*, 22: 619, 679–84. Also see Sebastiano Mulioni di Gemona, *Chronicon glemonense dal 1300 al 1517*, 26.

48. Although a great many Udinesi enjoyed public office at least once, a handful of men dominated the more important jobs such as deputy, procurator of the communal grain office, judge, chancellor, and ambassador. Between 1505 and 1517 some 817 offices were filled in Udine. A majority of 54 percent of those elected held office more than once. In fact, some 20 percent of all the office holders obtained more than five positions during this period. Up until the treason of Antonio Savorgnan, these civic oligarchs included most prominently the partisans of the Zambarlani, such as the three Monticolo brothers who among them garnered twenty-five offices, the two Corbelli twenty, and Francesco Janis di Tolmezzo five. Even after Antonio's fall, Ascanio Sbroiavacca held on to serve in fifteen offices, his brother Giovanni Francesco managed ten, and Giovanni Francesco Torso secured thirteen. The lists of civic officials also include a few Strumieri, such as Antonio Brazzacco who held nine offices, Pietro Arcoloniano sixteen, Francesco Cergneu fourteen, and Francesco Colombatto twelve, but the Strumiero leadership is conspicuously absent from the registers. No member of the Colloredo clan ever held an office in Udine, and Alvise Della Torre garnered only three special offices, two times as a member of a delegation to Venice and once on the original commission to reform the city's statutes. The percentages of single and multiple office holders are based on a random sample of 122 names taken from the 817 names of officials listed in BCU, ACU, Annali, from reg. 41, fol. 15v (6 September 1505) to reg. 42, fol. 117r (12 March 1517).

49. On the legislation closing the Udinese nobility, see Nino Tenca Montini, *Le famiglie della nobiltà udinese e le cariche pubbliche (1513–1797)* (Udine: n.p., 1903). For a discussion of the reforms, see *DU, GA*, 234–35 (235 for quote), 252–53. Cf. Cergneu, *Cronaca delle guerre friulane*, 56–57, 78–79. For Girolamo's complaints about the erosion of his rights, see ASV, CCD, Lettere di condottieri (Savorgnan), busta 308, letter dated 27 April 1516. For his opposition to reforms, see BCU, MS Joppi 689d, vol. 4, fols. 176, 181r. For the attempt to reestablish the *arengo*, see ASV, CCD, Lettere rettori, busta 169, Udine, 159r–160v. For the general Venetian program of legal reform after the war, see Gaetano Cozzi, "Politica del diritto," in *Stato, società e giustizia*, ed. Gaetano Cozzi, 122–46.

50. For the luogotenente's announcement, see Sanuto, *I diarii*, 27: 625, dated 5 September 1519.

51. On Girolamo's late career, see Bonati Savorgnan D'Osoppo, "Aspetti della personalità di Gerolamo Savorgnan," 84–85. One sign of the erosion of his privileges and influence was that he eventually lost the toll station at Osoppo, which

was returned to Gemona. In compensation, Udine was supposed to pay him four hundred ducats per year, but the city failed to meet its obligation. See ASV, CCD, Lettere di condottieri (Savorgnan), busta 308, letter from Girolamo dated 22 January 1520. On the 1526 affair and decline of his support, see *DU*, GA, 286–88, 300, 304. For the quote about his enemies, see Savorgnan, "Lettere sulla guerra," 41. The Council of Ten promised Bernardino and Francesco their property as early as 1523, but Girolamo would apparently not give it up. See BCU, MS Joppi 592, fol. 2r. On their return and requests for compensation, see ASV, CD, Parti comuni, filza 11, fascicoli 41 (8 April 1530) and 60 (30 April 1530). On resulting property arrangements, also see ASU, AT, cartella 19, colto 26, fascicolo 3.

52. Although discussed frequently, the origins of the *contadinanza* are best explained in Andreina Stefanutti, "Udine e la contadinanza: Solidarietà e tensioni sociali nel Friuli del '500 e 600," which supplants the traditional accounts by Pier Silverio Leicht, "Movimento agrario nel Cinquecento," 15–19 and "La rappresentanza dei contadini presso il Veneto luogotenente della Patria del Friuli." On rural burdens, see Cozzi, "Ambiente veneziano, ambiente veneto," 114–15. On Memmo, see Mallett and Hale, *Military Organization*, 419.

53. On the assassination of Nicolò, see *DU*, GA, 234n, 250; *DU*, GAH, 504, 542n.

54. On Tolmezzo and Monticolo, see *DU*, GA, 229n, 234n, 268–70; *DU*, GAH, 498n.

55. For examples of criminal violence, see ASV, CD, Parti criminali, reg. 3, fol. 172v (Cividale case); fols. 220v, 228 (uprising in Piera sotto Oderzo); reg. 4, fol. 152v (charges against Giulio Savorgnan); fols. 214, 221r–223v (murder of captain of Venzone); fols. 239v–240v (murder of Constantino Savorgnan); reg. 5, fols. 85v–86r (defamation of rector of Sacile). On the trial of Pagano Savorgnan, see ASV, Avogaria di Comun, Miscellanea, Penale, busta 254, filza 11 and busta 284, filza 8. For the activities of exiled Strumieri, see Archivio Eredi di Irene Spilimbergo-Spanio, pergamena dated 10 July 1526 (on Francesco Candido and Giacomo di Spilimbergo); BSU, Archivio Capitolare, Raccolta Bini, Miscellanea, 19: 115 (for appeal to the emperor from a Della Torre orphan).

Chapter 8: Toward the Duel

1. On attempts to isolate the implicit rules of revenge, see Raymond Verdier, "De l'une a l'autre vengeance," in *La vengeance: Études d'ethnologie, d'histoire et de philosophie*, Vol. 2: *Vengeance et pouvoir dans quelques sociétés extraoccidentales*, ed. Raymond Verdier (Paris: Éditions Cujas, 1980), 7–13; Robin Fox, *The Tory Islanders: A People of the Celtic Fringe* (Cambridge, United Kingdom: Cambridge University Press, 1978), 186–88; idem, "The Inherent Rules of Violence," in *Social Rules and Social Behavior*, ed. Peter Collett (Totowa, N.J.: Rowan and Littlefield, 1977), 132–49; and Margaret Hasluck, *The Unwritten Law in Albania*, 219–37. For an attempt to catalogue the rules of vendetta in Renaissance Italy, see Anna Maria Enriques, "La vendetta nella vita e nella legislazione fiorentina," 87–117. Cf. Pierre Bourdieu, *Outline of a Theory of Practice*, 1–27, 182–95.

2. Long intervals, some lasting for two or more generations, are not unusual in feuding societies. Cf. Stephen Wilson, *Feuding, Conflict, and Banditry in Nineteenth-*

Century Corsica, 199–200. In this section I closely follow the narration of assaults and murders in Ernesto Degani, *I partiti in Friuli nel 1500 e la storia di un famoso duello*, 79–116. There are, however, several errors in his account which have been corrected by the archival documents cited below. Ercole Della Rovere, a supporter of the Colloredo clan, had wounded a Savorgnan in a scuffle during the War of the League of Cambrai and been freed from banishment at the request of the assassins of Nicolò Savorgnan, but otherwise his career as a Strumiero partisan is obscure. On Ercole, see *DU*, GA, 250. On the loss of Savorgnan jurisdiction over the streams, see Strassoldo, *Cronaca dal 1509 al 1603*, 26–27.

3. On the banishment of Germanico Savorgnan, see ASV, CD, Parti criminali, reg. 7, fols. 96v–97v.

4. For the sentences, see ASV, CD, Parti criminali, reg. 7, fols. 143, 146v–147v. Cf. Soldoniero di Strassoldo, *Cronaca dal 1509 al 1603*, 84–85; and Prospero Antonini, *I baroni di Waldsee o Walsee, i visconti di Mels, i signori di Prodolone e di Colloredo: Accenni genealogici e note storiche*, 88–90, 154–55. Degani, *I partiti in Friuli*, 81 gives the date incorrectly as 1548 and confuses Colloredo's sentence with Della Torre's.

5. A traveling English knight, one Thomas Hoby, picked up a rather garbled version of the story. Although a great deal seems to have been lost in translation, he certainly understood from his Venetian informants that the crime was an episode in a long vendetta. Thomas Hoby, *The Travels and Life of Sir Thomas Hoby, K.t of Bisham Abbey, Written by Himself, 1547-64*, ed. Edgar Powell, The Royal Historical Society, Camden Miscellany (London: The Society, 1902), 10: 15. I wish to thank Steven Masello for bringing Hoby's book to my attention. On Tristano at Pinzano, see ASV, CCD, Lettere di condottieri (Savorgnan), busta 308, letters from Pietro Morosini, 6 and 12 August 1549.

6. On the sentences against Tristano and others, see ASV, CD, Parti criminali, reg. 7, fols. 153v–155v, 158r, 168r–169v, 180, 182r. Tristano's sentence is published in Antonini, *I baroni di Waldsee*, 156–59, doc. no. 6; and in Cesare Cantù, "Recenti lavori di erudizione storica," *ASI*, ser. 3, 19 (1874): 154–56. Also see ASU, AT, cartella 19, colto 26, fascicolo 1. On the destruction of the Udine palace, see ASV, CCD, Lettere di condottieri (Savorgnan), busta 308, letter from Vicenzo Diedo, dated 9 December 1549. On the legal tradition of destroying houses as a punishment, see Antonio Pertile, *Storia del diritto italiano dalla caduta dell'Impero Romano alla codificazione*, 5: 350–55.

7. On the motto, see Nicolò, Tristano, and Federigo Savorgnan, *Difesa de gli Illustri Signori, Nicolò, Tristano, & Federigo Savorgnani dalle false imputationi date loro, & all'honorata sua famiglia, dal Signor Martio Colloreto*, 25v. On Tristano in Crete, see ASU, AT, cartella 19, colto 26, fascicolo 3, doc. dated 29 January 1550.

8. On the confrontation between the Colloredo and Marco da Carpi, see ASV, CCD, Lettere di condottieri (Savorgnan), busta 308, for a letter from Luogotenente Francesco Michiel, dated 21 May 1551.

9. On the murder of Antonio Savorgnan the younger and Marzio's violations of his ban, see ASV, CD, Parti criminali, reg. 8, fols. 50, 60, 67v, 148v–150r, 236. Also see 112v for a fight between the servants of the Colloredo and Savorgnan. On the reaction in Udine to Antonio's murder, see *Relazioni*, 1: 47.

10. For a renewal of Marzio's ban in 1560, the Tagliamento attack, and murders

at the luogotenente's palace, see ASV, CD, Parti criminali, reg. 9, fols. 62v–64v, 113r–115v, 182r–184v, 188r. On the murder of Francesco, see Strassoldo, *Cronaca dal 1509 al 1603*, 48. Cf. Degani, *I partiti in Friuli*, 109–14. On Marzio's late career, which culminated in his governorship of Siena, see Pier Silverio Leicht, "Marzio Colloredo governatore di Siena," which omits unseemly references to his involvement in the vendetta; and the more useful entry in *Dizionario biografico degli Italiani*, s.v. "Colloredo, Marcio."

11. To be accurate courtly manners should perhaps be described more as renewed than as new. A code of behavior for the ideal knight, who epitomized both courage and courtesy, emerged during the Ottonian and Salian periods from the German cathedral schools and the royal chapel, in which the clerics who formed the administrative élite of the empire received their training. See C. Stephen Jaeger, *The Origins of Courtliness: Civilizing Trends and the Formation of Courtly Ideals, 939–1210* (Philadelphia: University of Pennsylvania Press, 1985); Norbert Elias, *The History of Manners*, 85, 90, 117–20; Giovanni Della Casa, *Galateo*, 9. Marvin B. Becker argues that the roots of the "civility" of the the sixteenth-century courts can be found in the civic culture of fourteenth-century Florence; *Civility and Society in Western Europe, 1300–1600*, passim. Although a culture of civilities similar to Florence's evolved in Venice, it had far less influence on Friulan aristocratic mores than did the courtly versions of the principalities. One of the deficiencies of Venetian civic culture was its weakness outside the home city. In contrast, Elias may overstate the influence of the court in France. See Daniel Gordon, "The Idea of Sociability in Pre-Revolutionary France" (Ph.D. diss., University of Chicago, 1990), 1: 84–102. I wish to thank Dena Goodman for lending me her copy of Gordon's dissertation.

12. On Erasmus, see Elias, *The History of Manners*, 78–79. Cf. Jacques Revel, "The Uses of Civility," 170.

13. Della Casa, *Galateo*, xi–xiii, xxi–xxii, 10–11, 19–24. On the success of *Galateo* in reforming manners, see Elias, *The History of Manners*, 81–82. Cf. Gianluca Prosperi, "Per una lettura antropologica del *Galateo* di Della Casa," *Studium* 10 (1980): 379–86. On the proliferation of formalities, see Peter Burke, *The Historical Anthropology of Early Modern Italy: Essays on Perception and Communication*, 90–92; and Frederick Robertson Bryson, *The Point of Honor in Sixteenth-Century Italy: An Aspect of the Life of the Gentleman*, 15–17. On the theme of honest dissimulation, see Pietro Redondi, *Galileo Heretic*, trans. Raymond Rosenthal (Princeton: Princeton University Press, 1987), 24; and Perez Zagorin, *Ways of Lying: Dissimulation, Persecution, and Conformity in Early Modern Europe* (Cambridge: Harvard University Press, 1990). On courtesies in France, see Orest Ranum, "Courtesy, Absolutism, and the Rise of the French State, 1630-60," 443–51. On the distinction between dignity and honor, see Peter L. Berger, Brigette Berger, and Hansfried Kellner, *The Homeless Mind: Modernization and Consciousness* (New York: Random House, 1973), 83–96. For a useful application of this distinction to the United States, see Edward L. Ayers, *Vengeance and Justice: Crime and Punishment in the Nineteenth-Century American South*, 3–33.

14. Annibale Romei, "Dell'Onore," in his *Ferrara e la corte estense nella seconda*

metà del secolo decimosesto. I Discorsi, 82–108. Cf. Gabriel Maugain, *Moeurs italiennes de la Renaissance: La vengeance*, 169, 176; and Werner L. Gundersheimer, "Trickery, Gender, and Power: The *Discorsi* of Annibale Romei." By insisting that the ideal male courtier must make a profession of arms, Castiglione emphasized the necessity of physical courage: "And, just as among women the name of purity, once stained, is never restored, so the reputation of a gentleman whose profession is arms, if ever in the least way he sullies himself through cowardice or other disgrace, always remains defiled before the world and covered with ignominy." *The Book of the Courtier*, trans. Charles S. Singleton (Garden Ctiy, N.Y.: Anchor Books, 1959), 32. On the character of Renaissance honor, see Jules Kirshner, "Pursuing Honor While Avoiding Sin: The *Monte delle Doti* of Florence," *Studi senesi* 87 (1977): 177–258; Curtis Brown Watson, *Shakespeare and the Renaissance Concept of Honor*, 2–12; and Ruth Kelso, *The Doctrine of the English Gentleman in the Sixteenth Century* (Urbana: University of Illinois Press, 1929). It should be noted, however, that whatever the claims of the courtesy books, honor was just as important for artisans and peasants as for aristocrats. See Natalie Zemon Davis, "Charivari, Honor and Community in Seventeenth-Century Lyon and Geneva," 50; and idem, *Fiction in the Archives: Pardon Tales and Their Tellers in Sixteenth-Century France*, 42. On modern examples of honor among industrial workers, see Charles F. Sabel, *Work and Politics: The Division of Labor in Industry* (New York: Cambridge University Press, 1982).

15. On the values of the court, see Norbert Elias, *Court Society*. Also see idem, *The History of Manners*, 191–205. On compensatory measures, see René Girard, *Violence and the Sacred*, 20–21. On the effects of the duel in reducing criminal violence, see V. G. Kiernan, *The Duel in European History: Honour and the Reign of Aristocracy*, 6.

16. On the details of the new dueling, the two best sources are Frederick Robertson Bryson, *The Sixteenth Century Italian Duel: A Study in Renaissance Social History*, xi–xxiii, 21–22, 37; and Kiernan, *The Duel*, 46–47. Far less satisfactory is Robert Baldick, *The Duel: A History of Duelling* (London: Chapman and Hall, 1965). On the technical literature on dueling, see François Billacois, *Le duel dans la société française de XVIe–XVIIe siécles: Essai de psychosociologie historique*, 70–72, trans. into English as *The Duel: Its Rise and Fall in Early Modern France*, ed. and trans. Trista Selous (New Haven: Yale University Press, 1990). On the market for dueling books in the Veneto, see Claudio Donati, *L'idea di nobiltà in Italia secoli XIV–XVIII*, 95–97; and Francesco Erspamer, *La biblioteca di Don Ferrante: Duello e onore nella cultura del Cinquecento*, 55–73. Probably the most extensive description of actual duels in Italy and discussion of their implications for the code of honor are in Seigneur de Brantôme (Pierre de Bourdeille), *Mémoires touchant les duels*, in his *Oeuvres complètes* (Paris, 1823), 6: 1–239. On the ways in which the duel thrived in a culture that valued appearances over reality, see Kenneth S. Greenberg, "The Nose, the Lie, and the Duel in the Antebellum South," *American Historical Review* 95 (1990): 57–74.

17. On the stages of the challenge, see Bryson, *The Sixteenth-Century Italian Duel*, 3–23.

18. Possevino is quoted and translated in Bryson, *Point of Honor*, 55. See Girolamo Muzio, *Il duello del Mutio Justinopolitano*, 10r–18v on kinds of lies. On the total number of kinds of lies, see Kiernan, *The Duel*, 48.

19. On the form of challenges, see Muzio, *Il duello*, 24r–26r. For examples of some early challenges, see Carlo Milanesi, "Cartelli di querela e di sfida tra Lodovico Martelli, Dante da Castiglione e Giovanni Bandini, Rubertino Aldobrandi al tempo dell'assedio di Firenze 1530," *ASI*, n.s., vol. 4, pt. 2 (1857): 3–25.

20. On rules, see Bryson, *The Sixteenth-Century Italian Duel*, 72–74.

21. Bourdieu describes three corollaries to the general principle of the equality of honor: (1) the challenger confers honor on the challenged; (2) a man who challenges someone incapable of accepting dishonors himself; and (3) a man need only accept a challenge from someone worthy of making it. See *Outline of a Theory of Practice*, 11–12.

22. Paris de Puteo (Paride del Pozzo), *Duello: Libro de Re, Imperatori, Principi, Signori, Gentil'homini; & de tutti Armigeri, continente Disfide, Concordie, Pace, Casi accadenti; & iudicii con ragione, Exempli, Philosophi, Legisti, Canonisti, & Eccesiastici. Opera dignissima, et utilissima ad tutti gli spiriti gentili* (Venice, 1525), book 1, ch. 10, unpaginated. On Fausto, Donati, *L'idea di nobiltà*, 97. Muzio, *Il duello*, 38v (for quote), 41v–43v. See Antonio Possevino, *Libro . . . nel qual s'insegna a conoscer le cose pertinenti all'honore, et a ridurre ogni querela alla pace*, 4–7; Giovanni Battista Possevino, *Dialogo dell'honore . . . nel quale si tratta a pieno del duello*, 266–80. Cf. Bryson, *The Sixteenth-Century Italian Duel*, xxii–xxiv, 27, 87–95; and Billacois, *Le duel dans la société française*, 357–61.

Fausto da Longiano, one of the principal theorists of courtesy and the duel, authored *Il gentilhuomo* (Venice, 1542) and *Il duello regolato a le leggi de l'honore* (Venice, 1551). He was also well known in Friulan circles, having taught Latin and Greek in Udine. He dedicated the second volume of his translations of Cicero's orations to Nicolò Savorgnan. On Longiano, see A. Scarpellini, "Fausto da Longiano," *Studi romagnoli* 10 (1959): 283–300; and idem, "Fausto da Longiano traduttore di Erasmo," *Convivium* 30 (1962): 338–42.

23. Antonio Massa, *Contra l'uso del duello*, 42v–45v. On vendetta versus clemency, see Giorgio de Piaggi, *Società militare e mondo femminile nell'opera di Brantôme* (Salerno: Edizioni "Beta," 1970), 286–87.

24. Fabio Albergati, *Del modo di ridurre a' pace l'inimicitie private*, 118–24, 179–80 (quote on 179). On his career, see *Dizionario biografico degli italiani*, s.v. "Albergati, Fabio." His arguments are borrowed and amplified in Scipione Maffei, *Della scienza chiamata cavalleresca* (Rome, 1710), 358–61. Romanello Manin wrote in 1726 a similar antidueling argument, adapting it to the specifically Friulan context of the struggle between Udine and the castellans. See Andreina Stefanutti, "Il 'Dialogo tra un nobile cittadino udinese e un castellano della Patria': Appunti e note," 15–17.

25. On laws against the duel, Maugain, *Moeurs italiennes*, 170–75; and Bryson, *The Sixteenth-Century Italian Duel*, xvii–xviii, xxiv–xxvii, 102–19, 129 (on Mantova). On Venetian legislation, see L. C. Borghi, "La legislazione," ASV, Compilazione leggi, busta 182-D, Disfide e duelli, filza cxxxi, n. 12, pp. 10–13; and *Novissimum statutorum*, pt. 2, fol. 33v.

26. Emilio Candido, *Cronaca udinese dal 1554 al 1564*, 23–24.

27. On the rapier, Lawrence Stone, *The Crisis of the English Aristocracy, 1558–1641* (Oxford: Clarendon Press, 1965), 244–45. For an excellent parallel discussion of the causes for the dueling craze in France, see Robert A. Schneider, "Swordmaking and Statemaking: Aspects of the Campaign against the Duel in Early Modern France," in *Statemaking and Social Movements*, ed. C. Bright and S. Harding (Ann Arbor: University of Michigan Press, 1984), 268–72. On the military revolution, see Michael Roberts, "The Military Revolution, 1560–1660," *Essays in Swedish History* (London: Weidenfeld and Nicolson, 1967), 209; and Geoffrey Parker, "The 'Military Revolution,' 1560–1660: A Myth?," *Journal of Modern History* 48 (1976): 195–214. Kiernan devalues the role of military developments in the spread of the duel; see *The Duel*, 46–67.

28. The *cartelli* and *manifesti* between the two sides written between 10 May 1563 and 17 February 1568 have been collected together in "Contese cavalleresche tra i Savorgnan e i Coloredo avvenute negli anni 1563-'66-'68," BCU, MS Joppi 116. On the challenges and duels that followed these, also see Degani, *I partiti in Friuli*, 117–71. The quote comes from Marzio Colloredo, *Successo di quanto e passato fra li illu. signori Martio Colloreto, Nicolò, et Federigo Savorgnan*, 66v. On the Accademia degli Storditi, see Michele Maylender, *Storia delle accademie d'Italia* (Bologna: L. Cappelli, 1930), 5: 264.

29. For Marzio's involvement in a challenge to a duel in Milan as early as 1553, see Donati, *L'idea di nobiltà*, 103.

30. Degani, *I partiti in Friuli*, 119. Nicolò's initial response, entitled *Manifesto dell'Illustr. Nicolo Savorgnano a lettori* and dated 12 July 1563 in Ferrara, can be found in BCU, MS Joppi 116, fols. 2r–8v and Biblioteca Universitaria, Bologna, MS 1938, opuscolo 1, unpaginated; quote is from the beginning. For the physical description of the document, I relied on the Bologna example. According to the rules, a cavalier must refuse a challenge from a person under a ban, but since Nicolò had also been banished for his past crimes, he never raised that point in rejecting Marzio's challenge.

31. BCU, MS Joppi 116, fols. 9r–22r. Also see Degani, *I partiti in Friuli*, 121–23.

32. For an account of the duel by the seconds and judge, see BCU, MS Joppi 116, fols. 27r–36v, quote on fol. 30v.

33. For the postduel debate, see BCU, MS Joppi 116, fols. 38v–118r. The anonymous pro-Savorgnan pamphlet is *Copia d'una lettera ch' e stata mandata a Roma, per un gentil'huomo del Friuli, in materia delle cose passate, fra li Signori Martio Colloreto, Federigo Savorgnano, & Gio. Maria Gonzaga, Doppò quella quistione di Renzano*, with a prefatory letter by Troiano Archano (n.p., 1565). Marzio Colloredo's tract is *Successo di quanto e passato fra li illu. signori Martio Colloreto, Nicolo, et Federigo Savorgnan*.

34. On Tristano's challenge, see BCU, MS 1247, fascicolo titled, "Cartelli per il duello tra Marzio Colloreto e Tristano Savorgnano, 1565." Also see ASU, AT, cartella 19, colto 26, fascicoli, 5–6. On the appropriateness of substitutes in duels, see Bryson, *The Sixteenth-Century Italian Duel*, 24–26.

35. Marzio Colloredo, *Giustificatione di tutte le cose narate dal S. Martio Colloreto, del S. Tristano Savorgnano*; and idem, *Cartelli passati nel ultima querella fra li Ill.*

Signori Martio, & Camillo Colloreti, con i Sig. Tristano Savorgnano con la giustificatione di tutte le cose che narrò il S. Martio nel suo manifesto sopra il particolare del S. Tristano. Copies are in BCU, MS Joppi 116.

36. Nicolò, Tristano, and Federigo Savorgnan, *Difesa degli Illustri Signori, Nicolò, Tristano, & Federigo Savorgnani, dalle false imputationi date loro, & all'honorata sua famiglia, dal Signor Martio Colloreto,* 3r–18r for Nicolò, 19r–31r for Tristano (27r for quote), and 37r–59v for Federigo. Foliation numbers come from the copy in the BMV.

37. Marzio Colloredo, *Risposta del Sig. Martio Colloreto, a tre manifesti de' signori Savorgnani* (Augusta, 1568), copies found in BCU, MS Joppi 116 and BMV.

38. Degani, *I partiti in Friuli,* 134–36.

39. The peace was anticipated on 15 May by a general revocation of all licenses to bear arms for six months. See ASV, CD, Parti comuni, register for 1567–68, fol. 110. Based on the ms copy in BSU, Archivio capitolare di Udine, Collezione Bini, Miscellanea, vol. 19, Degani published the peace agreement in *I partiti in Friuli,* 155–71. The peace among the Friulans followed a broader pattern of a decline of dueling in Italy during and after the 1560s; Billacois, *Le duel dans la société française,* 75–78.

Conclusion

1. In contrasting the situation in Friuli to tribal feuding, I am thinking primarily of Jacob Black-Michaud, *Cohesive Force: Feud in the Mediterranean and the Middle East.* Cf. on these same issues, Elisabeth Claverie and Pierre Lamaison, *Impossible mariage: Violence et parenté en Gévaudan XVIIe, XVIIIe, et XIXe siècles*; and Chris Wickham, "Comprendere il quotidiano: Antropologia sociale e storia sociale." For quote about "deliberate social engineering," see Christopher Boehm, *Blood Revenge: The Anthropology of Feuding in Montenegro and Other Tribal Societies,* 87–88.

2. On Scotland, see Keith M. Brown, *Bloodfeud in Scotland, 1573–1625: Violence, Justice and Politics in an Early Modern Society*; on Iceland, see Kirsten Hastrup, *Culture and History in Medieval Iceland: An Anthropological Analysis of Structure and Change*; on Corsica, see Stephen Wilson, *Feuding, Conflict, and Banditry in Nineteenth-Century Corsica.* Similar to my view about the importance of the political and economic context of the feud and the ability of outside government to influence its course is Altina L. Waller, *Feud: Hatfields, McCoys, and Social Change in Appalachia, 1860–1900.*

3. The spectrum of European feud types is suggested by Jenny Wormald, "The Blood Feud in Early Modern Scotland," 104. On the increase of violence on the terraferma in the late sixteenth century, see A. D. Wright, "Venetian Law and Order: A Myth?," *Bulletin of the Institute of Historical Research* 53 (1980): 192–202.

4. On social homicide, see Barbara A. Hanawalt, "Community Conflict and Social Control: Crime and Justice in the Ramsey Abbey Villages," *Medieval Studies* 39 (1977): 402–23.

5. Gabriel Maugain, *Moeurs italiennes de la Renaissance: La vengeance,* 213–320.

6. On the identity formation of males in traditional Mediterranean societies, see David D. Gilmore, *Manhood in the Making: Cultural Concepts of Masculinity,* 30–55.

Cf. my "The Double Binds of Manly Revenge in Renaissance Italy," in *Gendering Rhetorics: Postures of Dominance and Submission in History*, ed. Richard C. Trexler (Binghamton, N.Y.: Medieval and Renaissance Texts and Studies, 1993).

7. On women in Corsican feuds, see Wilson, *Feuding*, 19, 31, 35, 36, 101, 211–23.

Bibliography

Entries include sources cited more than once and those used extensively in preparing this book. Publishers are provided only for editions from the twentieth century.

Primary Sources

Albergati, Fabio. *Del modo di ridurre à pace l'inimicitie private.* Rome, 1583.

Amaseo, Leonardo; Amaseo, Gregorio; and Azio, Giovanni Antonio. *Diarii udinesi dell'1508 al 1541.* Edited by Antonio Ceruti. Monumenti storici publicati dalla R. Deputazione Veneta di Storia Patria, ser. 3, vol. 2, Cronache e diarii, vol. 1. Venice, 1884.

"Autentiche testimonianze intorno alla famiglia Savorgnan." In *Antonio Savorgnan,* edited by Fabia Savini. *MSF* 27–29 (1931–33): 300–305.

Belloni, Antonio. *De clade Turriana.* Appendix to Dionisio Tassini, "La rivolta del Friuli nel 1511 durante la sua guerra contro i tedeschi." *NAV,* n.s., 39 (1920): 151–54.

Berselli, Ieronimo [Gerolamo]. *Lodi del porco opera piacevole et ridicolosa. Nella quale a pieno si descrive la perfettione, la bontà, l'eccelenza, l'industria, la magnanimità, la valorosità & la fierezza del porco.* Bologna, ca. 1590.

Bilanci generali della repubblica di Venezia. 3 vols. Venice: Visentini, 1912.

Biondo, Michelangelo. *De canibus et venatione libellus.* In *Arte della caccia,* edited by G. Innamorati, 1: 214–86. Milan: Il Polifilo, 1965.

Canal, Martin da. *Les estoires de Venise: Cronaca veneziana in lingua francese dalle origini al 1275.* Edited by Alberto Limentani. Civiltà veneziana fonti e testi, 12, ser. 3, no. 3. Florence: Leo S. Olschki, 1972.

Candido, Emilio. *Cronaca udinese dal 1554 al 1564.* Edited by Vincenzo Joppi. Udine, 1886.

Candido, Giovan. *Commentarii de i fatti d'Aquileja.* Venice, 1544.

Cergneu, Giovanni Battista di. *Cronaca delle guerre friulane coi germani dal 1507 al 1524.* Edited by Vincenzo Joppi and Vincenzo Marchesi. Accademia di Udine: Croniche antiche friulane, no. 1. Udine, 1895.

Chronicon Spilimbergense. Edited by P. J. Bianchi. Udine, 1856.

Chronicon Spilimbergense. In L. Pognici, *Guida Spilimbergo e suo distretto,* 196–234. Pordenone, 1872.

Colloredo, Agostino di. "Chroniche friulane, 1508–18." *Pagine friulane* 2 (1889): 5–6.

Colloredo, Marzio. *Cartelli passati nel ultima querella fra li Ill. Signori Martio, & Camillo Colloreti, con i Sig. Tristano Savorgnano con la giustificatione di tutte le cose che narrò il S. Martio nel suo manifesto sopra il particolare del S. Tristano.* Mantua, 1566.

————?. *Copia d'una lettera ch' e stata mandata a Roma, per un gentil'huomo del Friuli, in materia delle cose passate, fra li Signori Martio Colloreto, Federigo Savorgnano, & Gio. Maria Gonzaga, doppò quella quistione di Renzano,* with prefatory letter by Troiano Archano. N.p., 1565.

————. *Giustificatione di tutte le cose narate dal S. Martio Colloreto, del S. Tristano Savorgnano.* Verona, 1566.

————. *Risposta del Sig. Martio Colloreto, a tre manifesti de' signori Savorgnani.* Augusta, 1568.

————. *Successo di quanto e passato fra li illu. signori Martio Colloreto, Nicolo, et Federigo Savorgnan.* Brescia, 1565.

Croce, Giulio Cesare. *L'eccellenza et il trionfo del porco.* Bologna, 1594?.

————. *Le sottilissime astuzie di Bertoldo. Le piacevoli e ridicolose simplicità di Bertoldino.* Edited by Piero Camporesi. Turin: Giulio Einaudi, 1978.

Della Casa, Giovanni. *Galateo.* Translated, with an introduction and notes, by Konrad Eisenbichler and Kenneth R. Bartlett. Toronto: Centre for Reformation and Renaissance Studies, 1986.

Emiliani, Marcantonio, and Emiliani, Lapro. *Cronaca udinese dal 1532 al 1616.* Edited by G. A. Pirona. Udine, 1881.

Forgiarini, Giovanni, ed. "Quattro lettere storiche di Antonio Savorgnano (1457–1512)." *MSF* 9 (1913): 301–8.

Joppi, Vincenzo, and Wolf, Alessandro, eds. *Statuti e ordinamenti del comune di Udine.* Udine, 1898.

Leggi per la Patria e Contadinanza del Friuli compilate novamente, e stampate. Udine, 1686.

Lemaire de Belges, Jean. *La légende des Vénitiens.* In *Oeuvres* 3: 361–409. Louvain, 1885. 1st ed., Lyon, 1509.

Machiavelli, Niccolò. *Machiavelli: The Chief Works and Others.* Translated by Allan Gilbert. 3 vols. Durham, N.C.: Duke University Press, 1965.

Massa, Antonio. *Contra l'uso del duello.* Venice, 1555.

Mocenigo, Andrea. *La guerra di Cambrai fatta a'tempi nostri in Italia.* Venice, 1562.

Monticoli, Nicolò. *Cronaca delle famiglie udinesi.* Udine: Privately published, 1911.

———. *Descrittione del sacco MDXI seguito in Udine il giovedì XXVII febbraio.* Edited by Gian Giuseppe Liruti. Udine, 1857.

Mulioni di Gemona, Sebastiano. *Chronicon glemonense dal 1300 al 1517.* Udine, 1887.

Muzio, Girolamo. *Il duello del Mutio Justinopolitano.* Venice, 1550.

Novissimum statutorum ac Venetarum legum volumen, duabus in partibus divisum, Aloysio Mocenico Venetiarum Principi dicatum. Venice, 1729.

Partenopeo, Giovanni. *La guerra del Friuli contro i tedeschi (1508-13).* Edited by Dionisio Tassini. Udine: Privately published, 1916.

Porcìa, Girolamo di. *Descrizione della Patria del Friuli con l'utile che cava il serenissimo principe e con le spese che fa.* Udine, 1897.

Porto, Luigi da. *Alcune lettere inedite scritte dall'anno MDIX al MDXIII.* Padua, 1829.

———. *Lettere storiche dall'anno 1509 al 1528.* Edited by Bartolomeo Bressan. Florence, 1857.

Possevino, Antonio. *Libro . . . nel qual s'insegna a conoscer le cose pertinenti all'honore, et a ridurre ogni querela alla pace.* Venice, 1559.

Possevino, Giovanni Battista. *Dialogo dell'honore . . . nel quale si tratta a pieno del duello.* Venice, 1559.

Relazioni dei rettori veneti in terraferma. Vol. 1, *La Patria del Friuli (Luogotenenza di Udine).* Vol. 5: *Provveditorato di Cividale del Friuli, Provveditorato di Marano.* Milan: Giuffrè, 1973, 1976.

Romei, Annibale. *Ferrara e la corte estense nella seconda metà del secolo decimosesto. I Discorsi.* Città di Castello, 1891.

Ruzante [Angelo Beolco]. *Teatro.* Edited, translated into Italian, and annotated by Ludovico Zorzi. Turin: Giulio Einaudi, 1967.

Sanuto, Marino [Sanudo, Marin]. *Descrizione della Patria del Friuli (1502–3).* Edited by Leonardo Manin. Venice, 1853.

———. *I diarii.* Edited by Rinaldo Fulin et al. 58 vols. Venice, 1879–1903.

———. "Frammento inedito dell'itinerario." Edited with an introduction by Rinaldo Fulin. *AV* 22 (1881): 1–28.

———. *Itinerario . . . per la terraferma veneziana nell'anno MCCCCLXXXIII.* Edited by Rawdon Brown. Padua, 1847.

―――. "Viaggio in Spagna di Francesco Janis da Tolmezzo." Edited with an introduction by Rinaldo Fulin. *AV* 22 (1881): 63–103.

Savorgnan, Girolamo. "Lettere sulla guerra combattuta nel Friuli dal 1510 al 1528 scritte alla signoria di Venezia." Edited by Vincenzo Joppi. *ASI*, n.s., vol. 2, pt. 2 (1855): 3–59; vol. 3, pt. 1 (1856): 3–35; vol. 4, pt. 1 (1856): 13–42.

Savorgnani, Nicolò, Tristano, and Federigo. *Difesa de gli Illustri Signori, Nicolò, Tristano, & Federigo Savorgnani dalle false imputationi date loro, & all'honorata sua famiglia, dal Signor Martio Colloreto.* Ferrara, 1566.

Savorgnano, Mario. *Del governo della sua famiglia: Lettera a Luigi Cornaro.* Udine, 1863.

Sini, Girolamo. *Cronaca della terra di S. Daniele dai primi tempi all'anno 1515.* Udine, 1862.

Spilimbergo, Roberto de' Signori di. *Cronaca de' suoi tempi dal 1499 al 1540.* Edited by Vincenzo Joppi. Udine, 1884.

Stainer, Jacobus. *Patria del Friuli restaurata.* Venice, 1595.

Strassoldo, Niccolò Maria di. *Cronaca: Anni 1469–1509.* Edited by Vincenzo Joppi. Udine, 1876.

Strassoldo, Soldoniero di. *Cronaca dal 1509 al 1603.* Edited by Ernesto Degani. Accademia di Udine: Cronache antiche friulane, no. 2. Udine, 1895.

Secondary Sources

Accati, Luisa. "La rivolta contadina del 1511 in Friuli: Una possibile lettura." In *Società e cultura del Cinquecento nel Friuli occidentale: Studi,* edited by Andrea Del Col, 131–38. Pordenone: Edizioni della Provincia di Pordenone, 1984.

―――. "'Vive le roi sans taille et sans gabelle': Una discussione sulle rivolte contadine." *QS* 21 (1972): 1071–1103.

Anderson, J. K. *Hunting in the Ancient World.* Berkeley and Los Angeles: University of California Press, 1985.

Antonini, Prospero. *I baroni di Waldsee o Walsee, i visconti di Mels, i signori di Prodolone e di Colloredo: Accenni genealogici e note storiche.* Florence, 1877.

―――. *Il Friuli orientale: Studi.* Milan: Francesco Vallardi, 1865.

Ardrey, Robert. *The Hunting Hypothesis: A Personal Conclusion Concerning the Evolutionary Nature of Man.* New York: Atheneum, 1976.

Atti del convegno: Venezia e la terraferma attraverso le relazioni dei rettori, Trieste, 23–24 ottobre 1980, edited by Amelio Tagliaferri. Milan: Giuffrè, 1981.

Ayers, Edward L. *Vengeance and Justice: Crime and Punishment in the Nine-*

teenth-Century American South. New York: Oxford University Press, 1984.

Bakhtin, Mikhail. *Rabelais and His World.* Translated by Helen Iswolsky. Cambridge: MIT Press, 1968.

Baldissera, G. *Il contegno del famigerato Antonio Savorgnan all'espugnazione de' castelli di Vipulzano e S. Martino di Quisca nel 1510: Rimostranze della comunità di Cividale alla Veneta Repubblica.* Venice: Istituto Veneto di Arti Grafiche, 1913.

Banfield, Edward C., with the assistance of Banfield, Laura Fasano. *The Moral Basis of a Backward Society.* New York: Free Press, 1967.

Barbina, Guido. "La centralità di Udine nel sistema insediativo friulano: Analisi di un processo." In *Udin: Mil agn tal cûr dal Friûl,* edited by Gian Carlo Menis, 43–49. 60n Congress—25 di setembar 1983, Societât Filologjche Furlane. Udine: Società Filologica Friulana, 1983.

Baruzzi, Marina, and Montanari, Massimo, eds. *Porci e porcari nel Medioevo: Paesaggio, economia, alimentazione.* Bologna: CLUEB, 1981.

Basaglia, Enrico. "Il controllo della criminalità nella repubblica di Venezia. Il secolo XVI: Un momento di passaggio." In *Atti del convegno: Venezia e la terraferma attraverso le relazioni dei rettori, Trieste, 23–24 ottobre 1980,* edited by Amelio Tagliaferri, 65–78. Milan: Giuffrè, 1981.

Battistella, Antonio. "Udine nel secolo XVI: L'edilizia, l'igiene e la polizia urbana." *MSF* 19 (1923): 1–36.

———. "Udine nel secolo XVI: L'ordinamento interno della città." *MSF* 18 (1922): 149–92.

———. "Udine nel secolo XVI: La religione e i provvedimenti economico-sociali." *MSF* 20 (1924): 1–40.

Becker, Marvin B. *Civility and Society in Western Europe, 1300–1600.* Bloomington: Indiana University Press, 1988.

Benedetti, Andrea. *Storia di Pordenone.* Edited by Daniele Antonini. Pordenone: "Il Noncello," 1964.

———. "Il trattato della caccia, uccellagione e pesca del Conte Jacopo di Porcìa." *Il Noncello* 19 (1962): 47–81.

Benvenuti, Angelo de. *Inchiesta sugli archivi del Friuli: Archivi comunali.* Udine: Arti Grafiche Friulane, 1942.

Bernheimer, Richard. *Wild Men in the Middle Ages.* Cambridge: Harvard University Press, 1952.

Bertolini, Gian Lodovico, and Rinaldi, Umberto, eds. *Carta politico-amministrativa della Patria del Friuli al cadere della repubblica veneta.* Udine: Società Storica Friulana, 1913.

Bertolla, P. "Il castello di Cergneu." *Pagine friulane* 3 (1890): 148–50.

Billacois, François. *Le duel dans la société française de XVIe–XVIIe siècles:*

Essai de psychosociologie historique. Civilisations et sociétés, no. 73. Paris: Ecole des Hautes Etudes en Sciences Sociales, 1986. In English as *The Duel: Its Rise and Fall in Early Modern France*, edited and translated by Trista Selous. New Haven: Yale University Press, 1990.

Black-Michaud, Jacob. *Cohesive Force: Feud in the Mediterranean and the Middle East.* New York: St. Martin's, 1975.

Blanshei, Sarah R. "Criminal Law and Politics in Medieval Bologna." *Criminal Justice History* 2 (1981): 1–30.

Blok, Anton. "Rams and Billy-Goats: A Key to the Mediterranean Code of Honour." *Man* 16 (1981): 427–40.

Boehm, Christopher. *Blood Revenge: The Anthropology of Feuding in Montenegro and Other Tribal Societies.* Lawrence: University Press of Kansas, 1984.

Boissevain, Jeremy. "Patronage in Sicily." *Man* 1 (1966): 19–33.

Boissevain, Jeremy, and Mitchell, J. Clyde, eds. *Network Analysis: Studies in Human Interaction.* The Hague: Mouton, 1973.

Bonati Savorgnan D'Osoppo, Fulvio. "Aspetti della personalità di Gerolamo Savorgnan," *MSF* 47 (1966): 81–90.

———. "Di una famiglia storica del Friuli: I Savorgnano." *AV*, ser. 5, vol. 100 (1973): 5–18.

Borelli, Giorgio. *Un patriziato della terraferma veneta tra XVII e XVIII secolo: Ricerche sulla nobiltà veronese.* Milan: Giuffrè, 1974.

Borghese, Cinzia. "Castellani e contadini del Friuli orientale negli anni della rivolta: Le proprietà dei Colloredo e dei Savorgnan (Feudo di Buia)." Tesi di laurea, Facoltà di lettere e filosofia, Università degli Studi di Venezia, anno accademico 1985–86.

Bossy, John, ed. *Disputes and Settlements: Law and Human Relations in the West.* Cambridge, United Kingdom: Cambridge University Press, 1983.

Bourdieu, Pierre. *Outline of a Theory of Practice.* Translated by Richard Nice. Cambridge, United Kingdom: Cambridge University Press, 1977.

Braudel, Fernand. *The Mediterranean and the Mediterranean World in the Age of Philip II.* Translated by Siân Reynolds. 2 vols. New York: Harper and Row, 1972.

Bristol, Michael D. *Carnival and Theater: Plebeian Culture and the Structure of Authority in Renaissance England.* New York: Methuen, 1985.

Brown, Keith M. *Bloodfeud in Scotland, 1573–1625: Violence, Justice and Politics in an Early Modern Society.* Edinburgh: John Donald, 1986.

Bryson, Frederick Robertson. *The Point of Honor in Sixteenth-Century Italy: An Aspect of the Life of the Gentleman.* New York: Publications of the Institute of French Studies, Columbia University, 1935.

———. *The Sixteenth Century Italian Duel: A Study in Renaissance Social History.* Chicago: University of Chicago Press, 1938.

Burke, Peter. *The Historical Anthropology of Early Modern Italy: Essays on Perception and Communication.* Cambridge, United Kingdom: Cambridge University Press, 1987.

———. *Popular Culture in Early Modern Europe.* New York: Harper and Row, 1978.

Burkert, Walter. *Greek Religion: Archaic and Classical.* Translated by John Raffan. Oxford: Basil Blackwell, 1985.

———. *Homo Necans: The Anthropology of Ancient Greek Sacrificial Ritual and Myth.* Translated by Peter Bing. Berkeley and Los Angeles: University of California Press, 1983.

———. *Structure and History in Greek Mythology and Ritual.* Berkeley and Los Angeles: University of California Press, 1979.

Byock, Jesse. *Feud in the Icelandic Saga.* Berkeley and Los Angeles: University of California Press, 1982.

Cacciavillani, Ivone. *Le leggi veneziane sul territorio, 1471–1789: Boschi, fiumi, bonifiche e irrigazioni.* Limena: Signum, 1984.

Cammarosano, Paolo. "Il paesaggio agrario del tardo medioevo." In *Contributi per la storia del paesaggio rurale nel Friuli-Venezia Giulia,* 125–136. Pordenone: Grafiche Editoriali Artistiche Pordenonesi, 1980.

———. "Strutture d'insediamento e società nel Friuli dell'età patriarchina." *Metodi e ricerche* 1 (1980): 5–22.

———, ed. *Le campagne friulane nel tardo medioevo: Un'analisi dei registri di censi dei grandi proprietari fondiari.* Udine: Casamassima, 1985.

Campbell, J. K. *Honour, Family, and Patronage: A Study of Institutions and Moral Values in a Greek Mountain Community.* Oxford: Clarendon Press, 1964.

Camporesi, Piero. *Alimentazione folklore società.* Le forme del discorso, no. 20. Parma: Pratiche, 1980.

———. *La carne impassibile.* Milan: Il Saggiatore, 1983. In English as *The Incorruptible Flesh: Bodily Mutilation and Mortification in Religion and Folklore.* Cambridge, United Kingdom: Cambridge University Press, 1988.

———. *La maschera di Bertoldo: B. C. Croce e la letteratura carnevalesca.* Turin: Giulio Einaudi, 1976.

———. *Il paese della fame.* Saggi, no. 178. Bologna: Il Mulino, 1978.

———. *Il pane selvaggio.* Saggi, no. 195. Bologna: Il Mulino, 1980.

———. *Il sugo della vita: Simbolismo e magia del sangue.* Milan: Edizione di Comunità, 1982.

Canetti, Elias. *Crowds and Power.* Translated by Carol Stewart. New York: Continuum, 1981.

Cargnelutti, Liliana. "Antonio Savorgnan e l'insurrezione del 1511." In *I Savorgnan e la Patria del Friuli dal XIII al XVIII secolo,* 121–25. Udine: Provincia di Udine, Assessorato alla Cultura, 1984.

Carreri, Ferruccio Carlo. *Breve storia di Valvasone e dei suoi signori dagli inizi al 1806*. Venice: Nuovo Archivio Veneto, 1906. Also published in *NAV*, n.s., 11 (1906).

———. "Del buon governo spilimberghese." *AV* 36 (1888): 299–310; 37 (1889): 43–58, 321–39.

Carroll, Linda L. *Angelo Beolco (Il Ruzante)*. Boston: Twayne, 1990.

———. "Authorial Defense in Boccaccio and Ruzante: From Liminal to Liminoid." *Romance Quarterly* 34 (1987): 103–16.

———. "Carnival Rites as Vehicles of Protest in Renaissance Venice." *Sixteenth Century Journal* 16 (1985): 487–502.

———. "Giorgione's *Tempest*: Astrology is in the Eyes of the Beholder." In *Reconsidering the Renaissance*, edited by Mario A. Di Cesare. Binghamton: Medieval and Renaissance Texts and Studies. 1992.

———. *Language and Dialect in Ruzante and Goldoni*. Ravenna: Longo, 1981.

———. "Linguistic Variation and Social Protest in the Plays of Ruzante." *Allegorica* 8 (1983): 201–17.

———. "Ruzante's Early Adaptations from More and Erasmus." *Italica* 66 (1989): 29–34.

———. "Who's on Top?: Gender as Societal Power Configuration in Italian Renaissance Painting and Drama." *Sixteenth Century Journal* 20 (1989): 531–58.

Certeau, Michel de. *The Practice of Everyday Life*. Translated by Steven F. Rendall. Berkeley and Los Angeles: University of California Press, 1984.

Cervelli, Innocenzo. *Machiavelli e la crisi dello stato veneziano*. Naples: Guida, 1974.

Cessi, Roberto. "Venezia e la preparazione della guerra friulana (1381-5)." *MSF* 10 (1914): 414–73.

Chojnacki, Stanley. "Marriage Legislation and Patrician Society in Fifteenth-Century Venice." In *Law, Custom, and the Social Fabric in Medieval Europe: Essays in Honor of Bryce Lyon*, edited by Bernard S. Bachrach and David Nicholas, 163–84. Medieval Culture, no. 28. Kalamazoo, Mich.: Medieval Institute Publications, 1990.

Ciriacono, S. "Irrigazione e produttività agraria nella terraferma veneta tra Cinque e Seicento." *AV*, ser. 5, vol. 112 (1979): 73–136.

Claverie, Elisabeth, and Pierre Lamaison. *L'impossible mariage: Violence et parenté en Gévaudan XVIIe, XVIIIe, et XIXe siècles*. Collection "La mémoire du temps," edited by Jean Guilaine. Paris: Hachette, 1982.

Clifford, James, and Marcus, George E., eds. *Writing Culture: The Poetics and Politics of Ethnography.* Berkeley and Los Angeles: University of California Press, 1986.

Cogo, G. "La sottomissione del Friuli alla signoria di Venezia." *Atti dell'Accademia di Udine,* ser. 3, vol. 3 (1896): 95–146.

Cohn, Esther. "Law, Folkore, and Animal Lore." *Past and Present* 110 (1986): 6–37.

Concina, E. *La macchina territoriale: La progettazione della difesa nel '500 Veneto.* Rome: Laterza, 1983.

Contributi per la storia del paesaggio rurale nel Friuli-Venezia Giulia. Pordenone: Grafiche Editoriali Artistiche Pordenonesi, 1980.

Cozzi, Gaetano. "Ambiente veneziano, ambiente veneto." In *L'uomo e il suo ambiente,* edited by Stefano Rosso-Mazzinghi, 93–146. Florence: Sansoni, 1973.

———. "Authority and the Law in Renaissance Venice." In *Renaissance Venice,* edited by J. R. Hale, 293–345. London: Faber and Faber, 1973.

———. *Repubblica di Venezia e stati italiani: Politica e giustizia dal secolo XVI al secolo XVIII.* Turin: Giulio Einaudi, 1982.

———, ed. *Stato, società e giustizia nella Repubblica Veneta (sec. XV–XVIII).* 2 vols. Rome: Jouvence, 1980, 1985.

Cozzi, Gaetano, and Knapton, Michael. *Storia della Repubblica di Venezia.* Turin: UTET, 1986.

Cracco, Giorgio. *Società e stato nel medioevo veneziano (secoli XII–XIV).* Florence: Leo S. Olschki, 1967.

Cracco, Giorgio, and Knapton, M., eds. *Dentro la "Stado Italico": Venezia e la terraferma fra Quattro e Seicento.* Special volume of *Civis: Studi e testi,* vol. 8, no. 24 (December 1984).

Darnton, Robert. *The Great Cat Massacre and Other Episodes in French Cultural History.* New York: Basic Books, 1984.

———. "The Symbolic Element in History." *Journal of Modern History* 58 (1986): 218–34.

Davies, Wendy, and Fouracre, Paul, eds. *The Settlement of Disputes in Early Medieval Europe.* Cambridge, United Kingdom: Cambridge University Press, 1986.

Davis, James C. *A Venetian Family and Its Fortune, 1500–1900: The Donà and the Conservation of Their Wealth.* Memoirs of the American Philosophical Society, vol. 106. Philadelphia: American Philosophical Society, 1975.

Davis, John H. R. *People of the Mediterranean: An Essay in Comparative Social Anthropology.* London: Routledge and Kegan Paul, 1977.

Davis, Natalie Zemon. "Charivari, Honor, and Community in Seventeenth-Century Lyon and Geneva." In *Rite, Drama, Festival, Spectacle:*

Rehearsal Toward a Theory of Cultural Performance, edited by John J. MacAloon, 42–57. Philadelphia: ISHF, 1984.

―――. *Fiction in the Archives: Pardon Tales and Their Tellers in Sixteenth-Century France*. Stanford: Stanford University Press, 1987.

―――. "The Reasons of Misrule" and "The Rites of Violence." In *Society and Culture in Early Modern France*, edited by Natalie Zemon Davis, 97–123 and 152–88, respectively. Stanford: Stanford University Press, 1975.

Degani, Ernesto. "Un comune friulano sotto il Veneto dominio." *MSF* 10 (1914): 182–206.

―――. *I partiti in Friuli nel 1500 e la storia di un famoso duello*. Udine, 1900.

Del Col, Andrea, ed. *Società e cultura del Cinquecento nel Friuli occidentale: Studi*. Pordenone: Edizioni della Provincia di Pordenone, 1984.

Del Giudice, Pasquale. "La vendetta nel diritto longobardo." *Archivio storico lombardo* 2 (1875): 217–52, 365–80; 3 (1876): 157–81.

Del Lungo, Isidoro. "Una vendetta in Firenze il giorno di San Giovanni 1295." *ASI*, ser. 4, vol. 18 (1880): 355–409.

Donati, Claudio. *L'idea di nobiltà in Italia secoli XIV–XVIII*. Bari: Laterza, 1988.

Dorigo, Wladimiro. *Venezia origini: Fondamenti, ipotesi, metodi*. 2 vols. Milan: Electa, 1983.

Douglas, Mary, "Deciphering a Meal." In *Myth, Symbol and Culture*, edited by Clifford Geertz, 61–81. New York: Norton, 1971.

Dudley, Edward, and Novak, Maximilian E., eds. *The Wild Man Within: An Image in Western Thought from the Renaissance to Romanticism*. Pittsburgh: University of Pittsburgh Press, 1972.

Edgerton, Samuel Y., Jr. *Pictures and Punishment: Art and Criminal Prosecution during the Florentine Renaissance*. Ithaca: Cornell University Press, 1985.

Elias, Norbert. *The Court Society*. New York: Pantheon, 1983.

―――. *The History of Manners*. Translated by Edmund Jephcott. *The Civilizing Process*, vol. 1. New York: Pantheon, 1978.

Enriques, Anna Maria. "La vendetta nella vita e nella legislazione fiorentina." *ASI*, ser. 7, vol. 19 (1933): 85–146, 181–223.

Erspamer, Francesco. *La biblioteca di Don Ferrante: Duello e onore nella cultura del Cinquecento*. Centro Studi "Europa delle Corti," Biblioteca del Cinquecento, no. 18. Rome: Bulzoni, 1982.

Evans, Edward P. *The Criminal Prosecution and Capital Punishment of Animals*. London: Faber and Faber, 1987.

Evans-Pritchard, E. E. *The Nuer: A Description of the Modes of Livelihood and Political Institutions of a Nilotic People*. Oxford: Clarendon Press, 1940.

Ferrari, Giovanni. *Il Friuli: La popolazione dalla conquista veneta ad oggi.* Udine: Camera di commercio-industria-agricoltura, 1963.

Finlay, Robert. *Politics in Renaissance Venice.* New Brunswick: Rutgers University Press, 1980.

Francescato, Giuseppe, and Salimbeni, Fulvio. "Per un'analisi della situazione linguistica e culturale del Friuli nel '500." *MSF* 58 (1978): 111–32.

———. *Storia, lingua e società in Friuli.* Udine: Casamassima, 1976.

Gellner, Ernest, and Waterbury, John, eds. *Patrons and Clients in Mediterranean Societies.* London: Duckworth, 1977.

Gilmore, David D. *Aggression and Community: Paradoxes of Andalusian Culture.* New Haven: Yale University Press, 1987.

———. *Manhood in the Making: Cultural Concepts of Masculinity.* New Haven: Yale University Press, 1990.

Ginzburg, Carlo. "Charivari, associazioni giovanili, caccia selvaggia." *QS* 49 (1982): 164–77.

———. *The Cheese and the Worms: The Cosmos of a Sixteenth-Century Miller.* Translated by John and Anne C. Tedeschi. Baltimore: Johns Hopkins University Press, 1980.

———. *Miti, emblemi, spie: Morfologia e storia.* Turin: Giulio Einaudi, 1986. In English as *Clues, Myths, and the Historical Method*, translated by John and Anne C. Tedeschi. Baltimore: Johns Hopkins University Press, 1989.

———. *The Night Battles: Witchcraft and Agrarian Cults in the Sixteenth and Seventeenth Centuries.* Translated by John and Anne C. Tedeschi. Baltimore: Johns Hopkins University Press, 1983.

———. *Storia notturna: Una decifrazione del Sabba.* Turin: Giulio Einaudi, 1989. In English as *Ecstasies: Deciphering the Witches' Sabbath*, translated by Raymond Rosenthal, edited by Gregory Elliott. London: Hutchinson Radius, 1990.

Girard, René. "Generative Scapegoating." In *Violent Origins: Walter Burkert, René Girard, and Jonathan Z. Smith on Ritual Killing and Cultural Formation*, edited by Robert G. Hamerton-Kelly, 73–105. Stanford: Stanford University Press, 1987.

———. *Job: The Victim of His People.* Translated by Yvonne Freccero. Stanford: Stanford University Press, 1987.

———. *Things Hidden Since the Foundation of the World.* Translated by Stephen Bann and Michael Meteer. Stanford: Stanford University Press, 1987.

———. *"To Double Business Bound": Essays on Literature, Mimesis, and Anthropology.* Baltimore: Johns Hopkins University Press, 1978.

————. *Violence and the Sacred.* Translated by Patrick Gregory. Baltimore: Johns Hopkins University Press, 1977.

Giummolè, R. "I poteri del luogotenente della Patria del Friuli nel primo cinquentenario: 1420-70." *MSF* 45 (1962–64): 57–124.

Gluckman, Max. *Custom and Conflict in Africa.* Oxford: Basil Blackwell, 1955.

————. "The Peace in the Feud," *Past and Present* 7 (1955): 1–14. Reprinted in *Custom and Conflict in Africa,* 1–26.

Gobet, Sergio. "1511: Agitazioni contadine nelle campagne del Friuli." Tesi di Laurea in Etnologia, Facoltà di Lettere e Filòsofia, Università degli Studi di Trieste, anno accademico 1977-78.

————. "La rivolta contadina del 1511 in Friuli: Le cause e gli avvenimenti." In *Società e cultura del Cinquecento nel Friuli occidentale: Studi,* edited by Andrea Del Col, 119–30. Pordenone: Edizioni della Provincia di Pordenone, 1984.

Goffman, Erving. "The Nature of Deference and Demeanor." *American Anthropologist* 58 (1956): 473–502.

Gorn, Elliott J. " 'Gouge and Bite, Pull Hair and Scratch': The Social Significance of Fighting in the Southern Backcountry." *American Historical Review* 90 (1985): 18–43.

Gortani, G. "I Turchi in Friuli." *Pagine friulane* 14 (1901): 111–14.

Gottardi, Michele. "La struttura politico-amministrativa del Friuli occidentale nel XVI secolo." In *Società e cultura del Cinquecento nel Friuli occidentale: Studi,* edited by Andrea Del Col, 75–103. Pordenone: Edizioni della Provincia di Pordenone, 1984.

Grendi, Edoardo. "Il sistema politico di una comunità ligure: Cervo fra Cinquecento e Seicento." *QS* 46 (1981): 92–129. In English as "The Political System of a Community in Liguria: Cervo in the Late Sixteenth and Seventeenth Centuries." In *Microhistory and the Lost Peoples of Europe,* edited by Edward Muir and Guido Ruggiero and translated by Eren Branch, 119–58. Selections from *QS,* vol. 2. Baltimore: Johns Hopkins University Press, 1991.

Gri, Gian Paolo. "Giurisdizione e vicinia nell'età moderna: Il caso di Buia." In *I Savorgnan e la Patria del Friuli dal XIII al XVIII secolo,* 177–97. Udine: Provincia di Udine, Assessorato alla Cultura, 1984.

Grubb, James S. *Firstborn of Venice: Vicenza in the Early Renaissance State.* Johns Hopkins University Studies in Historical and Political Science, ser. 106, no. 3. Baltimore: Johns Hopkins University Press, 1988.

————. "When Myths Lose Power: Four Decades of Venetian Historiography," *Journal of Modern History* 58 (1986): 43–94.

Guaitoli, Alessandro. "Beni comunali e istituti di compascuo nel Friuli agli inizi del secolo XVII: Con particolari riferimenti alla montagna e alta pianura della destra Tagliamento." In *Società e cultura del Cinquecento nel Friuli occidentale: Studi*, edited by Andrea Del Col, 33–55. Pordenone: Edizioni della Provincia di Pordenone, 1984.

———. *Comunità rurale e territorio: Per una storia delle forme del popolamento in Friuli*. Udine: Istituto di studi territoriali, Coop. Edit. "il Campo," 1983.

Gundersheimer, Werner L. "Trickery, Gender, and Power: The *Discorsi* of Annibale Romei." In *Urban Life in the Renaissance*, edited by Susan Zimmerman and Ronald F. E. Weissman, 121–41. Newark, Del.: University of Delaware Press, 1989.

Hale, J. R., ed. *Renaissance Venice*. London: Faber and Faber, 1973.

Hamerton-Kelly, Robert G., ed. *Violent Origins: Walter Burkert, René Girard, and Jonathan Z. Smith on Ritual Killing and Cultural Formation*. Stanford: Stanford University Press, 1987.

Hanlon, Gregory. "Les rituels de l'agression en Aquitaine au XVIIe siècle." *Annales: E. S. C.* 40 (1985): 244–68.

Hasenfratz, Hans-Peter. *Die Toten Lebenden: Eine religionsphänomenologische Studie zum sozialen Tod in archaischen Gesellschaften: Zugleich ein kritischer Beitrag zur sogenannten Strafopfertheorie*. Zeitschrift für Religions- und Geistesgeschichte, Beiheft 24. Leiden: E. J. Brill, 1982.

Hasluck, Margaret. *The Unwritten Law in Albania*. Edited by J. H. Hutton. Cambridge, United Kingdom: Cambridge University Press, 1954.

Hastrup, Kirsten. *Culture and History in Medieval Iceland: An Anthropological Analysis of Structure and Change*. Oxford: Clarendon Press, 1985.

Heers, Jacques. *Family Clans in the Middle Ages: A Study of Political and Social Structures in Urban Areas*. Translated by Barry Herbert. Amsterdam: North-Holland, 1977.

Herde, Peter. *Guelfen und Neoguelfen zur Geschichte einer Nationalen Ideologie vom Mittelalter zum Risorgimento*. Sitzungsberichte der Wissenschaftlichen Gesellschaft an der Johann Wolfgang Goethe-Universität Frankfurt am Main, vol. 22, no. 2. Stuttgart: Franz Steiner Verlag Wiesbaden GMBH, 1986.

Huizinga, Johan. *Homo Ludens: A Study of the Play-Element in Culture*. Translated by R. F. C. Hull. New York: Roy Publishers, 1950.

Ivanoff, Nicola. "Il problema iconologico degli affreschi." In *Il Palazzo della Ragione di Padova*, 69–84. Venice: Neri Pozza, 1964.

Jacoby, Susan. *Wild Justice: The Evolution of Revenge*. New York: Harper and Row, 1983.

Joppi, Vincenzo. *I signori ed il comune di Valvasone nel secolo XVI: Documenti e note*. Venice, 1889.

Kellner, Hans. "Narrativity in History: Post-Structuralism and Since." *History and Theory* 26 (1987): 1–29.

Kete, Kathleen. "*La Rage* and the Bourgeoisie: The Cultural Context of Rabies in the French Nineteenth Century." *Representations* 22 (Spring 1988): 89–107.

Kiernan, V. G. *The Duel in European History: Honour and the Reign of Aristocracy.* Oxford: Oxford University Press, 1988.

King, Margaret L. *Venetian Humanism in an Age of Patrician Dominance.* Princeton: Princeton University Press, 1986.

Kinser, Samuel. "Presentation and Representation: Carnival at Nuremberg, 1450–1550." *Representations* 13 (1986): 1–42.

———. *Rabelais's Carnival: Text, Context, Metatext.* Berkeley and Los Angeles: University of California Press, 1990.

Kroll, Jerome, and Bachrach, Bernard S. "Medieval Dynastic Decisions: Evolutionary Biology and Historical Explanation." *The Journal of Interdisciplinary History* 21 (1990): 1–28.

Kuehn, Thomas. "Honor and Conflict in a Fifteenth-Century Florentine Family." *Ricerche storiche* 10 (1980): 287–310.

Lane, Frederic C. *Venice: A Maritime Republic.* Baltimore: Johns Hopkins University Press, 1973.

Larner, John. "Order and Disorder in Romagna, 1450–1500." In *Violence and Civil Disorder in Italian Cities, 1200–1500*, edited by Lauro Martines, 38–71. Berkeley and Los Angeles: University of California Press, 1972.

Law, John Easton. "Verona and the Venetian State in the Fifteenth Century." *Bulletin of the Institute of Historical Research*, vol. 52, no. 125 (1979): 9–22.

Le Roy Ladurie, Emmanuel. *Carnival in Romans.* Translated by Mary Feeney. New York: George Braziller, 1979.

Leach, Edmund R. "Anthropological Aspects of Language: Animal Categories and Verbal Abuse." In *New Directions in the Study of Language*, edited by Eric H. Lenneberg, 23–63. Cambridge: MIT Press, 1964.

Lebe, Reinhard. *Quando San Marco approdò a Venezia: Il culto dell'Evangelista e il miracolo politico della Repubblica di Venezia.* Rome: Il Veltro, 1981.

Leicht, Pier Silverio. "Aneddoti sul Friuli al tempo della Lega di Cambray." *MSF* 5 (1909): 183–84.

———. "La difesa del Friuli nel 1509, con appendice di documenti." *MSF* 5 (1909): 97–126.

———. "L'esilio di Tristano di Savorgnano." *MSF* 35–36 (1939–40): 37–68; 37 (1941): 1–50.

———. "La figura di Girolamo Savorgnan." *MSF* 24 (1928): 73–83.

———. "Marzio Colloredo governatore di Siena." *MSF* 4 (1908): 34–39.

———. "Un movimento agrario nel Cinquecento." *Rivista italiana di so-*

ciologia 12 (1908): 824–44. Reprinted in Leicht, *Scritti vari di storia del diritto italiano*, 73–91. Milan: Del Bianco, 1943.

———. *Parlamento Friulano*. 2 vols. Bologna: Nicola Zanichelli, 1917, 1925.

———. "Un programma di parte democratica in Friuli nel Cinquecento." In Leicht, *Studi e frammenti*, 105–21. Udine: Del Bianco, 1903.

———. "La rappresentanza dei contadini presso il Veneto luogotenente della Patria del Friuli." In Leicht, *Studi e frammenti*, 123–44. Udine: Del Bianco, 1903.

———. "La riforma delle costituzioni friulane nel primo secolo della dominazione veneziana." *MSF* 39 (1943–51): 73–84.

———. "Lo stato veneziano e il diritto comune." In *Miscellanea in onore di Roberto Cessi*, vol. 1, 203–11. Rome: Edizioni di storia e letteratura, 1958.

———. "Il tramonto dello stato patriarcale e la lotta delle parti in Friuli durante le tregue del 1413–1418." In *Miscellanea Pio Paschini*, vol. 2, 83–108. Rome: Lateranum, 1949.

Levi, Giovanni. *Inheriting Power: The Story of an Exorcist*. Translated by Lydia G. Cochrane. Chicago: University of Chicago Press, 1988.

Lincoln, Bruce. *Discourse and the Construction of Society: Comparative Studies of Myth, Ritual, and Classification*. Oxford: Oxford University Press, 1989.

Mallett, M. E., and Hale, J. R. *The Military Organization of a Renaissance State: Venice c. 1400 to 1617*. Cambridge, United Kingdom: Cambridge University Press, 1984.

Manzano, Francesco di. *Annali del Friuli ossia raccolta delle cose storiche appartenenti a questa regione*. 7 vols. Udine, 1858–79.

Marchesi, Vincenzo. "Il Friuli al tempo della Lega di Cambrai." *NAV*, n.s., 6 (1903): 501–37.

Marcuzzi, Giorgio. "Demaecologia delle isole linguistiche tedesche delle alpi and prealpi orientali (Sauris, Timau e Sappada)." *CF* 60 (1984): 207–39.

Martin, John. "A Journeymen's Feast of Fools." *The Journal of Medieval and Renaissance Studies* 17 (1987): 149–74.

Martines, Lauro, ed. *Violence and Civil Disorder in Italian Cities, 1200–1500*. Berkeley and Los Angeles: University of California Press, 1972.

Maugain, Gabriel. *Moeurs italiennes de la Renaissance: La vengeance*. Publications de la Faculté des Lettres de Strasbourg, ser. 2, vol. 14. Paris: Les Belles Lettres, 1935.

Mazzacane, Aldo. "Lo stato e il dominio nei giuristi veneti durante il 'secolo della terraferma.'" In *Storia della cultura veneta*. Vol. 3: *Dal primo quattrocento al Concilio di Trento*, pt. 1, 577–650. Vicenza: Neri Pozza, 1980.

Mazzi, Maria Serena, and Raveggi, Sergio. *Gli uomini e le cose nelle campagne fiorentine del Quattrocento*. Florence: Leo S. Olschki, 1983.

Menis, Gian Carlo. *Storia del Friuli dalle origini alla caduta dello stato patriarcale (1420)*, ed. 5. Udine: Società Filologica Friulana, 1984.

———, ed. *Udin: Mil agn tal cûr da Friûl*. 60n Congress—25 di setembar 1983, Societât Filologjche Furlane. Udine: Società Filologica Friulana, 1983.

Micelli, Francesco. "I Savorgnan e la difesa della Patria." In *I Savorgnan e la Patria del Friuli dal XIII al XVIII secolo*, 133–60. Udine: Provincia di Udine, Assessorato alla Cultura, 1984.

Miotti, Tito. *Castelli del Friuli*. 6 vols. Udine: Del Bianco, 1977–84.

———. "Udinesi e friulani ribelli: Dal patriarcato d'Alençon alle lotte fra Zambarlani e Strumieri." In *Udin: Mil agn tal cûr da Friûl*, edited by Gian Carlo Menis, 119–28. 60n Congress—25 di setembar 1983, Societât Filologjche Furlane. Udine: Società Filologica Friulana, 1983.

Molmenti, Pompeo. "I bandi e i banditi della repubblica veneta." *Nuova Antologia*, ser. 3, vol. 46 (1893): 124–51, 307–34, 508–33.

Mor, Carlo Guido. "L'ambiente agrario friulano dall'XI alla metà del XIV secolo." In *Contributi per la storia del paesaggio rurale nel Friuli-Venezia Giulia*, 163–218. Centro per lo Studio del Paesaggio Agrario, Istituto di Geografia, Università di Udine. Pordenone: Grafiche Editoriali Artistiche Pordenonesi, 1980.

———. "Aristocrazia veneziana e nobiltà di terraferma." In *Atti del Convegno: Venezia e la terraferma attraverso le relazioni dei rettori, Trieste, 23–24 ottobre 1980*, edited by Amelio Tagliaferri, 353–59. Milan: Giuffrè, 1981.

———. "Nascita di una capitale." In *Udin: Mil agn tal cûr da Friûl*, edited by Gian Carlo Menis, 79–90. 60n Congress—25 di setembar 1983, Societât Filologjche Furlane. Udine: Società Filologica Friulana, 1983.

———. "Problemi organizzativi e politica veneziana nei riguardi dei nuovi acquisti di terraferma." In *Umanesimo europeo e umanesimo veneziano*, edited by V. Branca, 1–10. Florence: Leo S. Olschki, 1963.

Muir, Edward. "The Cannibals of Renaissance Italy." *Syracuse Scholar*, vol. 5, no. 2 (fall 1984): 5–14.

———. *Civic Ritual in Renaissance Venice*. Princeton: Princeton University Press, 1981.

———. "Manifestazioni e cerimonie nella Venezia di Andrea Gritti." In *"Renovatio Urbis": Venezia nell'età di Andrea Gritti (1523–1538)*, edited by Manfredo Tafuri, 59–77. Rome: Officina Edizioni, 1984.

———. "The Virgin on the Street Corner: The Place of the Sacred in

Italian Cities." In *Religion and Culture in the Renaissance and Reformation*, edited by Steven Ozment, 25–40. Sixteenth Century Essays and Studies, edited by Charles G. Nauert, Jr., vol. 11. Kirksville, Mo.: Sixteenth Century Journal Publishers, 1989.

Muir, Edward, and Ruggiero, Guido, eds. *Microhistory and the Lost Peoples of Europe*. Translated by Eren Branch. Selections from *QS*, vol. 2. Baltimore: Johns Hopkins University Press, 1991.

Muir, Edward, and Weissman, Ronald F. E. "Social and Symbolic Places in Renaissance Venice and Florence." In *The Power of Place: Bringing Together Geographical and Sociological Imaginations*, edited by John A. Agnew and James S. Duncan, 81–103. Boston: Unwin Hyman, 1989.

Musoni, Francesco. *Sulle incursioni dei Turchi in Friuli*. Udine, 1890.

———. "Le ultime incursioni dei Turchi in Friuli." *Atti della Accademia di Udine*, ser. 3, vol. 1 (1893–94): 99–125.

Niccoli, Ottavia. "The End of Prophecy." *Journal of Modern History* 61 (1989): 667–82.

———. *Prophecy and People in Renaissance Italy*. Translated by Lydia G. Cochrane. Princeton: Princeton University Press, 1990.

———. "Il re dei morti sul campo di Agnadello." *QS* 51 (1982): 929–58. In English as "The Kings of the Dead on the Battlefield of Agnadello." In *Microhistory and the Lost Peoples of Europe*, edited by Edward Muir and Guido Ruggiero and translated by Eren Branch, 71–100. Selections from *QS*, vol. 2. Baltimore: Johns Hopkins University Press, 1991.

Nicholas, David. *The Van Arteveldes of Ghent: The Varieties of Vendetta and the Hero in History*. Ithaca: Cornell University Press, 1988.

Ortalli, Gherardo, ed. *Bande armate, banditi, banditismo e repressione di giustizia negli stati europei di antico regime*. Atti del Convegno, Venezia 3–5 novembre 1985. Rome: Jouvence, 1986.

Otterbein, Keith F., and Otterbein, Charlotte Swanson. "An Eye for an Eye, a Tooth for a Tooth: A Cross-Cultural Study of Feuding." *American Anthropologist* 67 (1965): 1470–82.

Ozment, Steven E. *The Reformation in the Cities: The Appeal of Protestantism to Sixteenth-Century Germany and Switzerland*. New Haven: Yale University Press, 1975.

Ozoeze Collodo, S. "Attila e le origini di Venezia nella cultura veneta tardo-medioevale." *Atti dell'Ist. Veneto di Scienze, Lettere ed Arti* 131 (1972–73): 531–67.

Palladio degli Olivi, Gio. Francesco. *Historie della provincia del Friuli*. Udine, 1660.

Paschini, Pio. *Storia del Friuli*, ed. 2, 2 vols. Udine: "Aquileia," 1953–54.

Peristiany, J. G., ed. *Honour and Shame: The Values of Mediterranean Society*. Chicago: University of Chicago Press, 1966.

Pertile, Antonio. *Storia del diritto italiano dalla caduta dell'Impero Romano alla codificazione.* 6 vols. Padua, 1873–87.

Perusini, Gaetano. "L'amministrazione della giustizia in una giurisdizione friulana del Cinquecento." *MSF* 40 (1952–53): 205–18.

————. "Le condizioni di vita in un paese della pianura friulana nel secolo XVI." *CF* 26 (1948–49): 165–74.

————. *I contratti agrari nel Friuli durante il dominio veneto.* Osservatorio italiano di diritto agrario: Studi giuridici, no. 3. Rome: Edizione Universitarie, 1939.

————. "Il contratto di soccida in Friuli," *Archivio Vittorio Scialoja* 10 (1944): 1ff.

————. *Vita di popolo in Friuli: Patti agrari e consuetudini tradizionali.* Biblioteca di "Lares," vol. 8. Florence: Leo S. Olschki, 1961.

Pieri, Piero. *Il rinascimento e la crisi militare italiana.* Turin: Giulio Einaudi, 1952.

Pitt-Rivers, Julian, ed. *Mediterranean Countrymen: Essays in the Social Anthropology of the Mediterranean.* Paris: Mouton, 1963.

Povolo, Claudio. "Aspetti e problemi dell'amministrazione della giustizia penale nella repubblica di Venezia, secoli XVI–XVII." In *Stato, società e giustizia nella Repubblica Veneta (sec. XV–XVIII)*, edited by Gaetano Cozzi, 1: 153–258. Rome: Jouvence, 1980.

————, ed. *Lisiera: Immagini, documenti e problemi per la storia e cultura di una comunità veneta, strutture—congiunture—episodi,* 2 vols. Lisiera: Edizioni Parrocchia di Lisiera, 1981.

Preto, Paolo. *Venezia e i Turchi.* Florence: G. C. Sansoni, 1975.

Pullan, Brian. *The Jews of Europe and the Inquisition of Venice, 1550–1670.* Totowa, N.J.: Barnes and Noble, 1983.

————. *Rich and Poor in Renaissance Venice: The Social Institutions of a Catholic State, to 1620.* Oxford: Basil Blackwell, 1971.

Queller, Donald E. *The Venetian Patriciate: Reality versus Myth.* Urbana, Ill.: University of Illinois Press, 1986.

Raggio, Osvaldo. *Faide e parentele: Lo stato genovese visto dalla Fontanabuona.* Turin: Giulio Einaudi, 1990.

Ranum, Orest. "Courtesy, Absolutism, and the Rise of the French State, 1630–1660," *Journal of Modern History* 52 (1980): 426–51.

————. "The French Ritual of Tyrannicide in the Late Sixteenth Century." *Sixteenth Century Journal* 11 (1980): 63–81.

Revel, Jacques. "The Uses of Civility." In *A History of Private Life*, edited by Philippe Ariès and Georges Duby. Vol. 3: *Passions of the Renaissance*, edited by Roger Chartier and translated by Arthur Goldhammer, 167–205. Cambridge: Belknap Press of Harvard University Press, 1989.

Roberts, Simon. "The Study of Dispute: Anthropological Perspectives."

In *Disputes and Settlements: Law and Human Relations in the West*, edited by John Bossy, 1–24. Cambridge, United Kingdom: Cambridge University Press, 1983.

Romano, Dennis. "The Aftermath of the Querini-Tiepolo Conspiracy in Venice." *Stanford Italian Review* 7 (1987): 147–59.

————. *Patricians and Popolani: The Social Foundations of the Venetian Renaissance State*. Baltimore: Johns Hopkins University Press, 1987.

Romano, Giovanni Battista. "Strumieri e Zamberlani." *Il Friuli*, 7, 8, 10 May 1902 and reprinted as a separate volume. Udine: Marco Bardusco, 1902.

Romano, R.; Spooner, F. C.; and Tucci, U. "Le finanze di Udine e della Patria del Friuli all'epoca della dominazione veneziana." *MSF* 44 (1960–61): 235–67.

Rosaldo, Renato. *Ilongot Headhunting, 1883–1974: A Study in Society and History*. Stanford: Stanford University Press, 1980.

Rotunda, Dominic Peter. *Motif-Index of the Italian Novella in Prose*. Bloomington, Ind.: Indiana University Press, 1942.

Ruggiero, Guido. *The Boundaries of Eros: Sex Crime and Sexuality in Renaissance Venice*. Oxford, United Kingdom: Oxford University Press, 1985.

————. *Violence in Early Renaissance Venice*. New Brunswick: Rutgers University Press, 1980.

Sacchetti, Armida. "Un entusiasta di Cividale (Giorgio Gradenigo)." *MSF* 3 (1907): 78–96.

Sardella, Pierre. *Nouvelles et spéculations à Venise au début du XVIe siècle*. Paris: Armand Colin, 1948.

Savage, H. L. "Hunting in the Middle Ages." *Speculum* 8 (1933): 30–41.

Savini, Fabia. "Antonio Savorgnan." *MSF* 27–29 (1931–1933): 265–305.

Savorgnan di Brazzà, Alvise. *"Maledetti Savorgnan": Mille anni di simbiosi con Udine*. Udine: Arti Grafiche Friulane, 1983.

I Savorgnan e la Patria del Friuli dal XIII al XVIII secolo. Udine: Provincia di Udine, Assessorato alla Cultura, 1984.

Savorgnani, Aurelia de. "Antonio Savorgnano e l'insurrezione friulana del 1511." Tesi di Laurea, Facoltà di Magistero, Università degli Studi di Trieste, anno accademico, 1969–70.

Scarabello, Giovanni. "Nelle relazioni dei rettori veneti in terraferma: Aspetti di una loro attività di mediazione tra governanti delle città suddite e governo della dominante." In *Atti del Convegno: Venezia e la terraferma attraverso le relazioni dei rettori, Trieste, 23–24 ottobre 1980*, edited by Amelio Tagliaferri, 485–91. Milan: Giuffrè, 1981.

Scheff, Thomas J. "Micro-linguistics and Social Structure: A Theory of Social Action." *Sociological Theory* 4 (1986): 71–83.

————. "Shame and Conformity: The Deference-Emotion System." *American Sociological Review* 53 (1988): 395–406.

————. "The Shame/Rage Spiral: A Case Study of an Interminable Quarrel." In *The Role of Shame in Symptom Formation*, edited by H. B. Lewis. Hillsdale, N.J.: LEA, 1987.

Scott, James C. *Weapons of the Weak: Everyday Forms of Peasant Resistance.* New Haven: Yale University Press, 1985.

Stallybrass, Peter, and White, Allon. *The Politics and Poetics of Transgression.* Ithaca: Cornell University Press, 1986.

Starn, Randolph, *The Contrary Commonwealth: The Theme of Exile in Medieval and Renaissance Italy.* Berkeley and Los Angeles: University of California Press, 1982.

Stearns, Carol Z., and Stearns, Peter N. *Anger: The Struggle for Emotional Control in America's History.* Chicago: University of Chicago Press, 1986.

Stearns, Peter N. *Be a Man!: Males in Modern Society.* New York: Holmes and Meier, 1979.

Stefanutti, Andreina. "Consorti feudali, 'cittadini' e 'popolani' a Spilimbergo: Spunti per la storia di una società tra XVI e XVII secolo." In *Spilimbèrc*, 95-108. Udine: Società Filologica Friulana, 1984.

————. "Il 'Dialogo tra un nobile cittadino udinese e un castellano della Patria:' Appunti e note." *CF* 55 (1979): 7–17.

————. "Giureconsulti friulani tra giurisdizionalismo veneziano e tradizione feudale." *AV*, ser. 5, no. 142 (1976): 75–93.

————. "Maniago nell'età moderna e contemporanea: Linee e tempi di una ricerca storica." In *Maniago: Pieve, feudo, comune*, 75–108. Maniago: Comitato per il millenario 981–1981, 1981.

————. "Udine e la contadinanza: Solidarietà e tensioni sociali nel Friuli del '500 e '600." In *Udin: mil agn tal cûr dal Friûl*, edited by Gian Carlo Menis, 111–17. 60n Congress—25 di setembar 1983, Societât Filologjche Furlane. Udine: Società Filologica Friulana, 1983.

Tafuri, Manfredo. *Venezia e il Rinascimento: Religione, scienza, architettura.* Turin: Giulio Einaudi, 1985. In English as *Venice and the Renaissance.* Translated by Jessica Levine. Cambridge: MIT Press, 1989.

Tagliaferri, Amelio. "L'amministrazione veneziana in terraferma: Deroghe e limitazioni al potere giudiziario dei rettori." *MSF* 56 (1976): 111–34.

————. "I caratteri dell'habitat rurale ed il trend demografico." In *Contributi per la storia del paesaggio rurale nel Friuli-Venezia Giulia*, 235–41. Pordenone: Grafiche Editoriali Artistiche Pordenonesi, 1980.

————. "Castelli, giurisdizioni, economie." In *Castelli del Friuli*, edited by Tito Miotti, 4: 7–22. Udine: Del Bianco, 1980.

————. "Cenni introduttivi e quadro storico preliminare allo studio del paesaggio agrario." In *Contributi per la storia del paesaggio rurale nel Friuli-Venezia Giulia*, 221–33. Pordenone: Grafiche Editoriali Artistiche Pordenonesi, 1980.

———. "Idee nuove per un vecchio problema: La caduta dello stato patriarcale." *CF* 52 (1976): 211–17.

———. "Ordinamento amministrativo dello stato di terraferma." In *Atti del Convegno: Venezia e la terraferma attraverso le relazioni dei rettori, Trieste, 23–24 ottobre 1980*, edited by Amelio Tagliaferri, 15–43. Milan: Giuffrè, 1981.

———. "Rettori veneti e castellani nella Patria del Friuli." *CF* 58 (1982): 191–96.

———. *Struttura e politica sociale in una comunità veneta del '500 (Udine)*. Milan: Giuffrè, 1969.

———. *Udine nella storia economica*. Udine: Casamassima, 1982.

———, ed. *Venezia e il Friuli: Problemi storiografici*. Milan: Giuffrè, 1982.

Tassini, Dionisio. "La rivolta del Friuli nel 1511 durante la guerra contro i tedeschi." *NAV*, n.s., 39 (1920): 142–54.

Tassini, Giuseppe. *Feste, spettacoli, divertimenti e piaceri degli antiche veneziani*, ed. 2. Venice: Filippi, 1961.

Thomas, Keith. *Man and the Natural World: A History of the Modern Sensibility*. New York: Pantheon Books, 1983.

Thompson, E. P. "The Moral Economy of the English Crowd in the Eighteenth Century." *Past and Present* 50 (1971): 76–136.

Torre, Angelo. "Faide, fazioni e partiti, ovvero la ridefinizione della politica nei feudi imperiali della Longhe tra Sei e Settecento." *QS* 63 (1986): 775–810.

Trebbi, Giuseppe. *Francesco Barbaro, patrizio veneto e Patriarca di Aquileia*. Udine: Casamassima, 1984.

Trexler, Richard C. "Correre la Terra: Collective Insults in the Late Middle Ages." *Mélanges de l'École Française de Rome. Moyen âge-Temps modernes* 96 (1984): 845–902.

———. "Follow the Flag: The Ciompi Revolt Seen from the Streets." *Bibliothèque d'Humanisme et Renaissance* 46 (1984): 357–92.

———. *Public Life in Renaissance Florence*. New York: Academic Press, 1980.

———, ed. *Persons in Groups: Social Behavior as Identity Formation in Medieval and Renaissance Europe*. Binghamton: Medieval and Renaissance Texts and Studies, 1985.

Ventura, Angelo. "Il dominio di Venezia nel Quattrocento." In *Florence and Venice: Comparisons and Relations*, edited by Sergio Bertelli, Nicolai Rubinstein, and Craig Hugh Smyth. Vol. 1: *Quattrocento*, 167–90. Florence: La Nuova Italia, 1979.

————. *Nobiltà e popolo nella società veneta del '400 e '500.* Bari: Laterza, 1964.

Venuti, Tarcisio. "I 32 capitoli della sentenza arbitraria tra i consorti e il popolo di Valvasone nel 1580." *CF* 60 (1984): 21–37.

Wallace-Hadrill, J. M. "The Bloodfeud of the Franks." *Bulletin of the John Rylands Library* 41 (1959): 459–87.

Waller, Altina L. *Feud: Hatfields, McCoys, and Social Change in Appalachia, 1860–1900.* Chapel Hill: University of North Carolina Press, 1988.

Watson, Curtis Brown. *Shakespeare and the Renaissance Concept of Honor.* Princeton: Princeton University Press, 1960.

Weissman, Ronald F. E. "The Importance of Being Ambiguous: Social Relations, Individualism, and Identity in Renaissance Florence." In *Urban Life in the Renaissance*, edited by Susan Zimmerman and Ronald F. E. Weissman, 269–80. Newark: University of Delaware Press, 1989.

————. "Reconstructing Renaissance Sociology: The 'Chicago School' and the Study of Renaissance Society." In *Persons in Groups: Social Behavior as Identity Formation in Medieval and Renaissance Europe*, edited by Richard C. Trexler, 39–46. Binghamton: Medieval and Renaissance Texts and Studies, 1985.

White, Hayden. "The Forms of Wildness: Archaeology of an Idea." In *The Wild Man Within: An Image in Western Thought from the Renaissance to Romanticism*, edited by Edward Dudley and Maximilian E. Novak, 3–38. Pittsburgh: University of Pittsburgh Press, 1972.

Wickham, Chris. "Comprendere il quotidiano: Antropologia sociale e storia sociale." *QS* 60 (1985): 839–57.

Wilson, Stephen. *Feuding, Conflict, and Banditry in Nineteenth-Century Corsica.* Cambridge, United Kingdom: Cambridge University Press, 1988.

Wormald, Jenny. "The Blood Feud in Early Modern Scotland." In *Disputes and Settlements: Law and Human Relations in the West*, edited by John Bossy, 101–44. Cambridge, United Kingdom: Cambridge University Press, 1983.

Zacchigna, Michele. "I Savorgnano di Udine: L'espansione fondiaria (sec. XIII–XIV)." *Metodi e ricerche* 2 (1981): 43–56.

Zannier, Giancarlo. "L'amministrazione del feudo spilimberghese fino al 1509." Tesi di Laurea, Facoltà di Giurisprudenza, Università degli Studi di Padova, anno accademico 1962-63.

Zug Tucci, Hannalore. "La caccia, da bene comune a privilegio." In *Storia d'Italia: Annali.* Vol. 6: *Economia naturale, economia monetaria*, edited by Ruggiero Romano and Ugo Tucci, 397–445. Turin: Giulio Einaudi, 1983.

Index

Badoer, Antonio, 5–6
Bakhtin, Mikhail, 198, 291
Balbi, Alvise, 183
Bandit, 60, 73–76, 127, 180, 228, 306, 309–10, 318, 350
Barbeano, 99, 314
Barozzi, Bishop Pietro, 53–54
Bassano, Venetian income from, 64
Beheading, 167
Belgrado, Savorgnan fief of, 136, 239–40
Belluno: millenarian movement in, 193; Venetian income from, 65
Bembo, Pietro, 158–59, 267
Benandanti. See Dead, armies of
Bergamo, Venetian income from, 63–65
Bernstein, Basil, 72
Blasphemy, punishment for, 204–5
Boldù, Giacomo, 217
Bondimier, Alvise, 181–82
Brazzacco castle, 170, 172
Brazzacco, Giacoma, 11
Brescia, Venetian income from, 62–66
Brugnera, 11, 182
Bruni, Leonardo, 70
Buia, 28, 35, 41–42, 120, 122–23, 321, 329; resistance to peasant revolt in, 176–77
Burckhardt, Jacob, Renaissance state model of, 49, 302
Burial, denial of, 168–69. See also Corpse, dismembering of
Burkert, Walter, 235–36

Cadore, victory of, 25–26, 131, 239
Cambrai. See League of Cambrai
Canal, Bernardo, 184
Candido, Francesco, 155, 157
Candido, Giovanni, 214, 223
Candido, Giovanni Battista, 157, 162, 167, 330
Candido, Ugo, 262–63
Cannibalism, as revenge, 236–37, 347–48
Capello, Pietro, 116–18, 218
Caporiacco, castle of, 174–75
Caporiacco, Nicolò Maria, 155
Capriglie, Giovanni di Leonardo Marangone di (Vergon), 9, 162, 166, 168, 201, 325

Carnia, militiamen of, 26
Carnic Alps, strategic importance of, 24–26
Carnival: body-centered imagery in, 168–69, 194–200, 222, 334; death and resurrection themes in, 194–95, 334; Fat and Lean themes in, 195, 197, 277; playacting and masking in, 10, 196, 198; social functions of, 196–97, 323, 335. See also Giovedì Grasso
Carpi, Marco da, 251, 351
Castellans: definition of, xxiv; as dynamic process, xxiv, 77–78, 85, 310; economic power of, 37, 39–43, 99–100, 314; foreign connections of, 273; parliament dominated by, 35; peasant attacks on, 135–51, 153, 169–88; after Sterpo assault, 153; structure of families of, 37–38; subdivision of public authority by, 16, 34–35, 38–40; vendetta among, xxiv, 78, 90–97. See also Clans; Factions
Castello, Giacomo, 155, 177–78, 219
Castiglione, Baldassare, 252, 255, 279
Castles, burning of, in peasant revolt, 169–88
Cellini, Benvenuto, 202
Cergneu castle, in peasant revolt, 177
Cergneu, Francesco, 155, 157, 159–60, 162, 166–67, 172, 177, 324
Cergneu, Giovanni Battista, 161, 177, 214, 221, 313
Cernide. See Militia
Chabod, Federico, 49
Chiribin, Nicolò. See Savorgnan, Nicolò (d. 1518)
Chittolini, Giorgio, 50
Chiusaforte, fortress at, 25–26, 298
Chojnacki, Stanley, 87
Christianity, vendetta rationalization in, 69–71
Church: attitudes of, toward hunting, 234–36; in Friuli, 36–37, 54, 299; Savorgnan as patrons of, 79
Cichiare, Leonardo di, 94
Cipernio, Giovanni, 181, 330
Cividale: attitudes in, toward Antonio Savorgnan, 113–15; after Giovedì Grasso, 245; representation of, in parliament, 35; role of, in Savorgnan-

Designed by Martha Farlow

Composed by G & S Typesetters, Inc., in Bembo

Printed by The Maple Press Company, Inc., on 50-lb. Glatfelter Eggshell Cream
and bound in Rainbow Linique with Rainbow Texture endsheets